Selected Works of
MARY SIDNEY
HERBERT
Countess of Pembroke

MEDIEVAL AND RENAISSANCE
TEXTS AND STUDIES

VOLUME 290

MRTS TEXTS FOR TEACHING

VOLUME 1

Selected Works of
MARY SIDNEY
HERBERT
Countess of Pembroke

Edited by

Margaret P. Hannay, Noel J. Kinnamon,
and Michael G. Brennan

Arizona Center for Medieval and Renaissance Studies
Tempe, Arizona
2005

Library of Congress Cataloging-in-Publication Data

Pembroke, Mary Sidney Herbert, Countess of, 1561–1621.
    [Selections. 2005]
    Selected works of Mary Sidney Herbert, Countess of Pembroke / edited
by Margaret P. Hannay, Noel J. Kinnamon, and Michael G. Brennan.
    p. cm.—(Medieval and Renaissance texts and studies ; 290)
    Includes bibliographical references.
    ISBN-13: 978–0–86698–333–4 (alk. paper)
    ISBN-10: 0–86698–333–3 (alk. paper)
    I. Hannay, Margaret P., 1944–. II. Kinnamon, Noel J. III. Brennan,
Michael G. IV. Title. V. Series: Medieval & Renaissance Texts & Studies
(Series) ; v. 290.

PR2329.P2A6 2005
821'.3—dc22

                         2005011607

TABLE OF CONTENTS

A Note on the Cover   vii

List of Plates   ix

Abbreviations   x

Preface   xi

Editorial Procedures   xiv

Chronology   xvi

Introduction:
    Life and Works   1
    Process of Revision   21
    Circulation and Reception of the Texts   27

I. Works Circulated in Print

Antonius by Robert Garnier   41

A Discourse of Life and Death by Philippe de Mornay   112
    Supplemental material: Précis by Elizabeth
       Ashburnham Richardson   130

The Doleful Lay of Clorinda (disputed)   136

A Dialogue between Two Shepherds, *Thenot* and *Piers*,
    in Praise of *Astrea*   144
    Supplemental material: Countess of Pembroke's
       Letter to Queen Elizabeth   151

II. Works Circulated in Manuscript

Even Now That Care   155

To the Angel Spirit of the Most Excellent Sir Philip Sidney   164
    Supplemental material: Variant printed in
       Samuel Daniel's 1623 *Works*   172

The Psalms of David   175
   Psalm 44 and Variant   186
   Psalm 45   192
   Psalm 51   195
   Psalm 53   198
    Supplemental material: Philip Sidney's Psalm 14 199
   Psalm 55   200
   Psalm 57   203
   Psalm 58   205
   Psalm 68   206
   Psalm 71 and Variant   210
   Psalm 73   217
   Psalm 82   220
   Psalm 84   221
   Psalm 88   223
   Psalm 100   226
   Psalm 101   227
   Psalm 102   228
   Psalm 104   231
   Psalm 107   236
   Psalm 111   241
   Psalm 117   242
   Psalm 119 F, K and O   242
   Psalm 124 and Variant   246
    Supplemental material: Psalm 124 from the Book
     of Common Prayer   248
   Psalm 130   248
   Psalm 131 and Variant   250
   Psalm 137   251
   Psalm 139   253
   Psalm 143   256
   Psalm 148   259
   Psalm 150   261

The Triumph of Death by Francis Petrarch   262

Bibliography   280

A NOTE ON THE COVER

This portrait of a lady is said to be "Mary Wife of Henry Herbert, Earl of Pembroke" on an inscription added later. The portrait is more than life size, 78 by 42 inches. The sitter, dressed magnificently in silk and velvet, with dramatic (and very expensive) lace on her collar and sleeves protected by a fine gauze overlay, poses before a view of Antwerp across the river Scheldt, and her hand rests on an elaborate clock.

The portrait was sold at Christie's on 23 June 1933 by "Miss Molineux Montgomerie owing to the death of the Late Mrs Molineux Montgomerie of Garboldisham Old Hall, Norfolk," to Spink, and then sold to Sir Felix Cassel, grandfather of the current owner, Mrs. Harriet Tuckey. Based on the costume of a long wasted doublet bodice with tight sleeves worn with a farthingale, the portrait has been dated circa 1610, and it has been variously attributed to Marcus Gheeraerts II, Paulus Van Somer, and Frans Pourbus II.

The portrait has been exhibited three times since its purchase by Cassel:

- *Seventeenth Century Art in Europe*, Burlington House, 1938, No. 24
- Luton Hoo, Luton, Beds, 1953–63, ten-year loan (on public exhibition with the *Wernher Collection* for the full ten years)
- *In the Public Eye: Treasures from Collections in the East of England*, Fitzwilliam Museum, Cambridge, May–August 1999.

Sir Roy Strong has questioned the identity of the sitter based on her age, since in 1610 the countess of Pembroke was 49. It may, however, have been painted during her sojourn in the Low Countries from 1614 to 1616. She wrote a letter to Sir Tobie Matthew during 1616 after she had completed a course of physic at Spa, saying "that whereas you thought and told me, that the Spa would do no body good; this last season, I owe too much, both to it and to you, to let you go away with that errour. For if you saw me now, you would say, it had created a new creature. Therefore, let all Pictures now hide themselves; for, believe me, I am not now, as I was then." If she thought that all her previous portraits should "hide themselves," she may well have decided to have a new one painted while she was in the Low Countries. On 2 August 1616 Dudley Carleton comments that he has visited the countess of Pembroke in Spa, "who complains chiefly of a common disease and much troublesome to fair women, *Senectus* [old age], otherwise we see nothing amiss in her."[1] Clearly, if

---

[1] Sir Dudley Carleton to Sir John Chamberlain, 2 August 1616, *Dudley Carleton to John Chamberlain, 1603–1624: Jacobean Letters* (New Brunswick, N.J.: Rutgers University Press, 1971), 209.

(as seems likely) she did indeed have her portrait painted about that time, then it seems pretty certain that the anonymous painter would have found himself in front of a client who was complaining (as she must have done to Carleton) about looking old. If, then, a portrait taken in that time appears to have a sitter who looks rather younger than the dowager countess of Pembroke would have looked at that date, it would not be surprising. Surely a painter who accepted a commission from a foreign member of the aristocracy would have been at some pains to please his client, avoiding what might be regarded as ruthless artistic verisimilitude. The sitter is not in her first youth, but she is depicted as a woman of mature beauty and grace. If it is the countess of Pembroke it could well have been painted at this time to flatter her, presenting her as she wished to see herself.

The face fits the two authenticated portraits, the Nicholas Hilliard miniature (c. 1590) and the much less flattering Simon van de Passe engraving (1618). The hair is equally curly in all three portraits, and the coloring is close to that in the miniature, although the hair in the miniature seems more blonde than red. (Red hair could be a conscious choice for coloring grey.) The set of pearls matches that in the van de Passe engraving. Her wealth is evident. That she wears black could be appropriate for a widow, although her gold and silver braid, patterned silk, and Irish mantle with black beads (hung in clusters of five) are far from mourning attire. She is wearing a broken ring that signifies a widow, and the black "thread" tied about the jewel on her sleeve may actually be the hair of her beloved, perhaps another sign of a widow. The jewels themselves were probably originally diamond rather than black, since the silver paint used to depict diamonds tarnishes. (See also the necklace in the Hilliard miniature.)

She wears an unusual diamond jewel on the bodice, perhaps a pomander to hold scent, or else a small vase to hold a flower, although other examples are not known before the eighteenth century.

Her hand rests on an elegant clock probably manufactured in Nuremberg, possibly after 1575, although it would be tempting to think that it is a family heirloom, the clock left to her mother, Lady Mary Dudley Sidney, by her mother, Jane Guildford Dudley, duchess of Northumberland, mentioned in the duchess' 1555 bequest to Lady Sidney as "her clock . . . she did so much set by, that was the Lord her father's, praying it her to keep it as a jewel." Such a "jewel" would normally pass from mother to daughter through many generations.

Thus the identification of the sitter as Mary Sidney Herbert, countess of Pembroke, while not certain, remains an intriguing possibility.

LIST OF PLATES

1. Sir Henry Sidney in Ireland from John Derrick, *The Image of Ireland* (1581), Plate 10. Courtesy of Edinburgh University Library.

2. Mary Sidney Herbert, Countess of Pembroke. Miniature by Nicholas Hilliard. Courtesy of the National Portrait Gallery, London.

3. Mary Sidney Herbert, Countess of Pembroke. Engraving by Simon van de Passe. Courtesy of the National Portrait Gallery, London.

4. a & b. First publication of "The Doleful Lay of Clorinda" in Edmund Spenser, *Astrophel* (1595). Courtesy of the Brotherton Library, University of Leeds.

5. Musical setting of Psalm 130 from British Library ADD 15.117. By permission of The British Library.

6. Modernized musical setting of Mary Sidney Herbert's Psalm 130 from British Library 15117. Courtesy of Allan Alexander.

7. *The Triumph of Death.* Courtesy of the Brotherton Library, University of Leeds.

ABBREVIATIONS

CERES	Cambridge English Renaissance Electronic Service
ELH	*English Literary History*
ELR	*English Literary Renaissance*
EMS	*English Manuscript Studies, 1100–1700*
HLQ	*Huntington Library Quarterly*
HMC	Historical Manuscripts Commission
HMSO	Her Majesty's Stationery Office
JES	*Journal of European Studies*
JMRS	*Journal of Medieval and Renaissance Studies*
MLN	*Modern Language Notes*
MLA	Modern Language Association
MRTS	Medieval and Renaissance Texts and Studies
N&Q	*Notes and Queries*
OED	*Oxford English Dictionary*
PMLA	*Publications of the Modern Language Association*
PRO, SP	Public Record Office (now The National Archives), State Papers
RES	*Review of English Studies*
RETS	Renaissance English Text Society
RQ	*Renaissance Quarterly*
SEL	*Studies in English Literature, 1500–1900*
SP	*Studies in Philology*

PREFACE

This selected edition of the writings of Mary Sidney Herbert, countess of Pembroke, is specifically intended for the student and general reader interested in early-modern women writers and the remarkable literary productivity of the Sidney circle during the Tudor and Stuart periods. Our 1998 Oxford English Texts edition of her collected works offered to its readers complete, old-spelling versions of all her known writings, accompanied by the detailed textual and critical apparatus standard to this academic series. In contrast, we have now sought in this edition to illustrate the impressive range and quality of her literary endeavors by means of readily accessible modern-spelling (and re-edited) texts, with new introductions and commentaries specifically aimed at the needs of the student or general reader. We hope that this selection of Pembroke's dramatic and prose translations, original poetry, verse translations, and versifications of the Psalms of David will serve to demonstrate for a wider audience her standing alongside her elder brother, Sir Philip Sidney, as a major figure in the development of early-modern English literature during the 1580s and 1590s.

The volume is organized to guide the reader through the biographical, literary and historical significance of Pembroke's life and writings. The Introduction draws together a fresh assessment of the defining elements of her life as a daughter of the illustrious Sidney family, as the wife of a high-ranking and politically active aristocrat, and as the mother of William and Philip Herbert, third and fourth earls of Pembroke, the joint patrons of the First Folio (1623) of Shakespeare's works. It also considers her powerful role as a patron of other writers, a reputation generated in no small measure by her unwavering and highly productive commitment to the preservation of the memory of her gifted and iconic brother, Philip, whose literary productivity in significant English poetry and prose (it could be argued) was unsurpassed during the first half of the 1580s. Her own talents as a writer were similarly diverse and firmly founded upon a high degree of technical and imaginative accomplishment. In conjunction with illustrating the impressive diversity of her work, this edition has been organized to place special emphasis upon how her compositions circulated among her contemporaries in both print and manuscript (see "Circulation and Reception of the Texts" and Elizabeth Ashburnham's summary of and meditation on her translation of de Mornay). We have also sought to elucidate the often complex but informative textual evidence through which it is possible to trace how she composed, and then often heavily revised, her own work (see "Process of Revision"). This edition, therefore, seeks to present not only a selection of the rich diversity of Pembroke's writings but also offers to the reader opportunities for exploring how she drafted, revised, and polished her own writings, especially the most ambitious and technically brilliant of all her works, the completion of the versification of the Psalms of David begun by her brother Philip.

Mary Sidney Herbert is the modern form of her full name. After her marriage she continued to identify herself as a Sidney and to use the Sidney *pheon*, or arrowhead, as her seal; the 1618 engraving by Simon van de Passe identifies her late in her life as "Mary Sidney, Countess of Pembroke" (see Plate no. 3). Her relative John Harington also identified her as "Mary Sidney, Countess of Pembroke," when he sent copies of her work to their cousin Lucy, countess of Bedford. She was not known as "Mary Herbert" or "Lady Herbert," an inferior title that belonged to her sister-in-law Mary Stanley Herbert, the wife of the earl of Pembroke's younger brother Sir Edward Herbert. Her signature was "M. Pembroke"; after her daughter-in-law Mary Talbot Herbert adopted that signature, Mary Sidney Herbert signed her name simply "Pembroke." We call her "Mary" when referring to her childhood; otherwise we use either her full modernized name or, following her own self-designation, her title (frequently abbreviated to "Pembroke") when speaking of her after her marriage.

Our collaborative work on this edition has been generously supported by our own employers, and valuable periods of leave from teaching and administrative duties have been granted to Margaret Hannay by Siena College and to Michael Brennan by the Study Leave in the Humanities Scheme at the University of Leeds. Various private and institutional owners have allowed us to examine their holdings of manuscript and printed materials. Our greatest and longstanding debt in our collaborative work on the Sidney family is to Viscount De L'Isle, MBE, DL (and also to his late father, Viscount De L'Isle, VC, KG), for their sustained generosity in allowing us access to their family papers at the Centre for Kentish Studies and for permission to use their manuscript of the Sidney *Psalms* (MS. *A*) as our copy-text. We are also most grateful to Dr. Bent E. Juel-Jensen for his permission to include versions of his unique texts of the two dedicatory poems ("Even Now That Care" and "To the Angel Spirit") from the Tixall MS. Similarly, we thank the Masters and Bench of the Inner Temple for permission to include Pembroke's translation of Petrarch's *The Triumph of Death* from their unique manuscript; the Master and Fellows of Trinity College, Cambridge, for permission to print material from their manuscript (MS. *G*) of the Sidney *Psalms*; the Folger Shakespeare Library, Washington, D.C., for permission to include Elizabeth Ashburnham's manuscript on Pembroke's translation of *A Discourse of Life and Death*; and the marquess of Salisbury for permission to include Pembroke's letter to Queen Elizabeth. We have been greatly assisted by the staff of the following libraries: the British Library, London; British Library Lending Division, Boston Spa;

Brotherton Library, University of Leeds; Centre for Kentish Studies, Maidstone; Edinburgh University Library; the Folger Shakespeare Library, Washington, D.C.; Lambeth Palace Library, London; Leeds Library, Leeds; Longleat House Library, Warminster; The National Archives (PRO), Kew; Renfro Library, Mars Hill; and Standish Library, Siena College. The following individuals have readily responded to our enquiries and offered valuable advice of various kinds: Allan Alexander, Carol Boggess, Geraldine Brennan, Mary Kim Cumming, Beth Fisher, Douglas Gordon, Ruth Hannay, Judith Herz, W. Speed Hill, William Kennedy, Roger Kuin, Roy McGinnis, Harriet McGinnis, Mary Moore, Rebeccah K. Neff, Harry M. Neff, Elizabeth Patton, Anne Lake Prescott, Debra Rienstra, Donna Robertson, Eve Rachele Sanders, Christopher Sheppard, Betty Travitsky, Jessica Weeks, and Georgianna Ziegler. We are particularly grateful to our editors, William Gentrup and Robert Bjork, and book designer, Dorothy Bungert. We also owe a considerable debt to David Hannay, for his constant and reliable advice on all matters concerning the technical production of our word-processed drafts.

EDITORIAL PROCEDURES

This edition is intended primarily for the student and the general reader. With that in mind, we have modernized the text wherever possible, but we have tried also to avoid "translation" and have sought to preserve distinctive features of the originals. The following principles have guided us.

1. Modern American spelling is normally adopted for words included in standard dictionaries. Otherwise, the text is emended when there is support in the manuscript tradition, in the sources, or, in the case of the translations, in the original texts. Quotations from other works of the period are similarly modernized (except for the titles of Edmund Spenser's works), as are titles except for those quoted in the titles of modern books and articles.

2. We retain common words or forms for which there is no exact modern English equivalent, but we regularize the spelling according to the *Oxford English Dictionary*: e.g., "affy" ("trust"), "amate" ("dismay"), "erst" ("formerly"), "sith" ("since"). In cases where both older and modern forms occur, however, we normally adopt the modern form throughout (except when an older form is required by the rhyme; see item 3 below): e.g., "worldly" for "wordly," "helped" for "holp," "chariot" for "charet." We retain common early verb forms such as "makest" and "goeth" and the second person singular "shalt" and "wilt." In words like "Caesar," "ae" is substituted for "æ."

3. Special cases are certain early words or forms that we retain for the sake of rhyme: e.g., "pight" ("pitched, placed"), "regreet" ("regret"), "slidden" ("slid"). In a few instances, we retain early forms for the sake of rhyme, but we use modern forms elsewhere: e.g., "bare" (*Triumph* 1.117, 2.185; Ps. 131.2) and "bore," "spake" (*Triumph* 2.11) and "spoke," "mo" (*Triumph*, 2.8; Ps. 45.46) and "more."

4. We normally retain the apostrophe to indicate elision of vowels and syllables for the sake of the meter: e.g., "car'st," "giv'st," "heav'nly," "th'other" ("the other"), "t'increase" ("to increase"), "by't" ("by it"), "is't" ("is it"). We also insert the apostrophe where the spelling indicates elision: e.g., "flow'r" for "flowre," "heav'n" for "heavn." When a syllable is silent in modern English, however, we expand the spelling and delete the apostrophe: e.g., "turned," "foiled," "obscured." We assume that most speakers of modern English will pronounce certain common polysyllabic words as disyllabic: e.g., "every," "evening," "fiery," "interest." We regularize the spelling of modal and auxiliary verbs without an apostrophe: e.g., "canst,"

"couldst," "didst." We also regularly use the apostrophe to signal the elision of vowels and syllables at the beginnings of words. Because Pembroke's verse is metrically regular to an extraordinary degree, we do not insert the apostrophe routinely to mark elisions not indicated by the spelling. In the case of the rare metrically ambiguous line, readers can make their own decisions regarding scansion, as at *Antonius* 1129: "Vexed with my evils, I never more had care." In one instance, for the sake of consistency within a single passage, we indicate elision by inserting an apostrophe: "go'st" for "goest" in Psalm 139.15 (cf. "com'st" in line 16). We do not routinely note older pronunciations required by the meter: e.g., "evils" (monosyllabic), *Antonius*, 281; "glued" (disyllabic), Ps. 137.21; "world" (disyllabic: "wordle" in the original), *Antonius*, 491; "dyed" (disyllabic), *Antonius*, 512; "supplied" (trisyllabic), Ps. 104.96; "nations" (trisyllabic), *Antonius*, 131. We add the apostrophe to possessive forms: "company's," "fathers'," "poet's."

5. We regularize the use of "O" and "oh": "O" in vocative constructions; "oh" in exclamations.

6. Punctuation is modernized and is occasionally emended to clarify the sense of a passage. We add quotation marks to indicate direct discourse but replace them with italics to indicate *sententiae* in one of the choruses of *Antonius* (807–17).

7. We adopt modern conventions for capitalization and the use of italics. We retain uppercase for personifications, and we retain the contrasting font (italic in this case) for the *sententiae* in *Antonius*.

8. We use modern conventions of paragraphing for prose.

9. In *Antonius* we retain both "Antonius" and "Antony" where they occur in the text; similarly, we retain the Latin and modern forms of the name of the city "Mutina"/ "Modena." We do not replace the names "Eras," "Charmion," and "Dircetus" (as in Garnier) with forms more familiar from Shakespeare's *Antony and Cleopatra*, "Iras," "Charmian," and "Dercetas."

10. Because the text is modernized, we list only verbal emendations of errors, not those of spelling and punctuation, in the printing or transcription of copy-texts.

11. We use the title *Psalms* to distinguish the full collection of the Sidneys' metaphrases, or metrical psalm paraphrases, from the biblical Psalms. Following convention we use a period for metrical psalms (e.g. Psalm 51.12) and a colon for biblical psalm citations (e.g. Psalm 51:3). Variant Psalms are numbered with roman numerals, as in the original.

12. In glossing, we use a comma between synonyms and semicolons between words that represent varying uses of the same word (or words with similar spelling) in different senses.

CHRONOLOGY

1551 (29 Mar)	Henry Sidney marries Mary Dudley, daughter of John, duke of Northumberland, and is knighted (11 Oct).
1552 (25 Apr)	King Edward VI grants Penshurst Place, Kent, to Sir William Sidney (d.1554).
1553	accession of Queen Mary I
1554 (30 Nov)	birth of Philip Sidney (d.1586)
1556 (?)	birth of Margaret (Mary) Sidney (d.13 Apr 1558)
1558 (17 Nov)	accession of Queen Elizabeth I
1560–86	Sir Henry Sidney, Lord President of the Council in the Marches of Wales
1560 (?)	birth of Elizabeth Sidney (d.1566)
1561 (27 Oct)	birth of Mary Sidney (d.1621) at Tickenhall near Bewdley, Worcestershire
1562 (autumn)	Lady Mary Dudley Sidney catches smallpox while nursing the queen.
1563 (19 Nov)	birth of Robert Sidney (d.1626) at Penshurst Place
1564 (?)	birth of Ambrosia Sidney (d.1575)
1565–71	Sir Henry Sidney, Lord Deputy of Ireland
1569 (25 Mar)	birth of Thomas Sidney (d.1595)
1572 (May)	Sir Henry Sidney declines a barony due to its related expenses.
1575–78	Sir Henry Sidney, Lord Deputy of Ireland
1575 (22 Feb)	death of Ambrosia Sidney at Ludlow. Soon afterwards, Queen Elizabeth invites Mary Sidney to court.
1577 (21 Apr)	Mary Sidney marries Henry Herbert (d.1601), second earl of Pembroke.
1578 (27 Oct)	Mary Sidney's seventeenth birthday, marked by a gathering of the Sidneys, Dudleys, and Herberts at Wilton House.
1580 (8 Apr)	birth of William Herbert (d.1630), later third earl of Pembroke
1581 (15 Oct)	birth of Katherine Herbert (d.1584)
1583 (9 Mar)	birth of Anne Herbert (d.1606?)

1584 (16 Oct)	birth of Philip Herbert (d.1650), later fourth earl of Pembroke; his sister Katherine had died several hours earlier.
1586 (1 or 5 May)	death of Sir Henry Sidney at Worcester (John Stow, *The Annals of England* (1592), sig. LIII2r = 1 May; Raphael Holinshed *Chronicles* (1587), III.1548 = 5 May)
(9 Aug)	death of Lady Mary Dudley Sidney at London
(7 Oct)	Robert Sidney is knighted by the earl of Leicester for valor at the battle of Zutphen.
(17 Oct)	death of Sir Philip Sidney from wounds received at Zutphen
1587 (16 Feb)	funeral of Sir Philip Sidney at St Paul's Cathedral, London
(?) (18 Oct)	birth of Mary Sidney (d.1653?), later Lady Mary Wroth
1588 (Aug)	Mary Sidney Herbert at Wilton during the Spanish Armada crisis
(4 Sept)	death of Robert Dudley, earl of Leicester
(Nov)	Mary Sidney Herbert and her children return to London for Accession Day.
1589–1616	Robert Sidney, Governor of Flushing
1590	publication of *The Countess of Pembroke's Arcadia* and Books I–III of Edmund Spenser's *The Faerie Queene*
1592	publication of Mary Sidney Herbert's translation of *A Discourse of Life and Death* and *Antonius*
1593	*The Countess of Pembroke's Arcadia*, with Books I–III from 1590 edition and IV–V from manuscript; publication of "The Doleful Lay" in Spenser's *Astrophel* (printed with his *Colin Clouts Come Home Againe*)
1598	publication of *The Countess of Pembroke's Arcadia*, with *Defence of Poetry* and *Astrophil and Stella*
1599	proposed royal visit to Wilton House for which "A Dialogue" and the Tixall Manuscript of the *Psalms* may have been prepared
1600	transcription of Mary Sidney Herbert's translation of Petrarch's *Triumph of Death*
1601 (19 Jan)	death of Henry Herbert, second earl of Pembroke
1602	publication of Mary Sidney Herbert's "A Dialogue" in Francis Davison's *Poetical Rhapsody*

1603 (24 Mar)	death of Queen Elizabeth and accession of King James VI of Scotland and I of England
(13 May)	Sir Robert Sidney created Baron Sidney of Penshurst and appointed Chamberlain to Queen Anne.
(Aug–Nov)	King James visits Wilton House.
1604 (27 Sept)	Mary Sidney marries Sir Robert Wroth at Penshurst.
(4 Nov)	William Herbert marries Mary Talbot at Wilton.
(27 Dec)	Philip Herbert marries Susan de Vere at London.
1605 (4 May)	Robert Sidney is created Viscount Lisle, and Philip Herbert is created earl of Montgomery.
1608 to 1613	hiatus in biographical records for Mary Sidney Herbert
1614 (June)	Mary Sidney Herbert arrives at Flushing before sailing on to Antwerp. She remains on the continent for about two years.
1618	Simon van de Passe engraving of Mary Sidney Herbert's portrait
(2 Aug)	Robert Sidney created earl of Leicester.
1619 (13 May)	Robert Sidney and Mary Sidney Herbert attend the funeral of Queen Anne.
1621 (21 July)	King James visits Mary Sidney Herbert's Houghton House.
(25 Sept)	Mary Sidney Herbert dies from smallpox at her house in Aldergate Street, London. After her funeral at St Paul's, she is taken to Wiltshire and buried at Salisbury Cathedral next to her husband, Henry Herbert, earl of Pembroke.

INTRODUCTION

Life and Works

Mary Sidney Herbert, countess of Pembroke, was famous in her own day as a writer. Edmund Spenser, for example, proudly said that he had read one of her poems in manuscript, thereby claiming to be part of her literary coterie.[1] William Shakespeare borrows from her translation *Antonius* in his *Antony and Cleopatra* for the drama's structure and characterization, and apparently echoes *A Discourse of Life and Death* in *Measure for Measure*.[2] John Donne wrote a poem praising the Sidneian *Psalms*, in which he called Philip and Mary Sidney "David's successors," saying that "their sweet learned labors" would serve to inspire sacred poetry.[3] Aemilia Lanyer said that Mary Sidney far surpassed her famous brother Philip "For virtue, wisdom, learning, dignity."[4] She was known for her translations, for her poems praising Queen Elizabeth and mourning her brother Philip, and especially for her metrical paraphrase of the biblical Psalms. How did she achieve such recognition in an era when even highly educated English women were often instructed to be silent in public and most of their writings were kept private?

She had great talent as a writer, like her brothers Philip and Robert, but that in itself was insufficient to overcome gender restrictions on women's public speech. Her ability to conceptualize herself as a writer and to circulate her works in elegant manuscripts and in print seems to have come from a combination of five major factors: her social position, her education, her desire to memorialize her slain brother Philip by taking up his work, the presence of female role models, and her own self-assertion.

---

[1] Edmund Spenser, *The Ruines of Time* (London, 1591), lines 316–22.

[2] See Michael Steppat, "Shakespeare's Response to Dramatic Tradition in *Antony and Cleopatra*," in *Shakespeare—Text, Language, Criticism: Essays in Honour of Marvin Spevack*, ed. Bernhard Fabian and Kurt Tetzeli von Rosador (Hildesheim: Olms-Weidmann, 1987), 254–79, 475–9, and *Collected Works*, 39–40; William Shakespeare, *Measure for Measure*, 1.3.43–44, in *William Shakespeare: The Complete Works*, ed. Stanley Wells and Gary Taylor (Oxford: Clarendon Press, 1986), 907. See also Katherine Duncan-Jones, "Stoicism in *Measure for Measure*: A New Source," *RES* 28 (1977): 441–46.

[3] John Donne, "Upon the Translation of the Psalms by Sir Philip Sidney, and the Countess of Pembroke His Sister," in *John Donne: The Divine Poems*, ed. Helen Gardner (Oxford: Clarendon Press, 1952), 34–35.

[4] *The Poems of Aemilia Lanyer: Salve Deus Rex Judaeorum*, ed. Susanne Woods (New York: Oxford University Press, 1993), 28.

Her social position was the first important factor, for while a talented woman of lower rank like Isabella Whitney might write and publish, Whitney was not in a position to become celebrated by the literary community. The countess of Pembroke held the rank and wealth to attract international attention for her writing and her patronage. By birth she was a Sidney, daughter of Sir Henry Sidney and Lady Mary Dudley Sidney. She was born on 27 October 1561 at Tickenhall near Bewdley, one of her father's official residences as Lord President of the Council in the Marches of Wales; he served as Lord President from 1560 to 1586 and concurrently as Lord Deputy of Ireland from 1565 to 1571 and 1575 to 1578. She thus grew up seeing her father in positions of authority. When he traveled from one official residence to another, he was honored with processions and flattering speeches. (See, for example, Plate no. 1, "Sir Henry Sidney in Ireland.") When he was at court he was constantly surrounded by people seeking positions or other favors, as his wife explained. They needed separate office and living space at court, she argued, because of the "multitude of Irish and Welsh people, that follow him."[5] When Queen Elizabeth saw Henry Sidney entering London in a splendid procession, she said it was well, for he held two of the highest offices in the kingdom. And yet even this magnificence was bittersweet, for the Sidneys never achieved the position that Mary Dudley had known in her youth, when her father was duke of Northumberland and, for a time, virtually ruled England for young King Edward.

When Mary Dudley married Henry Sidney on 29 March 1551, it may have been a less important alliance than her ambitious father wished, though Sidney did seem to have a promising future as one of King Edward's closest friends. The marriage may have been a love match, for the young newlyweds inscribed verses together in one of their books.[6] But their future depended on the king's favor, and the young king became ill with a pulmonary disease; on 6 July 1553 Edward died in Henry Sidney's arms.[7] Northumberland attempted to retain power by marrying his son Guildford to Lady Jane Grey and supporting her claim to the English throne. (As part of the same arrangement, little Katherine Dudley was married to Henry Hastings, later earl of Huntingdon, and young Henry Herbert, later earl of Pembroke, was married to Lady Jane's sister Katherine Grey; Herbert later repudiated the marriage, no doubt for political reasons as well as her affair with Edward Seymour.) On 9 July Lady

[5] Lady Mary Sidney to Edmund Molineux, "Monday" [1578], De L'Isle MS. U1475 C7/7. The De L'Isle manuscripts are now at the Centre for Kentish Studies, Maidstone, Kent.

[6] Edward Hall, *The Union of the Two Noble ... Families of Lancaster and York* (London: Richard Grafton, 1548). The Folger Library's copy 2 has verses inscribed by Mary Dudley Sidney and Sir Henry Sidney on Rr8 and KKK7.

[7] Sir Henry Sidney to Sir Francis Walsingham, 1 March 1583, PRO SP12/159, fol. 39v.

Sidney was sent to bring Jane, her young sister-in-law, to Syon, where Northumberland was waiting. The next day Jane was taken by barge to the Tower of London to be declared queen, and for several days it looked as if she might rule. When Mary Tudor was crowned instead, the Dudleys were declared traitors, their property was confiscated, their titles lost, and Northumberland, Guildford, and Lady Jane Grey eventually executed; their brother John also died as a result of imprisonment. In 1553 Lady Sidney had been the daughter of the most powerful and richest nobleman in England, and she had five brothers who held varying positions of wealth and power. A year later she was the daughter of a traitor, her father and two brothers were dead, and the entire family was under attainder, a punishment that abolished many of their civil rights, including the right to own property.

Queen Mary rapidly strengthened her own position by her engagement to Philip of Spain, son of the Holy Roman Emperor Charles V. The Sidneys worked to ingratiate themselves with Mary and to protect the rest of the Dudley family, though Sidney described his situation as "neither liking nor liked as I had been."[8] Fortunately for them, Henry Sidney's sisters, Mabel and Elizabeth, were attendants to the queen, as was his niece Jane Dormer, later countess of Feria.[9] No doubt they interceded with the queen for Henry Sidney, for the queen entrusted him with her marriage settlement. The queen sent Sidney to Spain with John Russell, earl of Bedford, to negotiate with Philip; during that visit Sidney enlisted Philip's support for the Dudleys. Astutely, the Sidneys named their first child Philip (born 30 November 1554) and asked Philip of Spain, as well as Bedford, to be his godfathers. Continuing their efforts to maintain friendly relations with the new queen, they named their daughter Mary Margaret in 1556; little Mary died in infancy, perhaps from the influenza epidemic. By this time Mary Dudley Sidney's surviving brothers had been released from prison and succeeded in winning the queen's favor by their participation in the battle of St. Quentin. Henry Dudley died in the battle, but the two surviving brothers, Ambrose and Robert, were released from attainder, although they were not restored to their former position or wealth. When Henry Sidney's father died in 1554, the queen allowed him to inherit Penshurst Place, which remains the home of the Sidney family.

By the time the second Sidney girl was born in 1560, Mary Tudor had died and Elizabeth had come to the throne; that daughter was appropriately named Elizabeth and the queen was her godmother. Queen Elizabeth had counted the Dudleys among her childhood friends. She rewarded them by restoring to Ambrose, the eldest surviving Dudley brother, his father's title of earl of

---

[8] Sir Henry Sidney to Sir Francis Walsingham, 1 March 1583, PRO SP12/159, fol. 39v.

[9] Katherine Duncan-Jones, *Sir Philip Sidney: Courtier Poet* (New Haven: Yale University Press, 1991), 9.

Warwick, and she particularly favored Robert, whom she later made earl of Leicester. (Elizabeth was widely believed to have been in love with "Robin," as she called Leicester.) Lady Sidney was a close friend of Elizabeth, serving her at court and entering into various political negotiations for her. The third Sidney daughter was given the name of her dead sister, Mary (as was customary at the time), and their fourth daughter (born c. 1564) was named Ambrosia, for her powerful uncle and godfather Ambrose Dudley. That same year the queen caught smallpox. Lady Sidney nursed her through the disease, but caught it herself and was badly scarred. Since a woman's beauty was thought to consist primarily in her complexion, her altered appearance was devastating for her and led her to withdraw from most court activities. Henry Sidney later said that she was "a full fair lady, in mine eye at least the fairest" when he left the court on the queen's business, but when he returned, "I found her as foul a lady as the small pox could make her."[10] (Philip Sidney gives a fictionalized account of such disfigurement in the Argalus and Parthenia story in *The Countess of Pembroke's Arcadia*, though in that version the wife's beauty is miraculously restored.) Robert, named for Robert Dudley, whose title of earl of Leicester he eventually achieved, was born in 1563, a few months after Lady Sidney recovered. Thomas, born prematurely in London in 1569, was the baby of the family. None of the younger children—Elizabeth, Mary, Ambrosia, Robert, or Thomas—would have remembered their mother without scars.

Elizabeth never gave Lady Sidney the reward she deserved for risking her own life and health to nurse the queen. She did invest Henry Sidney with the Order of the Garter in 1565, and appointed him as her representative to administer Ireland and Wales, but he never held an aristocratic title. In 1572 he was offered a barony, the lowest of the aristocratic orders, but was so strapped financially that he could not accept that expensive promotion. For Lady Sidney, daughter of a duke, writing to say that the honor would be their "utter ruin" without financial reward must have been a bitter task indeed; they were never granted the money and apparently never again offered a title.[11]

Education was designed to fit a child for his or her place in society and thus differed by rank and by gender. Boys in the upper ranks of society were prepared for public service, with emphasis on military and rhetorical training; Latin was the primary language of instruction. Girls in the highest ranks of society were prepared to ornament the court in their youth and then to manage a large household after their marriage. The Sidney boys were schooled at home until they were about seven, when they were sent to Shrewsbury School and then on to university. (Robert seems to have stayed at home longer, since

---

[10] Sir Henry Sidney to Sir Francis Walsingham, 1 March 1583, PRO SP12/159, fol. 38v.

[11] Mary Dudley Sidney to William Cecil, Lord Burghley, 2 May 1572, PRO SP 12/86, fol. 159.

Shrewsbury School has no record of his attendance.) The girls studied at home with tutors, but they also received an excellent education, analogous to that of Queen Elizabeth, the learned Cook sisters, Lady Jane Grey, and their own mother. Their mother was fluent enough in Italian to converse with the Spanish ambassador in that language and was known for her wise advice and for her eloquence. Edward Molineux said that she exceeded her sex in "good speech . . . excellency of wit, and notable eloquent delivery (for none could match her, and few or none come near her, either in the . . . frame of orderly writing . . . or facility of gallant, sweet, delectable, and courtly speaking)."[12]

Lady Sidney may well have helped to instruct the girls herself, but they also had tutors, including Mr. Thornton and "Mistress Maria, the Italian." Unfortunately, no records of their texts or lessons have been found, but we know from her later writing that Mary was schooled in scripture and the classics, trained in rhetoric, and was fluent in French, Italian, and Latin; she may also have known some Greek and Hebrew. The children may also have picked up some Celtic words from their residence in Wales and Ireland. Like other aristocratic girls, Mary was also trained in household medicine and administration, and she excelled in the feminine accomplishments of needlework and music—voice, lute, and the virginals, an instrument like an early piano. The account books for the Sidney children show that they practiced archery, went through many lute strings in their attempt to master that instrument, and needed their virginals tuned regularly. They apparently had a happy childhood, largely at Penshurst, where they must have played in the Baron's Hall on rainy days. They were entertained by singers on May Day, by players who performed the adventures of Robin Hood, and by minstrels on Midsummer's Day. Each child evidently had his or her own prayerbook, and they would have grown up attending daily worship and singing the Psalms. They frequently traveled with their father to his official residences in Wales or Ireland, and occasionally their parents took them all to London, sometimes even visiting the queen. The children saw their mother act as hostess at Ludlow Castle and other official residences; years later, when Mary Sidney's husband, the earl of Pembroke, was given her father's position as Lord President of the Council in the Marches of Wales, she assumed the duties there that had been her mother's.

As a young child, Mary Sidney was one of three sisters, but when Mary was six her older sister Elizabeth died in Dublin. The two younger girls, Mary and Ambrosia, studied and played together, and even dressed alike, as in their warm winter gowns of purple mockado (imitation velvet) with woolen petticoats, or their more formal dresses of crimson satin. Even more striking

---

[12] Edward Molineux in Raphael Holinshed's *Chronicles of England, Scotland, and Ireland* (1586: repr. 1808; repr. New York: AMS Press, 1965), 4:879.

were their matching dresses of changeable orange and purple taffeta made when Mary was nine; the same fabric was used to make cloaks for their little brothers Robert and Thomas.[13] Their parents usually dressed in rich velvets and satins in the black and white favored at Elizabeth's court, trimmed with fur for winter, and their older brother Philip also had clothes of black velvet and taffeta, with some flashes of blue or crimson, largely for linings.[14] Philip, seven years older than Mary, was held up as a model for the younger children. Sir Henry later instructed Robert, "Imitate [Philip's] virtues, exercises, studies, and actions; he is a rare ornament of this age."[15] When Philip came home from school he must have been admired by his little sisters and brothers, but they probably also found him intimidating. Their father's evaluation of his sons is reflected in his description of them as "one [Philip] of excellent good proof, the second [Robert] of great good hope, and the third [Thomas] not to be despaired of, but very well to be liked."[16] Perhaps Thomas, who was not to be despaired of, had been spoiled like so many youngest children.

The family again suffered tragedy when Ambrosia died at Ludlow on 22 February 1575. Her childless godfather Ambrose Dudley showed his grief by erecting a magnificent tomb for her in Ludlow, decorated with his own coat of arms and initials as well as the Sidney arms. Mary must have found Ambrosia's death even more devastating. The two girls, so close in age, had spent their lives playing and studying together. Queen Elizabeth was concerned that the Sidneys not lose their one remaining daughter, a girl "of very good hope," and therefore invited young Mary to court to get her away from the "unpleasant air" of Wales, where her sister had died, presumably from disease. The queen promised that "we will have a special care of her...if you will send her unto us."[17] At fourteen Mary was the right age to become one of the queen's waiting maids, or Maids of Honor, a descriptive term that, according to the *OED* was used first by Mary Sidney herself, in Psalm 45.54.[18] Their duties included standing with the queen on ceremonial occasions, escorting her to chapel, accompanying her on progresses, participating in court dances, and, in the private chambers, playing cards and other games. They held no official political position, but because they and the older women who made up the queen's Privy Chamber were the queen's constant companions, courtiers sought their favor

---

[13] De L'Isle MS. U1475 A36 Clothing accounts for Henry and Mary Sidney, 1571.

[14] De L'Isle MS. U1475 A36 Clothing accounts for Henry and Mary Sidney, 1568.

[15] Sir Henry Sidney to "Robin" Sidney, 25 March 1578, De L'Isle MS. Z 53/22.

[16] Sir Henry Sidney to Sir Francis Walsingham, 1 March 1583, PRO SP12/159, fol. 41.

[17] Queen Elizabeth to Sir Henry Sidney, preserved in a copy in the warrant book, PRO SP 41/1, fol. 83.

[18] References to verses in the biblical Psalms are given in the form Psalm 51:5; references to lines in metrical psalm paraphrases are given in the form Psalm 51.5.

to gain access to Elizabeth. As Elizabeth Brown argues, "that [the queen] was able to use the Privy Chamber women simultaneously as an extension of her body for political display and as a way to reinforce her remoteness and inaccessibility reveals her understanding of the complex management of power."[19] For an intelligent girl like Mary Sidney, the days at court were an apprenticeship in courtiership. As an adult she was known for her effective political letters. Her mastery of court rhetoric and etiquette is apparent in her letter to Elizabeth (see page 151), and her brother Robert's agent Rowland White praised an intercessory letter on his behalf: "The copy of her letter [to the Lord Treasurer] she did vouchsafe to send unto me of her own handwriting. I never read anything that could express an earnest desire like unto this."[20]

Though the queen was usually reluctant, and often angry, to have her Maids leave her to marry, their families sent them to court in the hopes that they would make advantageous marriages. Mary was particularly well placed to make a splendid match, since her uncle Robert Dudley, earl of Leicester, was the queen's favorite. When Leicester provided magnificent entertainment for the queen at Kenilworth, Mary and her mother were honored guests. When the queen and her court proceeded on to Woodstock, Mary was given the first ·of many poems praising her. This one celebrated her youth and her promise, saying "Though young in years yet old in wit, a gest [deportment or behavior] due to your race [family], / If you hold on as you begin, who is't you'll not deface?"[21] Leicester arranged her marriage on 21 April 1577 to his friend and contemporary, Henry Herbert, second earl of Pembroke, one of the richest men in England. She left no statement on her feelings about this marriage, except perhaps a hint in her paraphrase of Psalm 45, advice to a young bride on an arranged marriage to the king. The bride is told to transfer her affection from her own "house and folk" to her husband. If she will listen to and obey her husband, then she is promised a loving spouse: "So in the king, thy king, a dear delight / Thy beauty shall both breed, and bred maintain." Yet she need obey *only* her husband, "for only he on thee hath lordly right / Him only thou with awe must entertain" (40–44). If she will obey him, then she will command others who will come "with humble suit thy royal grace to gain, /

---

[19] Elizabeth A. Brown, "'Companion Me with My Mistress': Cleopatra, Elizabeth I, and Their Waiting Women," in *Maids and Mistresses, Cousins and Queens: Women's Alliances in Early Modern England*, ed. Susan Frye and Karen Robertson (New York: Oxford University Press, 1999), 134.

[20] Rowland White to Robert Sidney, 4 February 1598, De L'Isle MS. U1475 C12/129. Like all of her voluminous correspondence to, from, and for her brothers, this letter has been lost.

[21] Quoted in J. W. Cunliffe, "The Queen's Majesty's Entertainment at Woodstock," *PMLA* 26 (1911): 99–100.

To thee shall do such homage as they owe" (47–48). Her earliest extant letter, written to Leicester when she was a young bride, poignantly shows her learning to call the earl of Pembroke her lord. She first writes "he was" and crosses it out to write above the line "my lord was."[22] But like the young queen in the psalm, she found that learning such obedience to her husband would give her some derivative power and considerable wealth. None of her brothers ever achieved the wealth that she gained by marriage, and only Robert was able to attain a rank equal to hers as countess of Pembroke—though not until he was fifty-four, after many long years of lawsuits.

The bride in the psalm is dressed in cloth of gold, but we do not have any details about the wedding ceremony or what Mary Sidney wore. The bills for her trousseau include a skirt with purple and gold embroidery, a skirt with black and silver embroidery, and a pair of "night court shoes." Her brother Robert wore a splendid outfit of black velvet, white satin, and carnation velvet, and had his best hat restyled to match.[23] Philip was travelling abroad and missed the wedding but visited his sister and her husband that August and many times thereafter.

Herbert was of Welsh descent, spoke both English and Welsh, and owned vast properties in England and Wales. Mary Sidney thereby became, at the age of fifteen, countess of Pembroke and official mistress of the many Herbert homes, including Cardiff Castle, an enormous country home near Salisbury called Wilton House, and the smaller Wiltshire estates of Ramsbury and Ivychurch. Most impressive was Baynard's Castle in London, once a royal palace, a splendid building on the banks of the Thames that covered many city blocks and had an inner courtyard with a garden. Her stepmother-in-law, Anne Talbot Herbert, lived with them for most of the first eleven years of her marriage; Henry Herbert's widowed sister Anne came to live with them after the death of her husband, Francis Lord Talbot, in 1582 and stayed with them much of the time at least through 1587, "much made of and cherished" as Roger Manners reported.[24] No doubt these older women taught young Mary how to deal with the hierarchies of hundreds of servants, entertain distinguished guests,

---

[22] Mary Sidney, countess of Pembroke, to Robert Dudley, earl of Leicester, undated (probably 15 August 1578), Dudley Papers II, fol. 187, Longleat. Correspondence I, *The Collected Works of Mary Sidney Herbert, Countess of Pembroke*, ed. Margaret P. Hannay, Noel J. Kinnamon, and Michael G. Brennan, 2 vols. (Oxford: Clarendon Press, 1998), 1:285. Subsequent references will be to *Collected Works*.

[23] De L'Isle MS. U1475 A57.

[24] Roger Manners to the earl of Rutland, 26 October 1582, HMC, *The Manuscripts of His Grace the Duke of Rutland, G.C.B., Preserved at Belvoir Castle* (London: HMSO, 1888), 1:143.

and supervise the migrations of the household between estates. Some tension among the women must have been inevitable.

The earl of Pembroke was about forty-five when he married Mary Sidney; he had been married twice before, but he had no heir. When Mary bore him a long-awaited son on 8 April 1580, he was so thrilled that he installed a large tablet in the village church, recording the birth of this "first child of the noble Henry Herbert earl of Pembroke by his most dear wife Mary," concluding "God bless [him] with his mother above named with prosperous life in all happiness." (William succeeded his father as third earl of Pembroke and became an important political figure in the Stuart court, as well as a prominent literary patron; the First Folio edition of Shakespeare's works, for example, was dedicated to him and his brother Philip.) The Pembrokes had three other children in rapid succession: Katherine (1581); Anne (1583); and Philip (1584), later earl of Montgomery and fourth earl of Pembroke. These early years of their marriage were a time of great joy—and great tragedy. Little Katherine apparently died just a few hours before Philip was born in October 1584. In the Sidney family psalter all the births, marriages, and deaths seem to be recorded by a professional secretary, except for the entries for this one day, which appear to be in the hand of Lady Mary Dudley Sidney. Of her little granddaughter she wrote, "a child [who] promised much excellency if she might have lived."[25] In May 1586 Sir Henry Sidney died from "an extreme cold"; his body was buried at Penshurst but his heart in Ambrosia's tomb in Ludlow.[26] That same year her mother died in London in August. Edmund Molineux later described Lady Sidney's exemplary death. Her godly eloquence "astonished the hearers [those family and friends gathered around her deathbed] to hear." She "left the world most confidently" and went "to God (no doubt) most gloriously."[27] Mary herself was reportedly near death, perhaps from the same illness that took her mother. She was the only child present at her mother's death, for her three brothers were all in the Netherlands with Leicester's troops, fighting to rescue the Dutch from the rule of Spain. And then, in that same year, her brother Philip died on 17 October from wounds received in a battle at Zutphen. The mourning for his death was international and cut across social class. He became a hero to the Dutch as well as to the English and was mourned by

---

[25] Sidney family psalter, Trinity College Library, Cambridge, R.17.2, fol. 5v.

[26] Molineux, in *Chronicles of England, Scotland, and Ireland*, 4:878. The lead heart casket, inscribed "Hart Sidney L[ord] P[resident] Anno Domini 1586," is now on view in the British Museum.

[27] Edward Molineux, in Holinshed, *Chronicles*, 4:879.

both Queen Elizabeth and her enemy Philip of Spain, who wrote on the dispatch announcing Sidney's death, "He was my godson."[28] Sidney's European friends—including Hubert Languet and Philippe de Mornay—were devastated. His body was ceremonially transported from Holland in a ship with black sails and hung with black cloth decorated with his coat of arms. His funeral in St. Paul's Cathedral was conducted with a magnificence befitting royalty. Some seven hundred mourners, all male, marched in the procession. The chief mourner was his brother Robert Sidney, accompanied by young Thomas Sidney.[29] In this public funeral there was no place for Philip Sidney's sister, who was represented by her husband. Nor could she participate in the public poetic mourning for him, including four volumes of elegies published by the universities of Oxford, Cambridge, and Leiden in the months just after his death in October 1586; contributors included many of Sidney's friends, and many who did not know him well—or at all—but of course no women, because none attended university.

The public attention to Sidney's death made him virtually a cult figure. As Roger Howell summarizes the outpouring of grief, "Elizabeth's England, small and weak on the edges of European power, needed a hero-figure, and in Sidney it found what it needed."[30] In addition to the university elegies in English and Latin, several eyewitness accounts of his death were published, popular ballads mourned for him, and Thomas Lant published a book of engravings that showed the entire funeral procession. Mr. Singleton of Gloucester pasted the prints together (they were the length of a room) and mounted them above the mantel in his parlor; he turned the figures on pins to make them march for young John Aubrey.[31] All the public attention must have been both gratifying and disorienting for Philip Sidney's family. Overcome by illness and grief, Mary Sidney Herbert remained at the Pembroke country estates in Wiltshire for two years.

This bleak time was also a national crisis. The execution of Mary Stuart, queen of Scotland, had offered an excuse for Philip of Spain to attack England, restore it to Catholicism, and reassert the power that he had lost there when his wife Mary Tudor, queen of England, had died. Pembroke's husband and uncles and her brother Robert were all actively engaged in preparing to

---

[28] Roger Howell, *Sir Philip Sidney: The Shepherd Knight* (Boston: Little, Brown, and Co, 1968), 264.

[29] Sander Bos, Marianne Lange-Meyers, and Jeanine Six, "Sidney's Funeral Portrayed," in *Sir Philip Sidney: 1586 and the Creation of a Legend*, ed. Jan Van Dorsten, Dominic Baker-Smith, and Arthur Kinney (Leiden: Brill, 1986), 38–61.

[30] Howell, *Sir Philip Sidney*, 267.

[31] John Aubrey, *Brief Lives*, ed. Oliver Lawson Dick (London: Secker & Warburg, 1949), 280.

defend England against the Spanish Armada in the summer of 1588. She stayed in Wiltshire to take care of her teenage brother Thomas and her brother Robert's family—his wife Barbara Gamage Sidney and their infant daughter Mary, later Lady Mary Wroth. Then, shortly after the dispersal of the Armada, her powerful uncle Leicester died of malaria in September. In less than four years she had lost her daughter, mother, father, older brother, and the uncle who had sponsored her at court. She gathered her courage, and, in November 1588 she returned to London for the triumphant celebration of the English victory against the Spanish. She arrived in a magnificent procession that marked her reentry into public life. According to the Spanish ambassador:

> Before her went 40 gentlemen on horseback, two by two, all very finely dressed with gold chains. Then came a coach in which was the Countess and a lady, then another coach with more ladies, and after that a litter containing the children, and four ladies on horseback. After them came 40 or 50 servants in her livery with blue cassocks. [32]

Her ability for self-promotion is already evident in this splendid return to court. (The Nicholas Hilliard miniature portraying her youthful beauty was probably painted about this time; see Plate no. 2.)

All of her surviving writings were evidently completed in the twelve years between that reentry and the death of her husband in January 1601. She seems to have returned with the determination to become her brother's literary executor and heir, thereby honoring her Dudley/Sidney family after so many losses. She began her public literary activities to commemorate her brother Philip by serving as patron to those who wrote in his praise, including Edmund Spenser, Thomas Moffet, and Abraham Fraunce. Spenser wrote for her *The Ruines of Time*, praising not only Philip, but also others whom she had lost. It was her family that was honored, but it was her husband's wealth and influence that allowed her to serve as a literary patron in place of her brother Philip, for when poets sought her favor they were really asking her to convince her husband to give them a gift or a position. The extent of her literary patronage has sometimes been exaggerated, but she did encourage those in her family and household to write, including her brothers Philip and Robert; her children's tutor Samuel Daniel; her physician Thomas Moffet; her son William; and her niece and namesake Mary Sidney, later Lady Wroth, author of *The Countess of Montgomery's Urania, Pamphilia to Amphilanthus*, and *Love's*

---

[32] *Calendar of State Papers Relating to English Affairs Preserved in...the Archives of Simancas* (London, 1899; repr. Nendeln, Liechtenstein: Kraus Reprint, 1971), 4:488.

Victory. The lengthy list of dedications to her indicates that many other writers sought her favor and that of her wealthy husband.[33]

The most important of the writers that she inspired was her brother Philip, who said that he had written *The Countess of Pembroke's Arcadia* at her request. His working copy was given to her as it was written, "being done in loose sheets of paper, most of it in your presence, the rest, by sheets, sent unto you, as fast as they were done."[34] The first version of the *Arcadia*, usually known as the *Old Arcadia*, is full of asides to "fair ladies," his sister and her friends and relatives who were at Wilton.[35] When she was pregnant, he wrote her riddles for which the answer was "a pregnant woman."[36] He gave her the only complete manuscript of his sonnet sequence *Astrophil and Stella*, the one that revealed the secret that "Stella" was Penelope Devereux, Lady Rich, who "hath no misfortune, but that Rich she is."[37] This shared private context for some of Philip Sidney's writings may have extended to her own early writings. She may have contributed ideas for the *Arcadia* as he read portions to her, she may have written some early pieces that have been lost, and they may have begun the psalm paraphrase together, though the evidence is ambiguous. (See headnote for "Even Now That Care.")

She may have been among the first to write an elegy for Philip Sidney. In *The Ruines of Time* (1591) Spenser said that no one could better praise Sidney than "thine own sister, peerless Lady bright, / Which to thee sings with deep heart's sorrowing." Her poetry is so moving "That her to hear I feel my feeble spright [spirit]/ Robbed of sense, and ravished with joy, / O sad joy made of mourning and annoy."[38] She had not yet published any works by 1591, so Spenser was here claiming to have seen one of her poems in manuscript, probably the early elegy mentioned in her 1594 letter to Sir Edward Wotton as having been written "long since" in "those sad times."[39] This appears to be "The

---

[33] Franklin Williams, "The Literary Patronesses of England," *N&Q* 207 (1962): 364–66; Mary Ellen Lamb, "The Countess of Pembroke's Patronage," *ELR* 12 (Spring 1982): 162–79; Michael G. Brennan, *Literary Patronage in the English Renaissance: The Pembroke Family* (London: Routledge, 1988), 59–82.

[34] Sir Philip Sidney, "To my Dear Lady and Sister, the Countess of Pembroke," in *The Countess of Pembroke's Arcadia* (London: William Ponsonby, 1593), A3v.

[35] Mary Ellen Lamb, *Gender and Authorship in the Sidney Circle* (Madison: University of Wisconsin Press, 1990), 72–80.

[36] Wendy Gibson, "Sidney's Two Riddles," *N&Q* 24 (1977): 520–21.

[37] *Astrophil and Stella*, Sonnet 37, in *The Poems of Sir Philip Sidney*, ed. William A. Ringler, Jr. (Oxford: Clarendon Press, 1962), 183.

[38] Edmund Spenser, *The Ruines of Time* (London, 1591), lines 316–22.

[39] Mary Sidney Herbert, countess of Pembroke, to Sir Edward Wotton, endorsed 1594, Correspondence III, *Collected Works*, 1:387.

Doleful Lay of Clorinda," later published with poems by Spenser and others in the *Astrophel* volume of elegies for Philip Sidney (1595). Spenser may be alluding to that poem when he talks about the paradoxical pleasure of reading her elegy as "sad joy" that comes from "mourning and annoy," transmuting the "Lay's" statement that Sidney's death had "reft from me my joy...and left sad annoy" (ll. 50, 52). (Her authorship is disputed; see headnote for "The Doleful Lay.") She honored her brother by supervising the publication of *The Countess of Pembroke's Arcadia* that he had originally written for her (1593 and, with additional works, 1598); by translating *A Discourse of Life and Death*, written by his friend Philippe de Mornay; by writing two poems in his praise, an early elegy and her 1599 dedicatory poem "To the Angel Spirit of the Most Excellent Sir Philip Sidney"; and by completing the metrical psalms paraphrase that he had begun.

Philip and Mary Sidney became so closely associated in the public mind that an eighteenth-century manuscript of Sidney's epitaph identified him as the "brother of the Countess of Pembroke."[40] Nearly a century after Philip Sidney's death, the royalist John Aubrey attacked Philip Herbert by saying that he had heard old men say that "there was so great love" between Sir Philip Sidney and "his fair sister that . . . they lay together, and it was thought the first Philip earl of Pembroke was begot by him." Aubrey adds to a substantial body of satire against Philip Herbert, who had switched from the king to Parliament during the Civil War, by saying that "he inherited not the wit of either brother or sister."[41] His uncorroborated and politically motivated account of an incestuous relationship between Philip and Mary Sidney has led some modern critics to assert that there is something "disturbing" about their love.[42] No such suspicion was recorded during their lives, however, nor has evidence been found that Aubrey's accusation was taken seriously before late twentieth-century critics produced Freudian readings of their words.[43] Philip Herbert's royalist enemies also directed sexual slander at his pious widow, Lady Anne Clifford. Alan Stewart has recently suggested that "there is nothing to support this accusation, or to suggest that the rumor was ever current." It might, however "betray a real anxiety," that "something untoward" was happening at Wilton,

---

[40] Thomas Archer, 1760, British Library Additional MS. 5830, fol. 179v.

[41] Aubrey, *Brief Lives*, 139. See, for comparison, a satirical elegy that invites those who want to mourn Herbert's "death at his grave" to "draw near and make water upon an old knave," in *The Last Will and Testament of Philip Herbert . . . Vulgarly Called the Earl of Pembroke and Montgomery* (London, 1650), 4v.

[42] Gary Waller, *Mary Sidney, Countess of Pembroke: A Critical Study of Her Writings and Literary Milieu* (Salzburg: University of Salzburg Press, 1979), 99.

[43] See, for example, R. E. Pritchard, "Sidney's Dedicatory Poem: 'To the Angel Spirit of the Most Excellent Sir Philip Sidney,'" *Explicator* 54 (1995): 2–4.

which "did seem to attract some of England's most politically dangerous figures," like Leicester, Warwick, and other members of their circle.[44]

In addition to honoring her brother, Mary Sidney Herbert honored her queen, who was not only her monarch, but also a role model as a writer and translator.[45] Two original poems praise Queen Elizabeth. They were both apparently written in 1599, when her husband was seriously ill and she was beginning to seek a position at court for her son William, as indicated by her later letter to Elizabeth. "Even Now That Care," which dedicates the Sidneys' poetic paraphrase of the *Psalms* to Elizabeth (1599), exists in only one manuscript and may have been written for the queen's eyes alone. "A Dialogue between Two Shepherds, *Thenot* and *Piers*, in Praise of *Astrea*" is a pastoral dialogue evidently written for the queen's intended visit to Wilton in 1599.[46] She also completed three translations: *Antonius* and *A Discourse of Life and Death*, printed together in 1592; and *The Triumph of Death*, which survives only in a transcription of a copy that John Harington of Kelston sent to Lucy Harington Russell, countess of Bedford.

Pembroke's own literary works thus fit approved categories for women—translation, elegy, encomium (poem of praise), and psalm paraphrase—thereby allowing her to stretch the boundaries for women even while she appeared to remain within them. Translation, an important art form in the Renaissance, was often thought to be more suitable for women than original composition, particularly if the translation contributed to the cause of the true faith. Protestants and Catholics differed on which was the true faith, but both believed that the highest use of scholarship and art was to contribute to it. Among sixteenth-century English women who translated religious works were Margaret More Roper, daughter of Sir Thomas More, who translated Erasmus's *Devout Treatise upon the Pater Noster* [Lord's Prayer]; Anne Lock, who translated sermons by John Calvin and Jean Taffin; and Queen Elizabeth, who as a girl had translated the *Mirror or Glass of the Sinful Soul* by Marguerite de Navarre. The most remarkable family of translators were the Cook sisters: Anne Cook Bacon, who translated into English sermons by Bernadino Ochino and *An Apology of Answer in Defence of the Church of England* by Bishop John Jewel and others; Mildred Cook Cecil, who translated a sermon of St. Basil's from Greek; and Elizabeth Cook Russell, who translated Bishop John Ponet's *A Way of Reconciliation Touching the True Nature and Substance*

---

[44] Alan Stewart, *Philip Sidney: A Double Life* (London: Chatto & Windus, 2000), 202.

[45] See *Elizabeth I: Collected Works*, ed. Leah S. Marcus, Janel Mueller, and Mary Beth Rose (Chicago: University of Chicago Press, 2000).

[46] Mary C. Erler, "Davies's *Astraea* and Other Contexts of the Countess of Pembroke's 'A Dialogue,'" *SEL* 30 (1990): 41–61.

of the Body and Blood of Christ in the Sacrament.[47] Pembroke's translation of
A Discourse of Life and Death, a Christian/Senecan meditation by the French
Huguenot Philippe de Mornay, followed in this tradition.

Secular translation was somewhat more problematic for a woman, espe-
cially in England. Although Queen Elizabeth had translated selections from
works by Plutarch, Euripides, Horace, Boethius, and Xenophon, among oth-
ers, those works were not publicly circulated. The women who lived with her
may have seen them, however, or at least known of them. If Pembroke knew of
Elizabeth's translation of part of Petrarch's *Triumph of Eternity*, that might have
encouraged her own translation of *The Triumph of Death*. If she knew of Lady
Joanna Lumley's translation of Euripides' *Iphigenia at Aulis* or Queen Elizabeth's
translation of Seneca's *Hercules Oetaeus*, that might have encouraged her own
translation of the neo-Senecan drama *Marc Antoine* by the avant garde French
playwright Robert Garnier. The only secular translation printed by a woman
in England prior to Pembroke's *Antonius* was Margaret Tyler's translation of
Ortunez de Calahorra Diego's *Mirror of Princely Deeds and Knighthood* (1578).
Tyler's preface attempts to justify her translation of a "story profane, and a mat-
ter more manlike then becometh my sex." Her critics, she says, would "enforce
me necessarily either not to write or to write of divinity." A romance has value,
Tyler argues, because it gives examples of virtuous behavior; it is the same argu-
ment that Philip Sidney uses in his *Defence of Poetry*. A woman should be per-
mitted to translate or even to write romance, Tyler contends, because "it is all
one for a woman to pen a story, as for a man to address his story to a woman."[48]
Pembroke, whose brother had dedicated *The Countess of Pembroke's Arcadia*
to her, may have agreed; certainly her niece Lady Wroth did, for she wrote *The
Countess of Montgomery's Urania* loosely modeled on the *Arcadia*. Pembroke's
Antonius was historical drama rather than romance, though the portrayal of
Antony and Cleopatra is not unlike that of lovers in romance.

In England her poems praising a queen had precedent in the 104 Latin
distichs (couplets) honoring Marguerite de Navarre by Anne, Margaret, and
Jane Seymour, daughters of the Lord Protector Somerset (published 1551).[49]

---

[47] Mary Ellen Lamb, "The Cooke Sisters: Attitudes toward Learned Women in the
Renaissance," in *Silent but for the Word: Tudor Women as Patrons, Translators, and Writ-
ers of Religious Works*, ed. Margaret P. Hannay (Kent, Ohio: Kent State University Press,
1985), 107–25; Louise Schleiner, *Tudor and Stuart Women Writers* (Bloomington: Indiana
University Press, 1994), 34–51.

[48] Margaret Tyler, trans. *The Mirror of Princely Deeds and Knighthood* (London:
Thomas East, 1578), A3, A4v.

[49] Brenda M. Hosington, "England's First Female-Authored Encomium: The Sey-
mour Sisters' *Hecatodistichon* (1550) to Marguerite de Navarre. Text, Translation, Notes,
and Commentary," *SP* 93 (1996): 117–63.

Women had also dedicated works to other women, such as Anne Lock's dedication of translations to the duchess of Suffolk and to the countess of Warwick. Pembroke wrote a dedicatory poem, "Even Now That Care," that was also a poem of political advice, using admonitory flattery. She also composed a pastoral dialogue honoring Elizabeth, "A Dialogue between Two Shepherds, *Thenot* and *Piers*, in Praise of *Astrea*," as her brother Philip had done in "The Lady of May," and Edmund Spenser had done in "April" of his *Shepheardes Calender*.

Elegies by women for dead relatives also had precedent. Pembroke may have known the Italian poems Vittoria Colonna wrote for her dead husband, for example, or the Latin and Greek verse of Elizabeth Cook Russell, who wrote to mourn the deaths of her husband, her sister Katherine, and her son.[50] Perhaps the closest parallel was Marguerite de Navarre's poetic lament for her brother Francis I, king of France. So when Pembroke joined in the chorus of poets eulogizing Philip Sidney, she did have some female models, even though the scores of poets who had published poems praising Sidney were all, to our knowledge, male.[51]

The poetic work that established her literary reputation was her completion of the metrical *Psalms* begun by Philip. He had composed Psalms 1–43; she completed Psalms 44–150, including the 22 parts of Psalm 119, using a dazzling array of 126 different verse forms. Her *Psalms* are notable for their metrical complexity, inspired by the elegant French *Psaumes* of Clément Marot and Theodore Beza; for their witty word play and use of rhetorical figures; for their expansion of metaphors to reflect her own experience at court and as an aristocratic wife and mother; and for their careful scholarship in the many psalm versions and commentaries that she consulted in English, Latin, and French.

Metrical psalms were an important literary genre in early modern Europe, rivaling the Petrarchan sonnet in prestige and popularity. Among those who composed psalm paraphrases were Thomas Wyatt, Edmund Spenser (his psalm paraphrases are now lost), and later Francis Bacon and John Milton in England, as well as Martin Luther, Clément Marot, Theodore Beza, Laura Battiferri, Pietro Aretino, and many others on the Continent. Although most of the hundreds of psalm meditations and paraphrases were written by men, they formed an accepted literary genre for English women as well. In the fifteenth century, for example, Dame Eleanor Hull had translated a lengthy

---

[50] Lady Russell's verses are reprinted in Schleiner, *Tudor and Stuart Women Writers*, 47–51.

[51] Anne Bradstreet wrote "An Elegy upon the Honorable and Renowned Knight Sir Philip Sidney" many years later. *The Works of Anne Bradstreet*, ed. Jeannine Hensley (Cambridge: Harvard University Press, 1967), 189–91.

French commentary on the penitential psalms into English.[52] Two anonymous psalm translations—of Savonarola's exposition of Psalm 51 and of John Fisher's psalms—may have been the work of Katherine Parr.[53] The previous psalm meditations and paraphrases by English women that the countess of Pembroke could have known included those by Elizabeth Fane (1550; no longer extant) as well as paraphrases of psalm sections attributed by John Bale to Anne Askew and Queen Elizabeth. (Bale himself may have composed them, but they were circulated as the work of these women and so legitimized women's participation in the genre.)[54] Pembroke must have known the works by women included in Thomas Bentley's collection *The Monument of Matrons* (1582), particularly the "Second Lamp," or volume, that includes religious works and psalm meditations by Katherine Parr, Queen Elizabeth, Lady Jane Grey, Elizabeth Fane, Elizabeth Tyrwhit, Frances Abergavennie, and Dorcas Martin. Bentley says that he includes the works of these "heroical authors and worthy women" to serve "as perfect presidents [precedents] of true piety and godliness in woman kind to all posterity."[55] Bentley's collection validated such writing by women. When Pembroke began to write metrical psalm paraphrases, she thus had numerous works by English women to serve as examples for her content, although not for her array of literary forms. Anne Lock, who wrote a sonnet sequence on Psalm 51 that Pembroke echoed in her own metrical paraphrase of that psalm, may have been her most immediate female model, although she may also have known Laura Battiferri's Italian metrical paraphrases of the penitential psalms with their varied stanzaic forms.[56]

Pembroke never apologizes for her role as a woman writer, instead presenting her own works as part of this rich English and Continental literary tradition. She modeled her work primarily on that of her brother Philip, including a similar choice of rhetorical devices, numerous scattered allusions to his verse, and the recasting of *Astrophil and Stella* 5 in her paraphrase of Psalm 73. She is also particularly indebted to Spenser, as signaled by her diction and poetic style, her use of Spenserian characters in "A Dialogue," and specific allusions to *The Faerie Queene* in Psalms 78, 104, and 107. Both her

---

[52] Dame Eleanor Hull, *The Seven Psalms: A Commentary on the Penitential Psalms*, ed. Alexandra Barratt (Oxford: Clarendon Press, 1996).

[53] Susan James, *Kateryn Parr: The Making of a Queen* (Aldershot, England and Burlington, Vt.: Ashgate, 1999), 200–9.

[54] John King, *English Reformation Literature: The Tudor Origins of the Protestant Tradition* (Princeton: Princeton University Press, 1982), 219.

[55] Thomas Bentley, ed., *The Monument of Matrons: Containing Seven Several Lamps of Virginity* (London, 1582), B1.

[56] Margaret Hannay, "'Unlock my lipps': the *Miserere Mei Deus* of Anne Vaughan Locke and Mary Sidney Herbert, Countess of Pembroke," in *Privileging Gender in Early*

genre, the metrical psalm, and her sophisticated literary forms established her
Psalms as part of the mainstream of the English poetic tradition. (See *Psalms*
headnote.)

Except for some correspondence, nothing survives that she may have
written after her husband's death in 1601. During Henry Herbert's final ill-
ness she had helped to secure young William's future by arranging a position
for him at court.[57] But after Queen Elizabeth died in 1603, Pembroke's influ-
ence at court waned; as her sons achieved positions of prominence under King
James VI and I, they took over her role as literary patron. In her twenty years
as a widow she attempted to put down insurrections in Cardiff, administered
her properties, continued writing and translating (although the later works
alluded to in her correspondence have been lost), built herself the architectur-
ally innovative Houghton House in Bedfordshire (identified by local tradition
as John Bunyan's House Beautiful), carried on a flirtation with her handsome
and learned younger doctor (Sir Matthew Lister), and took the waters for her
health in the fashionable Continental town of Spa, frequented by European
aristocracy such as Louise de Coligny, dowager princess of Orange, and Pem-
broke's friend the countess of Barlemont. She continued to take part in some
major state occasions, including the funeral for Queen Anne.[58] Her relation-
ship with her natural grandchildren, the children her son William had with
her niece Mary Sidney Wroth, is unknown. Wroth hints in the second part of
Urania that Pembroke approved of the affair and loved the children, but that
may have been wishful thinking.

Letters printed as Pembroke's by John Donne the Younger show her hav-
ing her portrait painted (perhaps the Antwerp portrait now owned by Har-
riet Tuckey; see cover illustration), continuing to write and translate, and ex-
changing manuscripts with friends. She says of one manuscript, "as this copy
is the first, so also is it to be the last," which would help explain why any works
from this period have been lost.[59] Similarly, her earlier letter to Sir Edward

---

Modern England, ed. Jean R. Brink, Sixteenth-Century Essays and Studies. Kirksville,
Mo.: Sixteenth Century Journal Publishers, 23 (1993): 19–36; Laura Battiferri, *I Sette Salmi
Penitentiali des Santissimo Profeta Davit* (Florence, 1566).

[57] Michael G. Brennan, "The Queen's Proposed Visit to Wilton House in 1599 and the
'Sidney Psalms,'" *Sidney Journal* 21 (2003): 1–28.

[58] At the funeral the countess of Pembroke walked with other women of her rank
from Somerset House to Westminster Abbey, wearing the required heavy black gown
made of sixteen yards of broadcloth. See James Nichols, *The Progresses, Processions, and
Magnificent Festivities, of King James the First* (London, J. B. Nichols, 1828), 2: 540–41.

[59] John Donne the Younger, ed., *A Collection of Letters Made by Sir Tobie Matthew,
Knight* (London: Henry Herringman, 1660), 85–92; *Collected Works*, 1:300.

Wotton had pleaded with him to return her elegy, for she had lost her own copy: "if your care of these follies of such a toy have chanced to keep that which myself have lost, my earnest desire is that I may again see it."[60] Mary Sidney Wroth dramatizes the extemporaneous and ephemeral quality of this verse in *The Countess of Montgomery's Urania*. She shadows the countess of Pembroke in the Queen of Naples, who is "as perfect in poetry and all other princely virtues as any woman that ever lived, to be esteemed excellent in any one, [but] she was stored with all, and so the more admirable."[61] Hearing a nightingale, she recites a poem, included as "verses framed by the most incomparable Queen, or Lady of her time, a nightingale most sweetly singing, upon which she grounded her subject." After hearing her poem, Perissus exclaims "that he never had heard any like them, and in so saying, he did right to them, and her who knew when she did well, and would be unwilling to lose the due unto herself, which he gave her, swearing he never heard any thing finelier worded, nor wittilier written on the sudden."[62] This is the desired reward for such social verse: not publication, but praise within her own social group.

This does not necessarily indicate humility. Indeed, we may guess that Wroth's description of "her who knew when she did well, and would be unwilling to lose the due unto herself" might well be an accurate description of her aunt, who had received much public praise for her writing. Such a portrait fits the tone of her own writings, which are humble only on the surface. "Angel Spirit" is "quietly subversive," as Beth Wynn Fisken notes, managing "to camouflage the assertiveness of her style with the self-abnegation of her subject matter."[63] According to Gavin Alexander, "Even Now That Care" demonstrates similarly "aggressive humility."[64] Like Queen Elizabeth, Pembroke understood public relations. Like the queen, she crafted a self-image through

---

[60] Mary Sidney Herbert, countess of Pembroke, to Sir Edward Wotton, undated, probably 1594. Scribal copy. Bacon Papers. Lambeth Palace MS. 650/346. Correspondence III, *Collected Works*, 1:287.

[61] Lady Mary Wroth, *The First Part of The Countess of Montgomery's Urania*, ed. Josephine A. Roberts, RETS, 7th ser., vol. 17 (Binghamton, N.Y.: MRTS, 1995), 371.

[62] Wroth, *The First Part of The Countess of Montgomery's Urania*, 490.

[63] Beth Wynne Fisken, "'To the Angel Spirit . . .': Mary Sidney's Entry into the 'World of Words,'" in *The Renaissance Englishwoman in Print: Counterbalancing the Canon*, ed. Anne M. Haselkorn and Betty S. Travitsky (Amherst: University of Massachusetts Press, 1990), 265–66.

[64] Gavin Alexander, "Five Responses to Sir Philip Sidney, 1586–1628" (Ph.D. diss., University of Cambridge, 1996), 33. See also Suzanne Trill, "Spectres and Sisters: Mary

her own writings and through her patronage. Part of that image is her position as Sidney's sister. As she says in the autograph postscript to a business letter written by her secretary: "it is the Sister of Sir Philip Sidney who you are to right [i.e., to champion] and who will worthily deserve the same."[65] Far from abasing herself as merely Sidney's sister, she proudly claims both family connections and personal worth.

A similar combined claim is made in the 1618 portrait engraved by Simon van de Passe. Dressed in the velvet, pearls, and ermine appropriate to her wealth, she is described by her rank (signified by the inscription in Latin and English and by the coronet), and by her Sidney heritage (signified in her name "Mary Sidney," rather than "Mary Herbert," and in the Sidney *pheon*, or arrowhead crest, above the portrait), yet she is most prominently signified as a poet. The sides of the cartouche, or frame, appear to be quill pens in ink-wells, as Anne Lake Prescott suggests.[66] It is crowned with the poet's laurel wreath—above the *pheon* and above the coronet. And lest we miss the symbolism, Pembroke holds out to us the work on which her poetic reputation is founded, *"David's Psalms"* (see Plate no. 3).

Like Lady Anne Clifford, Mary Sidney Herbert seems to have been quiet and sweet as a young girl, when such behavior was rewarded, but to have become a formidable presence in her later years. Class was, in many ways, more important than gender in the social hierarchy, and the man of lower rank who crossed her would have been brave indeed, as records of her court cases against Edmund Matthew and Peter Samyn indicate.[67] She died from smallpox on 25 September 1621 at her home in London, traditionally Crosby Hall. (The Great Hall, which is all that survives, has since been moved to Chelsea.) After a funeral "according to her quality" in St. Paul's Cathedral, a magnificent torchlight procession took her to Wiltshire for burial beside her husband in Salisbury Cathedral.[68]

During her life Pembroke was celebrated as a writer. Among the male contemporaries who praised her works and/or borrowed from them are Samuel

---

Sidney and the 'Perennial Puzzle' of Renaissance Women's Writing," in *Renaissance Configurations: Voices/Bodies/Spaces, 1580–1690*, ed. Gordon McMullan (London: Macmillan, 1998), 202–5.

[65] Mary Sidney Herbert, countess of Pembroke, to Sir Julius Caesar, 8 July 1603, Correspondence XII, *Collected Works*, 1:294–95.

[66] Anne Lake Prescott, discussion at the meeting of the Society for the Study of Women in the Renaissance, City University of New York, 20 April 1998.

[67] Margaret Hannay, *Philip's Phoenix: Mary Sidney, Countess of Pembroke* (New York: Oxford University Press, 1990), 174–84, 203.

[68] Robert Sidney, earl of Leicester, to Robert Sidney, Viscount L'Isle, 30 September 1621, De L'Isle MS. U1475 Z53/81.

Daniel, John Davies, John Donne, Michael Drayton, Gabriel Harvey, George Herbert, Henry Lock (Lok), Henry Parry, William Shakespeare, and Edmund Spenser. Her importance as a role model for younger women writers is seen in Aemilia Lanyer's lengthy dedicatory poem in *Salve Deus Rex Judaeorum* (1611), and, as we have seen, in her niece Mary Wroth's affectionate portrayals of her in *Urania*. She was the first English woman to achieve such recognition as a poet.

Process of Revision

We have more information on Pembroke's process of revision than we have for most early modern writers—because of accidents. In 1695, approximately a century after Pembroke completed the *Psalms*, Samuel Woodford's brother bought some old "broken books" so that he could use the pages "to put up coffee powder." Samuel Woodford rescued part of a manuscript that turned out to be the Sidneys' working copy of their *Psalms*. Or at least Woodford says that it was, for "the very manner of this Psalm's being crossed and altered almost in every line and in many words twice makes me believe this was an original book . . . for none but an author could or would so amend any copy."[69] Woodford thus rescued what remained—Psalms 1–87 and 102–30. The rest had already been torn out. Because of his respect for Sir Philip Sidney, Woodford undertook the task of tidying up the manuscript, copying the whole volume, including (he says) all the variants. This is the version known as manuscript B, Bodleian Library MS. Rawl. Poet. 25. Then he evidently discarded the original manuscript. So his rescue is complicated by his blindness in thinking that his neat copy was more valuable than the authors' original. Nevertheless, we can get a sense of Pembroke's methods of revision by comparing her versions of Psalms 44–87 and 102–30 in this manuscript, or in later manuscripts, with the more polished versions in the authoritative Penshurst manuscript that was copied, under her direction, by the professional calligrapher John Davies of Hereford. For psalms like 71 we see that she has rethought the entire poem, including the length, rhyme, and meter. For other psalms, like 44 and 68, the changes are somewhat subtler. Eighteen manuscripts of the Sidney *Psalms* have been found; later manuscripts provide interesting opportunities to examine the history of transmission, as one version is copied from another.

"To the Angel Spirit of the Most Excellent Sir Philip Sidney" also exists in two forms because of a mistaken attribution. An early draft was found with Samuel Daniel's papers after his death in 1619 and erroneously printed as his

---

[69] Samuel Woodford, Bodleian MS. Rawl. poet. 25, fol. ii.

in *The Whole Works of Samuel Daniel Esquire in Poetry* (1623). The final version of the poem exists only as the dedicatory poem to the Tixall manuscript of the Sidneian *Psalms*.

We print six of Pembroke's works with other drafts or versions to demonstrate her process of revision: "Angel Spirit," Psalm 44, a portion of Psalm 68 (included in this introduction), Psalm 71, Psalm 124, and Psalm 131. Each presents opportunities for comparative study.

In Pembroke's revision of "Angel Spirit" she retained the same seven-line pattern of rhymes (*abbabba*) and the same meter (iambic pentameter), though the second version is longer. The most significant change is a shift of emphasis from her grief to presentation of Philip Sidney and herself as writers. She removes lines 22–35 of the variant, including images that allude to Spenser's *The Ruines of Time* ("Angel Spirit" Variant, 31) and Petrarch's *Triumph of Death* ("Angel Spirit" Variant, 35). She then adds four stanzas on Sidney and on her role as writer ("Angel Spirit," 50–70, 78–84). For example, in both versions her love "hath never done," but in the first version that love "Nor can enough, though justly here controlled" ("Angel Spirit" Variant, 41–42). What it can never do enough—praise Sidney—is clarified in the revision: "Nor can enough in world of words unfold" (28). She extends the images of wounds from her grief ("Angel Spirit" Variant, 19–20) to include Philip Sidney's work on the *Psalms*, which become "This half-maimed piece" (18). The wounds of her grief still bleed, but that blood is now "dissolved to ink" as she writes the poem (79). Praising Sidney not as a warrior but as a poet, she declares that his own works are so well written "as art could not amend" them and "no wit can add" to them (67–68).[70] The problem of her inadequacy to complete his *Psalms* becomes generalized: no one could complete them as he would have. She uses the same rhetorical strategy in saying that she is inadequate to praise him, for she is not alone: "There lives no wit that may thy praise become" ("Angel Spirit," 49; "Angel Spirit" Variant, 63). In both statements she places herself in the same position as other *poets*. She is claiming a place among authors of belles lettres that no Englishwoman before her had held. Protesting that she writes only from "simple love / Not art nor skill" ("Angel Spirit," 82–83) is also less self-effacing than it appears, for she is alluding to *Astrophil and Stella* 1, wherein Astrophil learns to write not from art but from his heart. By such echoes of her brother's words, she honors him and presents herself as a writer. Like Philip Sidney's Astrophil, the speaker here paradoxically uses modesty for self-assertion.

---

[70] Elaine Beilin, *Redeeming Eve: Women Writers of the English Renaissance* (Princeton: Princeton University Press, 1987), 148.

In her revision she strengthens the poem, although her syntax becomes even more complex.[71] She amplifies metaphors, adds characteristic rhetorical questions, adds repetition, and adds her usual exclamations "oh" and "ah." She also eliminates her harsh criticism of previous psalters as "what the vulgar formed," an uncomplimentary reference to the repetitive rhythms of the ubiquitous, and often poorly printed, Sternhold and Hopkins Psalter designed for congregational singing ("Angel Spirit" Variant, 10–11).[72] Donne later drew a similar contrast, but it was not tactful for one of the authors herself to do so.[73] She revises those lines to praise the original Hebrew Psalms, traditionally ascribed to David ("Angel Spirit," 10–14), and to honor biblical scholars because "all of tongues [all who know the scholarly languages—Greek, Latin, and here especially Hebrew] with soul and voice admire / These sacred hymns the kingly prophet formed" (13–14).

In an attempt to refute the charge that she is partial to her own "blood" or family, she invokes "Truth." Not only Sidney's sister, but also anyone who is not blind as an owl in daylight can see his worth, she says (50–56). The revision appears to add a final couplet, but those lines may well have been part of the early version as well—the rest of that last stanza was revised less than most. (The lines could have been written on a separate sheet, for example, and so lost when Daniel's works were printed.) The couplet appropriately concludes the poem with the traditional aspiration that she could join her brother in heaven.[74] The poem declares that her work was written only for Philip Sidney and has no "other purpose but to honor thee" (29–30), but like most such poetic statements, it is only a partial truth. "Angel Spirit" is placed beside a poem dedicating the *Psalms* to Queen Elizabeth, implying that this particular manuscript would reach royal eyes, and, as Pembroke obviously hoped, the *Psalms* themselves established her own poetic reputation by circulating widely in manuscript.

---

[71] Louise Schleiner includes a modernized version of the revised poem in her discussion of its syntax, *Tudor and Stuart Women Writers*, 77–79.

[72] Despite such comments, Hannibal Hamlin establishes the wide popularity of the Sternhold and Hopkins Psalter across all social classes. "'Very Mete to be Used of all Sortes of People': The Remarkable Popularity of the 'Sternhold and Hopkins' Psalter," *The Yale University Library Gazette* 75 (2000): 37–51. See also his *Psalm Culture and Early Modern English Literature* (Cambridge: Cambridge University Press, 2004).

[73] Donne, "Upon the Translation of the Psalms," in *John Donne: The Divine Poems*, ed. Gardner, 34–35.

[74] This conventional wish that the mourner could join the departed in heaven appears frequently in elegies for Sidney. See, for example, "Another of the Same," lines 21–22, in *Astrophel*, or, less plausibly, the city Verlame's wish in Spenser's *The Ruines of Time*, lines 307–8.

Her revision of Psalm 68 also demonstrates her reflection on her own role as writer, this time in connection with gender restrictions rather than in tribute to her brother Philip. This is a particularly difficult psalm to translate, with much controversy over just who is speaking the psalm of praise. The Geneva Bible, saying that this psalm describes the celebration when David brought the ark to Jerusalem (1 Chron. 15), translates verses 11–13 as follows:

> 11. The Lord gave matter to the women to tell of the great army.
> 12. Kings of the armies did flee . . . and she that remained in the house, divided the spoil.
> 13. Though ye have lain among pots, yet shall ye be as the wings of a dove that is covered with silver, and whose feathers are like yellow gold.

A note to verse 11 explains that "the fashion then was that women sang songs after the victory, as Miriam, Deborah, Judith and others." Their biblical songs, as well as this sixty-eighth Psalm, did seem to empower women writers, including Pembroke and, a century later, Anne Finch, countess of Winchilsea.[75] Yet in this very difficult psalm there is no direct connection between the women singers, the women dividing the spoil with the soldiers, and some unidentified persons lying near the pots who will be like doves. The Geneva Bible says that those persons near the pots represent the church lying "in black darkness" that God will make "shining and white" (note v. 13). One of the few commentators who does read the passage as referring to women is Theodore Beza, Calvin's successor at Geneva, a Hebrew scholar whose commentary Pembroke frequently consulted: "O ye damsels, ye have lived hitherto amongst the soot of the pots, even sitting at home, but now ye may come forth, shining and glittering no otherwise than the doves as white as snow, do cast forth a certain golden glistering as they flee in the air" (v. 13). Pembroke adapts that version into a moving statement about the plight of women, who are confined to the house and household duties.

> 11.   A virgin army there, with chasteness armed best
>   While armies fled, by thee was taught this triumph song to sing.
>
> 12.   These kings, these sons of war—lo, lo—they fly, they fly,
>   We house-confined maids with distaffs share the spoil

---

[75] Anne Finch, countess of Winchilsea, "The Introduction," *Miscellany Poems, on Several Occasions* (London: J. B., 1713), repr. in *Early Modern Women Poets: An Anthology*, ed. Jane Stevenson and Peter Davidson (Oxford: Oxford University Press, 2001), 458–60.

13.   Whose hue though long at home the chimney's gloss did
              foil
      Since now as late enlarged doves we freer skies do try
          As that gold-feathered fowl, so shall our beauties shine
          With beating wavy air with oar of silvered wing
          So dazzleth gazing eyes that eyes cannot define
      If those sweet lovely, glittering streams from gold or silver
              spring.

(VARIANT PSALM LXVIII, LINES 31–40)

She interprets living among the soot as spinning by an open hearth, adding to the original biblical verse the symbolic distaff used for this traditional female occupation. Though she retains the cliché that chastity is a woman's best armor, she rejects the restriction of women's poetic voice, making them empowered by their song of praise, so that "we freer skies do try." In the traditional equation of flight/song/poetry, these women become writers, whose works dazzle the eyes. What makes this image even more striking is the apparent identification of the speaker with the women. Pembroke uses indirect discourse, that is, the women say "we," but this seems to be the only gendered use of that pronoun in her *Psalms*. We women, she says, we poets who sing God's praise, we who have been confined to the household. In her revision she improved the poetry, but she also eliminated this statement, either because she herself thought it too strong, or because she was advised to change it by Daniel, who had read this early draft, or by someone else. In her revised version (lines 25–32) the women are "weak" rather than "house-confined," implying that they remain at home because of their own inadequacy rather than gender restrictions. "We" becomes "you," distancing the poet from the women singers. The doves, rather than a symbol of empowerment, become stereotypically feminine. They are conventionally "lovely" rather than "enlarged" in the "freer skies," and "shine . . . gracefully" rather than dazzling the eye. Even the doves' flight is less assertive. They "glide" rather than "beating" the air with their wings.[76] It is a remarkable shift in emphasis, as the writer retreats to contemporary gender norms.

Other revisions raise a variety of poetic and social issues. Assuming, as seems feasible, that Psalm 44 was the first she had paraphrased, we have included the earliest extant draft, from Woodford's transcription, to give a

---

[76] See Margaret Hannay, "'House-confined Maids': The Presentation of Woman's Role in the *Psalms* of the Countess of Pembroke," *ELR* 24 (1994): 44–71.

sense of where she began.[77] (Pembroke's work on the *Psalms* may have begun as early as the mid 1580s and seems to have been essentially complete by 1594.)[78] Variant Psalm 71 is another early draft from that manuscript; note particularly the faulty rhyme that remains in stanza five of this working draft. (See page 213.) We have included an alternate version of Psalm 131 from manuscript *N* (Bibliothèque de la Sorbonne, MS. 1110), which also preserves some early wording. A different study in revision is represented by the two versions of Psalm 124, the original quantitative version in the Penshurst manuscript and the simplified rhyming version found in two later manuscripts. The later version of Psalm 124 reverses her normal pattern of composition. We can see from Woodford's transcriptions that she usually begins with a paraphrase of the biblical text, either from the Geneva Bible of 1560 or from Coverdale's version in the Book of Common Prayer, or sometimes from *Les Psaumes mis en rime Français* of Marot and Beza (see particularly Psalm 55). Then she consults a wide variety of scholarly sources, relying most heavily on the commentaries (in Latin and in English translation) of Calvin and of Beza. Where the commentaries differed she tends to choose the reading that was closest to the Hebrew.[79] She polishes the poetic form, improves the rhyme and meter, smooths phrasing, and adds or intensifies her usual patterns of alliteration, compound words, rhetorical questions, and sophisticated patterns of repetition, particularly chiasmus (reversal of phrases), and polyptoton (repeating the same word in a different form).[80] In two later manuscripts, *G* (Trinity College, Cambridge, MS. R. 3. 16) and *M* (Huntington Library MS. HM 117), the replacement poems for Psalms 120–27 reverse this pattern. In the Penshurst manuscript these psalms are paraphrased as unrhymed quantitative verse, an attempt to reproduce classical meters in English. In these two seventeenth-

---

[77] On her progression as a writer see Waller, *Mary Sidney*, 75–106 and 152–78, and Beth Wynne [Fisken], "The Education of Mary Sidney" (Ph.D. diss., Rutgers University, 1979), and "Mary Sidney's *Psalms*: Education and Wisdom," in *Silent but for the Word*, ed. Hannay, 166–83.

[78] Michael G. Brennan, "The Date of the Countess of Pembroke's Translation of the Psalms," *RES* 33 (1982): 434–36.

[79] She may have relied on the translations closest to the Hebrew, consulted with Hebrew scholars, or even have had some knowledge of Hebrew. Theodore Steinberg, "The Sidneys and the Psalms," *SP* 92 (1995): 1–17; *Collected Works*, 2:16–19. Chanita Goodblatt argues that the most important question was her access to Hebrew scholarship; the Geneva notes, which relied heavily on rabbinical commentary, were a primary source. See her "Dialogue and David's Voice: Jewish Exegesis and Christian Hebraism in the Sidneian Psalms," paper read at "David in Medieval and Renaissance Culture," Barnard College, 7 December 2003.

[80] "Methods of Composition and Translation," *Collected Works*, 1:55–77.

century manuscripts these eight sophisticated poems are replaced with short rhymed stanzas that closely parallel the prose psalms in the Book of Common Prayer. (We have included both versions of Psalm 124, as well as the psalm from the Book of Common Prayer.) These simplified poems seem to be intended for congregational singing. Psalm 124, for example, can be sung to the Huguenot tune known to English speakers as "Old Hundredth," often now sung as the Doxology ("Praise God from whom all blessings flow"). We do not believe that this late revision of Psalms 120–27 is authorial, but it demonstrates the social context of the collection, transmission, and use of the Sidney *Psalms*.

Circulation and Reception of the Texts

This modern-spelling anthology includes all of her original poems, *Antonius*, approximately half of *A Discourse of Life and Death*, *The Triumph of Death*, and twenty-nine of her psalms from the Penshurst manuscript, plus four variants from other manuscripts to demonstrate her writing process (Psalms 44, 71, and 131) and the transmission history of her work (Psalm 124). We have also included supplemental material for the study of these works: Elizabeth Ashburnham Richardson's précis of and meditation on *A Discourse of Life and Death*, the countess of Pembroke's letter to Queen Elizabeth, a variant of "To the Angel Spirit of the Most Excellent Sir Philip Sidney" printed in Samuel Daniel's 1623 *Works*, and Philip Sidney's Psalm 14.

We present the countess of Pembroke's works along with supplemental materials to indicate how her works may have been disseminated and read in the early modern period. She was a liminal figure in the shift from manuscript to print circulation of belles lettres in court circles, gradually gaining control of the works by her brother, and then making careful decisions about which works by her brother and herself would circulate in manuscript and which in print. Philip Sidney's works had, during his life, circulated only in manuscript among a coterie of friends and relatives, as was customary in the higher levels of court society. Shortly after Sidney's death, his friend Fulke Greville was warned by the stationer William Ponsonby that an unauthorized edition of *The Countess of Pembroke's Arcadia* was about to be issued. Greville therefore asked Sidney's widow to return to him the corrected manuscript that Sidney had originally left with him.[81] Assuming the role of Sidney's literary executor, he then published with Ponsonby in 1590 an edition of the *Arcadia* that included the revised version that Sidney had left unfinished at his death

---

[81] Sir Fulke Greville to Sir Francis Walsingham, November 1586, PRO SP12/195. Greville and Pembroke quarreled over control of Sidney's work; John Florio and Matthew

(known as the *New Arcadia*), with the conclusion supplied from the earlier version (the *Old Arcadia*); it also added chapter headings and rearranged the poems. In 1591 an unauthorized and corrupt edition of *Astrophil and Stella* appeared, printed from an incomplete manuscript. These publications distressed Pembroke so much that they prompted her to undertake a corrected publication of Sidney's work, beginning with the work that Sidney had originally dedicated to her, *The Countess of Pembroke's Arcadia*. The Pembrokes' secretary Hugh Sanford worked with her. He claimed that the 1593 edition published by William Ponsonby was "most by her doing, all by her directing," concluding that "it is now by more than one interest *The Countess of Pembroke's Arcadia*: done, as it was for her: as it is, by her."[82] This is not the last of the efforts she will undertake on her brother's behalf, Sanford said, and five years later Ponsonby reissued the 1593 *Arcadia*, adding to it Sidney's *Defence of Poetry, Certain Sonnets*, the *Lady of May*, and the first complete edition of all the Astrophil sonnets.[83] The 1598 *Arcadia* is thus virtually the collected literary works of Sir Philip Sidney. Pembroke decided to omit his religious works, his translation of Du Bartas' *Divine Weeks*, since lost, and his *Psalms*, reserved for manuscript circulation.[84]

In the midst of her efforts to print her brother's literary works and so stabilize the text, she allowed Ponsonby to print two of her own, with her name as part of the title: *A Discourse of Life and Death. Written in French by Ph[ilippe de] Mornay. Antonius, A Tragedy Written Also in French by Ro[bert] Garnier. Both Done in English by the Countess of Pembroke* (1592). Her rank and her position as the sister of Sir Philip Sidney, whose magnificent funeral had been held at St. Paul's Cathedral just five years earlier, insured an interested audience for this work. Both works, in the Christian/Stoical tradition, emphasized reason over emotion and public duty over private relationships. In *Antonius* she introduced to English audiences several aspects of avant-garde French drama, including the focus on Cleopatra (the subject of numerous

---

Gwinne, who had evidently worked on the 1590 *Arcadia*, also became involved in the dispute. See introduction to *The Countess of Pembroke's Arcadia [The New Arcadia]*, ed. Victor Skretkowicz (Oxford: Clarendon Press, 1987), lviii–lxiii.

[82] H. S., "To the Reader," *The Countess of Pembroke's Arcadia* (1593), A4.

[83] On the editions of *Astrophil and Stella* as a struggle over patronage, see Arthur F. Marotti, *Manuscript, Print, and the English Renaissance Lyric* (Ithaca, N.Y.: Cornell University Press, 1995), 312–14.

[84] Debra Rienstra and Noel Kinnamon, "Circulating the Sidney-Pembroke Psalter," in *Women's Writing and the Circulation of Ideas: Manuscript Publication in England, 1550–1800*, ed. George Justice and Nathan Tinker (Cambridge: Cambridge University Press, 2002), 50–72; Margaret Hannay, "Mary Sidney and Scribal Publication," in *Women's Writing and the Circulation of Ideas*, 17–49.

plays in France and Italy), the use of Roman history to comment on contemporary events, and the form of neo-Senecan drama (sometimes termed "closet drama"), usually intended for reading aloud or private performance rather than the public stage. She was also innovative in her verse form, translating Robert Garnier's French rhymed couplets into English blank verse (unrhymed iambic pentameter), recently used for English drama by Christopher Marlowe. (She also uses occasional couplets for emphasis in the body of the drama and employs complex rhymes for the choruses.) *Antonius* was widely praised and popular enough to be reprinted in 1595 as *The Tragedy of Antony*. Pembroke's depiction of Cleopatra influenced Shakespeare's *Antony and Cleopatra*, although he combined the English stage tradition of action with the character development of neo-Senecan drama.[85] Elizabeth Cary seems to have used *Antonius* as a model for her original drama (the first by a woman in English), *The Tragedy of Mariam, the Fair Queen of Jewry*, which is set in Israel during the era of Cleopatra.[86] (See *Antonius* headnote.)

A Discourse of Life and Death, reprinted three times and reissued once by 1608, was valued by its English readers for its religious and philosophical meditations. Mornay had combined Stoic ideas, particularly from Seneca's moral essays and letters, with biblical reflections on death as our entry into eternal life. Gabriel Harvey, Michael Drayton, Wroth, and Shakespeare mention or allude to it, and it was obviously widely read.[87] One of the most interesting surviving responses is Elizabeth Ashburnham Richardson's recently rediscovered summary of and meditation on Pembroke's translation. We have included this rare surviving response by one early modern woman writer to the work of another to demonstrate how a reader adapted the text for her own use.

Three years later "The Doleful Lay of Clorinda," a poem of mourning probably originally written shortly after Philip Sidney's death in 1586, appeared

---

[85] Ernest Schanzer, "'Antony and Cleopatra' and the Countess of Pembroke's 'Antonius,'" *N&Q* 201 (1956): 152–54; Michael Steppat, "Shakespeare's Response to Dramatic Tradition in *Antony and Cleopatra*," in *Shakespeare—Text, Language, Criticism: Essays in Honour of Marvin Spevack*, ed. Bernhard Fabian and Kurt Tetzeli von Rosador (Hildesheim: Olms-Weidmann, 1987), 254–79.

[86] Nancy Cotton, *Women Playwrights in England c. 1363–1750* (Lewisburg, Pa.: Bucknell University Press, 1980), 36; Marta Straznicky, "'Profane Stoical Paradoxes': *The Tragedie of Mariam* and Sidneian Closet Drama," *ELR* 24 (1994): 103–34.

[87] Gabriel Harvey, *A New Letter of Notable Contents. With a Strange Sonnet, Entitled Gorgon, or the Wonderful Year* (1593), A4v–B1; Michael Drayton, *Idea: The Shepherds Garland*, in *The Works of Michael Drayton*, ed. J. William Hebel. Introductions, notes and variant readings, ed. Kathleen Tillotson and Bernard Newdigate (Oxford: Basil Blackwell, 1931–1941), 1:74, 76; Wroth, *The First Part of The Countess of Montgomery's Urania*, 332.

in Edmund Spenser's *Astrophel* (1595), an anthology of poems memorializing Sidney. Spenser introduces the poem, which is set off in its original publication by decorative borders, as the work of Sidney's sister "Clorinda." When Spenser editors raised the issue of authorship at all, it was generally accepted as hers until Ernest de Selincourt attributed it to Spenser and included it in *Spenser: Poetical Works* (1912).[88] He and some subsequent critics, who knew little about early modern women writers, erroneously assumed that she would not have had the rhetorical training to write such a work. The "Lay," however, is much simpler in form and style than her later poems, some of which are equally Spenserian in style.[89] The "Lay" does appear to be her earliest extant poem, though perhaps reworked in collaboration with Spenser for the *Astrophel* volume. (See page 136.)

The only other complete work to appear as hers in print in her own lifetime was "A Dialogue between Two Shepherds, *Thenot* and *Piers*, in Praise of *Astrea*," a pastoral dialogue praising Elizabeth that had evidently been written for Elizabeth's projected visit to Wilton in 1599. Sir John Davies seems to have seen a manuscript version, as Mary Erler notes, for his *Hymns of Astraea* (1599) have many parallels to Pembroke's "Dialogue."[90] Francis Davison included it, along with poems by Philip Sidney and others, in *A Poetical Rhapsody* (1602), which he dedicated to the countess of Pembroke's son William Herbert. A popular anthology, *A Poetical Rhapsody* was reprinted three times by 1621.

A few other pieces were printed in the seventeenth century. Fragments of her works, including scattered selections from *Antonius* and "The Doleful Lay," were included by John Bodenham in *Bel-vedére or the Garden of the Muses* (1600). Bodenham did not print entire poems, but rather gathered

---

[88] We can find no instance of a Spenser editor raising the question of authorship prior to 1805, when Henry John Todd notes on lines 215–16 of "Astrophel": "From this avowal I conclude that the following poem was not written by Spenser, but by the sister of Sir Philip, the accomplished Mary Countess of Pembroke, here poetically called *Clarinda* [sic]. We have already seen that she was particularly skilled in poetry. . . . All the subsequent poems on the death of Sir Philip are evidently a collection brought together by Spenser." *The Works of Edmund Spenser* (London: F. C. & J. Rivington, 1805), 8:61. Nineteenth-century editors generally followed Todd, except for a question raised by John Payne Collier in *The Works of Edmund Spenser* (London: Bickers, 1873), 5:76.

[89] Margaret Hannay, "The Countess of Pembroke as a Spenserian Poet," in *Pilgrimage for Love: Essays in Early Modern Literature in Honor of Josephine A. Roberts*, ed. Sigrid M. King, RETS (Tempe, Ariz.: MRTS, 1999), 41–62.

[90] Erler, "Davies's *Astraea*," 41–61. See also Steven May, *The Elizabethan Courtier Poets: The Poems and Their Contexts* (Asheville, N.C.: Pegasus Press, 1999), 177–78.

lines to be printed under headings such as "Of Pride" and "Of Courage."[91] Such poetic anthologies, as Wendy Wall notes, were designed to give the book purchaser the sense of entering "an enclosed or secret sphere."[92] Bodenham makes the analogy explicit when he invites the reader into "the Muses' garden (a place that may beseem the presence of the greatest prince in the world)."[93] Some lines from Pembroke's Psalm 97 seem to have been adapted in *All the French Psalm Tunes with English Words* (1623).[94] As we have seen, an early draft of her dedicatory poem "Angel Spirit" was found in Daniel's papers after his death and printed as his in *The Whole Works of Samuel Daniel Esquire in Poetry* (1623). Three letters to Tobie Matthew said to be hers appeared in print in 1660, published by John Donne the Younger as examples for composition.[95] More doubtful is "The Nightingale," a poem included in Lady Wroth's *Urania* (1621) as the work of the Queen of Naples (who shadows the countess of Pembroke), although it may have been jointly written with Wroth.

An educated seventeenth-century reader thus had access to a substantial body of work by Mary Sidney Herbert, countess of Pembroke. Nevertheless, her reputation as a poet was established not by these works that circulated in print, but by her metrical *Psalms*, 128 poems that she reserved for the aristocratic medium of scribal publication. She would lend a copy, often a draft in progress to a friend, such as her son's tutor Samuel Daniel, or her cousin John Harington, who would copy (or have a scribe copy) it for his own use. They could then give a copy to someone else, as Harington did when he sent excerpts from her works to his cousin Lucy, countess of Bedford. She might give a later draft to another friend, who would in turn share it with others. Several slightly different versions were simultaneously passed from hand to hand, with each copyist making additional changes, both intentional and unintentional. The transmission history of the eighteen extant manuscripts of the *Psalms* thus becomes exceedingly complex.[96] In addition, some psalms circulated in correspondence as individual poems, including three sent by

---

[91] John Bodenham, *Bel-vedére or the Garden of the Muses*, [ed.] A. M.[unday?] (1600), A3v.

[92] Wendy Wall, *The Imprint of Gender: Authorship and Publication in the English Renaissance* (Ithaca, N.Y.: Cornell University Press, 1993), 177.

[93] Bodenham, *Bel-vedére*, A3–A4v.

[94] Jim Doelman, "A Seventeenth-Century Publication of Three of Sir Philip Sidney's Psalms," *N&Q* 38 (1991): 162–63.

[95] *A Collection of Letters made by Sir Tobie Matthew, Knight* (1660); *Collected Works*, 1:298–301.

[96] "Manuscripts of the *Psalms*" and "Relationship of the Texts of the *Psalms*" in *Collected Works*, 2:308–57.

Harington to the countess of Bedford.[97] Some of these psalms in manuscript circulation were set to music. Two of the penitential psalms that she paraphrased, Psalms 51 and 130, were set for soprano voice and lute in what Linda Austern suggests is part of a collection compiled by an individual woman for her own performance.[98] (See Plates 5 and 6 of the settings for Psalm 130.) As her version of Psalm 97 was adapted for congregational song in *All the French Psalm Tunes with English Words*, so her complex quantitative verse for Psalms 120–27 was simplified in some later manuscripts, presumably also for congregational singing.[99] We may deduce that the Sidney *Psalms* were also considered appropriate for private devotional use, as indicated by their rubrication for Morning and Evening Prayer, as in the Book of Common Prayer, in one of John Harington's manuscripts.[100]

Her *Psalms* also became a literary model for seventeenth-century devotional verse by writers including George Herbert, Aemilia Lanyer, and John Donne.[101] George Herbert, brother of Edward, Lord Herbert of Cherbury, and Sir Henry Herbert, Master of the Revels, was a distant blood relative of the Pembroke branch of the family. Philip Herbert, fourth earl of Pembroke, asked King Charles to give him the position as parish priest at Bemerton, a short walk from Wilton, in 1630. George Herbert must have exchanged manuscripts with his relatives there, for the Sidney *Psalms* influenced his poems, including his quotation of the phrase "My God, my king" (Psalm 59.88) in "Jordan" (I).[102] Other parallels include Psalm 104 and "Providence," Pembroke's acrostic Psalm 117 and Herbert's "Coloss. 3:3," and Psalm 88 and Herbert's "Affliction" (IV).[103] The most direct parallel may be Herbert's two-part "Easter" and Psalm

---

[97] Sir John Harington of Kelston to Lucy, countess of Bedford, 19 December 1600, Library of the Inner Temple Petyt MS. 538.43.14, fols. 284–86.

[98] British Library Additional MS. 15117; Linda Austern, private correspondence.

[99] *Collected Works*, 2:355–56.

[100] British Library Additional MS. 12047; "Manuscripts of the Psalms," *Collected Works*, 1:317–19.

[101] Debra Rienstra, "Aspiring to Praise: The Sidney-Pembroke Psalter and the English Religious Lyric" (Ph.D. diss., Rutgers University, 1995).

[102] Louis Martz, *Poetry of Meditation* (New Haven: Yale University Press, 1962), 273–79; John C. A. Rathmell, "A Critical Edition of the Psalms of Sir Philip Sidney and the Countess of Pembroke" (Ph.D. diss., University of Cambridge, 1964), lxxvi; Chana Bloch, *Spelling the Word: George Herbert and the Bible* (Berkeley: University of California Press, 1985), 233–35; Alice Ostriker, "Song and Speech in the Metrics of George Herbert," *PMLA* 80 (1965): 62–68; Heather Asals, "The Voice of George Herbert's 'The Church,'" *ELH* 36 (1969): 511–28. See also Bloch's chart of his references to specific psalms, *Spelling*, 308–10.

[103] Waller, *Mary Sidney*, 226–27; *The Psalms of Sir Philip Sidney and the Countess of Pembroke*, ed. J. C. A. Rathmell (New York: New York University Press, 1963), xviii–xix.

57, which includes "consort" and "bear a part," as well as her adaptation of Wyatt's phrase, "awake my lute."[104] The form of Psalms 88 and 130 anticipates Herbert's psalm-like lyrics, such as "Longing," "Home," "Dullness," "Giddiness," "The Method," "Complaining," and "The Glance." The Sidney *Psalms* also influenced both Herbert's style and content, his "tone, stance of speaker, rhythmic effects, and deceptively simple formulations of staggering religious paradoxes," as Barbara Lewalski observes.[105]

The influence of Pembroke's *Psalms* on Aemilia Lanyer was more a matter of example than of specific parallels, as she gives her prominence in the dedications that comprise her "community of good women."[106] In her dedicatory poem to Pembroke, Lanyer presents her as singing her *Psalms* with a company of women, says that she surpasses her famous brother, and then asks her to favor her work. As Pembroke compared her work to the "little streams" and Sidney's to the "great sea" ("Angel Spirit," 32–33), so Lanyer says that her works are simple honey in contrast to the imported "finer, higher prized" sugar of Pembroke's works.[107] Yet in her plea that Pembroke will accept her lines that are "unlearned" compared to hers, she seeks a model, both of poetic composition and of "feminine spiritual achievement," as Rienstra says – or perhaps she seeks even to displace Pembroke, as Kari Boyd McBride argues.[108] Her long preface echoes, in stanzas 8–10, "a mélange of Psalm texts . . . in what seems to be a gesture of discipleship to the Countess of Pembroke."[109] Her lyrics themselves are psalmic, particularly in her praise of God in "Salve Deus," lines 73–144, and in her preface.[110]

---

[104] Noel Kinnamon, "A Note on Herbert's 'Easter' and the Sidneian Psalms," *George Herbert Journal* 1 (1978): 44–48, and "Notes on the Psalms in Herbert's *The Temple*," *George Herbert Journal* 4 (1981): 10–29; Bloch, *Spelling the Word*, 250–51; Coburn Freer, *Music for a King: George Herbert's Style and the Metrical Psalms* (Baltimore: Johns Hopkins University Press, 1972), 240; Susanne Woods, *Natural Emphasis: English Versification from Chaucer to Dryden* (San Marino, Calif.: Huntington Library, 1984), 171.

[105] Barbara Kiefer Lewalski, *Protestant Poetics and the Seventeenth-Century Religious Lyric* (Princeton: Princeton University Press, 1979), 244.

[106] Barbara Kiefer Lewalski, *Writing Women in Jacobean England* (Cambridge: Harvard University Press, 1993), 213; see also Susanne Woods, *Lanyer: A Renaissance Woman Poet* (New York: Oxford University Press, 1999), 106.

[107] Aemilia Lanyer, "The Author's Dream to the Lady Marie, the Countess Dowager of Pembroke," in *Poems of Aemilia Lanyer*, ed. Woods, 30.

[108] Rienstra, "Aspiring to Praise," 222; Kari McBride, "Remembering Orpheus in the Poems of Aemilia Lanyer," *SEL* 38 (1998): 87–108.

[109] Lewalski, *Writing Women*, 228.

[110] Kari Boyd McBride and John C. Ulreich, "Aemilia Lanyer's Psalm of Psalms," read at Renaissance Society of America conference, Chicago, 29–31 March 2001.

Donne also saw the Sidney *Psalms* as a literary model, saying they "tell us *why,* and teach us *how* to sing."[111] His most characteristic stylistic elements are also found in the Sidney *Psalms,* including dramatically abrupt openings, argumentative structure, and vivid imagery.[112] (There are a few verbal parallels as well. In Holy Sonnet 10 ["Death be not proud"], for example, his phrase "why swellst thou thus" seems to recall Pembroke's Psalm 52.1, "Tyrant, why swell'st thou thus.") Now that God "hath translated these translators," Donne says, "We thy Sydnean Psalms shall celebrate."[113] Similarly, Daniel promises that Pembroke's *Psalms* will give her fame on earth and in heaven:

> Those h*ymns* that thou dost consecrate to heaven,
> Which *Israel's* Singer to his God did frame:
> Unto thy voice eternity hath given,
> And makes thee dear to him from whence they came.
> In them must rest thy ever reverent name,
> So long as *Zion's* God remaineth honored.[114]

Emphasizing her own role in completing the *Psalms,* and adapting the architectural metaphor that she herself had used in the dedicatory poems, he says "this is that which thou mayest call thine own," work that will endure even after "*Wilton* lies low leveled with the ground." Her Psalms are a "monument" that "cannot be over-thrown."[115]

Despite this comparatively wide manuscript circulation, not everyone who referred to the Sidney *Psalms* would have seen them. To have read them, or better yet, to have been given a copy, was a sign of membership in a prestigious literary coterie. Francis Davison, among others, wanted to make this work available to the print audience, but no print edition appeared during Pembroke's life. Some twenty years after her death John Langley, an official licenser of printed books, had approved the printing of the Sidney *Psalms,* but no such edition is known to be extant.[116] John Harington's descendant eventually printed seven psalms from his papers in the eighteenth-century

---

[111] Donne, "Upon the Translation of the Psalms," in *John Donne: The Divine Poems,* ed. Gardner, 34.

[112] Lewalski, *Protestant Poetics,* 241–43; Rathmell, "Critical Edition," xx–xxii.

[113] Donne, "Upon the Translation of the Psalms," in *John Donne: The Divine Poems,* ed. Gardner, 35.

[114] Samuel Daniel, *Delia and Rosamond Augmented. Cleopatra* (1594), H6. Cf. Beilin, *Redeeming Eve,* 126.

[115] Daniel, *Delia,* H6v.

[116] Michael G. Brennan, "Licensing the Sidney Psalms for the Press in the 1640s," *N&Q* 31 (1984): 304–5.

collection *Nugae Antiquae.* This was their only known appearance in print before the nineteenth century. In 1823 the first complete edition of the Sidney *Psalms* appeared in print. Selections from the *Psalms,* usually attributed solely to Philip Sidney, were published in at least five nineteenth-century anthologies, including forty-four psalms in John Ruskin's *Rock Honeycomb,* and only six in Robert Barnwell's misleadingly titled volume *The Works of Mary Sidney, Countess of Pembroke* (1865), but they soon passed once again into obscurity. J. C. A. Rathmell's 1963 edition provided the foundation for modern studies of the Sidney *Psalms.*

Pembroke's two poems dedicating the *Psalms*—"To the Angel Spirit of the Most Excellent Sir Philip Sidney," which is as much a meditation on her role as writer as it is elegy for Sidney; and "Even Now That Care," which dedicates the Sidneys' poetic paraphrase of the Psalms to Queen Elizabeth (1599)—had far less circulation. They are included in just one of the eighteen surviving manuscripts of the Sidney *Psalms,* MS. *J,* the manuscript once at Tixall, now owned by Dr. Bent Juel-Jensen. The Tixall manuscript was copied from the Penshurst *Psalms* manuscript. The Penshurst manuscript was transcribed for Pembroke herself in the most elegant Italian style (highlighted with gold ink) by the calligrapher John Davies of Hereford. Because the Penshurst manuscript is missing the opening leaves, it is unclear whether the dedicatory poems were originally included there as well. But perhaps they were, for Davies later refers to his work writing "in gold, what thou, in ink hadst writ," saying that her *Psalms* will live eternally, for "the angels . . . shall chant it in their quires [perhaps with a pun on choirs and quires of paper]," in a near quotation from "Angel Spirit."[117] Angel references were common in sacred poetry, but references to her *Psalms* are frequently paired with such references to angels, saying they were penned with an "angel's quill," or were sung by angels, or that Philip Sidney "doth shine midst angels bright."[118] Donne says that the angels themselves will learn to sing those *Psalms* by listening to "what the Church does here."[119] Daniel, who owned a copy of an early draft of "Angel Spirit," complimented Pembroke by echoing in *Delia* Sonnet 1 her own phrasing.[120] It is thus

[117] John Davies, *Muses Sacrifice,* in *The Poems of Sir John Davies,* ed. Robert Krueger (Oxford: Clarendon Press, 1975), 2:4

[118] Nathaniel Baxter, *Sir Philip Sidney's Ouránia, that is, Endimion's Song and Tragedy. Containing all Philosophy* (1606), N2v; Lanyer, *Poems,* 27; Drayton, *Works,* 1:76; Henry Lok, *Ecclesiastes, Otherwise Called the Preacher. Containing Solomon's Sermons or Commentaries* (London: Richard Field, 1597), Y1v.

[119] Donne, "Upon the Translation of the Psalms," in *John Donne: The Divine Poems,* ed. Gardner, 34.

[120] Lars-Håkan Svensson, *Silent Art: Rhetorical and Thematic Patterns in Samuel Daniel's Delia,* Lund Studies in English, vol. 57 (Lund: Lund University Press, 1980), 35–49.

quite possible that others read the poem as well. In contrast, her dedication to Queen Elizabeth seems to have been intended for the queen's eyes alone, combining praise with admonition; no contemporary references to this poem have as yet been found.

Although contemporary references indicate that she wrote other poems and translations, the only other work that has survived is her translation of Petrarch's *The Triumph of Death*. John Harington sent a copy to Lucy, countess of Bedford, as we have seen. All that survives is a corrupt transcription of his copy, accompanying a letter dated 1600.[121] Some of Pembroke's household had read her Petrarch translation, including her niece Mary Wroth and her physician Thomas Moffet.[122] Apparently it was known to some others as well, including Aemilia Lanyer, Michael Drayton, and Gabriel Harvey, so it may have had some limited circulation.[123]

In an era that treated the personal letter as both a significant literary form and a vital political tool, her correspondence was widely celebrated. Francis Osborn, for example, praises the literary quality of the "incomparable letters of hers" that he had seen, and Robert Sidney's agent Rowland White told him that his sister's letters on his behalf would be efficacious.[124] To our great loss, these letters and most of her other correspondence have disappeared, including all the letters that she exchanged with her brothers Philip and Robert; only one of her family letters, written to her sister-in-law Barbara Gamage Sidney, has been preserved, along with a scattering of her other correspondence.[125] (Barbara Sidney also preserved at Penshurst some 332 of her husband's letters to her.)[126] All the papers Pembroke herself had saved at Wilton and at Baynard's Castle were probably burned in the mid-seventeenth-century fires that

---

[121] Library of the Inner Temple Petyt MS. 538.43.14, fols. 286–89.

[122] On possible allusions to *The Triumph of Death* by Wroth and by Lanyer, see Lynn Moorhead Morton, "'Vertue Cladde in Constant Love's Attire': The Countess of Pembroke as a Model for Renaissance Women Writers" (Ph.D. diss., University of South Carolina, 1993), 134–38; Thomas Moffet, *The Silkworms and Their Flies (1599)*, facsimile, introd. Victor Houliston, RETS (Binghamton, N.Y.: MRTS, 1989), A2.

[123] Lanyer, *Poems*, 22; Drayton, *Works*, 1:76; Harvey, *Letter*, A4v.

[124] Francis Osborn, *Historical Memoirs on the Reigns of Queen Elizabeth and King James* (1683), 455; Rowland White to Robert Sidney, 14 January 1598, De L'Isle MS. U1475 C12/121.

[125] Mary Sidney Herbert, countess of Pembroke, to Lady Barbara Gamage Sidney, 9 September 1590, *Collected Works*, 1:286.

[126] Margaret P. Hannay, Noel J. Kinnamon, and Michael G. Brennan, eds., *Domestic Politics and Family Absence: The Correspondence (1588–1621) of Robert Sidney, First Earl of Leicester, and Barbara Gamage Sidney* (Aldershot, England, and Burlington, Vt.: Ashgate, 2005).

destroyed those residences. Nevertheless, since 1999 one additional *Psalms* manuscript and two brief letters in private hands have been recovered, giving us hope that more of her work is as yet undiscovered (or incorrectly attributed) in various attics and archives.[127] Even so, her known works run to some five hundred pages in print, a remarkable body of work to have survived for any early modern writer.

---

[127] Gavin Alexander, "A New Manuscript of the Sidney Psalms; A Preliminary Report," *Sidney Journal* 18 (2000): 43–56; Steven W. May, "Two Unpublished Letters by Mary Herbert, Countess of Pembroke," *EMS* 9 (2000): 88–97.

I.

WORKS CIRCULATED
IN PRINT

ANTONIUS

In each of her translations the countess of Pembroke imported sophisticated literary forms and techniques. By translating Robert Garnier's drama *Marc Antoine* (1578, revised 1585) she brought to England the Continental use of Roman history to comment on contemporary political events. Garnier, a member of the Pléiade and among the avant garde of French playwrights, was also a magistrate who intended his historical works to apply to the current French civil war. The subtitle of *Porcie* (1568), for example, emphasizes that it represents the cruel and bloody season of the Roman civil wars as parallel to the calamity of his own time, and the dedication of *Marc Antoine* similarly warns that its representation of the result of the Roman civil wars demonstrates the horrors of such conflict for France.[1]

When the countess of Pembroke translated *Marc Antoine* in 1590, civil war and foreign invasion were constant threats to England. In 1587 Mary Queen of Scots had been executed because of repeated plots to assassinate Elizabeth and put Mary on the English throne. The Spanish Armada had been sent by Philip of Spain to attack England in 1588, and there were frequent threats of invasion throughout the following decade. (The earl of Pembroke was charged with defending Milford Haven on the coast of Wales, thought to be the most probable site for invasion.) There was a real fear that England would also soon face another civil war because the aged Elizabeth refused to name her successor. The civil wars in France also had a new urgency. Henri IV (still Protestant) was now king, but Catholic conservatives were fighting him and calling in the Spanish. Elizabeth helped to fund Henri, as she helped the Dutch to fight against their Spanish conquerors. The English fixation on the French civil wars was energized by fear that such wars could happen in England when Elizabeth died or the Spanish tried again to invade. Since Garnier's drama was written in the shadow of earlier religious civil wars, it was thus already relevant to contemporary politics.

By the time Pembroke translated *Marc Antoine*, the tragedy of Antony and Cleopatra had been the subject of at least six plays written in Italian,

---

[1] Robert Garnier, *Porcie: tragedie françoise, représentant la cruelle et sanglante saison des guerres civiles de Rome: propre et convenable pour y voir depeincte la calamité de ce temps* (Paris: Robert Estienne, 1568); "A Monseigneur de Pibrac," *Two Tragedies: Hippolyte and Marc Antoine*, ed. Christine M. Hill and Mary G. Morrison (London: Athlone Press, 1975), 104.

French, and Spanish since 1550. Each of these dramas had been based on Plutarch's *Life of Antony*, which presents Antony as a great Roman destroyed by his passion for the Egyptian queen. In this early modern example of Orientalism, Roman virtues of honor and self-discipline, represented by Octavius Caesar and (at first) Antony, are contrasted with Egyptian luxury and decadence, represented by a manipulative Cleopatra who corrupts Antony for political gain. *Marc Antoine* shifts the emphasis by including an Egyptian perspective, by portraying Cleopatra as a constant lover, and by portraying Octavius Caesar, through the eyes of Antony, as a devious coward (1109–24). Both Plutarch and Garnier compare the warrior ideal with a degrading love of pleasure. Garnier gives Antony a speech comparing the proverbial symbol of decadence, the warrior's arms covered with spider's webs (1177), with his achievements, described earlier in terms of "piled carcasses" (966). Garnier challenges that masculine ideal, however, by presenting the viewpoints of other characters and by showing such slaughter as negative, even for the soldiers themselves (chorus of Act 4). The play thus demonstrates considerable ambiguity towards the warrior code, even as it emphasizes Stoic virtues of self-control.

Garnier used the fashionable neo-Senecan dramatic form to compose a drama apparently intended for dramatic reading or private performance rather than for presentation on the popular stage. Such tragedies focus on character rather than action, banishing violence off stage. Caesar describes Antony's defeat at Actium in a flashback, for example, and Dircetus carries in a bloody sword as he comes to report Antony's death. A full stage production is certainly possible, but less formal performance would be simple: no crowd scenes, no special effects, and usually only one or two characters onstage. No more than four actors have speaking parts in any given scene. The most crowded scene is the climax in Act 5, involving six characters, but even that could be staged in sequence, so that Cleopatra is on stage with her two (silent) children and her children's tutor; after they leave, her two waiting women could enter. The entire group could recite the choruses. Pembroke's translation of Garnier's *Marc Antoine* is thus ideal for informal performance at home, perhaps one reason it was popular enough to go through two editions in three years.

Neo-Senecan tragedies were comprised of three main structural elements: extended speeches by the major characters; formal debates on moral issues, often in the form of *stichomythia*, two characters talking in alternate lines; and meditations by the chorus, as in Greek drama. In keeping with this dramatic form, there are no direct confrontations between Antony and his enemy Octavius Caesar, or even between Antony and Cleopatra, who do not appear together until Cleopatra and her women haul the dead body of Antony into her own tomb. Garnier deliberately ranges across social classes to present a variety of perspectives—the rulers Antony, Cleopatra, and Octavius Caesar; their faithful servants and retainers; the aristocrat Philostratus, a *rhetor*, or rhetorician, whose sole function in the play is to give the long speech that opens Act 2; and the chorus representing the people, "first, Egyptians, and after, Roman soldiers." Classical mythology is typically used as a sort of code, so that the Furies, for example, represent the passions of lust, ambition, and rage that lead to disaster. Cleopatra is repeatedly compared to Circe, who changed men into swine, and Antony's love for her is compared to Hercules' love for Omphale, who dressed him in women's clothes and set him to the traditionally female task of spinning. Comparisons to the fall of Troy evoke a classical context for the fall of Egypt.

In the Argument, or opening explanation, Pembroke does not translate Garnier so much as provide a fuller explanation for English audiences who might well be unfamiliar with the political details of the Antony and Cleopatra story. Antony and Octavius Caesar had defeated the republicans Cassius and Brutus, who had murdered Julius Caesar. Antony and Octavius were then appointed, with Lepidus, to rule Rome as a triumvirate. A serious quarrel between Antony and Octavius was repaired when Antony married Octavius's sister for political reasons, even though he had previously had a passionate affair with the Egyptian queen Cleopatra. The empire was divided between Octavius in the west and Antony in the east. Antony set off on a military campaign to the east, but instead of conquering the Parthians, he returned to Cleopatra. (According to Dio Cassius he divorced Octavia and married Cleopatra; other records disagree, hence the ambiguity about Cleopatra's "wifely love . . . scarce wifely" in lines 597–98.) Octavius avenged the honor of his sister by attacking Antony, thereby causing a civil war that spread over the Roman empire. Antony was winning the great sea battle off Actium, on the western coast of Greece, when he saw Cleopatra flee with her sixty ships. Following her rather than continuing to lead his troops, he lost everything in one of the greatest military defeats in history (31 B.C.). Octavius then besieged Alexandria.

As the drama opens, Octavius is on his way to capture Antony and Cleopatra so that he can display them in his triumph, or victory parade, in Rome. External action is largely suspended while the besieged lovers await the conquering Octavius, and the primary conflict becomes internal. Faced with disaster, they can only determine their own attitudes towards each other and towards their past actions, and then decide whether to allow themselves to be humiliated as Octavius's captives or to commit suicide. Antony blames Cleopatra in his long opening soliloquy that comprises Act 1, which culminates in four lines of standard misogyny blaming all women as defective. In Act 2, after Philostratus and the chorus present an Egyptian perspective,

Cleopatra appears with her women. Her first words are a defense against Antony's charge that she has betrayed him; she has given up everything for him, and her flight at Actium was the result of cowardice rather than treachery, but she does admit that she is the "sole cause" (455) of his overthrow. Cleopatra and Charmion debate fate and free will, and then consider whether or not suicide is justified.[2] (The Roman acceptance of suicide is challenged from a Christian perspective in the accompanying translation, *A Discourse of Life and Death*.) In Act 3 Antony calls her his "fair enticing foe" (1151), but he begins to accept some responsibility for choosing pleasure over honor (1149–78). He realizes that he lost all by "one disordered act at Actium" (1125) and decides that he has now no honorable recourse but suicide. The chorus meditates on the difficulties of life and the benefits of death, paralleling *A Discourse of Life and Death*. Act 4 opens with a speech by Octavius Caesar, who reviles Antony for "his lewd delights" (1398) with Cleopatra and proclaims his own supremacy over the entire world. Caesar and Agrippa debate the wisdom of killing rivals to the throne, a debate topical in England after the execution of Mary Queen of Scots and in France after the assassination of two chief rivals for the throne. Dircetus, a messenger, reports the death of Antony and describes Cleopatra and her women hauling his body up into her tomb. Act 5 belongs to Cleopatra's speeches, interspersed with dialogue with her women and her children as she prepares to die. As Antony is given the first words, accusing Cleopatra, Cleopatra is given the last, mourning for Antony.

In Garnier's play Cleopatra is not merely the traditional seductress but a constant lover. Her love for Antony is genuine, she worries about her children, and she regrets her dereliction of duty to her country. Remarkably, as Eve Sanders notes, she is presented as admirable without being conventionally chaste. Instead, "she is by turns regal, maternal, defiant, loyal, physically courageous, and sensual," and she "demonstrates her virtue by the arduous feat

---

[2] Mary Ellen Lamb, "The Countess of Pembroke and the Art of Dying," in *Women in the Middle Ages and the Renaissance: Literary and Historical Perspectives*, ed. Mary Beth Rose (Syracuse, N.Y.: Syracuse University Press, 1986), 207–26.

[3] Eve Rachele Sanders, *Gender and Literacy on Stage in Early Modern England* (Cambridge: Cambridge University Press, 1998), 97, 100. See also Tina Krontiris, *Oppositional Voices: Women as Writers and Translators of Literature in the English Renaissance* (London and New York: Routledge, 1992), 69–73; Howard B. Norland, "Englishing Garnier: Mary Sidney's *Antonie* and Daniel's *Cleopatra*," *Tudor Theatre: Emotion in the Theatre*, Collection Theta 3 (Bern: Peter Lang, 1996), 161–69; and May, *Elizabethan Courtier Poets*, 168–69.

of raising Antoine from the ground to the top of the monument."[3] Pembroke subtly alters this scene to emphasize Cleopatra's strength and physicality.

In twentieth-century criticism Pembroke was often criticized for setting up the form of neo-Senecan drama (sometimes called "closet drama") to combat Shakespeare and the popular stage.[4] This is most unlikely, since Pembroke and her family arranged for dramatic performances and served as patrons to a theater company; she herself paid the players on at least one occasion, and her sons William and Philip were the "incomparable pair of brethren" to whom the First Folio of Shakespeare's works was dedicated, because they had shown their author "so much favor."[5] It would be more accurate to say that her importation of French vernacular neo-Senecan drama, with its emphasis on character, helped to encourage greater sophistication on the English stage, particularly as Shakespeare combined the English tradition of stage action with character development through soliloquy and dialogue. Shakespeare's *Antony and Cleopatra* is indebted to her *Antonius* for some phrasing and for elements of characterization, including, perhaps, the questioning of the warrior ideal of masculinity.[6] Pembroke's translation also inspired other neo-Senecan dramas on Roman themes, notably Samuel Daniel's *Cleopatra*, written at her request, and Elizabeth Cary's *Mariam*, the first original play by an English woman. Like Cleopatra, Mariam is queen of a land (Israel, in this case) under Roman domination.[7] Rather than present as a heroine a woman notorious for her love affairs, however, Cary presents a pure but impolitic Mariam in contrast to her promiscuous and manipulative enemy Salome. Both dramas address issues of politics and gender.

Pembroke translates the body of the drama line by line, for the most part quite accurately.[8] She uses the new (for drama) form of English blank verse

---

[4] See particularly Alexander Maclaren Witherspoon, *The Influence of Robert Garnier on Elizabethan Drama* (New Haven: Yale University Press, 1924), 65–83, 181–89. His conspiracy theory was answered by Mary Ellen Lamb, "The Myth of the Countess of Pembroke: The Dramatic Circle," *Yearbook of English Studies* 11 (1981): 194–202.

[5] *William Shakespeare: The Complete Works*, ed. Stanley Wells and Gary Taylor (Oxford: Clarendon Press, 1986), xlii; Hannay, *Philip's Phoenix*, 119–29.

[6] *A New Variorum Edition of Shakespeare: Antony and Cleopatra*, ed. Marvin Spevak (New York: MLA, 1990), 477–79.

[7] For a detailed analysis of these plays, see Sanders, *Gender and Literacy*, 89–137; see also Elizabeth Patton, "Seven Faces of Cleopatra," in *Teaching Tudor and Stuart Women Writers*, ed. Susanne Woods and Margaret Hannay (New York: MLA, 2000), 289–94.

[8] Coburn Freer, "Mary Sidney, Countess of Pembroke," in *Women Writers of the Renaissance and Reformation*, ed. Katharina A. Wilson (Athens, Ga.: University of Georgia Press, 1987), 486–87; Brennan, *Literary Patronage*, 67; "*Antonius*: Fidelity to Originals," *Collected Works*, 1:147–51.

(unrhymed iambic pentameter), to translate Garnier's rhyming couplets in alexandrines (twelve-syllable lines). She saves rhyme for emphasis, sometimes at the close of paragraphs (as in 927–28), or for *stichomythia* (as in 554–65) and *sententiae* (proverbial statements, as in 887–88). Her renderings of the choruses are freer. They retain the same number of lines as Garnier, and, except for Act 4, the same number of stanzas, but all except the chorus in Act 3 change the poetic forms. The chorus in Act 1 has eleven stanzas of eight lines, iambic trimeter, with varying use of four rhymes: *abcdadcb, abcbadcd*, etc. In Act 2 the first chorus has eleven stanzas of six lines, iambic trimeter, rhymed *ababcc*, and the second chorus has eleven stanzas of eleven lines, headless iambic tetrameter with a trochaic effect, rhymed *ababcddcede* or *ababcddcece*. In Act 3 the chorus has sixteen stanzas of six lines, each two lines of tetrameter followed by one line of trimeter with a feminine ending, rhymed *aabccb*. In Act 4, the chorus has eighty lines of iambic trimeter in rhymed couplets.

Antonius and *A Discourse of Life and Death* were appropriately published together. Both set forth the Stoic ideal that elevates reason over emotion, public duty over private relationships, and detachment from the external world over pleasure and materialism. *A Discourse* warns against the worldly life; *Antonius* dramatizes the disastrous consequences of such a life.[9]

As in the *Collected Works of Mary Sidney Herbert, Countess of Pembroke* we have retained the through-line numbering of the text adopted from Marvin Spevack's edition in the New Variorum *Antony and Cleopatra*.

COPY-TEXT: *Antonius* (1592). Verbal emendations of *1592* (most obvious printing errors, including turned letters, are silently corrected, occasionally with the support of *1595*): 566 *them (them not)*, 572 *left (lest)*, 632 *high estate (high st ate)*, 727 *to th'enchanting (th'e'nchanting)*, 894 *wears (weare)*, 998 *on (one)*, 1103 *should be (should)*, 1281 *our (or* [perhaps a spelling variant]*)*, 1449 *Cilicia (Cicilia)*, 1649 *help (helpt)*, 1664 *half-dead (life-dead)*, 1905 *Eras (Cl.)*.

⁹ Beilin, *Redeeming Eve*, 128. See also Betty S. Travitsky, "The Possibilities of Prose," in *Women and Literature in Britain, 1500–1700*, ed. Helen Wilcox (Cambridge: Cambridge University Press, 1996), 244.

ANTONIUS

The Argument

After the overthrow of Brutus and Cassius, the liberty of Rome being now utterly oppressed, and the empire settled in the hands of Octavius Caesar and Marcus Antonius (who for knitting a straiter[10] bond of amity[11] between them, had taken to wife Octavia, the sister of Caesar), Antonius undertook a journey against the Parthians, with intent to regain on them the honor won by them from the Romans, at the discomfiture and slaughter of Crassus. But coming in his journey into Syria, the places renewed in his remembrance the long intermitted love of Cleopatra, queen of Egypt, who before time had both in Cilicia[12] and at Alexandria entertained him with all the exquisite delights and sumptuous pleasures which a great prince and voluptuous lover could to the uttermost desire. Whereupon omitting his enterprise, he made his return to Alexandria, again falling to his former loves, without any regard of his virtuous wife Octavia, by whom nevertheless he had excellent children. This occasion Octavius took of taking arms against him, and preparing a mighty fleet, encountered him at Actium,[13] who also had assembled to that place a great number of galleys of his own, besides sixty which Cleopatra brought with her from Egypt. But at the very beginning of the battle Cleopatra with all her galleys betook her to flight, which Antony seeing could not but follow, by his departure leaving to Octavius the greatest victory which in any sea battle hath been heard of. Which he not negligent to pursue, follows them the next spring and besiegeth them within Alexandria, where Antony finding all that he trusted to fail him, beginneth to grow jealous and to suspect Cleopatra. She thereupon enclosed herself with two of her women in a monument she had before caused to be built, thence sends him word she was dead, which he believing for truth, gave himself with his sword a deadly wound, but died not until a messenger came from Cleopatra to have him brought to her to the tomb. Which she not daring to open lest she should be made a prisoner to the Romans and carried in Caesar's triumph, cast down a cord from a high window, by the which (her women helping her) she trussed up Antonius half dead,

---

[10] *straiter:* closer.

[11] *amity:* friendship, alliance.

[12] *Cilicia.* A division of southeast Asia Minor on the Mediterranean coast, of importance to both the Romans and the Egyptians.

[13] *Actium.* A promontory and town in western Greece.

and so got him into the monument. The stage supposed Alexandria; the chorus, first, Egyptians, and after, Roman soldiers. The history to be read at large in Plutarch, in *The Life of Antonius.*

The Actors

Antonius
Cleopatra
Eras and Charmion, Cleopatra's women
Philostratus, a philosopher
Lucilius
Diomed, secretary to Cleopatra
Octavius Caesar
Agrippa
Euphron, teacher of Cleopatra's children
Children of Cleopatra
Dircetus, the messenger

[Act 1]

Antonius

Since cruel heav'ns against me obstinate,[14]
Since all mishaps of the round engine[15] do
Conspire my harm, since men, since powers divine,
Air, earth, and sea are all injurious,
And that my queen herself, in whom I lived,
The idol of my heart, doth me pursue,
It's meet[16] I die. For her have I forgone
My country, Caesar unto war provoked
(For just revenge of sister's wrong, my wife,)
Who moved my queen—ay me!—to jealousy
For love of her, in her allurements caught,
Abandoned life, I honor have despised,

10

---

[14] *obstinate.* A verb in this construction: are *obstinate against me.*

[15] *round engine:* the earth. Cf. Lucretius, *De Rerum Natura,* 5.96: *machina mundi* (engine of the world).

[16] *meet:* fitting, appropriate.

Disdained my friends, and of the stately Rome
Despoiled the empire of her[17] best attire,
Contemned[18] that power that made me so much feared,
A slave become unto her feeble face.
    O cruel traitress, woman most unkind,
Thou dost, forsworn, my love and life betray
And giv'st me up to rageful enemy,   20
Which soon (O fool!) will plague thy perjury.
    Yielded Pelusium[19] on this country's shore,
Yielded thou hast my ships and men of war,
That naught remains (so destitute am I)
But these same arms which on my back I wear.
Thou shouldst have had them, too, and me unarmed
Yielded to Caesar naked of defense,
Which[20] while I bear, let Caesar never think
Triumph of me shall his proud chariot grace,
Not think with me his glory to adorn,   30
On me alive to use his victory.
    Thou only, Cleopatra, triumph[21] hast,
Thou only hast my freedom servile made,
Thou only hast me vanquished: not by force
(For forced I cannot be) but by sweet baits
Of thy eyes' graces, which did gain so fast
Upon my liberty, that naught remained.
None else henceforth, but thou my dearest queen,
Shall glory in commanding Antony.
    Have Caesar fortune and the gods his friends,   40
To him have Jove and fatal sisters[22] given
The scepter of the earth: he never shall
Subject my life to his obedience.

---

[17] *her*, i.e., the empire's.

[18] *Contemned:* held in contempt, viewed contemptuously.

[19] *Pelusium.* According to Plutarch's account, Cleopatra was said to have consented to the yielding of this city at the mouth of the Nile to Octavius in 30 B.C.

[20] *Which*, i.e., Antony's arms. He claims that Cleopatra has so destroyed him that she might as well have taken his arms and turned him over to Caesar. But while he has his weapons, he has the option of choosing suicide rather than the humiliation of being displayed in Caesar's "triumph," or victory parade.

[21] *triumph.* Cf. Petrarch, *Triumph of Love,* in which Cleopatra is presented as gaining conquest over Julius Caesar.

[22] *Jove and fatal sisters,* i.e., Jupiter and the Fates. Cf. lines 670–71.

But when that Death, my glad refuge, shall have
Bounded the course of my unsteadfast life,
And frozen corpse under a marble cold
Within tomb's bosom, widow of my soul,
Then at his will let him it subject make,
Then what he will let Caesar do with me:
Make me limb after limb be rent, make me
My burial take in sides of Thracian wolf.[23]

    Poor Antony! Alas, what was the day,
The days of loss that gained thee thy love!
Wretch[24] Antony! Since then Megaera,[25] pale
With snaky hairs, enchained thy misery!
The fire thee burnt was never Cupid's fire
(For Cupid bears not such a mortal brand):
It was some Fury's torch, Orestes'[26] torch,
Which sometimes burnt his mother-murdering soul
(When wandering mad, rage boiling in his blood,
He fled his fault which followed as he fled),
Kindled within his bones by shadow pale
Of mother slain returned from Stygian lake.

    Antony, poor Antony! Since that day
Thy old good hap[27] did far from thee retire.
Thy virtue[28] dead, thy glory made alive
So oft by martial deeds is gone in smoke;
Since then the bays[29] so well thy forehead knew

50

60

---

[23] *Thracian wolf.* A reference to the joining of Thrace, near Macedonia, with Brutus and Cassius against Antony and Octavius in the struggle for power following the assassination of Julius Caesar.

[24] *Wretch.* An adjective in this construction: wretched.

[25] *Megaera.* A Fury, or avenging spirit, often portrayed with torches and snakes; the other Furies are Tisiphone and Allecto. Cf. 58, 241.

[26] 58–63. Orestes avenged the death of his father Agamemnon by killing his mother Clytemnestra, who had killed Agamemnon upon his return from the Trojan War. In some versions of the story, the Furies pursue Orestes, madly wandering and boiling with rage (60). The *Stygian lake* is a reference to Styx, one of the rivers of the underworld in classical mythology.

[27] *hap:* luck, fortune. Cf. 1070, 1381.

[28] *virtue:* power.

[29] *bays.* Leaves of the bay-laurel, used in wreaths to crown the head of a conqueror (or poet).

To Venus' myrtles[30] yielded have their place,
Trumpets to pipes, field tents to courtly bowers,   70
Lances and pikes to dances and to feasts.
Since then, O wretch, instead of bloody wars
Thou shouldst have made upon the Parthian kings
For Roman honor 'filed by Crassus' foil,[31]
Thou threw'st thy cuirass off, and fearful helm,
With coward courage unto Egypt's queen
In haste to run, about her neck to hang
Languishing in her arms thy idol made:
In sum given up to Cleopatra's eyes.
Thou break'st at length from thence, as one encharmed   80
Breaks from th'enchanter that him strongly held.
For thy first reason (spoiling of their force[32]
The poisoned cups of thy fair sorceress)
Recured[33] thy sprite:[34] and then on every side
Thou mad'st again the earth with soldiers swarm.
All Asia hid, Euphrates' banks do tremble
To see at once so many Romans there
Breathe horror, rage, and with a threat'ning eye
In mighty squadrons cross his swelling streams.
Naught seen but horse, and fire-sparkling arms: 90
Naught heard but hideous noise of mutt'ring troops.
The Parth, the Mede,[35] abandoning their goods,
Hide them for fear in hills of Hyrcany,[36]
Redoubting[37] thee. Then willing to besiege

---

[30] *myrtles.* The myrtle is a shrub or small tree associated with Venus and love, hence, opposed in this context to victorious military exploits. Cf. the contrasts in the following lines.

[31] Because of the defiling of Roman honor by the defeat and death of Marcus Licinius Crassus in 53 B.C. at the hands of the Parthians.

[32] *spoiling of their force,* i.e., robbing the metaphorically poisoned cups of Cleopatra's allurement of their power over him. Cf. the implicit association of Cleopatra with Circe in Homer's *Odyssey* in 1166–72 below. Cf. also 1829–30.

[33] *Recured:* restored.

[34] *sprite:* spirit.

[35] *Parth . . . Mede.* Inhabitants of Parthia and Media, respectively. In Plutarch, Antony is said to have been distracted from his war with Parthia when he became enamored of Cleopatra.

[36] *Hyrcany.* Hyrcania adjoined Parthia and Media.

[37] *Redoubting:* fearing, standing in awe of, perhaps also with a pun on building redoubts, or fortifications.

The great Phraata[38] head of Media,
Thou camped'st at her walls with vain assault,
Thy engines fit[39] (mishap!) not thither brought.
 So long thou stay'st, so long thou dost thee rest,
So long thy love with such things nourished
Reframes, reforms itself and stealingly   100
Retakes his[40] force and rebecomes[41] more great.
For of thy queen the looks, the grace, the words,
Sweetness, allurements, amorous delights,
Entered again thy soul, and day and night,
In watch, in sleep, her image followed thee:
Not dreaming but of her, repenting still
That thou for war hadst such a goddess left.
 Thou car'st no more for Parth, nor Parthian bow,
Sallies, assaults, encounters, shocks, alarms,
For ditches, rampiers,[42] wards, entrenched grounds: 110
Thy only care is sight of Nilus[43] streams,
Sight of that face whose guileful semblant[44] doth
(Wandering in thee) infect thy tainted heart.
Her absence thee besots:[45] each hour, each hour
Of stay,[46] to thee impatient seems an age.
Enough of conquest, praise thou deem'st enough,
If soon enough the bristled[47] fields thou see
Of fruitful Egypt, and the stranger flood
Thy queen's fair eyes (another Pharos) lights.[48]

---

[38] *Phraata.* The principal city of Media, besieged by Antony in his war against the Parthians.

[39] *engines fit:* suitable weapons of war.

[40] *his,* i.e., its. *His* was the regular form of the singular neuter possessive, which was replaced by the modern form during the seventeenth century.

[41] *rebecomes:* again becomes.

[42] *rampiers:* ramparts.

[43] *Nilus.* The Latin form of *Nile.*

[44] *semblant:* outward appearance, as either countenance or demeanor.

[45] *besots:* causes to dote or stupefies.

[46] *stay:* pause, delay.

[47] *bristled:* filled with crops such as grain.

[48] The phrasing in Garnier suggests that *lights* is a verb with *eyes* as the subject, not an uncommon construction in early modern English. *Pharos* (with a pun on Pharaohs), an island near Alexandria, was the site of a lighthouse that was one of the Seven Wonders of the ancient world.

Returned, lo, dishonored, despised,   120
In wanton love a woman thee misleads
Sunk in foul sink,⁴⁹ meanwhile respecting naught
Thy wife, Octavia, and her tender babes,
Of whom the long contempt against thee whets
The sword of Caesar now thy lord become.
    Lost thy great empire, all those goodly towns
Reverenced thy name as rebels now thee leave,
Rise against thee, and to the ensigns flock
Of conqu'ring Caesar, who enwalls thee round
Caged in thy hold, scarce master of thyself,   130
Late master of so many nations.
    Yet, yet, which is of grief extremest grief,
Which is yet of mischief highest mischief,
It's Cleopatra—alas, alas, it's she,
It's she augments the torment of thy pain,
Betrays thy love, thy life, alas, betrays,
Caesar to please, whose grace she seeks to gain,
With thought her crown to save, and Fortune make
Only thy foe which common ought have been.⁵⁰
    If her I always loved, and the first flame   140
Of her heart-killing love shall burn me last,
Justly complain I, she disloyal is,
Nor constant is, even as I constant am,
To comfort my mishap, despising me
No more than when the heavens favored me.
    But ah, by nature women wav'ring are,
Each moment changing and rechanging minds.
Unwise, who blind in them, thinks loyalty
*Ever to find in beauty's company.*⁵¹

             Chorus   150

    The boiling tempest still
        Makes not sea-waters foam,
        Nor still the northern blast
        Disquiets quiet streams,

---

⁴⁹ *sink:* sewer.

⁵⁰ Cleopatra should suffer the same bad fortune as Antony does.

⁵¹ 146–49. One of several aphoristic passages, or *sententiae,* distinguished in the early texts by quotation marks or different type fonts. Cf. 749–50 and similar instances below.

Nor who his chest to fill
    Sails to the morning beams,
    On waves wind tosseth fast,
    Still keeps his ship from home;
Nor Jove still down doth cast
    Inflamed with bloody ire   160
    On man, on tree, on hill,
    His darts of thund'ring fire;
    Nor still the heat doth last
    On face of parched plain,
    Nor wrinkled cold doth still
    On frozen furrows reign;
But still as long as we
    In this low world remain,
    Mishaps,[52] our daily mates,
    Our lives do entertain,   170
    And woes which bear no dates
    Still perch upon our heads;
    None go, but straight[53] will be
    Some greater in their steads.
Nature made us not free
    When first she made us live;
    When we began to be,
    To be began our woe:
    Which growing ever more[54]
    As dying life doth grow,   180
    Do more and more us grieve,
    And tire us more and more.
No stay[55] in fading states,
    For more to height they retch,[56]
    Their fellow miseries
    The more to height do stretch.
    They cling even to the crown,

---

[52] *Mishaps*: misfortunes—such as those cited in 151–66, an extensive negative construction that reinforces the naturalness, or inevitability, of the often oppressive extremes of ordinary life such as storms, lightning, heat, and cold.

[53] *straight*: straightaway.

[54] *ever more*: ever greater. Cf. 895.

[55] *stay*: stop, end.

[56] *retch*: reach. The variant is retained here for the sake of the rhyme.

And threat'ning furious wise[57]
From tyrannizing pates[58]
Do often pull it down.   190
In vain on waves untried
To shun them go we should
To Scyths and Massagetes
Who near the Pole reside;[59]
In vain to boiling sands
Which Phoebus'[60] batt'ry beats,
For with us still they would
Cut seas and compass lands.[61]
The darkness no more sure
To join with heavy night   200
The light which guilds the days
To follow Titan[62] pure,
No more the shadow light
The body to ensue,[63]
Than wretchedness always
Us wretches to pursue.
Oh, blest who never breathed,
Or whom with pity moved,
Death from his cradle reaved,[64]
And swaddled in his grave;   210
And blessed also he
(As curse may blessing have)
Who low and living free
No prince's charge[65] hath proved.

---

[57] *furious wise*: furiously.

[58] *pates*: heads (of tyrants, whose rule, or crown, often succumbs to misfortunes).

[59] 193–94. The Scythians and Massagetes (Massagetai or Massagetae) were warlike people of northern Europe and Asia, thus imagined living near the north *Pole* at a great distance, but still not far enough away to escape misfortune.

[60] *Phoebus*, i.e., the sun, personified by the name of the sun god Phoebus Apollo.

[61] Sail through seas and traverse lands.

[62] *Titan*. Hyperion, father of the sun, although the name was often used for the sun itself.

[63] 203–4. The reference is to the *shadow*, which is *light* in the sense of being insubstantial, cast by (ensuing, or following) a *body*, a phenomenon as inevitable as the human experience of misfortune.

[64] *reaved*: robbed, seized.

[65] *charge*. Perhaps in the sense of both "duty" and "accusation."

By stealing sacred fire
    Prometheus[66] then unwise,
    Provoking gods to ire,
    The heap of ills did stir,
    And sickness pale and cold
    Our end which onward spur,   220
    To plague our hands too bold
    To filch the wealth of skies.
In heaven's hate since then
    Of ill with ill enchained
    We race of mortal men
    Full fraught[67] our breasts have borne,
    And thousand, thousand woes
    Our heav'nly souls now thorn,[68]
    Which free before from those
    No earthly passion pained.   230
War and war's bitter cheer
    Now long time with us stay,
    And fear of hated foe
    Still, still increaseth sore:
    Our harms worse daily grow,
    Less yesterday they were
    Than now, and will be more
    Tomorrow than today.

Act 2

Philostratus   240

What horrible Fury,[69] what cruel rage,
O Egypt, so extremely thee torments?
Hast thou the gods so angered by thy fault?
Hast thou against them some such crime conceived,
That their engrained[70] hand lift up in threats

---

[66] When Prometheus stole fire from heaven to give to human beings, the subsequent anger resulted in the misfortunes that *onward spur* our death (*end*).

[67] *fraught*: burdened, loaded.

[68] *thorn*: prick, pierce; vex (*OED,* citing this line). Cf. 486, 928.

[69] *Fury,* i.e., Megaera (in Garnier).

[70] *engrained:* dyed, in scarlet or crimson, i.e., blood (*rougissante* in Garnier). Cf. 246.

They should desire in thy heart blood to bathe?
And that their burning wrath which naught can quench
Should pitiless on us still lighten down?[71]
　　We are not hewn out of the monstrous mass
Of giants, those which heaven's wrack[72] conspired,　　　　250
Ixion's race, false prater of his loves,[73]
Nor yet of him who feigned lightnings found,[74]
Nor cruel Tantalus,[75] nor bloody Atreus,
Whose cursed banquet for Thyestes' plague
Made the beholding Sun for horror turn
His back, and backward from his course return,
And hastening his wing-footed horses' race,
Plunge him in sea for shame to hide his face,
While sullen night upon the wond'ring world
For midday's light her starry mantle cast.　　　　　　　260
　　But what we be, whatever wickedness
By us is done, alas, with what more plagues,
More eager torments could the gods declare
To heaven and earth that us they hateful hold?
With soldiers, strangers, horrible in arms
Our land is hid, our people drowned in tears.
But terror here and horror, naught[76] is seen,
And present death prizing[77] our life each hour.
Hard at our ports and at our porches waits
Our conquering foe: hearts fail us, hopes are dead;　　270
Our queen laments; and this great emperor

---

[71] *lighten down:* strike, as lightning hurled from Jupiter. Cf. 400.

[72] *wrack:* downfall, misfortune.

[73] *Ixion,* a *false prater* (deceiving idle talker), killed his father-in-law, apparently to avoid paying a bride-price, and also attempted to seduce Hera, the wife of Zeus, who deceived him with a phantom resembling her with whom he fathered the Centaurs. He was later punished by being attached to a revolving wheel.

[74] The reference is to Salmoneus, who used torches to imitate thunderbolts and was thus punished by Jupiter.

[75] 253–54. Having fed his sons to the gods, *Tantalus* was punished with eternal hunger and thirst in sight of tantalizing food and drink that he could not reach. *Atreus* and *Thyestes* are the grandsons of Tantalus. Out of revenge for the seduction of his wife by Thyestes, Atreus killed Thyestes' sons and served them to him as food, resulting in a curse on the house of Atreus. Philostratus's point is that the Egyptians do not deserve to suffer as such monstrous ancient figures do.

[76] *But . . . naught:* except for . . . nothing.

[77] *prizing:* bidding for (*OED,* citing this line).

Sometime[78] (would now they did) whom worlds did fear,
Abandoned, betrayed, now minds no more
But from his evils by hastened death to pass.
    Come, you poor people, tired with ceaseless plaints,
With tears and sighs make mournful sacrifice
On Isis'[79] altars, not ourselves to save,
But soften Caesar and him piteous make
To us, his prey, that so his lenity[80]
May change our death into captivity.[81]   280
    Strange are the evils the fates on us have brought.
Oh, but alas, how far more strange the cause!
Love, love (alas, whoever would have thought?)
Hath lost this realm inflamed with his fire.
Love, playing love, which men say kindles not
But in soft hearts, hath ashes made our towns.
And his sweet shafts, with whose shot none are killed,
Which ulcer not, with deaths our lands have filled.
    Such was the bloody, murdering, hellish love
Possessed thy heart, fair false guest, Priam's son,[82]   290
Firing a brand which after made to burn
The Trojan towers by Grecians ruinate.
By this love, Priam, Hector, Troilus,
Memnon, Deiphobus, Glaucus, thousands more,
Whom red Scamander's armor-clogged streams
Rolled into seas, before their dates are dead.[83]
So plaguy he,[84] so many tempests raiseth,
So murd'ring he, so many cities razeth,
When insolent, blind, lawless, orderless,
With mad delights our sense he entertains.   300

---

[78] *Sometime:* formerly.

[79] *Isis.* An Egyptian goddess, the wife of Osiris and mother of Horus. Cleopatra styled herself the "New Isis," according to Plutarch. See *Roman Lives,* trans. Robin Waterfield (Oxford, 1999), 406.

[80] *lenity:* leniency.

[81] 275–80. Unlike the high-ranking Antony and Cleopatra, the socially inferior Philostratus urges the ordinary Egyptians to pray for captivity not death.

[82] *Priam's son.* Paris, whose taking of Helen from Menelaus led to the destruction of Troy by the Greeks. Other figures associated with the Trojan War, as recounted in Homer's *The Iliad,* are mentioned in 293–94. *Scamander* (295) is a river near Troy.

[83] *before their dates are dead:* before their allotted life spans are ended.

[84] *plaguy he,* i.e., love.

All-knowing gods our wracks did us foretell
By signs in earth, by signs in starry spheres,
Which should have moved us, had not Destiny
With too strong hand warped our misery.
The comets flaming through the scattered clouds
With fiery beams, most like unbraided hairs:
The fearful dragon whistling at the banks,
And holy Apis'[85] ceaseless bellowing
(As never erst[86]) and shedding endless tears;
Blood raining down from heav'n in unknown showers;   310
Our gods' dark faces overcast with woe,
And dead men's ghosts appearing in the night.
Yea, even this night while all the city stood
Oppressed with terror, horror, servile fear,
Deep silence over all, the sounds were heard
Of diverse songs and diverse instruments,
Within the void of air, and howling noise,
Such as mad Bacchus' priests in Bacchus' feasts
On Nisa make:[87] and (seemed) the company,
Our city lost, went to the enemy.   320
    So we forsaken both of gods and men,
So are we in the mercy of our foes:
And we henceforth obedient must become
To laws of them who have us overcome.

Chorus

Lament we our mishaps,
    Drown we with tears our woe:
For lamentable haps
    Lamented easy grow,
        And much less torment bring   330
        Than when they first did spring.
We want that woeful song,
    Wherewith wood-music's queen[88]

---

[85] *Apis.* An Egyptian god appearing in the likeness of a bull.

[86] *erst*: formerly.

[87] *Nisa.* The place in India where Bacchus, the god of wine and revelry, was born.

[88] *wood-music's queen.* Philomel, who was transformed into a nightingale after being raped by Tereus, king of Thrace, who cut out her tongue to try to prevent her from exposing him. However, she used needlework to reveal the rape to her sister *Procne* (339), who

Doth ease her woes, among
Fresh springtime's bushes green,
On pleasant branch alone
Renewing ancient moan.
We want that moanful sound,
That prattling Procne makes
On fields of Thracian ground,   340
Or streams of Thracian lakes,
To empt[89] her breast of pain
For Itys by her slain.
Though halcyons[90] do still,
Bewailing Ceyx[91] lot,
The seas with plainings fill
Which his dead limbs have got,
Not ever other grave
Than tomb of waves to have;
And though the bird[92] in death   350
That most Meander loves
So sweetly sighs his breath
When Death his fury proves,[93]
As almost softs his heart,
And almost blunts his dart;
Yet all the plaints of those,
Nor all their tearful 'larms,[94]
Cannot content our woes,
Nor serve to wail the harms,
In soul which we, poor we,   360
To feel enforced be.

---

was subsequently turned into a swallow. *Itys* (343) was killed and served as food by the sisters to Tereus to avenge the crime.

[89] *empt:* empty, unburden.

[90] *halcyons.* Mythical birds, later identified with the kingfisher, supposed to have power to calm the seas.

[91] *Ceyx.* After his death by drowning, Alcyone, his wife, threw herself into the sea, and both were transformed into sea birds.

[92] *bird,* i.e., swan, supposed to sing just before it dies.

[93] *proves:* tests the limits of. Death's fury is nearly assuaged by the singing of the swan, but the sufferings of the Egyptians are not ameliorated by such singing or by the plaints of Philomel and Procne (356–61).

[94] *'larms:* alarms, with wordplay on *larmes* (tears).

Nor they of Phoebus bred[95]
 In tears can do so well,
 They for their brother shed,
 Who into Padus fell,
  Rash guide of chariot clear
  Surveyor of the year.
Nor she[96] whom heav'nly powers
 To weeping rock did turn,
 Whose tears distill in showers,   370
 And show she yet doth mourn,
  Where with his top to skies
  Mount Sipylus doth rise.
Nor weeping drops which flow
 From bark of wounded tree,
 That Myrrha's shame[97] do show
 With ours compared may be,
  To quench her loving fire
  Who durst[98] embrace her sire.
Nor all the howlings made   380
 On Cybele's sacred hill
 By eunuchs of her trade,
 Who "Attis, Attis" still
  With doubled cries resound,
  Which Echo[99] makes rebound.[100]

---

[95] The sisters of Phaethon, who mourned the death of their brother by drowning in *Padus* (the Italian river Po) after he failed in an attempt to drive the chariot of Phoebus Apollo, the god of the sun, and was struck with a thunderbolt by Jupiter before the chariot destroyed the earth by fire. The sisters were subsequently turned into alders. Cf. 1922.

[96] *she,* i.e., Niobe, who was transformed into a fountain on *Mount Sipylus* after her children were killed by Apollo. Cf. 1909–13.

[97] *Myrrha's shame.* Myrrha was transformed into a myrrh tree after committing incest with her father, Cinyras.

[98] *durst:* dared.

[99] *Echo.* A nymph who rebuffed the amorous overtures of Pan and was punished by becoming a voice capable only of repeating what others said.

[100] 380–85. *Attis,* a mortal who was loved by the goddess *Cybele,* castrated himself in a frenzy and joined the eunuchs who were her devotees. The hill sacred to her is Mount Dindymus in Phrygia.

Our plaints no limits stay,
    Nor more than do our woes:
Both infinitely stray
    And neither measure knows.
        In measure let them plain:[101]   390
        Who measured griefs sustain.

Cleopatra, Eras, Charmion, Diomed

Cleopatra

That I have thee betrayed, dear Antony,
My life, my soul, my sun? I had such thought?
That I have thee betrayed, my lord, my king?
That I would break my vowed faith to thee?
Leave thee, deceive thee, yield thee to the rage
Of mighty foe? I ever had that heart?
Rather sharp lightning lighten on my head;   400
Rather may I to deepest mischief fall;
Rather the opened earth devour me;
Rather fierce tigers feed them on my flesh;[102]
Rather, oh, rather let our Nilus send,
To swallow me quick,[103] some weeping crocodile.
    And didst thou then suppose my royal heart
Had hatched, thee to ensnare, a faithless love,
And changing mind, as Fortune changed cheer,
I would weak thee, to win the stronger, lose?[104]
Oh, wretch! Oh, caitiff! Oh, too cruel hap!   410
And did not I sufficient loss sustain
Losing my realm, losing my liberty,
My tender offspring, and the joyful light
Of beamy sun, and yet, yet losing more
Thee, Antony, my care, if I lose not
What yet remained? Thy love, alas, thy love,

---

[101] *plain*: complain, lament.

[102] Cf. Antony's reference to Thracian wolves (51). Both Cleopatra and Antony had rather die than be led captive by Caesar in his triumph. Cf. also 1847–68, where Cleopatra says that death or exile would even be better than captivity for her children.

[103] *quick*: alive.

[104] 406–9. Did you suppose that I pretended to love you to ensnare you, and would change my mind when your Fortune changed, losing you, when you were weak, to win stronger Caesar?

More dear than scepter, children, freedom, light.
 So ready I to row in Charon's barge,[105]
Shall lose the joy of dying in thy love;
So the sole comfort of my misery   420
To have one tomb with thee is me bereft.[106]
So I in shady plains shall plain alone,
Not (as I hoped) companion of thy moan.
O height of grief!
Eras.   Why with continual cries
Your griefful[107] harms do you exasperate;
Torment yourself with murdering complaints;
Strain your weak breast so oft, so vehemently;
Water with tears this fair alabaster;[108]
With sorrow's sting so many beauties wound?
Come of so many kings, want you the heart   430
Bravely, stoutly, this tempest to resist?
Cleopatra. My evils are wholly unsupportable,
No human force can them withstand but death.
Eras. To him that strives naught is impossible.
Cleopatra. In striving lies no hope of my mishaps.
Eras. All things do yield to force of lovely face.
Cleopatra. My face too lovely caused my wretched case.
My face hath so entrapped, so cast us down,
That for his conquest Caesar may it thank,
Causing that Antony one army lost,   440
The other wholly did to Caesar yield.
For not enduring (so his amorous sprite
Was with my beauty fired) my shameful flight,
Soon as he saw from rank wherein he stood
In hottest fight, my galleys making sail,
Forgetful of his charge (as if his soul
Unto his lady's soul had been enchained),
He left his men, who so courageously

---

[105] *Charon's barge.* The vessel in which Charon transported the dead to the underworld over the river Styx. Cf. 1297.

[106] 418–21. Thus, when I am ready for death (symbolized by *Charon's barge*), I will lose the joy of dying in your love and the comfort of being buried in the same tomb.

[107] *griefful:* painful; grievous (OED).

[108] *alabaster.* The Egyptian Cleopatra is imagined to have skin as white as the alabaster stone. See also the further descriptive details, including blond hair, in 721ff., which derive from Petrarchan tradition.

Did leave their lives to gain him victory.
And careless both of fame and army's loss,   450
My oared galleys followed with his ships,
Companion of my flight, by this base part
Blasting his former flourishing renown.
Eras. Are you therefore cause of his overthrow?
Cleopatra. I am sole cause: I did it, only I.
Eras. Fear of a woman troubled so his sprite?
Cleopatra. Fire of his love was by my fear inflamed.
Eras. And should he then to war have led a queen?
Cleopatra. Alas, this was not his offense, but mine.
   Antony (ay me, who else so brave a chief!)   460
Would not I should have taken seas with him,
But would have left me, fearful woman, far
From common hazard of the doubtful war.
     O that I had believed! Now, now of Rome
All the great empire at our beck should bend.
All should obey, the vagabonding[109] Scyths,
The feared Germans, back-shooting Parthians,[110]
Wand'ring Numidians,[111] Britons far removed,
And tawny nations scorched with the sun.
But I cared not: so was my soul possessed,   470
(To my great harm) with burning jealousy,
Fearing lest in my absence Antony
Should leaving me retake Octavia.
Charmion. Such was the rigor of your destiny.
Cleopatra. Such was my error and obstinacy.
Charmion. But since gods would not, could you do withal?
Cleopatra. Always from gods, good haps, not harms, do fall.
Charmion. And have they not all power on men's affairs?
Cleopatra. They never bow so low, as worldly cares,
   But leave to mortal men to be disposed   480
Freely on earth whatever mortal is.
If we therein sometimes some faults commit,

---

[109] *vagabonding:* wandering, nomadic.

[110] *back-shooting Parthians.* Plutarch describes the Parthians' practice of shooting arrows backward from their horses in his *Life of Crassus.* They are referred to simply as archers in Garnier. Cf. 1793. Cf. also Philip Sidney's similar description of Tartars in "A Shepherd's Tale" (350–51; *Poems,* ed. Ringler, 251).

[111] *Numidians.* Inhabitants of the ancient land of Numidia on the northern coast of Africa, now in Algeria.

We may them not to their high majesties,
But to ourselves impute, whose passions
Plunge us each day in all afflictions.
Wherewith when we our souls do thorned feel,
Flatt'ring ourselves we say they destinies are,
That gods would have it so, and that our care
Could not impeach[112] but that it must be so.
Charmion. Things here below are in the heav'ns begot,   490
Before they be in this our world born,[113]
And never can our weakness turn awry
The stayless[114] course of powerful Destiny.
Naught here—force, reason, human providence,
Holy devotion, noble blood—prevails,
And Jove himself whose hand doth heavens rule,
Who both to gods and men as king commands,
Who earth (our firm support) with plenty stores,
Moves air and sea with twinkling of his eye,
Who all can do, yet never can undo   500
What once hath been by their hard laws decreed.
   When Trojan walls, great Neptune's workmanship,
Environed were with Greeks, and Fortune's wheel
Doubtful ten years now to the camp did turn,
And now again towards the town returned,
How many times did force and fury swell
In Hector's veins egging him to the spoil
Of conquered foes, which at his blows did fly,
As fearful sheep at feared wolves' approach:
To save (in vain: for why? it would not be)   510
Poor[115] walls of Troy from adversaries' rage,
Who dyed them in blood, and cast to ground,
Heaped them with bloody burning carcasses.[116]
   No, madam, think that if the ancient crown
Of your progenitors that Nilus ruled,
Force take from you, the gods have willed it so,

---

[112] *impeach:* prevent.

[113] *begot . . . born.* Pembroke adds the connection between events being begotten, or conceived, in heaven in the minds of the gods, before they are *born* on earth.

[114] *stayless:* ceaseless; unhindered.

[115] *Poor:* weak, inadequate.

[116] 502–513. A summary of the story of the Trojan War, as told, for instance, in Homer's *The Iliad. Hector* (507) was one of the Trojan heroes.

To whom ofttimes princes are odious.
They have to everything an end ordained;
All worldly greatness by them bounded is,
Some sooner, later some, as they think best;   520
None their decree is able to infringe.
But, which is more, to us disastered men
Which subject are in all things to their will,
Their will is hid: nor while we live, we know
How, or how long, we must in life remain.
Yet must we not for that, feed on despair
And make us wretched ere[117] we wretched be,
But always hope the best, even to the last,
That from ourselves the mischief may not grow.
  Then, madam, help yourself, leave off in time   530
Antony's wrack, lest it your wrack procure:
Retire you from him, save from wrathful rage
Of angry Caesar both your realm and you.
You see him lost, so as your amity
Unto his evils can yield no more relief.
You see him ruined, so as your support
No more henceforth can him with comfort raise.
Withdraw you from the storm; persist not still
To lose yourself; this royal diadem
Regain of Caesar.   540

Cleopatra.   Sooner shining light
Shall leave the day, and darkness leave the night,
Sooner moist currents of tempestuous seas
Shall wave in heaven, and the nightly troops
Of stars shall shine within the foaming waves,
Than I thee, Antony, leave in deep distress.
I am with thee, be it thy worthy soul
Lodge in thy breast, or from that lodging part,
Crossing the joyless lake[118] to take her place
In place prepared for men, demigods.
  Live, if thee please; if life be loathsome, die: 550
Dead and alive, Antony, thou shalt see
Thy princess follow thee, follow, and lament,
Thy wrack, no less her own than was thy weal.[119]

---

[117] *ere:* before.
[118] *the joyless lake,* i.e., the river Styx. See the note on 418.
[119] *weal:* well-being.

Charmion. What helps his wrack this everlasting love?
Cleopatra. Help, or help not, such must, such ought I prove.
Charmion. Ill done, to lose yourself, and to no end.
Cleopatra. How ill think you to follow such a friend?
Charmion. But this your love naught mitigates his pain.
Cleopatra. Without this love I should be inhumane.
Charmion. Inhumane he, who his own death pursues.   560
Cleopatra. Not inhumane who miseries eschews.
Charmion. Live for your sons.
Cleopatra.   Nay, for their father die.
Charmion. Hard-hearted mother!
Cleopatra.   Wife kind-hearted I.
Charmion. Then will you them deprive of royal right?
Cleopatra. Do I deprive them? No, it's Dest'ny's might.
Charmion. Do you not them deprive of heritage,
     That give them up to adversary's hands,
     A man forsaken fearing to forsake,[120]
     Whom such huge numbers hold environed,
     T'abandon one 'gainst whom the frowning world   570
     Banded with Caesar makes conspiring war?
Cleopatra. The less ought I to leave him left of all.
     A friend in most distress should most assist.
     If that when Antony great and glorious
     His legions led to drink Euphrates' streams,
     So many kings in train redoubting him,
     In triumph raised as high as highest heav'n,
     Lord-like disposing as him pleased best,
     The wealth of Greece, the wealth of Asia:
     In that fair fortune had I him exchanged   580
     For Caesar, then men would have counted me
     Faithless, inconstant, light, but now the storm,
     And blust'ring tempest driving on his face,
     Ready to drown, alas, what would they say?
     What would himself in Pluto's mansion[121] say
     If I, whom always more than life he loved,
     If I, who am his heart, who was his hope,
     Leave him, forsake him (and perhaps in vain),
     Weakly to please who[122] him hath overthrown?

---

[120] *A man forsaken,* i.e., Antony.
[121] *Pluto's mansion,* i.e., the underworld, the house of Hades.
[122] *who,* i.e., Octavius Caesar.

Not light, inconstant, faithless should I be,   590
   But vile, forsworn, of treach'rous cruelty.
Charmion. Cruelty to shun, you self-cruel are.
Cleopatra. Self-cruel him from cruelty to spare.
Charmion. Our first affection to ourself is due.
Cleopatra. He is my self.
Charmion.   Next it extends unto
   Our children, friends, and to our country[123] soil.
   And you for some respect of wifely love,
   (Albe[124] scarce wifely)[125] lose your native land,
   Your children, friends, and (which is more) your life,
   With so strong charms doth love bewitch our wits;   600
   So fast in us this fire, once kindled, flames.
   Yet if his harm by yours redress might have—
Cleopatra. With mine it may be closed in darksome grave.
Charmion. And that,[126] as Alcest[127] to herself unkind,
   You might exempt him from the laws of death.
   But he is sure to die: and now his sword
   Already moisted is in his warm blood,
   Helpless for any succor you can bring
   Against death's sting, which he must shortly feel.
     Then let your love be like the love of old   610
   Which Carian queen did nourish in her heart
   Of her Mausolus, build for him a tomb
   Whose stateliness a wonder new may make.[128]
   Let him, let him have sumptuous funerals;
   Let grave[129] thereon the horror of his fights;

---

[123] *country:* country's (an uninflected genitive, not uncommon in the period).

[124] *Albe:* albeit.

[125] *scarce wifely.* Although Antony had married Cleopatra (a marriage not valid in Rome), Charmion acknowledges the ambiguity of the relationship and Cleopatra's behavior.

[126] *And that,* i.e., so that you might save him from death, although as the next lines state, that would not be the case.

[127] *Alcest.* Alcestis would have died as a substitute for her husband, Admetus, but she was rescued by Hercules and thus came to be viewed as the exemplar of the faithful wife.

[128] 610–13. Charmion advises Cleopatra to honor Antony by following the example of Artemisia, *Carian queen,* who built the great tomb for her husband, *Mausolus,* at Halicarnassus, another of the Seven Wonders of the ancient world. Parts of the Mausoleum are preserved in the British Museum.

[129] *grave:* engrave.

Let earth be buried with unburied heaps.
Frame there Pharsaly, and discolored streams
Of deep Enipeus; frame the grassy plain,
Which lodged his camp at siege of Mutina.[130]
Make all his combats and courageous acts,   620
And yearly, plays to his praise institute.[131]
Honor his memory. With doubled care
Breed and bring up the children of you both
In Caesar's grace, who as a noble prince
Will leave them lords of this most glorious realm.
Cleopatra. What shame were that! Ah gods! What infamy
  With Antony in his good haps to share,
  And overlive[132] him dead, deeming enough
  To shed some tears upon a widow tomb!
  The after-livers justly might report   630
  That I him only for his empire loved
  And high estate, and that in hard estate
  I for another did him lewdly[133] leave.
  Like to those birds wafted with wand'ring wings
  From foreign lands in springtime here arrive,
  And live with us so long as summer's heat
  And their food lasts, then seek another soil.
  And as we see with ceaseless fluttering
  Flocking of silly flies a brownish cloud
  To vintaged wine yet working in the tun,[134]   640
  Not parting thence while they sweet liquor taste,
  After, as smoke, all vanish in the air,
  And of the swarm not one so much appear.
Eras. By this sharp death what profit can you win?
Cleopatra. I neither gain, nor profit seek therein.
Eras. What praise shall you of after-ages get?
Cleopatra. Nor praise, nor glory in my cares are set.

---

[130] 615–19. Charmion suggests that Antony's tomb, like the Mausoleum, be adorned with friezes celebrating his battles at *Pharsaly* in Thessaly (near the river *Enipeus*) and *Mutina* (the modern Modena in Italy).

[131] 620–21. *Make plays*, or games (*jeux* in Garnier), of *all his combats and courageous acts, yearly* instituted *to his praise*. The use of *institute* as a past participle is attested in the *OED*.

[132] *overlive:* survive.

[133] *lewdly:* foolishly, wickedly.

[134] *tun:* barrel.

Eras. What other end ought you respect, than this?
Cleopatra. My only end my only duty is.
Eras. Your duty must upon some good be founded.   650
Cleopatra. On virtue it, the only good, is grounded.
Eras. What is that virtue?
Cleopatra.   That which us beseems.[135]
Eras. Outrage ourselves? Who that beseeming deems?
Cleopatra. Finish I will my sorrows dying thus.
Eras. 'Minish[136] you will your glories doing thus.
Cleopatra. Good friends, I pray you seek not to revoke
   My fixed intent of following Antony.
   I will die. I will die: must not his life,
   His life and death by mine be followed?
        Meanwhile, dear sisters, live: and while you live,   660
   Do often honor to our loved tombs.
   Strew them with flow'rs: and sometimes happily[137]
   The tender thought of Antony, your lord,
   And me, poor soul, to tears shall you invite,
   And our true loves your doleful voice commend.
Charmion. And think you, madam, we from you will part?
   Think you alone to feel death's ugly[138] dart?
   Think you to leave us, and that the same sun
   Shall see at once you dead and us alive?
   We'll die with you, and Clotho[139] pitiless   670
   Shall us with you in hellish boat embark.
Cleopatra. Ah, live, I pray you: this disastered woe
   Which racks my heart, alone to me belongs;
   My lot 'longs not to you; servants to be,
   No shame, no harm to you, as is to me.[140]
        Live, sisters, live, and seeing his suspect[141]
   Hath causeless me in sea of sorrows drowned,

---

[135] *us beseems:* is appropriate for us.

[136] *'Minish:* diminish.

[137] *happily:* by chance, perhaps.

[138] *ugly:* frightening, horrible.

[139] *Clotho.* One of the three Fates, who holds the distaff on which the thread of life is spun; it is drawn off by Lachesis, eventually to be cut by Atropos.

[140] 674–75. The sense is that Cleopatra's servants do not share her *lot*, which *'longs* (belongs) not to them—nor, therefore, do they suffer *shame* and *harm* because of it as she does.

[141] *suspect:* suspicion.

And that I cannot live, if so I would,
Nor yet would leave this life, if so I could,
Without his love, procure me, Diomed,   680
That 'gainst poor me he be no more incensed.
Wrest out of his conceit that harmful doubt,
That since his wrack he hath of me conceived
Though wrong conceived: witness, you reverend gods,
Barking Anubis,[142] Apis bellowing.
Tell him, my soul burning, impatient,
Forlorn with love of him, for certain seal
Of her true loyalty my corpse hath left,
T'increase of dead the number numberless.
     Go then, and if as yet he me bewail,   690
If yet for me his heart one sigh forth breathe,
Blest shall I be, and far with more content[143]
Depart this world, where so I me torment.
Mean season[144] us let this sad tomb enclose,
Attending here till death conclude our woes.
Diomed. I will obey your will.
Cleopatra.   So the desert[145]
The gods repay of thy true, faithful heart.

Diomed

     And is't not pity, gods, ah, gods of heav'n,
To see from love such hateful fruits to spring?   700
And is't not pity that this firebrand so
Lays waste the trophies of Philippi[146] fields?
Where are those sweet allurements, those sweet looks,
Which gods themselves right heart-sick would have made?
What doth that beauty, rarest gift of heav'n,
Wonder of earth? Alas, what do those eyes
And that sweet voice all Asia understood
And sunburnt Afric wide in deserts spread?
Is their force[147] dead? Have they no further power?
Cannot by them Octavius be surprised?   710

---

[142] *Anubis.* A jackal-headed Egyptian god.
[143] *Blest shall I be*, and *far* more blest *with more* contentment. . . .
[144] *Mean season*, i.e., the time before her death (in the meantime).
[145] *desert*: reward, payment, as in the phrase "just deserts."
[146] *Philippi.* A city founded by Philip of Macedon.
[147] *force*: strength, influence.

Alas, if Jove in midst of all his ire,
With thunderbolt in hand some land to plague,
Had cast his eyes on my queen, out of hand
His plaguing bolt had[148] fall'n out of his hand;
Fire of his wrath into vain smoke should turn,
And other fire within his breast should burn.
    Naught lives so fair. Nature by such a work
Herself should seem in workmanship hath passed.[149]
She is all heav'nly: never any man
But seeing her was ravished with her sight.   720
The alabaster covering of her face,
The coral color her two lips ingrains,[150]
Her beamy eyes, two suns of this our world,
Of her fair hair the fine and flaming gold,
Her brave straight stature, and her winning parts
Are nothing else but fires, fetters, darts.
    Yet this is nothing to[151] th'enchanting skills
Of her celestial sprite, her training[152] speech,
Her grace, her majesty, and forcing[153] voice,
Whether she it with fingers' speech[154] consort   730
Or hearing sceptered kings' ambassadors
Answer to each in his own language make.
    Yet now at need she aids her[155] not at all
With all these beauties, so her sorrow stings.
Darkened with woe, her only study is
To weep, to sigh, to seek for loneliness.
Careless of all, her hair disordered hangs;
Her charming eyes whence murd'ring looks[156] did fly,
Now rivers grown, whose wellspring anguish is,

---

[148] *had:* would have.

[149] *passed:* surpassed.

[150] *ingrains:* dyes indelibly (without cosmetics).

[151] *to.* Although the preposition is lacking in both the 1592 and 1595 editions of the play, the construction requires it, as does the meter.

[152] *training:* alluring.

[153] *forcing:* forceful, effective.

[154] *fingers' speech,* i.e., the music that results from Cleopatra's playing on an instrument.

[155] *her,* i.e., herself.

[156] *murd'ring looks.* According to the Petrarchan tradition, a lady's eyes could slay a man who loved her.

Do trickling wash the marble of her face. 740
Her fair discovered breast with sobbing swoll'n,
Self-cruel, she still martyreth with blows.
　　Alas, it's our ill hap, for if her tears
She would convert into her loving charms,
To make a conquest of the conqueror
(As well she might, would she her force employ),
She should us safety from these ills procure,
Her crown to her and to her race assure.[157]
Unhappy he, in whom self-succor lies,
Yet self-forsaken wanting succor dies. 750

Chorus

　　O sweet fertile land, wherein
　　　　Phoebus did with breath inspire
　　　　Man who men did first begin,
　　　　Formed first of Nilus' mire;
　　　　Whence of arts the eldest kinds,
　　　　Earth's most heavenly ornament,
　　　　Were as from their fountain sent,
　　　　To enlight our misty minds;
　　　　Whose gross sprite from endless time, 760
　　　　As in darkened prison pent,
　　　　Never did to knowledge climb;
　　Where the Nile, our father good,
　　　　Father-like doth never miss
　　　　Yearly us to bring such food,
　　　　As to life required is;
　　　　Visiting each year this plain,
　　　　And with fat slime[158] cov'ring it,
　　　　Which his seven mouths do spit,
　　　　As the season comes again, 770
　　　　Making thereby greatest grow
　　　　Busy reapers' joyful pain,
　　　　When his floods do highest flow;

---

[157] *assure:* insure.

[158] *fat slime:* rich, fertile mud—thought to be endowed with such miraculous powers of generation that crocodiles were supposedly hatched spontaneously from it. Cf. "Nilus' slime" (1.3) in Shakespeare's *Antony and Cleopatra,* as well as the statement in the same play (2.7) that "Your serpent of Egypt is bred now of your mud by the operation of your sun; so is your crocodile."

Wand'ring prince of rivers thou,
    Honor of the Ethiop's land,[159]
    Of a lord and master now
    Thou a slave in awe must stand.
    Now of Tiber, which is spread
    Less in force and less in fame,
    Reverence thou must the name,   780
    Whom all other rivers dread,
    For his children swoll'n in pride,
    Who by conquest seek to tread
    Round this earth on every side.[160]
Now thou must begin to send
    Tribute of thy wat'ry store,
    As sea paths thy steps shall bend,
    Yearly presents more and more.
    Thy fat scum,[161] our fruitful corn,
    Pilled[162] from hence with thievish hands   790
    All unclothed shall leave our lands
    Into foreign country borne,
    Which puffed up with such a prey
    Shall thereby the praise adorn
    Of that scepter Rome doth sway.[163]
Naught thee helps thy horns[164] to hide
    Far from hence in unknown grounds,
    That thy waters wander wide,
    Yearly breaking banks and bounds,
    And that thy sky-colored brooks   800
    Through a hundred peoples pass,
    Drawing plots for trees and grass
    With a thousand turns and crooks,

---

[159] *Ethiop's land:* Ethiopia.

[160] 778–84. The personified Nile (Egypt) must yield tribute to the *Tiber* (Rome).

[161] *fat scum:* fertile foam.

[162] *Pilled:* pillaged, stolen. Cf. 1196.

[163] 789–95. The Egyptians' grain (*corn*), which is produced from the fertile foam (*fat scum*) of the Nile, will be pillaged by foreigners and taken to *Rome*, leaving Egypt's lands *unclothed,* or barren, and therefore her people hungry.

[164] *horns.* The tributary streams that come from the unknown source of the Nile are described as cornucopia (from Latin *cornu,* or horn), an original adaptation of the horned river gods. Garnier: 'Rien ne te sert que tes cornes / se vont en terre cachantâ' (787–88).

Whom all weary of their way
Thy throats which in wideness pass
Pour into their Mother Sea.
Naught so happy hapless life
In this world as freedom finds;
Naught wherein more sparks are rife
To inflame courageous minds;   810
But if force must us enforce—
Needs a yoke to undergo,
Under foreign yoke to go—
Still it proves a bondage worse.
And doubled subjection
See we shall, and feel, and know
Subject to a stranger grown.
From henceforward for a king,
Whose first being from this place
Should his breast by nature bring   820
Care of country to embrace,
We at surly face must quake
Of some Roman madly bent,
Who, our terror to augment,
His proconsul's axe will shake,
Driving with our kings from hence
Our established government,
Justice' sword, and law's defense.
Nothing worldly of such might
But more mighty Destiny,   830
By swift Time's unbridled flight,
Makes in end his end to see.
Everything Time overthrows,
Naught to end doth steadfast stay:
His great scythe mows all away
As the stalk of tender rose.
Only immortality
Of the heav'ns doth it oppose
'Gainst his powerful deity.[165]

---

[165] 829–39. Cf. the struggle between Time and Eternity in Petrarch's *Triumph of Time* and *Triumph of Eternity*.

One day there will come a day   840
    Which shall quail[166] thy[167] fortune's flower,
    And thee ruined low shall lay
    In some barbarous prince's power;
    When the pity-wanting fire
    Shall, O Rome, thy beauties' burn,
    And to humble ashes turn
    Thy proud wealth and rich attire,
    Those gilt roofs which turretwise,
    Justly making Envy mourn,
    Threaten now to pierce skies.   850
As thy forces fill each land
    Harvests making here and there,
    Reaping all with ravening hand
    They find growing anywhere,
    From each land so to thy fall
    Multitudes repair shall make,
    From the common spoil to take
    What to each man's share may fall.
    Fingered[168] all thou shalt behold:
    No jot left for token's sake   860
    That thou wert so great of old.
Like unto the ancient Troy
    Whence derived thy founders be,
    Conqu'ring foe shall thee enjoy,[169]
    And a burning prey in thee.
    For within this turning ball[170]
    This we see, and see each day:
    All things fixed ends do stay,
    Ends to first beginnings fall,
    And that naught, how strong or strange,   870
    Changeless doth endure alway,
    But endureth fatal change.

---

[166] *quail*: destroy.

[167] *thy*, i.e., Rome's.

[168] *Fingered*: pilfered, stolen.

[169] 862–64. Aeneas, a warrior of *Troy*, was traditionally credited with founding Rome (although Romulus and Remus were the immediate founders) because he led a remnant of Trojan survivors to what would become Italy. See Virgil, *The Aeneid,* esp. Aeneas's vision of the future of his people in book 6. Troy itself was conquered by the Greeks.

[170] *turning ball*: the earth.

[Act 3]

M. Antonius, Lucilius

M. Antonius. Lucil, sole comfort of my bitter case,
    The only trust, the only hope I have,
    In last despair, ah, is not this the day
    That death should me of life and love bereave?
    What wait I for, that have no refuge left,
    But am sole remnant of my fortune left?   880
    All leave me, fly me; none, no, not of them
    Which of my greatness greatest good received,
    Stands with my fall: they seem as now ashamed
    That heretofore they did me aught regard;
    They draw them[171] back, showing they followed me,
    Not to partake my harms, but cozen[172] me.
Lucilius. In this our world nothing is steadfast found;
    In vain he hopes, who here his hopes doth ground.
Antonius. Yet naught afflicts me, nothing kills me so,
    As that I so my Cleopatra see   890
    Practice[173] with Caesar and to him transport
    My flame, her love, more dear than life to me.
Lucilius. Believe it not: Too high a heart she bears,
    Too princely thoughts.
Antonius.   Too wise a head she wears
    Too much inflamed with greatness, ever more
    Gaping for our great empire's government.
Lucilius. So long time you her constant love have tried.[174]
Antonius. But still with me good fortune did abide.
Lucilius. Her changed love what token makes you know?
Antonius. Pelusium lost, and Actian[175] overthrow,   900
    Both by her fraud: my well-appointed fleet,
    And trusty soldiers in my quarrel armed,
    Whom she, false she, instead of my defense,
    Came to persuade, to yield them to my foe;

---

[171] *them*, i.e., themselves.
[172] *cozen:* deceive.
[173] *Practice:* conspire.
[174] *tried:* tested, proven.
[175] *Actian*, adjective. Antony refers to the defeat at Actium. See the Argument.

Such honor Thyre[176] done, such welcome given,
Their long close talks I neither knew, nor would,
And treacherous wrong Alexas[177] hath me done,
Witness too well her perjured love to me.
But you, O gods (if any faith regard),
With sharp revenge her faithless change reward.   910
Lucilius. The dole[178] she made upon our overthrow,
Her realm given up for refuge to our men,
Her poor attire when she devoutly kept
The solemn day of her nativity,
Again the cost and prodigal expense
Shown when she did your birthday celebrate,
Do plain enough her heart unfeigned prove,
Equally touched,[179] you loving, as you love.
Antonius. Well, be her love to me or false or[180] true,
Once in my soul a cureless wound I feel.   920
I love, nay, burn in fire of her love:
Each day, each night her image haunts my mind,
Herself my dreams, and still I tired am,
And still I am with burning pincers nipped.
Extreme my harm, yet sweeter to my sense
Than boiling torch of jealous torment's fire:
This grief, nay, rage, in me such stir doth keep,
And thorns me still, both when I wake and sleep.

   Take Caesar conquest, take my goods, take he
The honor to be lord of the earth alone,   930
My sons, my life bent headlong to mishaps:
No force,[181] so not my Cleopatra take.
So foolish I, I cannot her forget,
Though better were I banished her my thought.[182]
Like to the sick, whose throat the fever's fire
Hath vehemently with thirsty drought inflamed,
Drinks still, albe the drink he still desires

---

[176] *Thyre,* i.e., Thyreus (or Thyrsus), sent by Caesar to charm Cleopatra with his eloquence.

[177] *Alexas.* Executed by Caesar because he betrayed Antony to Herod.

[178] *dole:* complaint, lament.

[179] *touched:* affected.

[180] *or . . . or:* either . . . or.

[181] *No force,* i.e., it is of no importance or consequence.

[182] It would be better if I banished her from my thought.

Be[183] nothing else but fuel to his flame:
He cannot rule himself; his health's respect
Yieldeth to his distempered stomach's heat.[184]   940
Lucilius. Leave off this love, that thus renews your woe.
Antonius. I do my best, but, ah, cannot do so.
Lucilius. Think how you have so brave a captain been,
    And now are by this vain affection fall'n.
Antonius. The ceaseless thought of my felicity
    Plunges me more in this adversity.
    For nothing so a man in ill torments,
    As who to him his good state represents.
    This makes my wrack, my anguish, and my woe
    Equal unto the hellish passions grow,   950
    When I to mind my happy puissance call
    Which erst[185] I had by warlike conquest won,
    And that good fortune which me never left,
    Which hard disaster now hath me bereft.

        With terror tremble all the world I made
    At my sole word, as rushes in the streams
    At waters' will; I conquered Italy,
    I conquered Rome, that nations so redoubt.[186]
    I bore (meanwhile besieging Mutina)
    Two consuls' armies for my ruin brought,   960
    Bath'd in their blood, by their deaths witnessing
    My force and skill in matters martial.

        To wreak[187] thy uncle, unkind Caesar, I
    With blood of enemies the banks imbrued[188]
    Of stained Enipeus, hindering his course
    Stopped with heaps of piled carcasses,
    When Cassius and Brutus,[189] ill betide,[190]
    Marched against us, by us twice put to flight,

---

[183] *Be,* i.e., even if it were.

[184] *distempered stomach's heat:* disordered or immoderate appetite's intensity. He yields to his appetite's intensity instead of respecting his health.

[185] *erst:* formerly.

[186] *redoubt:* dread, stand in awe of. ·

[187] *wreak:* avenge.

[188] *imbrued:* stained.

[189] *Cassius and Brutus.* After Antony defeated them at Philippi in 42 B.C., they committed suicide.

[190] *ill betide,* i.e., ill fortune having befallen them.

But by my sole conduct: for all the time
Caesar heart-sick with fear and fever lay.   970
Who knows it not, and how by everyone
Fame of the fact was giv'n to me alone?
  There sprang the love, the never changing love,
Wherein my heart hath since to yours been bound;
There was it, my Lucil,[191] you Brutus saved,
And for your Brutus Antony you found.
Better my hap in gaining such a friend,
Than in subduing such an enemy.
Now former virtue dead doth me forsake,
Fortune engulfs me in extreme distress;   980
She turns from me her smiling countenance,
Casting on me mishap upon mishap,
Left and betrayed of thousand, thousand friends
Once of my suit; but[192] you, Lucil, are left,
Remaining to me steadfast as a tower
In holy love, in spite of Fortune's blasts.
But if of any god my voice be heard,
And be not vainly scattered in the heav'ns,
Such goodness shall not gloryless be lost,
But coming ages still thereof shall boast.   990
Lucilius. Men in their friendship ever should be one,
And never ought with fickle Fortune shake,[193]
Which still removes, nor will, nor knows the way
Her rolling bowl in one sure state to stay.
Wherefore we ought as borrowed things receive
The goods light[194] she lends us to pay again:
Not hold them sure, nor on them build our hopes
As on such goods as cannot fail and fall;
But think again, nothing is durable,
Virtue except, our never failing host: 1000
So bearing sail when favoring winds do blow,

---

[191] *Lucil.* Lucilius gained Antony's favor by surrendering to Antony, thus saving Brutus.

[192] *but:* only.

[193] *shake:* shake hands. This use of "shake" without "hands" predates the first entry cited in the *OED* (Shakespeare, 1601).

[194] *goods light,* i.e., light, insubstantial goods. The sense of 995–96 is that we ought to receive as borrowed things those light, insubstantial goods that Fortune lends us to be repaid to her.

As frowning tempests may us least dismay
When they on us do fall, not over-glad
With good estate, nor over-grieved with bad,
Resist mishap.[195]

Antonius.   Alas, it is too strong.
Mishaps ofttimes are by some comfort borne,
But these, ay me, whose weights oppress my heart,
Too heavy lie, no hope can them relieve.
There rests no more, but that with cruel blade
For ling'ring death a hasty way be made.   1010

Lucilius. Caesar, as heir unto his father's state,
So will his father's goodness imitate,
To you-ward, whom he knows allied in blood,[196]
Allied in marriage, ruling equally
The empire with him, and with him making war
Have purged the earth of Caesar's murderers.
You into portions parted have the world
Even like coheirs their heritages part,
And now with one accord so many years
In quiet peace both have your charges ruled.   1020

Antonius. Blood and alliance nothing do prevail
To cool the thirst of hot ambitious breasts;
The son his father hardly can endure,
Brother his brother, in one common realm.
So fervent this desire to command,
Such jealousy it kindleth in our hearts,
Sooner will men permit another should
Love her they love, than wear the crown they wear.
All laws it breaks, turns all things upside down:
Amity, kindred, naught so holy is   1030
But it defiles. A monarchy to gain
None cares which way, so he may it obtain.

Lucilius. Suppose he monarch be and that this world
No more acknowledge sundry emperors,
That Rome him only fear, and that he join
The east with west, and both at once do rule:
Why should he not permit you peaceably

---

[195] 999–1005. A statement of the Stoic ideal: Since nothing except virtue lasts, we should remain unchanged by Fortune, good or bad.

[196] *allied in blood.* According to Plutarch, Antony and Octavius are related through Julius Caesar, who was Octavius's great-uncle and was also akin to Antony's mother.

Discharged of charge and empire's dignity,
Private to live reading philosophy,
In learned Greece, Spain, Asia, any land?   1040
Antonius. Never will he his empire think assured
    While in this world Mark Antony shall live.
    Sleepless Suspicion, pale Distrust, cold Fear
    Always to princes company do bear,
    Bred of reports, reports which night and day,
    Perpetual guests, from court go not away.
Lucilius. He hath not slain your brother Lucius,[197]
    Nor shortened hath the age of Lepidus,[198]
    Albeit both into his hands were fall'n,
    And he with wrath against them both inflamed.   1050
    Yet one, as lord in quiet rest doth bear
    The greatest sway in great Iberia;[199]
    The other with his gentle prince retains
    Of highest priest the sacred dignity.
Antonius. He fears not them; their feeble force he knows.
Lucilius. He fears no vanquished overfilled with woes.
Antonius. Fortune may change again.
Lucilius.   A downcast foe
    Can hardly rise, which once is brought so low.
Antonius. All that I can, is done; for last assay
    (When all means failed) I to entreaty fell   1060
    (Ah, coward creature!) whence again repulsed,
    Of combat I unto him proffer made,
    Though he in prime, and I by feeble age
    Mightily weakened both in force and skill.
    Yet could not he his coward heart advance,
    Basely afraid to try so praiseful chance.
    This makes me plain,[200] makes me myself accuse,
    Fortune in this her spiteful force doth use

---

[197] *Lucius.* Antony's brother Lucius and Antony's first wife, Fulvia, had taken arms against Octavius, but were forced out of Rome to Perugia, where they were starved into surrender. Fulvia died from disease; Lucius was spared and made governor of Spain.

[198] *Lepidus.* The third member of the second triumvirate (with Antonius and Octavius; the first triumvirate had been Julius Caesar, Pompey, and Crassus in 59 B.C.), Lepidus had been deposed in 36 B.C., though he retained until his death his position as *pontifex maximus*, or *highest priest* (1054).

[199] *Iberia:* ancient Spain.

[200] *plain:* complain.

'Gainst my gray hairs; in this unhappy I
Repine[201] at heav'ns in my haps pitiless.   1070
A man, a woman both in might and mind,
In Mars's[202] school who never lesson learned,
Should me repulse, chafe, overthrow, destroy,
Me of such fame, bring to so low an ebb?
Alcides' blood,[203] who from my infancy
With happy prowess crowned have my praise:
Witness, thou Gaul, unused to servile yoke,
Thou valiant Spain, you fields of Thessaly
With millions of mourning cries bewailed,
Twice watered[204] now with blood of Italy.   1080
Lucilius. Witness may Afric, and of conquered world
   All four quarters witnesses may be.
   For in what part of earth inhabited,
   Hungry of praise have you not ensigns spread?
Antonius. Thou know'st rich Egypt (Egypt of my deeds
   Fair and foul subject), Egypt, ah, thou know'st
   How I behaved me fighting for thy king,
   When I regained him his rebellious realm,
   Against his foes in battle showing force,
   And after fight in victory remorse.   1090
      Yet if to bring my glory to the ground,
   Fortune had made me overthrown by one
   Of greater force, of better skill than I—
   One of those captains feared so of old,
   Camill, Marcellus, worthy Scipio,
   This late great Caesar, honor of our state,
   Or that great Pompey aged grown in arms—[205]
   That after harvest of a world of men
   Made in a hundred battles, fights, assaults,

---

   [201] *Repine:* complain.
   [202] *Mars's.* Disyllabic, as the spelling *Marses* in the early printings indicates. Cf.
1322.
   [203] *Alcides' blood.* Antony was supposed to have been descended from Hercules. Cf.
1243–46, 1877–78.
   [204] *Twice watered.* Antony refers to two battles he fought in Thessaly: Pharsalus (48
B.C.) and Philippi (42 B.C.). Cf. 617–19.
   [205] 1095–97. A catalogue of successful Roman commanders: Marcus Furius Camil-
lus (*Camill*) defeated the Gauls; Marcus Claudius Marcellus captured Syracuse; *Scipio*
is either Aemilianus Scipio (Scipio Africanus Minor), who destroyed Carthage in 146

My body thorough[206] pierced with push of pike   1100
Had vomited my blood, in blood my life,
In midst of millions, fellows in my fall,
The less her wrong, the less should be my woe,
Nor she[207] should pain, nor I complain me so.[208]
     No, no, whereas I should have died in arms,[209]
And vanquished, oft new armies should have armed,
New battles given, and rather lost with me
All this whole world submitted unto me,
A man who never saw enlaced pikes
With bristled points against his stomach bent,   1110
Who fears the field and hides him cowardly,
Dead at the very noise the soldiers make;
His virtue—fraud, deceit, malicious guile—
His arms—the arts that false Ulysses[210] used—
Known at Modena, where the consuls both
Death-wounded were, and wounded by his men
To get their army, war with it to make
Against his faith, against his country soil;
Of Lepidus, which to his succors came,
To honor whom, he was by duty bound,   1120
The empire he usurped, corrupting first
With baits and bribes the most part of his men:
Yet me hath overcome, and made his prey,

B.C., or Publius Cornelius Scipio (Scipio Africanus Major), who battled the Carthaginians in 210 B.C.; *late great Caesar* is Julius Caesar, whose achievements in battle and politics were numerous; *Pompey* is Pompey the Great, who was particularly noted for his military genius.

[206] *thorough:* through. The disyllabic form is retained for the meter.

[207] *she:* Fortune.

[208] 1091–104. Antony regrets that he did not die a hero's death in battle against a worthier adversary than Octavius. Cf. 1065–74.

[209] The extended, syntactically complex passage that begins here and ends in 1124 reinforces Antony's regret that he has lost to the unworthy Octavius, who has used guile rather than heroic action to gain his ends: Whereas I should have died in arms … (1105–8), a man inexperienced and cowardly, whose only virtue is fraud, etc., and whose only arms are the wiles of a Ulysses; who acted against his faith and country to win at Modena; who overcame Lepidus by bribing those around him (1109–22)—yet such a man has defeated me and Rome (1123–24).

[210] *false Ulysses.* Known for his wily stratagems, Ulysses was not viewed favorably by the Trojans or their supposed descendants, the Romans, because of his plan to defeat Troy through the deceit of the Trojan Horse.

And state of Rome, with me hath overcome.
    Strange! One disordered act at Actium
The earth subdued, my glory hath obscured.
For since, as one whom heaven's wrath attaints,[211]
With fury caught, and more than furious
Vexed with my evils, I never more had care
My armies lost or lost name to repair: 1130
I did no more resist.
Lucilius.   All war's affairs,
But battles most, daily have their success
Now good, now ill, and though that Fortune have
Great force and power in every worldly thing,
Rule all, do all, have all things fast enchained
Unto the circle of her turning wheel,
Yet seems it more than any practice else
She doth frequent Bellona's[212] bloody trade,
And that her favor, wavering as the wind,
Her greatest power therein doth oft'nest show.   1140
Whence grows, we daily see, who in their youth
Got honor there, do lose it in their age,
Vanquished by some less warlike than themselves,
Whom yet a meaner man shall overthrow.
Her use is not to lend us still her hand,
But sometimes headlong back again to throw
When by her favor she hath us extolled[213]
Unto the top of highest happiness.
Antonius. Well ought I curse within my grieved soul,
Lamenting day and night, this senseless love,   1150
Whereby my fair enticing foe entrapped
My heedless Reason, could no more escape.
It was not Fortune's ever changing face,
It was not Dest'ny's changeless violence
Forged my mishap. Alas, who doth not know
They make, nor mar, nor anything can do.
Fortune, which men so fear, adore, detest,
Is but a chance whose cause unknown doth rest,
Although ofttimes the cause is well perceived,
But not th'effect the same that was conceived.   1160

---

[211] *attaints:* accuses, condemns.
[212] *Bellona.* War personified as a goddess.
[213] *extolled:* elevated.

Pleasure, naught else, the plague of this our life,
Our life which still a thousand plagues pursue,
Alone hath me this strange disaster spun,
Fall'n from a soldier to a chamberer,[214]
Careless of virtue, careless of all praise.
Nay, as the fatted swine in filthy mire
With glutted heart I wallowed in delights,
All thoughts of honor trodden under foot.
So I me[215] lost: for finding this sweet cup
Pleasing my taste, unwise I drank my fill,   1170
And through the sweetness of that poison's power
By steps I drove my former wits astray.[216]
I made my friends, offended, me forsake,
I helped my foes against myself to rise.
I robbed my subjects, and for followers
I saw myself beset with flatterers,
Mine idle arms fair wrought with spider's work,
My scattered men without their ensigns strayed:
Caesar meanwhile who never would have dared
To cope with me, me suddenly despised,   1180
Took heart to fight and hoped for victory
On one so gone, who glory had forgone.
Lucilius. Enchanting pleasure, Venus' sweet delights
Weaken our bodies, over-cloud our sprites,
Trouble our reason, from our hearts out-chase
All holy virtues, lodging in their place.
Like as the cunning fisher takes the fish
By traitor bait whereby the hook is hid;
So pleasure serves to vice instead of food
To bait our souls thereon too lickerish.[217]   1190
This poison deadly is alike to all,
But on great kings doth greatest outrage work,
Taking the royal scepters from their hands,

---

[214] *chamberer.* Probably a man who frequents ladies' chambers, a gallant, although the earliest use recorded in the *OED* is from Shakespeare (1604, *Othello*).

[215] *me*, i.e., myself.

[216] 1166–72. There is an implicit comparison of Cleopatra with Circe, the sorcerer and seducer in Homer's *The Odyssey,* whose role was often cited allegorically as woman overcoming men's reason through sexual appetite. Cf. 83, as well as the figure of Acrasia in Spenser's *The Faerie Queene*, book 2.

[217] *lickerish:* greedy. Garnier here uses *friande* (partial to).

Thenceforward to be by some stranger borne;
While that their people charged with heavy loads
Their flatt'rers pill, and suck their marrow dry,
Not ruled but left to great men as a prey,
While this fond prince himself in pleasures drowns,
Who hears naught, sees naught, doth naught of a king,
Seeming himself against himself conspired.   1200
Then equal Justice wand'reth banished,
And in her seat sits greedy Tyranny.
Confused disorder troubleth all estates,
Crimes without fear and outrages are done.
Then mutinous Rebellion shows her face,
Now hid with this, and now with that pretense,
Provoking enemies, which on each side
Enter at ease, and make them lords of all.
The hurtful works of pleasure here behold.
Antonius. The wolf is not so hurtful to the fold,   1210
 Frost to the grapes, to ripened fruits the rain,
 As pleasure is to princes full of pain.
Lucilius. There needs no proof, but by th' Assyrian king,[218]
 On whom that monster woeful wrack did bring.
Antonius. There needs no proof, but by unhappy I,
 Who lost my empire, honor, life thereby.
Lucilius. Yet hath this ill so much the greater force,
 As scarcely any do against it stand:
 No, not the demigods the old world knew,
 Who all subdued, could pleasure's power subdue. 1220
  Great Hercules, Hercules once that was
 Wonder of earth and heav'n, matchless in might,
 Who Antaeus, Lycus, Geryon overcame,
 Who drew from hell the triple-headed dog,
 Who Hydra killed, vanquished Achelous,
 Who heaven's weight on his strong shoulders bore:[219]

---

[218] *Assyrian king.* Either Sardanapalus, infamous for his excessive and self-indulgent behavior, or Sennacherib, who pursued futile martial exploits in Egypt, provoking a successful rebellion against him while he was away from Assyria. See Hill and Morrison, *Two Tragedies: Hippolyte and Marc Antoine*, 174; *Renaissance Drama by Women,* ed. Susan Cerasano and Marion Wynne-Davies (London and New York: Routledge, 1996), 184.

[219] 1221–26. Lucilius refers to the twelve labors of Hercules, including killing the giant Antaeus; helping Lycus in his struggle against the Bebryces; seizing cattle from the monster Geryon; slaying the many-headed Hydra; capturing Cerberus, the dog guarding the

Did he not under pleasure's burden bow?
Did he not captive to this passion yield,
When by his captive,[220] so he was inflamed,
As now yourself in Cleopatra burn,   1230
Slept in her lap, her bosom kissed and kissed,
With base, unseemly service bought her love,
Spinning at distaff, and with sinewy hand
Winding on spindles thread, in maid's attire?
His conqu'ring club at rest on wall did hang;
His bow unstringed he bent not as he used;
Upon his shafts the weaving spiders spun,[221]
And his hard cloak the fretting[222] moths did pierce.
The monsters free and fearless all the time
Throughout the world the people did torment,   1240
And more and more increasing day by day
Scorned his weak heart, become[223] a mistress's play.
Antonius. In only this like Hercules am I;
In this I prove me of his lineage right;
In this himself, his deeds I show in this;
In this, naught else, my ancestor he is.
        But go we: die I must, and with brave end
Conclusion make of all foregoing harms.
Die, die I must: I must a noble death,
A glorious death unto my succor call;   1250
I must deface the shame of time abused,
I must adorn the wanton loves I used
With some courageous act, that my last day
By mine own hand my spots may wash away.
        Come, dear Lucil: alas, why weep you thus?
This mortal lot is common to us all.
We must all die, each doth in homage owe

---

entrance to the underworld; marrying Deianeira after overcoming the river god Achelous,
her suitor; supporting the heavens in Atlas's place.

[220] *his captive.* After performing his twelve labors, Hercules fell in love with Omphale;
his heroic acts were replaced by spinning, and he wore a maiden's clothing. The latter
detail was added by Pembroke and echoed by Shakespeare.

[221] Cf. the parallel with Antony in 1177.

[222] *fretting:* eating.

[223] *become,* i.e., the heart of him who had become.

Unto that god[224] that shared the realms below.
Ah, sigh no more: alas, appease your woes,
For by your grief my grief more eager grows.   1260

Chorus

Alas, with what tormenting fire
Us martyreth this blind desire
        To stay our life from flying!
How ceaselessly our minds doth rack,
How heavy lies upon our back
        This dastard[225] fear of dying!
Death rather healthful succor gives,
Death rather all mishaps relieves
        That life upon us throweth: 1270
And ever to us doth unclose
The door, whereby from cureless woes
        Our weary soul out-goeth.
What goddess else more mild than she
To bury all our pain can be,
        What remedy more pleasing?
Our pained hearts when dolor stings,
And nothing rest, or respite brings,
        What help have we more easing?
Hope which to us doth comfort give,   1280
And doth our fainting hearts revive,
        Hath not such force in anguish:
For promising a vain relief
She oft us fails in midst of grief,
        And helpless lets us languish.
But Death who call on her at need
Doth never with vain semblant feed,
        But when them sorrow paineth,
So rids their souls of all distress
Whose heavy weight did them oppress,   1290
        That not one grief remaineth.

---

[224] *that god,* i.e., Hades, the god of the underworld, whose name is sometimes also used for the underworld itself.
[225] *dastard:* base, cowardly.

Who fearless and with courage bold
Can Acheron's[226] black face behold,
    Which muddy water beareth,
And crossing over, in the way
Is not amazed at peruke[227] gray
    Old rusty Charon weareth;
Who void of dread can look upon
The dreadful shades that roam alone,
    On banks where sound no voices,   1300
Whom with her fire-brands and her snakes
No whit afraid Allecto[228] makes,
    Nor triple-barking noises;[229]
Who freely can himself dispose
Of that last hour which all must close,
    And leave this life at pleasure,
This noble freedom more esteems,
And in his heart more precious deems,
    Than crown and kingly treasure.
The waves which Boreas'[230] blasts turmoil   1310
And cause with foaming fury boil,
    Make not his heart to tremble,
Nor brutish broil, when with strong head
A rebel people madly led
    Against their lords assemble,
Nor fearful face of tyrant wood,[231]
Who breathes but threats, and drinks but blood,
    No, nor the hand which thunder,
The hand of Jove which thunder bears,
And ribs of rocks in sunder tears,   1320
    Tears mountains' sides in sunder,
Nor bloody Mars's butchering bands,
Whose lightnings desert lay the lands
    Whom dusty clouds do cover,
From off whose armor sunbeams fly,

---

[226] *Acheron.* Another of the rivers of the underworld.

[227] *peruke:* head of hair.

[228] *Allecto.* Another of the Furies.

[229] A reference to the triple-headed dog Cerberus, who guarded the entrance to the underworld.

[230] *Boreas,* the north wind personified.

[231] *wood:* crazy, mad.

And under them make quaking lie
    The plains whereon they hover,
Nor yet the cruel murd'ring blade
Warm in the moisty bowels made
    Of people pell-mell[232] dying   1330
In some great city put to sack
By savage tyrant brought to wrack,
    At his cold mercy lying.
How abject him, how base think I,
Who wanting courage cannot die
    When need him thereto calleth,
From whom the dagger drawn to kill
The cureless griefs that vex him still
    For fear and faintness falleth?
O Antony, with thy dear mate   1340
Both in misfortunes fortunate,
    Whose thoughts to death aspiring
Shall you protect from victor's rage,
Who on each side doth you encage,
    To triumph much desiring.
That Caesar may you not offend,
Naught else but Death can you defend,
    Which his weak force derideth,
And all in this round earth contained,
Pow'rless on them whom once enchained   1350
    Avernus'[233] prison hideth,
Where great Psammetich's[234] ghost doth rest,
Not with infernal pain possessed,
    But in sweet fields detained,
And old Amasis' soul likewise,
And all our famous Ptolemies
    That whilom[235] on us reigned.

---

[232] *pell-mell:* in mingled confusion.

[233] *Avernus.* A lake near the cave through which Aeneas entered the underworld; also used to refer to the underworld itself.

[234] *Psammetich,* i.e., Psammetichus, one of the former kings of Egypt of the family of the *Ptolemies* (1356), as is also *Amasis* (1355).

[235] *whilom:* formerly.

Act 4

Caesar, Agrippa, Dircetus
the messenger

Caesar

You ever-living gods which all things hold
Within the power of your celestial hands,
By whom heat, cold, the thunder, and the wind,
The properties of interchanging months
Their course and being have; which do set down
Of empires by your destinied decree
The force, age, time, and subject to no change
Change all, reserving nothing in one state:
You have advanced, as high as thund'ring heav'n,   1370
The Romans' greatness by Bellona's might:
Mast'ring the world with fearful violence,
Making the world widow of liberty.
Yet at this day this proud exalted Rome
Despoiled, captived, at one man's will doth bend:
Her empire mine, her life is in my hand,
As monarch I both world and Rome command;
Do all, can all; forth my commandment cast
Like thund'ring fire from one to other Pole
Equal to Jove: bestowing by my word   1380
Haps and mishaps, as Fortune's king and lord.
      No town there is, but up my image sets,
But sacrifice to me doth daily make,
Whether where Phoebus join his morning steeds,
Or where the night them weary entertains,
Or where the heat the Garamants[236] doth scorch,
Or where the cold from Boreas' breast is blown:
All Caesar do both awe and honor bear,
And crowned kings his very name do fear.
      Antony knows it well, for whom not one   1390
Of all the princes all this earth do rule,
Arms against me, for all redoubt the power
Which heav'nly powers on earth have made me bear.

---

[236] *Garamants*, i.e., Garamantes, an African tribal people.

Antony, he poor man with fire inflamed
A woman's beauties kindled in his heart,
Rose against me, who longer could not bear
My sister's wrong he did so ill entreat,
Seeing her left while that his lewd delights
Her husband with his Cleopatra took
In Alexandry,[237] where both nights and days   1400
Their time they passed in naught but loves and plays.
    All Asia's forces into one he drew,
And forth he set upon the azured waves
A thousand and a thousand ships, which filled
With soldiers, pikes, with targets,[238] arrows, darts,
Made Neptune quake, and all the wat'ry troops
Of Glauces, and Tritons[239] lodged at Actium.
But mighty gods, who still the force withstand
Of him, who causeless doth another wrong,
In less than moment's space reduced to naught   1410
All that proud power by sea or land he brought.
Agrippa. Presumptuous pride of high and haughty sprite,
    Voluptuous care of fond and foolish love,
Have justly wrought his wrack: who thought he held
(By overweening[240]) Fortune in his hand.
Of us he made no count, but as to play,
So fearless came our forces to assay.
    So sometimes fell to sons of Mother Earth,[241]
Which crawled to heav'n war on the gods to make,
Olymp on Pelion, Ossa on Olymp,   1420
Pindus on Ossa loading by degrees,
That at handstrokes with mighty clubs they might
On mossy rocks the gods make tumble down,
When mighty Jove with burning anger chafed, . . .[242]

---

[237] *Alexandry*, i.e., Alexandria, abbreviated here for the meter.

[238] *targets*: shields (pronounced with a soft "g").

[239] *Glauces . . . Tritons*. Sea gods.

[240] *overweening*: presumption, arrogance.

[241] In 1418–26, Agrippa recounts the assault launched by the Giants (*Gyges, Briareus*): sons of Earth, against Mount Olympus by piling mountains (*Olymp[us], Pelion, Ossa, Pindus*) on top of one another. Jupiter (*Jove*) hurled thunderbolts at them, but they were eventually defeated by Hercules.

[242] A line in Garnier's text is missing at this point in the translation, probably the result of a printer's error: *Maint trait de foudre aigu desserra sur Typhé* (loosed many a

Disbrained with him Gyges and Briareus,
Blunting his darts upon their bruised bones.
For no one thing the gods can less abide
In deeds of men, than arrogance and pride.
And still the proud, which too much takes in hand,
Shall foulest fall, where best he thinks to stand.   1430
Caesar. Right as some palace, or some stately tower,
    Which over-looks the neighbor buildings round
    In scorning wise, and to the stars up grows,
    Which in short time his own weight overthrows.
        What monstrous pride, nay, what impiety
    Incensed him onward to the gods' disgrace,
    When his two children, Cleopatra's brats,
    To Phoebe and her brother he compared,
    Latona's race, causing them to be called
    The Sun and Moon?[243] Is not this folly right?   1440
    And is not this the gods to make his foes?
    And is not this himself to work his woes?
Agrippa. In like proud sort he caused his head to lose
    The Jewish king Antigonus,[244] to have
    His realm for balm, that Cleopatra loved,
    As though on him he had some treason proved.
Caesar. Lydia to her, and Syria he gave,
    Cyprus of gold, Arabia rich of smells,
    And to his children more—Cilicia,[245]
    Parths, Medes, Armenia, Phoenicia—   1450
    The kings of kings proclaiming them to be,
    By his own word, as by a sound decree.
Agrippa. What? Robbing his own country of her due
    Triumphed he not in Alexandria,
    Of Artabasus[246] the Armenian king,

---

sharp thunderbolt on Typhoeus). Typhoeus was a monster, often confused with the rebellious Giants.

[243] 1437-40. Two sources seem to be conflated here: Antony's calling his children Moon (*Phoebe*, a name sometimes used for Artemis) and Sun (*her brother*, Phoebus) is from Plutarch (44); his calling them Helios and Selene, children of the goddess Latona, is from Dio Cassius (50.24 and 51.21).

[244] *Antigonus.* Identified as king of the Jews in Plutarch (44).

[245] *Cilicia.* See the note on the Argument.

[246] *Artabasus.* After defeating Artabasus, Antony held a public celebration in Alexandria without first gaining authority from—and thereby offending—Rome.

Who yielded on his perjured word to him?
Caesar. Nay, never Rome more injuries received,
    Since thou, O Romulus,[247] by flight of birds
    With happy hand the Roman walls didst build,
    Than Antony's fond loves to it hath done.   1460
    Nor ever war more holy, nor more just,
    Nor undertaken with more hard constraint,
    Than is this war: which were it not, our state
    Within small time all dignity should lose,
    Though I lament (thou, Sun, my witness art,
    And thou, great Jove) that it so deadly proves,
    That Roman blood should in such plenty flow,
    Wat'ring the fields and pastures where we go.
    What Carthage in old hatred obstinate,
    What Gaul still barking at our rising state,   1470
    What rebel Samnite, what fierce Pyrrhus' power,
    What cruel Mithridate, what Parth hath wrought
    Such woe to Rome, whose commonwealth he had
    (Had he been victor) into Egypt brought?[248]
Agrippa. Surely the gods, which have this city built
    Steadfast to stand as long as time endures,
    Which keep the capitol, of us take care,
    And care will take of those shall after come,
    Have made you victor, that you might redress
    Their honor grown by passed mischiefs less.   1480
Caesar. The silly[249] man when all the Greekish Sea
    His fleet had hid, in hope me sure to drown,
    Me battle gave, where Fortune, in my stead,
    Repulsing him his forces disarrayed.

---

   [247] *Romulus.* According to legend, the founder of Rome, who chose the location through divination.

   [248] 1469–74. Caesar alludes to various cities, regions, persons posing threats to Rome: the long conflict with Carthage ended with the city's destruction in 146 B.C.; Gaul was annexed by Rome after an extended campaign by Julius Caesar; the rebellious Samnites of central Italy were defeated by Rome after three wars; Pyrrhus, attempting to revive the Macedonian empire founded by his cousin Alexander the Great, achieved a "Pyrrhic victory" by winning a battle against the Romans at great cost; Mithridates the Great, king of Persia, pursued a policy of expansion that reportedly included the killing of some 80,000 Italians living in Asia.

   [249] *silly:* foolish. Caesar in these lines recounts the crucial sea battle near Actium, when Antony followed the fleeing Cleopatra rather than continue the fight.

Himself took flight, soon as his love he saw
All wan through fear with full sails fly away.
His men, though lost, whom none did now direct,
With courage fought, fast grappled ship with ship,
Charging, resisting, as their oars would serve,
With darts, with swords, with pikes, with fiery flames.   1490
So that the darkened night her starry veil
Upon the bloody sea had over-spread,
Whilst yet they held, and hardly, hardly then
They fell to flying on the wavy plain.
All full of soldiers overwhelmed with waves;
The air throughout with cries and groans did sound;
The sea did blush with blood; the neighbor shores
Groaned, so they with shipwrecks pestered were,
And floating bodies left for pleasing food
To birds, and beasts, and fishes of the sea.[250]   1500
You know it well, Agrippa.

Agrippa.   Meet it was
The Roman Empire so should ruled be,
As heav'n is ruled, which turning over us,
All under things by his[251] example turns.
Now as of heav'n one only lord we know,
One only lord should rule this earth below.
When one self[252] *pow'r is common made to two,*
Their duties they nor suffer will, nor do,
In quarrel still, in doubt, in hate, in fear;
Meanwhile the people all the smart[253] *do bear.*   1510

Caesar. Then to the end none, while my days endure,
Seeking to raise himself may succors find,
We must with blood mark this our victory,
For just example to all memory.
Murder we must, until not one we leave,
Which may hereafter us of rest bereave.

Agrippa. Mark it with murders? Who of that can like?

Caesar. Murders must use, who doth assurance seek.

---

[250] 1481–500. Caesar's account of the defeat at Actium would evoke parallels with the recent defeat of the Spanish Armada.

[251] *his:* heaven's.

[252] *self:* same, sole.

[253] *smart:* pain.

Agrippa. Assurance call you enemies to make?
Caesar. I make no such, but such away I take.   1520
Agrippa. Nothing so much as rigor doth displease.
Caesar. Nothing so much doth make me live at ease.
Agrippa. What ease to him that feared is of all?
Caesar. Feared to be, and see his foes to fall.
Agrippa. Commonly fear doth breed and nourish hate.
Caesar. Hate without pow'r, comes commonly too late.
Agrippa. A feared prince hath oft his death desired.
Caesar. A prince not feared hath oft his wrong conspired.
Agrippa. No guard so sure, no fort so strong doth prove,
No such defense, as is the people's love.[254]   1503
Caesar. Naught more unsure, more weak, more like the wind,
Than people's favor still to change inclined.
Agrippa. Good gods! What love to gracious prince men bear!
Caesar. What honor to the prince that is severe!
Agrippa. Naught more divine than is benignity.
Caesar. Naught likes[255] the gods as doth severity.
Agrippa. Gods all forgive.
Caesar.   On faults they pains do lay.
Agrippa. And give their goods.
Caesar.   Ofttimes they take away.
Agrippa. They wreak them not, O Caesar, at each time
That by our sins they are to wrath provoked.   1540
Neither must you (believe, I humbly pray)
Your victory with cruelty defile.
The gods it gave, it must not be abused,
But to the good of all men mildly used,
And they be thanked, that having giv'n you grace
To reign alone, and rule this earthly mass,
They may henceforward hold it still in rest,
All scattered power united in one breast.
Caesar. But what is he, that breathless comes so fast,
Approaching us, and going in such haste?   1550

---

[254] *the people's love.* Pembroke quotes Elizabeth's oft repeated statement that she ruled by the love of her people, but choosing sides in this traditional debate between severity and gentleness as the best form of rule was perilous shortly after Elizabeth had ordered the execution of Mary Queen of Scots.

[255] *likes:* pleases.

Agrippa. He seems afraid, and under his arm I
    (But[256] much I err) a bloody sword espy.
Caesar. I long to understand what it may be.
Agrippa. He hither comes: it's best we stay and see.
Dircetus. What good god now my voice will reinforce,
    That tell I may to rocks, and hills, and woods,
    To waves of sea, which dash upon the shore,
    To earth, to heav'n, the woeful news I bring?
Agrippa. What sudden chance thee towards us hath brought?
Dircetus. A lamentable chance. Oh, wrath of heav'ns!   1560
    Oh, gods too pitiless!
Caesar.   What monstrous hap
    Wilt thou recount?
Dircetus.   Alas, too hard mishap!
    When I but dream of what mine eyes beheld,
    My heart doth freeze, my limbs do quivering quake,
    I senseless stand, my breast with tempest tossed
    Kills in my throat my words, ere fully born.
    Dead, dead he is: be sure of what I say,
    This murdering sword hath made the man away.
Caesar. Alas, my heart doth cleave, pity me racks,
    My breast doth pant to hear this doleful tale.   1570
    Is Antony then dead? To death, alas,
    I am the cause despair him so compelled.
    But, soldier, of his death the manner show,
    And how he did this living light forgo.
Dircetus. When Antony no hope remaining saw
    How war he might, or how agreement make,
    Saw him betrayed by all his men of war
    In every fight as well by sea, as land,
    That not content to yield them to their foes
    They also came against himself to fight,   1580
    Alone in court he 'gan[257] himself torment,
    Accuse the queen, himself of her lament,
    Called her untrue and traitress, as who sought
    To yield him up she could no more defend,
    That in the harms which for her sake he bore,
    As in his blissful state, she might not share.

---

[256] *But:* unless.
[257] *gan:* began.

But she again, who much his fury feared,
Got to the tombs, dark horror's dwelling place,
Made lock the doors, and pull the hearses[258] down.
Then fell she wretched, with herself to fight.   1590
A thousand plaints, a thousand sobs she cast
From her weak breast which to the bones was torn,
Of women her the most unhappy called,
Who by her love, her woeful love, had lost
Her realm, her life, and more, the love of him,
Who while he was, was all her woes' support.
But that she faultless was she did invoke
For witness heav'n, and air, and earth, and sea,
Then sent him word, she was no more alive,
But lay enclosed dead within her tomb.   1600
This he believed, and fell to sigh and groan,
And crossed his arms, then thus began to moan.
Caesar. Poor hopeless man!
Dircetus.   "What dost thou more attend—
Ah, Antony, why dost thou death defer,
Since Fortune, thy professed enemy,
Hath made to die, who only made thee live?"
Soon as with sighs he had these words upclosed,
His armor he unlaced, and cast it off,
Then all disarmed he thus again did say:
"My queen, my heart, the grief that now I feel,   1610
Is not that I your eyes, my sun, do lose,
For soon again one tomb shall us conjoin:
I grieve, whom men so valorous did deem,
Should now, than you, of lesser valor seem."
    So said, forthwith he Eros to him called,
Eros his man; summoned him on his faith
To kill him at his need. He[259] took the sword,
And at that instant stabbed therewith his breast,
And ending life fell dead before his feet.
"O Eros, thanks," quoth Antony, "for this   1620
Most noble act, who pow'rless me to kill,
On thee hast done, what I on me should do."
    Of speaking thus he scarce had made an end,
And taken up the bloody sword from ground,

---

[258] *hearses:* hearse cloths, funeral pall.
[259] *He:* Eros.

But he his body pierced, and of red blood
A gushing fountain all the chamber filled.
He staggered at the blow, his face grew pale,
And on a couch all feeble down he fell,
Swooning with anguish: deadly cold him took,
As if his soul had then his lodging left.   1630
But he revived, and marking all our eyes
Bathed in tears, and how our breasts we beat
For pity, anguish, and for bitter grief,
To see him plunged in extreme wretchedness,
He prayed us all to haste his ling'ring death,
But no man willing, each himself withdrew.
Then fell he new to cry and vex himself,
Until a man from Cleopatra came,
Who said from her he had commandment
To bring him to her to the monument.   1640
     The poor soul at these words even rapt with joy
Knowing she lived, prayed us him to convey
Unto his lady. Then upon our arms
We bore him to the tomb, but entered not.
For she, who feared captive to be made,
And that she should to Rome in triumph go,
Kept close the gate, but from a window high
Cast down a cord, wherein he was impacked.²⁶⁰
Then by her women's help the corpse she raised,
And by strong arms into her window drew.   1650
     So pitiful a sight was never seen.
Little and little Antony was pulled,
Now breathing death; his beard was all unkempt,
His face and breast all bathed in his blood.
So hideous yet, and dying as he was,
His eyes half-closed upon the queen he cast,
Held up his hands, and helped himself to raise,
But still with weakness back his body fell.
The miserable lady with moist eyes,
With hair which careless on her forehead hung,   1660
With breast which blows had bloodily benumbed,
With stooping head, and body downward bent,
Enlaced her in the cord, and with all force

---

²⁶⁰ *impacked:* fastened.

This half-dead[261] man courageously upraised.
The blood with pain into her face did flow,
Her sinews stiff, herself did breathless grow.
    The people which beneath in flocks beheld,
Assisted her with gesture, speech, desire,
Cried and encouraged her, and in their souls
Did sweat, and labor, no whit less than she,   1670
Who never tired in labor, held so long,
Helped by her women and her constant heart,
That Antony was drawn into the tomb,
And there (I think) of dead augments the sum.
    The city all to tears and sighs is turned,
To plaints and outcries horrible to hear:
Men, women, children, hoary-headed age
Do all pell-mell in house and street lament,
Scratching their faces, tearing off their hair,
Wringing their hands, and martyring their breasts.   1680
Extreme their dole, and greater misery
In sacked towns can hardly ever be:
Not if the fire had scaled the highest towers,
That all things were of force and murder full;
That in the streets the blood in rivers streamed;
The son his sire saw in his bosom slain,
The sire his son; the husband reft[262] of breath
In his wife's arms, who furious runs to death.
    Now my breast wounded with their piteous plaints
I left their town, and took with me this sword,   1690
Which I took up at what time Antony
Was from his chamber carried to the tomb,
And brought it you, to make his death more plain,
And that thereby my words may credit gain.
Caesar. Ah, gods, what cruel hap! Poor Antony,
Alas, hast thou this sword so long time borne
Against thy foe, that in the end it should
Of thee his lord the cursed murd'rer be?
O Death, how I bewail thee! We, alas,
So many wars have ended, brothers, friends,   1700

---

[261] *half-dead.* The word in the early editions, "life-dead," is likely a printer's error since the same compound in Garnier, *demy-mort,* is translated correctly as "half-dead" in line 1900.

[262] *reft*: robbed, taken.

Companions, cousins, equals in estate,
And must it now to kill thee be my fate?
Agrippa. Why trouble you yourself with bootless grief?
For Antony why spend you tears in vain?
Why darken you with dole your victory?
Me seems yourself your glory do envy.
Enter the town, give thanks unto the gods.
Caesar. I cannot but his tearful chance lament,
Although not I, but his own pride the cause,
And unchaste love of this Egyptian. 1710
Agrippa. But best we sought into the tomb to get,
Lest she consume in this amazed case[263]
So much rich treasure, with which happily[264]
Despair in death may make her feed the fire,
Suff'ring the flames her jewels to deface,
You to defraud, her funeral to grace.
Send then to her, and let some mean be used
With some device so hold her still alive,
Some fair large promises, and let them mark
Whether they may by some fine cunning sleight 1720
Enter the tombs.
Caesar.   Let Proculeius[265] go,
And feed with hope her soul disconsolate.
Assure her so, that we may wholly get
Into our hands her treasure and herself.
For this of all things most I do desire
To keep her safe until our going hence:
That by her presence beautified may be
The glorious triumph Rome prepares for me.

*Chorus of Roman
soldiers* 1730

Shall ever civil bate[266]
  Gnaw and devour our state?
  Shall never we this blade,
  Our blood hath bloody made,

---

[263] *amazed case:* dazed condition.
[264] *happily:* by chance.
[265] *Proculeius.* Octavius's messenger.
[266] *bate:* strife, discord.

Lay down, these arms down lay
As robes we wear alway,
But as from age to age,
So pass from rage to rage?
Our hands shall we not rest[267]
   To bathe in our own breast?   1740
   And shall thick in each land
   Our wretched trophies stand,
   To tell posterity,
   What mad impiety
   Our stony stomachs led
   Against the place us bred?
Then still must heaven view
   The plagues that us pursue,
   And everywhere descry
   Heaps of us scattered lie,   1750
   Making the stranger plains
   Fat with our bleeding rains,
   Proud that on their grave
   So many legions have,
And with our fleshes still
   Neptune his fishes fill
   And drunk with blood from blue
   The sea take blushing hue,
   As juice of Tyrian shell,[268]
   When clarified well   1760
   To wool of finest fields
   A purple gloss it yields.
But since the rule of Rome
   To one man's hand is come,
   Who governs without mate
   Her now united state,
   Late jointly ruled by three
   Envying mutually,
   Whose triple yoke much woe
   On Latins' necks did throw,   1770
I hope the cause of jar,[269]

---

[267] *rest*: cease.

[268] *Tyrian shell.* The reference is to molluscs from which a purple or crimson dye was made at Tyre.

[269] *jar*: disturbance, discord.

And of this bloody war,
And deadly discord gone
By what we last have done,
Our banks shall cherish now
The branchy pale-hued bow
Of olive, Pallas'[270] praise,
Instead of barren bays,
And that his[271] temple door,
 Which bloody Mars before   1780
Held open, now at last
Old Janus shall make fast,
And rust the sword consume,
And spoiled of waving plume,
The useless morion[272] shall
On crook hang by the wall.
At least if war return
 It shall not here sojourn,
To kill us with those arms
Were[273] forged for others' harms,   1790
But have their points addressed,
Against the Germans' breast,
The Parthians' feigned flight,
The Biscay'ns'[274] martial might.
Old Memory doth there
 Painted on forehead wear
Our fathers' praise, thence torn
Our triumphs' bays have worn,
Thereby our matchless Rome
Whilom of shepherds come   1800
Raised to this greatness stands,
The queen of foreign lands,
Which now even seems to face
 The heav'ns, her glories' place,

---

[270] *Pallas.* Part of the name or title of the goddess Athena.

[271] *his*, i.e., Janus's (1782). The reference in 1779–82 is to the tradition that the doors of the temple of Janus (the god of beginnings and endings, who had both a young and an old face) were open during times of war but closed when there was peace.

[272] *morion*: a kind of helmet, worn in the sixteenth and seventeenth centuries.

[273] *Were*, i.e., that were.

[274] *Biscay'ns*, i.e., Biscayans; in Garnier, *Cantabres* (1775), the people of Cantabri in Spain, conquered in campaigns led successively by Augustus and Agrippa.

Naught resting under skies
That dares affront her eyes,
So that she needs but fear
The weapons Jove doth bear,
Who angry at one blow
May her quite overthrow.   1810

Act 5

Cleopatra, Euphron, Children of Cleopatra,
Charmion, Eras

Cleopatra

Oh, cruel Fortune! Oh, accursed lot!
Oh, plaguy love! Oh, most detested brand!
Oh, wretched joys! Oh, beauties miserable!
Oh, deadly state! Oh, deadly royalty!
Oh, hateful life! Oh, queen most lamentable!
Oh, Antony by my fault buriable!   1820
Oh, hellish work of heav'n! Alas, the wrath
Of all the gods at once on us is fall'n.
Unhappy queen! Oh, would I in this world
The wand'ring light of day had never seen!
Alas, of mine the plague and poison I
The crown have lost my ancestors me left,
This realm I have to strangers subject made,
And robbed my children of their heritage.
     Yet this is naught, alas, unto the price
Of you, dear husband, whom my snares entrapped,   1830
Of you whom I have plagued, whom I have made
With bloody hand a guest of moldy tomb,
Of you whom I destroyed, of you, dear lord,
Whom I of empire, honor, life have spoiled.
     Oh, hurtful woman! And can I yet live,
Yet longer live in this ghost-haunted tomb?
Can I yet breathe? Can yet in such annoy,
Yet can my soul within this body dwell?
O sisters, you²⁷⁵ that spin the threads of death!

---

²⁷⁵ *you*, i.e., the Fates.

O Styx! O Phlegethon!²⁷⁶ You brooks of hell!   1840
   O imps of night!
Euphron.   Live for your children's sake:
   Let not your death of kingdom them deprive.
   Alas, what shall they do? Who will have care?
   Who will preserve this royal race of yours?
   Who pity take? Even now me seems I see
   These little souls to servile bondage fall'n,
   And borne in triumph.
Cleopatra.   Ah, most miserable!
Euphron. Their tender arms with cursed cord fast bound
   At their weak backs.
Cleopatra.   Ah, gods, what pity more!
Euphron. Their silly²⁷⁷ necks to ground with weakness bend.   1850
Cleopatra. Never on us, good gods, such mischief send.
Euphron. And pointed at with fingers as they go.
Cleopatra. Rather a thousand deaths!
Euphron.   Lastly his knife
   Some cruel caitiff in their blood imbrue.
Cleopatra. Ah, my heart breaks. By shady banks of hell,
   By fields whereon the lonely ghosts do tread,
   By my soul and the soul of Antony,
   I you beseech, Euphron, of them have care.
   Be their good father, let your wisdom let²⁷⁸
   That they fall not into this tyrant's hands.   1860
   Rather conduct them where their frizzed²⁷⁹ locks
   Black Ethiops to neighbor sun do show;
   On wavy ocean at the water's will;
   On barren cliffs of snowy Caucasus;
   To tigers swift, to lions, and to bears,
   And rather, rather unto every coast,
   To every land and sea, for naught I fear
   As rage of him, whose thirst no blood can quench.
      Adieu, dear children, children dear, adieu:
   Good Isis you to place of safety guide,   1870
   Far from our foes, where you your lives may lead

---

²⁷⁶ *Styx . . . Phlegethon.* Rivers of the underworld.

²⁷⁷ *silly:* innocent, pitiful.

²⁷⁸ *let:* prevent.

²⁷⁹ *frizzed:* curly (predating the earliest citation in the *OED* by nearly two centuries).

In free estate devoid of servile dread.
    Remember not, my children, you were born
Of such a princely race; remember not
So many brave kings which have Egypt ruled
In right descent your ancestors have been;
That this great Antony your father was,
Hercules' blood, and more than he in praise.
For your high courage such remembrance will,
Seeing your fall, with burning rages fill.   1880
    Who knows if that your hands false Destiny
The scepters promised of imperious Rome,
Instead of them shall crooked sheephooks bear,
Needles or forks, or guide the cart or plough?
Ah, learn t'endure: your birth and high estate
Forget, my babes, and bend to force of fate.
    Farewell, my babes, farewell, my heart is closed
With pity and pain, myself with death enclosed,
My breath doth fail. Farewell for evermore,
Your sire and me you shall see nevermore.   1890
    Farewell, sweet care, farewell.
Children.   Madam, adieu.
Cleopatra. Ah, this voice kills me. Ah, good gods! I swoon.
    I can no more, I die.
Eras.   Madam, alas!
    And will you yield to woe? Ah, speak to us.
Euphron. Come, children.
Children.   We come.
Euphron.   Follow we our chance.
    The gods shall guide us.
Charmion.   Oh, too cruel lot!
    Oh, too hard chance! Sister what shall we do,
What shall we do, alas, if murd'ring dart
Of death arrive while that in slumb'ring swoon
Half dead she lie with anguish overgone?   1900
Eras. Her face is frozen.
Charmion.   Madam, for god's love
    Leave us not thus: bid us yet first farewell.
    Alas, weep over Antony. Let not
    His body be without due rites entombed.
Cleopatra. Ah, ah!
Charmion.   Madam!

Cleopatra.   Ay me!
Eras.[280]   How faint she is!
Cleopatra. My sisters, hold me up. How wretched I,
    How cursed am! And was there ever one
    By Fortune's hate into more dolors thrown?
        Ah, weeping Niobe,[281] although thy heart
    Beholds itself enwrapped in causeful woe   1910
    For thy dead children, that a senseless rock
    With grief become, on Sipylus thou stand'st
    In endless tears, yet didst thou never feel
    The weights of grief that on my heart do lie.
    Thy children thou, mine I, poor soul, have lost,
    And lost their father, more than them I wail,
    Lost this fair realm; yet me the heavens' wrath
    Into a stone not yet transformed hath.
        Phaethon's sisters,[282] daughters of the Sun,
    Which wail your brother fall'n into the streams   1920
    Of stately Po: the gods upon the banks
    Your bodies to bank-loving alders turned.
    For me, I sigh, I ceaseless weep and wail,
    And heaven pitiless laughs at my woe,
    Revives, renews it still, and in the end
    (Oh, cruelty!) doth death for comfort lend.
        Die Cleopatra then,[283] no longer stay
    From Antony, who thee at Styx attends.[284]
    Go join thy ghost with his, and sob no more
    Without his love within these tombs enclosed.   ·   1930
Eras. Alas, yet let us weep, lest sudden death
    From him our tears and those last duties take
    Unto his tomb we owe.
Charmion.   Ah, let us weep
    While moisture lasts, then die before his feet.
Cleopatra. Who furnish will mine eyes with streaming tears

---

    [280] The mistaken assignment of this speech to Cleopatra in the 1592 edition is a print-er's error; the 1595 edition gives the speech to Charmion. We have adopted the assignment to Eras as in Garnier.

    [281] *Niobe.* See the note on 368.

    [282] 1919, 1921. *Phaethon's sisters . . . Po.* See the note on 362.

    [283] This is probably the point at which Cleopatra applies the asps, since they are pre-sumably sucking her *vital moisture* and *vital blood* in 1941–42.

    [284] *attends:* awaits.

My boiling anguish worthily to wail,
Wail thee, Antony, Antony my heart?
Alas, how much I weeping liquor want!
Yet have mine eyes quite drawn their conduits dry
By long beweeping my disastered harms.   1940
Now reason is that from my side they suck
First vital moisture, then the vital blood.
Then let the blood from my sad eyes outflow,
And smoking[285] yet with thine in mixture grow.
Moist it, and heat it new, and never stop,
All wat'ring thee, while yet remains one drop.
Charmion. Antony, take our tears: this is the last
    Of all the duties we to thee can yield
    Before we die.
Eras.   These sacred obsequies
    Take, Antony, and take them in good part.   1950
Cleopatra. O goddess, thou whom Cyprus doth adore,
    Venus of Paphos, bent to work us harm
    For old Julius' brood, if thou take care
    Of Caesar, why of us tak'st thou no care?
    Antony did descend, as well as he,
    From thine own son[286] by long enchained line,
    And might have ruled by one and selfsame fate,
    True Trojan blood, the stately Roman state.
        Antony, poor Antony, my dear soul,
    Now but a block, the booty[287] of a tomb,   1960
    Thy life, thy heat is lost, thy color gone,
    And hideous paleness on thy face hath seized.
    Thy eyes, two suns, the lodging place of love,
    Which yet for tents to warlike Mars did serve,
    Locked up in lids (as fair day's cheerful light
    Which darkness flies) do winking hide in night.
        Antony, by our true loves I thee beseech,

---

[285] *smoking*: emitting vapor.

[286] *thine own son.* Aeneas, the son of Anchises and Aphrodite (identified with Venus in Roman mythology). Both Antony and Octavius Caesar were supposedly descended from him and were thus members of *old Julius' brood* (the *gens Julia*), descendants of Venus according to imperial Roman tradition. Cf. 1951–54. Thus, Cleopatra says that Venus should favor Antony as well as Octavius.

[287] *block*, i.e., Antony's lifeless body; *booty*: plunder, usually in the sense of the spoils of war.

And by our hearts sweet sparks have set on fire,
Our holy marriage, and the tender ruth[288]
Of our dear babes, knot of our amity,   1970
My doleful voice thy ear let entertain,
And take me with thee to the hellish plain,
Thy wife, thy friend: hear, Antony, oh, hear
My sobbing sighs, if here thou be, or there.
    Lived thus long, the winged race of years
Ended I have as Destiny decreed,
Flourished and reigned, and taken just revenge
Of him who me both hated and despised.
Happy, alas, too happy! If of Rome
Only the fleet had hither never come!   1980
And now of me an image great shall go
Under the earth to bury there my woe.
What say I? Where am I? O Cleopatra,
Poor Cleopatra, grief thy reason reaves.
No, no, most happy in this hapless case,
To die with thee, and dying thee embrace,
My body joined with thine, my mouth with thine,
My mouth, whose moisture burning sighs have dried,
To be in one self[289] tomb, and one self chest,
And wrapped with thee in one self sheet to rest.   1990
    The sharpest torment in my heart I feel
Is that I stay from thee, my heart, this while.
Die will I straight[290] now, now straight will I die,
And straight with thee a wand'ring shade will be,
Under the cypress trees thou haunt'st alone,
Where brooks of hell do falling seem to moan.
But yet I stay, and yet thee overlive,
That ere I die due rites I may thee give.
    A thousand sobs I from my breast will tear,
With thousand plaints thy funerals[291] adorn;   2000
My hair shall serve for thy oblations,
My boiling tears for thy effusions,

---

[288] *ruth*: pity.

[289] *one self*, i.e., one and the same.

[290] *straight*: straightaway, without delay.

[291] *funerals*: funeral rites. In 1999–2004, Cleopatra says that since Antony will not have a public funeral, she must replace the usual *oblations* (sacrifices), *effusions* (libations), and *fire* with her own actions.

Mine eyes thy fire, for out of them the flame
(Which burnt thy heart on me enamored) came.
    Weep my companions, weep, and from your eyes
Rain down on him of tears a brinish stream.
Mine can no more, consumed by the coals
Which from my breast, as from a furnace, rise.
Martyr your breasts with multiplied blows,
With violent hands tear off your hanging hair,   2010
Outrage your face: alas, why should we seek
(Since now we die) our beauties more to keep?
    I spent in tears, not able more to spend,
But kiss him now, what rests me more to do?[292]
Then let me kiss you, you fair eyes, my light,
Front[293] seat of honor, face most fierce, most fair!
O neck, O arms, O hands, O breast where death
(Oh, mischief) comes to choke up vital breath.
A thousand kisses, thousand, thousand more
Let you my mouth for honor's farewell give,   2020
That in this office, weak my limbs may grow,
Fainting on you, and forth my soul may flow.

AT RAMSBURY, 26 OF NOVEMBER 1590.

---

[292] *what rests me more to do?* i.e., what more remains for me to do?
[293] *Front:* forehead.

A DISCOURSE OF LIFE AND DEATH

A *Discourse of Life and Death* is a type of meditation on the trials of our lives that was enormously appealing to early modern readers. It combines the wisdom of biblical and classical writers, particularly "Solomon" and Seneca, to offer consolation to those who were suffering from any kind of hardship or sorrow.[1] The prose of *A Discourse* is elegant, with vivid metaphors. Pembroke's translation was originally printed, as the first item in the volume, with *Antonius* (1592); the devotional text was thus followed by secularized classical drama. Both of these works present the Stoic ideal that emphasizes reason over emotion and public responsibility over personal relationships, both are strongly influenced by Seneca, both are connected with the *ars moriendi* or art of dying, and both encourage virtuous living. Similar Christian/Senecan meditations on life and death can be found throughout the devotional writings of the period, and were justified by allusions to Seneca in Christian authorities from Tertullian to Calvin.

The *Excellent discours de la vie et de la mort* (1576) was written by Philippe de Mornay, seigneur du Plessis-Marly, an aristocratic French Protestant soldier, theologian, and political theorist who was a dear friend of the countess of Pembroke's brother, Sir Philip Sidney. His theological works were widely translated into European vernacular languages. Sidney himself had begun a translation of Mornay's most popular work, *De la vérité de la religion chrestienne,* or "Trueness of the Christian Religion"; after Sidney's death, Arthur Golding published an English translation that he claimed was the completion of Sidney's work. Translating a work by Mornay was thus a way for Pembroke to honor her brother and, indirectly, to support the Protestant cause for which he died. *A Discourse*, as a Christian/Senecan meditation on life and death, may have particularly appealed to Pembroke in 1590 because of the recent deaths of her brother, mother, father, and three-year-old daughter.[2]

---

[1] Solomon was believed to be the author of the Song of Solomon, the Book of Proverbs, Psalms 72 and 117, and Ecclesiastes; the Wisdom of Solomon is attributed to him in the Apocrypha. Seneca, a Roman philosopher once believed to have been a Christian and a friend of St. Paul, praised a life that withdrew from the transitory goods of the world, cultivated inner virtue, and endured suffering. His work was ubiquitous in early modern Europe; Mornay in this essay draws particularly on Seneca's *Moral Epistles* and his *Moral Essays*. The first edition of *A Discourse of Life and Death* appended translations of Seneca from Latin to French.

[2] Lamb, "The Countess of Pembroke and the Art of Dying," 207–26.

Mornay's *Excellent discours* was so popular that it went through twelve French editions before 1600. It was printed with his translations from Seneca's works, particularly the epistles and the *Moral Essays*, on which much of Mornay's meditation is based. [3] *A Discourse* is part of the *ars moriendi* tradition, or meditations on the art of dying, although more than two thirds of the work meditates on life. It baptizes the ideas of the Stoics, particularly as transmitted by Seneca, emphasizing the virtuous life that is based on reason rather than on emotion so that the person remains unchanged by good or bad fortune. The wise person is not corrupted by riches or honor, nor destroyed by suffering. To this Stoic ideal Mornay adds thoughts from the Book of Ecclesiastes, traditionally attributed to Solomon, and from Christian doctrine. For the Christian, death is "not the end of life, but the end of death, and the beginning of life. 'Better,' saith *Solomon*, 'is the day of death, than the day of birth.' And why? Because it is not to us a last day, but the dawning of an everlasting day."

Mornay's wife, Charlotte d'Arbaleste, says in her *Memoirs* that he wrote the *Excellent discours* during their courtship at her request.[4] The work is dedicated to Mornay's sister, "Mademoiselle du Plessis," and would presumably be therefore particularly suited to a female audience. The reader is addressed by the title "mon ami" or my (male) friend, throughout, however, and the work is enlivened by Mornay's own experience as a courtier and a military officer. Nevertheless, the term "man" is used inclusively for all human beings, and most of the issues that *A Discourse* raises transcend divisions by gender or class: "Consider all the periods of this life. We enter it in tears, we pass it in sweat, we end it in sorrow. Great and little, rich and poor, not one in the whole world, that can plead immunity from this condition."

The work is structured according to the normal pattern of human life, adapted from Seneca: infancy, childhood, youth, maturity or "perfect age," and old age. *A Discourse* develops each stage according to the difficulties and moral dangers it presents. The infant is completely helpless. (Pembroke here alters a verb to describe the baby as unable to "support" itself, thereby needing the support of a mother or nurse.)[5] The child is under the stern guidance of a schoolmaster and longs for freedom. The youth is tempted by pleasure, and the adult by ambition and greed, the two primary temptations of a courtier; in fact, nearly one third of the entire essay is devoted to these temptations

---

[3] See *Collected Works*, 1:212–20.

[4] *Mémoires de Charlotte Arbaleste, sur la vie de Duplessis-Mornay son mari* is translated into English by Lucy Crump, *A Huguenot Family in the XVI Century: The Memoirs of Philippe de Mornay, Sieur du Plessis Marly, Written by His Wife* (London: Routledge, 1926), 169.

[5] Bornstein, ed., *Pembroke's Translation of Discourse of Life and Death*, 76.

that falsely promise "if we will adore them, perfect contentment of the goods and honors of this world." *A Discourse* demonstrates instead how these two sins will destroy all happiness. Like a prisoner, the courtier is fettered by his chains of office: "both are enchained . . . but that the one hath them of iron, the other of gold, and that the one is tied but by the body, the other by the mind." Greed is also imprisoning. The avaricious man loves his possessions with the ardor of a lover, but they do not bring him happiness: "He desired to have [riches], and now fears to lose them: he got them with burning ardor, and possesseth [them] in trembling cold." Whether one succumbs to these temptations, or chooses to devote oneself to scholarship, or withdraws from the world into religious retirement, old age "never fails to find us out." Old age is a second childhood, when "you are recompensed for the travails of mind, the watchings and cares of manhood, with loss of sight, loss of hearing, and all the senses one after another, except only the sense of pain."

Mornay, who wrote during the religious wars in France, is acutely conscious of human suffering, accepting misery as part of an ordinary life. "I will not here speak of the infinite evils wherewith men in all ages are annoyed, as loss of friends and parents, banishments, exiles, disgraces, and such others, common and ordinary in the world." He is also aware that he writes from a position of privilege, one that Pembroke shared: "We speak of none in this place but such as are esteemed . . . most happy" in the eyes of "the world." That is, the situation of the poor is so bad that it does not need further discussion; he evidently assumes that death would be preferable to such a life.

The final section of *A Discourse* meditates on death, explaining why we should not fear it, for it is the entrance to true life, when we return to our home. Plato's metaphor of the body as the prison of the soul is combined with Christian doctrine: "Our soul delivered out of this foul and filthy prison . . . shall again draw her own breath, recognize her ancient dwelling, and again remember her former glory and dignity. This flesh . . is not man: man is from heaven. . . . Man indeed is soul and spirit."

To die well is to die willingly. So attractive does Mornay make the ease and rest of death sound that he adds a caution against suicide. Developing a military metaphor, he says, "The Christian ought willingly to depart out of this life but not cowardly to run away. The Christian is ordained by God to fight therein, and cannot leave his place without incurring reproach and infamy. But if it please the grand captain to recall him, let him take the retreat in good part, and with good will obey it." The essay concludes with the memorable Christian paradox, " Die to live, / Live to die."

Edward Aggas, a printer and bookseller, made the only English translation printed before Pembroke's (1576); Pembroke seems to have known it, but is not indebted to its wordy style. Her translation remains close to her original, although she may make a phrase more concise by substituting a single adjective or noun for a doublet, or by omitting brief modifiers, or by using an adjective to replace an entire phrase, such as "false spectacles" for "de lunettes qui nous trompent." Pembroke retains much of Mornay's style, though alliteration, rhetorical questions, skillful repetition, wordplay, highly complex sentences, and parallel structures are also characteristic of her poetry. She is an accurate translator on the whole, but there are a few very minor slips.[6]

A Discourse was popular enough to be reprinted three times (1600, 1606, and 1608). In addition, the 1606 edition was reissued in 1607 and sold with *Six Excellent Treatises of Life and Death, Collected (and published in French) by Philip Mornay, Sieur du Plessis: And now (first) Translated into English* (1607).

The full old-spelling text of *A Discourse of Life and Death* is available from Renaissance Women Online <http://www.wwp.brown.edu/texts/rwoentry. html>, along with an earlier version of this headnote.

A Discourse of Life and Death is more about life than death. The first section (see page 118) recounts the hardships of life in the Senecan Ages of Man, perhaps most familiar in Shakespeare's adaptation to seven ages in Jaques' speech (*As You Like It*):

> All the world's a stage,
> And all the men and women merely players.
> They have their exits and their entrances,
> And one man in his time plays many parts,
> His acts being seven ages. At first, the infant,
> Mewling and puking in the nurse's arms.
> Then, the whining school-boy with his satchel
> And shining morning face, creeping like snail
> Unwillingly to school. And then the lover,
> Sighing like furnace, with a woeful ballad
> Made to his mistress' eyebrow. Then, a soldier,
> Full of strange oaths, and bearded like the pard,
> Jealous in honor, sudden, and quick in quarrel,
> Seeking the bubble reputation
> Even in the cannon's mouth. And then, the justice,
> In fair round belly, with good capon lined,
> With eyes severe, and beard of formal cut,

---

[6] See Bornstein, ed., *Pembroke's Translation of Discourse of Life and Death*, 8–21 and 73–97; Bornstein, "The Style of the Countess of Pembroke's Translation of Philippe de Mornay's *Discours de la vie et de la mort*," in *Silent but for the Word*, ed. Hannay, 126–48; and "*A Discourse of Life and Death*: Fidelity to Originals," *Collected Works*, 1:220–28.

Full of wise saws, and modern instances,
And so he plays his part. The sixth age shifts
Into the lean and slippered pantaloon,
With spectacles on nose, and pouch on side,
His youthful hose well saved, a world too wide
For his shrunk shank, and his big manly voice,
Turning again toward childish treble, pipes
And whistles in his sound. Last scene of all,
That ends this strange eventful history,
Is second childishness and mere oblivion,
Sans teeth, sans eyes, sans taste, sans everything. (2.7.139–66)

The middle section of *A Discourse* talks about the temptations that are most common for adults, avarice and ambition. The final section presents the benefits of death in Christian terms. The selection below abbreviates the essay, primarily by omitting portions of the lengthy meditations on avarice and ambition; it includes approximately half of the original work. Headings are supplied by the editors.

COPY-TEXT: *Discourse* (1592). Verbal emendation: "Adult Temptation: Ambition," last paragraph, *to man's (to to mans).*

A Discourse of Life and Death

*I*t seems to me strange and a thing much to be marveled, that the laborer to repose himself hasteneth as it were the course of the sun; that the mariner rows with all force[7] to attain the port, and with a joyful cry salutes the descried land; that the traveler is never quiet nor content till he be at the end of his voyage; and that we in the meanwhile tied in this world to a perpetual task, tossed with continual tempest, tired with a rough and cumbersome way, cannot yet see the end of our labor but with grief, nor behold our port but with tears, nor approach our home and quiet abode but with horror and trembling. This life is but a Penelope's web,[8] wherein we are always doing and undoing; a sea open to all winds, which sometime within, sometime without, never cease to torment us; a weary journey through extreme heats and colds, over high mountains, steep rocks, and thievish deserts.[9] And so we term it in weaving at this web, in rowing at this oar, in passing this miserable way.

Yet lo, when death comes to end our work, when she stretcheth out her arms to pull us into the port, when after so many dangerous passages, and loathsome lodgings she would conduct us to our true home and resting place, instead of rejoicing at the end of our labor, of taking comfort at the sight of our land, of singing at the approach of our happy mansion, we would fain (who would believe it?) retake our work in hand, we would again hoist sail to the wind, and willingly undertake our journey anew. No more, then, remember we our pains; our shipwrecks and dangers are forgotten; we fear no more the travails nor the thieves. Contrarywise, we apprehend death as an extreme pain, we doubt it as a rock,[10] we fly it as a thief. We do as little children, who all the day complain, and when the medicine is brought them, are no longer sick. . . . We have more sense of the medicine's bitterness soon gone, than of a bitter languishing long continued; more feeling of death the end of our miseries, than the endless misery of our life. And whence proceedeth this folly and simplicity? We neither know life, nor death. We fear that we ought to hope for,

---

[7] *force:* strength.

[8] *a Penelope's web.* In Homer's *The Odyssey,* Penelope, wife of Odysseus, told the suitors who were hoping to marry her and rule Ithaca in Odysseus's continuing absence that she would choose one of them after she finished weaving a burial shroud for Laertes, her father-in-law. Each evening, however, she unraveled what she had woven during the daytime and thus kept the suitors at bay.

[9] *thievish deserts,* i.e., deserted places where travelers are vulnerable to thieves.

[10] *doubt it as a rock:* fear it as something absolutely definite. The metaphor alludes to the shipwrecks above.

and wish for that we ought to fear. We call life a continual death: and death the issue of a living death, and the entrance of a never-dying life.

[Part 1: Meditation on Life]

Now what good, I pray you, is there in life, that we should so much pursue it? Or what evil is there in death, that we should so much eschew it? Nay, what evil is there not in life? And what good is there not in death? Consider all the periods of this life. We enter it in tears, we pass it in sweat, we end it in sorrow. Great and little, rich and poor, not one in the whole world, that can plead immunity from this condition.

[Infancy]

Man in this point worse than all other creatures, is born unable to support himself, neither receiving in his first years any pleasure, nor giving to others but annoy and displeasure, and before the age of discretion passing infinite dangers. Only herein less unhappy than in other ages, that he hath no sense nor apprehension of his unhappiness. Now is there any so weak minded, that if it were granted him to live always a child, would make account of such a life? So then it is evident that not simply to live is a good, but well and happily to live. But proceed.

[Childhood]

Grows he? With him grow his travails. Scarcely is he come out of his nurse's hands, scarcely knows he what it is to play, but he falleth into the subjection of some schoolmaster: I speak but of those which are best and most precisely brought up. Studies he? It is ever with repining.[11] Plays he? Never but with fear. This whole age while he is under the charge of another, is unto him but as a prison. He only thinks and only aspires to that time when freed from the mastership of another, he may become master of himself,[12] pushing onward (as much as in him lies) his age with his shoulder that soon he may enjoy his hoped liberty. In short, he desires nothing more than the end of this base age[13] and the beginning of his youth. And what else I pray you is the beginning of youth, but the death of infancy? The beginning of manhood, but the death of youth? The beginning of tomorrow, but the death of today?

---

[11] *repining*: complaining.

[12] *master of himself*. Cf. *Antonius*, 130.

[13] *base age*: low or early age, the years of childhood.

In this sort, then, desires he his death, and judgeth his life miserable, and so cannot be reputed in any happiness or contentment.

[Youth]

Behold him now, according to his wish, at liberty: in that age wherein Hercules[14] had the choice to take the way of virtue or of vice, reason or passion for his guide, and of these two must take one. His passion entertains him with a thousand delights, prepares for him a thousand baits, presents him with a thousand worldly pleasures to surprise him: and few there are that are not beguiled. But at the reckoning's end, what pleasures are they? Pleasures full of vice which hold him still in a restless fever; pleasures subject to repentance, like sweetmeats[15] of hard digestion; pleasures bought with pain and peril, spent and past in a moment, and followed with a long and loathsome remorse of conscience. And this is the very nature (if they be well examined) of all the pleasures of this world. There is in none so much sweetness, but there is more bitterness; none so pleasant to the mouth, but leaves an unsavory aftertaste and loathsome disdain; none (which is worse) so moderated but hath his corrosive and carries his punishment in itself. I will not here speak of the displeasures confessed by all, as quarrels, debates, wounds, murders, banishments, sickness, perils, whereinto sometimes the incontinency,[16] sometimes the insolency[17] of this ill-guided age conducts him. . . .

Now if he take and follow reason for his guide, behold on the other part wonderful difficulties: he must resolve to fight in every part of the field: at every step to be in conflict and at handstrokes,[18] as having his enemy in front, in flank, and on the rearward, never leaving to assail him. And what enemy? All that can delight him, all that he sees near or far off: briefly the greatest enemy of the world, the world itself. But which is worse, a thousand treacherous and dangerous intelligences among his own forces, and his passion within himself desperate, which in that age[19] grown to the highest, awaits but time, hour, and occasion to surprise him and cast him into all viciousness.[20] God

---

[14] *Hercules.* When he was eighteen years old and had to make a choice between female personifications of Pleasure and Virtue, Hercules wisely chose the latter, resulting in a life of labor that ended in honor and fame.

[15] *sweetmeats:* candy, less digestible than more nutritious food.

[16] *incontinency:* lack of self-restraint, hastiness.

[17] *insolency:* pride, contemptuous presumption.

[18] *handstrokes:* blows with the hand, particularly in combat as here, metaphorically. Cf. the reference to combat at the end of this paragraph.

[19] *that age,* i.e., youth, when passions can be especially strong.

[20] *viciousness:* vice, immoral behavior.

only, and none other, can make him choose this way; God only can hold him in it to the end; God only can make him victorious in all his combats. And well we see how few they are that enter into it, and of those few, how many that retire again.

Follow the one way or follow the other, he must either subject himself to a tyrannical passion or undertake a weary and continual combat, willingly cast himself to destruction or fetter himself as it were in stocks, easily sink with the course of the water or painfully swim against the stream. Lo, here the young man, who in his youth hath drunk his full draught of the world's vain and deceivable pleasures, overtaken by them with such a dull heaviness and astonishment, as drunkards the morrow after a feast. . . . Lo, him that stoutly hath made resistance: he feels himself so weary, and with this continual conflict so bruised and broken, that either he is upon the point to yield himself, or content to die, and so acquit himself. And this is all the good, all the contentment of this flourishing age, by children so earnestly desired and by old folks so heartily lamented.

[Perfect Age: Maturity]

Now cometh that which is called perfect age, in the which men have no other thoughts but to purchase themselves wisdom and rest. Perfect indeed, but herein only perfect, that all imperfections of human nature, hidden before under the simplicity of childhood or the lightness of youth, appear at this age in their perfection. We speak of none in this place but such as are esteemed the wisest and most happy in the conceit of the world. . . . Behold, now present themselves to us avarice and ambition, promising if we will adore them, perfect contentment of the goods and honors of this world. . . .

[Adult Temptation: Avarice]

But in the end, what is all this contentment? The covetous man makes a thousand voyages by sea and by land, runs a thousand fortunes, escapes a thousand shipwrecks in perpetual fear and travail, . . . and to gain wealth[21] loseth his life. Suppose he hath gained in good quantity, that he hath spoiled the whole East of pearls and drawn dry all the mines of the West:[22] will he therefore be settled in quiet? Can he say that he is content? All charges and jour-

---

[21] *gain wealth.* Cf. Luke 9:25.

[22] *he hath spoiled the whole East of pearls and drawn dry all the mines of the West.* References to new sources of wealth in the age of exploration and discovery: pearls from Asia, gold and silver from the New World.

neys past, by his passed pains[23] he heapeth up but future disquietness both of mind and body: from one travail[24] falling into another, never ending, but changing his miseries. He desired to have them and now fears to lose them; he got them with burning ardor, and possesseth in trembling cold; he adventured among thieves to seek them, and having found them, thieves and robbers on all sides run mainly on him; he labored to dig them out of the earth, and now is enforced to redig and rehide them. Finally, coming from all his voyages, he comes into a prison and for an end of his bodily travails, is taken with endless travails of the mind. And what at length hath this poor soul attained after so many miseries? . . . Is he therewith content?

Nay, . . . the greedy have goods and dare not use them; they have joys it seems and do not enjoy them; they neither have for themselves nor for another; but of all they have, they have nothing, and yet have want of all they have not. . . . The attaining of all these deceivable[25] goods is nothing else but weariness of body, and the possession for the most part, but weariness of the mind. . . . But the heap of all misery is when they come to lose them: when either shipwreck, or sacking, or invasion, or fire, or such like calamities, to which these frail things are subject, doth take and carry them from them. Then fall they to cry, to weep, and to torment themselves, as little children that have lost their play-game. . . . I will not here discourse of the wickedness and mischiefs whereunto the covetous men subject themselves to attain to these goods, whereby their conscience is filled with a perpetual remorse, which never leaves them in quiet: sufficeth that in this over-vehement exercise, which busieth and abuseth the greatest part of the world, the body is slain, the mind is weakened, the soul is lost without any pleasure or contentment.

[Adult Temptation: Ambition]

Come we to ambition, which by a greediness of honor fondly[26] holdeth occupied the greatest persons. . . . Of those that give themselves to court ambition, some are great about princes, others commanders of armies: both sorts according to their degree, you see saluted, reverenced, and adored of those that are under them. You see them appareled in purple, in scarlet, and in cloth of gold: it seems at first sight there is no contentment in the world but theirs. But men know not how heavy an ounce of that vain honor weighs, what

---

[23] *passed pains.* Perhaps not simply former pains, but pains passed through, endured.

[24] *travail:* hardship, oppressive or painful labor (cf. French *travaille,* "work"). In many passages, Pembroke plays on the ambiguities suggested by the spelling of this word in early modern English since it can also be used for "travel."

[25] *deceivable:* deceptive or deceiving, false.

[26] *fondly:* foolishly.

those reverences[27] cost them, and how dearly they pay for an ell[28] of those rich stuffs:[29] who knew them well, would never buy them at the price. The one hath attained to this degree,[30] after a long and painful service hazarding his life upon every occasion, with loss ofttimes of a leg or an arm, and that at the pleasure of a prince that more regards a hundred perches[31] of ground on his neighbor's frontiers, than the lives of a hundred thousand such as he: unfortunate to serve who loves him not, and foolish to think himself in honor with him that makes so little reckoning to lose him for a thing of no worth. Others grow up by flattering a prince and long submitting their tongues and hands to say and do without difference[32] whatsoever they[33] will have them: whereunto a good mind can never command itself. They shall have endured a thousand injuries, received a thousand disgraces, and as near as they seem about the prince, they are nevertheless always as the lion's keeper, who by long patience, a thousand feedings and a thousand clawings hath made a fierce lion familiar, yet gives him never meat but with pulling back his hand always in fear lest he should catch him. . . . Such is the end of all princes' favorites. When a prince after long breathings[34] hath raised a man to great height, he makes it his pastime, at what time he seems to be at the top of his travail, to cast him down at an instant: when he hath filled him with all wealth, he wrings him after as a sponge, loving none but himself and thinking everyone made but to serve and please him.

These blind courtiers make themselves believe that they have friends and many that honor them, never considering that as they make semblance to love and honor everybody, so others do by them. Their superiors disdain them and never but with scorn do so much as salute them. Their inferiors salute them because they have need of them (I mean of their fortune, of their food, of their apparel, not of their person), and for their equals between whom commonly friendship consists, they envy each other, accuse each other, cross each other, continually grieved either at their own harm or at others' good. . . .

Lastly, will you know what the diversity is between the most hardly entreated[35] prisoners and them? Both are enchained, both laden with fetters,

---

[27] *reverences:* exalted positions of honor; bows and curtsies.

[28] *ell:* a measure of length, a little longer than a yard.

[29] *stuffs:* fabrics, cloth.

[30] *degree:* position.

[31] *perches:* units for measuring land.

[32] *without difference:* without discrimination or discernment.

[33] *they,* i.e., the princes, or rulers, for whom an ambitious person will say or do anything.

[34] *breathings:* pauses, delays.

[35] *entreated:* treated, dealt with.

but that the one hath them of iron, the other of gold, and that the one is tied but by the body, the other by the mind. The prisoner draws his fetters after him, the courtier weareth his upon him. The prisoner's mind sometimes comforts the pain of his body, and sings in the midst of his miseries: the courtier tormented in mind wearieth incessantly his body, and can never give it rest.

And as for the contentment you imagine they have, you are therein yet more deceived. You judge and esteem them great, because they are raised high. . . . But could you enter into their minds, you would judge that neither they are great, true greatness consisting in contempt of those vain greatnesses, whereunto they are slaves, nor seem unto themselves so, seeing daily they are aspiring higher and never where they would be. . . . That which is beneath, he counts a toy: it is in his opinion but one step. He reputes himself low, because there is someone higher, instead of reputing himself high, because there are a million lower. And so high he climbs at last, that either his breath fails him by the way, or he slides from the top to the bottom. Or if he gets up by all his travail, it is but as to find himself on the top of the Alps: not above the clouds, winds, and storms, but rather at the devotion[36] of lightnings and tempests . . . which most commonly taketh pleasure to thunderbolt and dash into powder that proud height of theirs. . . .

But say you, such at least whom nature hath sent into the world with crowns on their heads and scepters in their hands . . . may call themselves happy. . . . Crowned they are indeed, but with a crown of thorns;[37] they bear a scepter, but it is of a reed, more than anything in the world pliable and obedient to all winds: it being so far off that such a crown can cure the migraines of the mind, and such a scepter keep off and fray[38] away the griefs and cares which hover about them, that it is contrarywise the crown that brings them, and the scepter which from all parts attracts them. "O crown," said the Persian monarch,[39] "who knew how heavy thou sittest on the head, would not vouchsafe to take thee up, though he found thee in his way." . . . Happy is he only who in mind lives contented: and he most of all unhappy, whom nothing he can have can content. . . .

---

[36] *devotion:* disposal, command.

[37] *crown of thorns.* A crown of thorns was placed on the head of Christ by his accusers to mock and humiliate him. See Matt. 27:29–30, which also recounts the placing of a reed in his hand for a scepter.

[38] *fray:* frighten, disperse.

[39] *the Persian monarch.* Xerxes I, or "the Great" (c. 519–465 B.C.), Persian king and son of Darius I, renowned for his violent suppression of Egypt (484 B.C.) and his invasion of Greece (480 B.C.) from across the Hellespont. He was murdered by members of his own court.

If you could hear the talk of the wisest and least discontent of this kind of men . . . one would gladly change garment with his tenant; another preacheth how goodly an estate it is to have nothing; a third complaining that his brains are broken with the noise of court or palace, hath no other thought, but as soon as he may to retire himself thence. So that you shall not see any but is displeased with his own calling and envieth that of another: ready nevertheless to repent him, if a man should take him at his word. None but is weary of the businesses whereunto his age is subject, and wisheth not to be elder, to free himself of them: albeit otherwise he keepeth off old age as much as in him lieth.

What must we then do in so great a contrariety and confusion of minds? Must we to find true humanity, fly the society of men and hide us in forests among wild beasts; . . . to pluck us out of the evils of the world, sequester ourselves from the world? Could we in so doing live at rest, it were something. . . . But the worst is, when we are out of these external wars and troubles, we find greater civil war within ourselves: the flesh against the spirit, passion against reason, earth against heaven, the world within us fighting for the world, evermore so lodged in the bottom of our own hearts, that on no side we can fly from it. . . . Retire we ourselves into ourselves, we find it there as unclean as anywhere. . . .

And as touching the contentment that may be in the exercises of the wisest men in their solitariness, as reading divine or profane books, with all other knowledges and learnings, . . . yet must they all abide the judgment pronounced by the wisest among the wise, Solomon,[40] that all this nevertheless applied to man's natural disposition, is to him but vanity and vexation of mind. Some are ever learning to correct their speech, and never think of correcting their life. . . . Another by geometry can measure fields, and towns, and countries: but cannot measure himself. . . . The philosopher discourseth of the nature of all other things: and knows not himself.[41] . . . These knowledges bring on the mind an endless labor, but no contentment: for . . . the more a man knows, the more knows he that he knows not: . . . all his knowledge consisting in knowing his ignorance, all his perfection in noting his imperfections, which who best knows and notes, is in truth among men the most wise and perfect. In short we must conclude with Solomon, that the beginning and

---

[40] *Solomon.* One of the kings of Israel, noted for his wisdom and traditionally thought to be the author of Proverbs and Ecclesiastes, two of the "wisdom" books of the Old Testament. For his observation that the human condition is *but vanity and vexation of the mind* (the spirit), see Eccles. 1:14.

[41] *knows not himself.* An allusion to "Know thyself," the maxim inscribed on the Temple of Apollo at Delphi, as mentioned in Plato's *Protagoras.*

end of wisdom is the fear of God:[42] that this wisdom nevertheless is taken of the world for mere folly.[43]

[Old Age]

But with what exercise soever we pass the time, behold old age unawares to us comes upon us: which whether we thrust ourselves into the press of men or hide us somewhere out of the way, never fails to find us out. . . . There you have the inability and weakness of infancy, and (which is worse) many times accompanied with authority; there you are paid for the excess and riotousness of youth, with gouts, palsies, and such like diseases, which take from you limb after limb with extreme pain and torment. There you are recompensed for the travails of mind, the watchings and cares of manhood, with loss of sight, loss of hearing, and all the senses one after another, except only the sense of pain. . . .

Conclude, then, that childhood is but a foolish simplicity; youth, a vain heat; manhood, a painful carefulness; and old age, a noisome languishing; that our plays are but tears; our pleasures, fevers of the mind; our goods, wracks[44] and torments; our honors, heavy vanities; our rest, unrest; that passing from age to age is but passing from evil to evil, and from the less unto the greater; and that always it is but one wave driving on another, until we be arrived at the haven of death. Conclude, I say, that life is but a wishing for the future and a bewailing of the past; a loathing of what we have tasted and a longing for that we have not tasted; a vain memory of the state past and a doubtful expectation of the state to come; finally, that in all our life there is nothing certain, nothing assured, but the certainty and uncertainty of death.

[Part 2: Meditation on Death]

Behold, now comes death unto us: behold her, whose approach we so much fear. . . . We have her in horror, but because we conceive her not such as she is, but ugly, terrible, and hideous, such as it pleaseth the painters to represent unto us on a wall. We fly before her, but it is because foretaken[45] with such vain imaginations, we give not ourselves leisure to mark her. But stay we, stand we steadfast, look we her in the face, we shall find her quite other than

---

[42] *the beginning and end of wisdom is the fear of God.* See Proverbs 1:7, 9:10, as well as Psalm 111:10.

[43] *this wisdom nevertheless is taken of the world for mere folly.* Cf. 1 Cor. 1:18–21, 3:19.

[44] *wracks:* misfortunes.

[45] *foretaken:* concerned beforehand, preoccupied.

she is painted us[46] and altogether of other countenance than our miserable life. Death makes an end of this life. This life is a perpetual misery and tempest: death then is the issue of our miseries[47] and entrance of the port where we shall ride in safety from all winds. . . . You will say, there is difficulty in the passage. So is there no haven, no port, whereinto the entrance is not strait[48] and cumbersome. No good thing is to be bought in this world with other than the coin of labor and pain. . . . All the pains our life yields us at the last hour we impute to death: not marking that life begun and continued in all sorts of pain, must also necessarily end in pain. Not marking (I say) that it is the remainder of our life, not death, that tormenteth us: the end of our navigation that pains us, not the haven we are to enter, which is nothing else but a safeguard against all winds. . . .

We think we die not, but when we yield up our last gasp. But if we mark well, we die every day, every hour, every moment. . . . Our living is but continual dying: look how much we live, we die; how much we increase, our life decreases. We enter not a step into life, but we enter a step into death. . . . One only difference there is between this life and that we call death: that during the one, we have always whereof to die; and after the other, there remaineth only whereof to live. In sum, even he[49] that thinketh death simply to be the end of man, ought not to fear it, inasmuch as who desireth to live longer, desireth to die longer: and who feareth soon to die, feareth (to speak properly) lest he may not longer die.

But unto us brought up in a more holy school, death is a far other thing: neither need we, as the pagans, of consolations against death,[50] but that death serve us as a consolation against all sorts of affliction, so that we must not only strengthen ourselves, as they, not to fear it, but accustom ourselves to hope for it. For unto us it is not a departing from pain and evil, but an access unto all good: not the end of life, but the end of death, and the beginning of life. "Better," saith Solomon, "is the day of death, than the day of birth."[51] And why? Because it is not to us a last day, but the dawning of an everlasting day. No more shall we have in that glorious light, either sorrow for the past or expectation of the future: for all shall be there present unto us, and that present shall never more pass. . . .

---

[46] *painted us*, i.e., depicted for us.

[47] *issue of our miseries*, i.e., the end result of our moral miseries.

[48] *strait:* narrow.

[49] *even he*, i.e., the Stoic, as opposed to those *brought up in a more holy school*.

[50] *consolations against death.* Probably a reference to works such as Seneca's *De Consolatione*, written for Polybius, who was mourning the death of his brother.

[51] Cf. Eccles. 7:1.

Our soul delivered out of this foul and filthy prison,[52] where, by long continuing it is grown into an habit of crookedness, shall again draw her own breath, recognize her ancient dwelling, and again remember her former glory and dignity. This flesh, my friend, which thou feelest, this body which thou touchest is not man: man is from heaven; heaven is his country and his air. That he is in his body, is but by way of exile and confinement. Man indeed is soul and spirit: man is rather of celestial and divine quality, wherein is nothing gross nor material. This body such as now it is, is but the bark and shell of the soul, which must necessarily be broken, if we will be hatched, if we will indeed live and see the light. We have, it seems, some life and some sense in us: but are so crooked and contracted, that we cannot so much as stretch out our wings, much less take our flight towards heaven, until we be disburdened of this earthly burden[53] . . . .

We say we are Christians: that we believe after this mortal, a life immortal; that death is but a separation of the body and soul; and that the soul returns to his happy abode, there to joy in God, who only is all good; that at the last day it shall again take the body, which shall no more be subject to corruption.[54] With these goodly discourses we fill all our books: and in the meanwhile, when it comes to the point, the very name of death as the horriblest thing in the world makes us quake and tremble. If we believe as we speak, what is that we fear? To be happy? To be at our ease? To be more content in a moment, than we might be in the longest mortal life that might be? Or must not we of force confess that we believe it but in part? That all we have is but words? . . .

Now to end well this life, is only to end it willingly: following with full consent the will and direction of God, and not suffering us to be drawn by the necessity of destiny.[55] To end it willingly, we must hope, and not fear death. To hope for it, we must certainly look after this life for a better life. To look for that, we must fear God, whom whoso well feareth, feareth indeed nothing in this world and hopes for all things in the other. To one well resolved in these points death can be but sweet and agreeable: knowing that through it he is to enter into a place of all joys. The grief that may be therein shall be allayed with sweetness: the sufferance[56] of ill, swallowed in the confidence of good. The

---

[52] *this foul and filthy prison,* i.e., the body.

[53] Cf. the Christian Neoplatonism in this paragraph with Laura's paradox in *The Triumph of Death*, 2.22–24 (see page 274).

[54] *that at the last day it shall again take the body, which shall no more be subject to corruption.* Cf. 1 Cor. 15:42–57.

[55] *following . . . destiny,* i.e., assenting willingly to God's will and direction, and not being compelled blindly to submit to fate.

[56] *sufferance:* acceptance, enduring.

sting of death[57] itself shall be dead, which is nothing else but fear. Nay, I will say more, not only all the evils conceived in death shall be to him nothing, but he shall even scorn all the mishaps men redoubt[58] in this life, and laugh at all these terrors. For, I pray, what can he fear, whose death is his hope? Think we to banish him his country? He knows he hath a country otherwhere, whence we cannot banish him, and that all these countries are but inns, out of which he must part at the will of his host. To put him in prison? A more strait prison he cannot have, than his own body, more filthy, more dark, more full of racks and torments. To kill him and take him out of the world? That is it he hopes for; that is it with all his heart he aspires unto. By fire, by sword, by famine, by sickness: within three years, within three days, within three hours, all is one to him; all is one at what[59] gate or at what time he pass out of this miserable life. For his businesses are ever ended, his affairs are dispatched, and by what way he shall go out, by the same he shall enter into a most happy and everlasting life. Men can threaten him but death, and death is all he promiseth himself: the worst they can do is to make him die, and that is the best he hopes for. The threatenings of tyrants are to him promises, the swords of his greatest enemies drawn in his favor: forasmuch as he knows that threatening him death, they threaten him life; and the most mortal wounds can make him but immortal. Who fears God, fears not death: and who fears it not, fears not the worst of this life.

By this reckoning, you will tell me death is a thing to be wished for: and to pass from so much evil, to so much good, a man should as it seemeth cast away his life. Surely, I fear not, that for any good we expect, we will hasten one step the faster: though the spirit aspire, the body it draws with it, withdraws it ever sufficiently towards the earth. Yet is it not that I conclude. We must seek to mortify our flesh in us and to cast the world out of us: but to cast ourselves out of the world is in no sort permitted us. The Christian ought willingly to depart out of this life but not cowardly to run away. The Christian is ordained by God to fight therein, and cannot leave his place without incurring reproach and infamy. But if it please the grand captain to recall him, let him take the retreat in good part, and with good will obey it. . . . Diest thou young? Praise God as the mariner that hath had a good wind, soon to bring him to the port. Diest thou old? Praise him likewise, for if thou hast had less wind, it may be thou hast also had less waves. But think not at thy pleasure to go faster or softer: for the wind is not in thy power, and instead of taking the shortest way

---

[57] *sting of death.* A reference to 1 Cor. 15:55: "O death, where is thy sting? O grave, where is thy victory?"

[58] *redoubt:* fear.

[59] *what,* i.e., whatever.

to the haven, thou mayest happily[60] suffer shipwreck. God calleth home from his work one in the morning, another at noon, and another at night. One he exerciseth till the first sweat, another he sunburneth, another he roasteth and drieth thoroughly. But of all his, he leaves not one without, but brings them all to rest and gives them all their hire, every one[61] in his time.[62] Who leaves his work before God call him, loses it: and who importunes him before the time, loses his reward. We must rest us in his will, who[63] in the midst of our troubles sets us at rest.

To end, we ought neither to hate this life for the toils therein, for it[64] is sloth and cowardice, nor love it for the delights, which is folly and vanity, but serve us of it, to serve God in it, who after it shall place us in true quietness and replenish us with pleasures which shall never more perish. Neither ought we to fly[65] death, for it is childish to fear it: and in flying from it, we meet it. Much less to seek it, for that is temerity: nor everyone that would die, can die: as much despair in the one, as cowardice in the other: in neither, any kind of magnanimity. It is enough that we constantly and continually wait for her[66] coming, that she may never find us unprovided. For as there is nothing more certain than death, so is there nothing more uncertain than the hour of death, known only to God, the only author of life and death, to whom we all ought[67] endeavor both to live and die.

> *Die to live,*
> *Live to die.*[68]

The 13 of May 1590.
At Wilton.

---

[60] *happily:* by chance, perhaps.

[61] *every one,* i.e., every worker in God's vineyard.

[62] *God calleth home . . . in his time.* See the parable of the vineyard in Matt. 20:1–16.

[63] *in his will, who,* i.e., in the will of him who.

[64] *it,* i.e., *to hate this life* is *sloth and cowardice.*

[65] *fly:* flee from.

[66] *her,* i.e., Death, which is grammatically feminine in French (*la mort*). Cf. the personification of death as a woman in Petrarch's *Trionfo della Morte.* See page 267.

[67] *ought:* ought to, with a sense of owing or obligation.

[68] *Die to live, / Live to die.* Cf. Laura in *Triumph,* 2.22–24. Shakespeare may be alluding to this passage in Claudio's statement, "To sue to live, I find I seek to die, / And seeking death, find life," in *Measure for Measure* 1.3.43–44 , and in the friar's advice to Hero, "Die to live," in *Much Ado about Nothing* 4.1.256. See Katherine Duncan-Jones, "Stoicism in *Measure for Measure*: A New Source," *RES* 28 (1977): 441–46.

Supplemental material:

A Discourse of the Tediousness of Life and Profit of Death

from Elizabeth Ashburnham, *Instructions for My Children, or Any Other Christian* (Washington, D.C., Folger Shakespeare Library), MS. V.a.511, fols. 84–85v.

This précis of and meditation on Pembroke's translation of *A Discourse of Life and Death* appears in a manuscript of prayers begun by Elizabeth Ashburnham (later Richardson) in 1606 (Folger MS. V.a.511). The manuscript, entitled "Instructions for my children, or any other Christian, Directing to the performance of our duties, towards God and Man—drawn out of the Holy Scripture," is one of the earliest examples of the mother's advice book, but it was kept privately in the family and not printed until 2000.[69] Her handwritten list of contents includes four sections; "A Discourse of the Tediousness of Life and Profit of Death" concludes the volume. She eliminated classical references, simplified the prose, and adapted the Senecan ages of man to fit the pattern of a woman's life, including an arranged marriage in youth.

In 1645 Richardson published *A Ladies Legacy to Her Daughters*, a later book of prayers and meditations in the tradition of the mother's advice book.[70] By then she had precedent for printing her words, since she probably knew such works as Elizabeth Grymeston's *Miscellanea, Meditations, Memoratives* (1604), Dorothy Leigh's *The Mother's Blessing* (1616), Elizabeth Clinton's *The Countess of Lincoln's Nursery* (1622), and Elizabeth Jocelin's *Mother's Legacy to Her Unborn Child* (1624).

---

[69] For an old spelling version see Margaret Hannay, "Elizabeth Ashburnham Richardson's Meditation on the Countess of Pembroke's *Discourse*," *EMS* 9 (2000): 114–28.

[70] Victoria E. Burke, "Elizabeth Ashburnham Richardson's 'Motherlie Endeavors' in Manuscript," *EMS* 9 (2000): 98–113.

A Discourse of the Tediousness of Life
and Profit of Death

 *H*ow cometh it to pass, that mankind only (amongst all other creatures) being endued with reason, should above all other living things, be most senseless and sensually affected in desiring and endeavoring with all their power, the long continuance of this present life (the vale of all mischief and misery) and so much fear and hate the approach of death, which is the beginning of all true and everlasting happiness. Oh, how many bend their ears unto the Siren song and listen to the pleasant voice of the Mermaid, till they sink in the gulf, unhappy wretches bewitched with the deceivable trains[71] and shows of this vain world, which if it be rightly considered with incorrupt eyes, is but a bottomless pit of errors, a market of deceit, a prison of darkness, a continual tempest of sundry storms and troubles, a sea of woes open to all winds, wherein we are tossed and continually tormented, sometimes within, sometimes without, a barren land wherein no good thing is attained but by great labor and care, a green and pleasant meadow full of serpents, ready to sting all that seek to take repast therein, a gallant and beautiful garden, but the flowers thereof are full of poison, a fountain of vanity, a false fable finely and cunningly framed, a spring of idle thoughts, a delightful dream wherein we see nothing but deceit: to conclude with wise Solomon, "vanity of vanities, all is but vanity, and vexation of spirit,"[72] wherein no good is to be found, nor any evil wanting, our purpose is restless, our hope frustrated, our security without safety, our intent failing of the event, our travails without end; all we enjoy is but abuse, and never do we attain to true content in any state or age.

Now all will grant that life in itself is not simple good, but to live well and happily is that which everyone aimeth at; yet if we take a view of the whole course of our lives, we shall hardly find one, that can or will confess to have attained thereunto. We all enter this life in crying and tears; we pass it with cares and pains, and end it in sorrow and fear. All men both high and low, have one manner of coming into life, and shall have a like going out. Everyone cometh from him that was first made of the dust of the ground[73] and falleth to the earth (which is of like nature) with lamentation, wrapped in swaddling clothes, nourished by the care and trouble of others, being least able of all creatures to help and support themselves, and only more happy in this age than afterwards, in that they have no sense nor apprehension of their own unhappiness.

---

[71] *trains:* snares.

[72] Eccles. 1:2, 14.

[73] *him that was first made of the dust of the ground,* i.e., Adam.

But when they grow to youth (which is the death of infancy) whereto are they inclined, or how like they to spend the time but in folly or mischief, being hardly brought unto anything that is good, but by the labor and diligence of their friends and with great repining and discontent in themselves. Come we to the next age so much desired and longed for of all, which freeth them from their subjection to others, and bringeth the hoped liberty, wherein they shall be at their own government and disposition (unless it be some unfortunate women, that are removed from the slavery of their youth's governors, to come under the tyranny of an indiscreet husband, which bondage seldom doth release during their lives) but who so enjoyeth this wished freedom, to take a course of life to their best liking, have it a doubtful choice whether to take the way of virtue or of vice, to have reason or passion for their guide, and few are they which by the especial grace of God choose the best way. And in seeking after virtue, we can expect but future, and not present happiness, for all that will live godly, must suffer persecution, and who so will follow Christ must take up a cross, for the life of a Christian is a continual warfare, having three most dangerous and deadly enemies: the devil, the world, and the flesh, with whom we can take no truce. That old serpent and destroyer of mankind, his malice and subtlety, his snares and baits, daily laid to endanger our souls is well known; the other two being but his companions and instruments, to work our utter destruction. The world entertains with a thousand delights, to persuade us to vanity, the flesh ever lusteth and rebelleth against the spirit, to lead us captive slaves to sin and all ungodliness; we cannot find a place in the world to retire ourselves, where the world will not find us; we may seek to avoid the infection and contagion of others' wickedness, and yet still be full of corrupt affections in ourselves, while we live. Let us change company, house, country, and all else, we shall still find evil and unquietness, till we be separate from ourselves by death. Now if we will let the reins loose to our unruly passion, and suffer ourselves to be allured by the deceitful enticements thereof, and run headlong into all vice and sensuality, hoping thereby to taste and enjoy all the pleasures and commodities of this vile world or the licentious flesh promiseth to their lovers in this life, [then] these seeming pleasures may more truly be called displeasures, having not so much sweetness as bitterness in them, gotten with pain and peril, spent and past in a moment, and followed with a long and heavy remorse of conscience, like sweetmeats that turn into choler,[74] none so pleasant to the mouth, but leaves an unsavory aftertaste, nor any so moderate, but hath his corrosive and carries his punishment in itself, and the best and happiest event is grievous repentance. And yet we pass over an infinite number of inconveniences and dangers, that this ill-guided age throws

---

[74] *choler:* bile, one of the four humors and a cause of anger.

them into; this is the age that children so earnestly desire, and the wisest old folks oftimes much lament.

Next followeth that which is called perfect age, wherein everyone seeketh to be accounted wise and discreet, and by their good carriage, to purchase credit and estimation in the world, and rest to themselves in future time; and indeed in this age are they able more perfectly to discern the imperfections of human nature, which the simplicity of childhood and lightness of youth could not discover; but now shall we have new assaults and combats, falling but from one mischief to another, like waves of the sea driving each other, thus changing but never ending our miseries. Then sues to them for entertainment, covetousness, pride, ambition, envy, vainglory, and the like, how many for lucre sake[75] adventure the loss of their lives, both temporal and eternal, thinking there is no other good to mortal men, but in getting mortal possessions, and when they have them, seldom use them, heaping up riches and cannot tell who shall enjoy them, setting all their heart and hope upon a vile excrement of the earth, of which the more they drink, the more thirsty, being never satisfied nor content, attaining them for the most part with great pains and weariness of the body and doth possess them with no less fear and trouble of mind: whereas if we obtain things necessary at God's hands, we ought to be satisfied, for we brought nothing into the world, and it is certain that we shall carry nothing out. Naked we came, and so we must return; for covetousness is the root of all evil[76] and the corruptions of their hoardings shall but serve to witness against them in the day of wrath.

Pride and ambition is hateful both to God and man, and envy fretteth the heart and drieth up the bones, being continually vexed, either at their own harms or at others' good, still discontented that they are not equal with the highest, and never are thankful that there are thousands under them. And what is that vain honor we so greedily hunt for, but a smoke and a blast of wind, which when the sun of fortune goes down upon us, it is quite gone, and the place thereof cannot be found? What doth pride profit us, or what good doth the pomp of riches bring us? All those things are passed away like a shadow, or a ship that goeth over the waves of the sea, the trace and path whereof cannot be seen. Why is earth and ashes proud, seeing when they die, they are but the heirs of serpents and food of worms? What have we that we have not received from God, and what honor can we have of ourselves, if others will not yield it unto us? But the glory and honor we aspire to at the best is

---

[75] *lucre sake*: money's sake. An example of an early modern possessive form without "s."

[76] I Timothy 6:7; Job 1:21; I Timothy 6:10. This précis is a pastiche of biblical quotation, often, as here, with each phrase of a sentence from a different passage.

but vain, and all that avarice can obtain but gross and base, for which we must suffer much ill, to get that which is ill. Only are they happy who in mind live content, and they most unhappy whom all they can have cannot content.

Now some few of the wisest spend much of this age in seeking for knowledge, wisdom, and learning, which indeed is the best bestowed time of all other, but these cannot be gotten without great and painful labor and diligence, and endless travail of the mind, for the more we know, the more we desire to know; the fuller the mind is, the emptier it finds itself, and who so increaseth knowledge increaseth sorrow in seeing his own ignorance; for the most we know, is to find that we know nothing, and our best perfection is to judge truly of our own imperfections. Yet knowledge in many puffeth them up, that in knowing much they forget themselves so turning the right and best use of our lives to their own hurt.

Then cometh old age which is but the post and messenger before death, and may fitter be called death than life, wherein all the senses grow weak and oft fail, except the sense of pain, repaying the riot of youth, with many infirmities, and finding a bitter aftertaste in mind or body, and oft in both of the former evils in all the ages past. And as by death we return again to the earth, from whence we came, so in this age we are come back to infancy, which was the first step we set on earth, being wearisome to ourselves and noisome to others. Therefore, Solomon wisheth us to remember our Creator in the time of youth, before the evil days come and the years approach wherein we shall say we have no pleasure in them, our days are then but sorrows, being tired with the perpetual task this life ties us to, wherein when we have done our best, we must begin again, passing from one evil to an other, grieving in the remembrance of [all] that is past, doubtful in the expectation of what is to come, and taking no content in the present time.

Now is there no hopeful comfort for the end and release of all these miseries, and the beginning of never ending happiness, but death only, than which nothing is more assured, though the time thereof be most uncertain unto us; for as soon as we are born, we begin to draw to our end, the increase of our days being the decrease of our lives. And once to die well, we had need to die daily in ourselves and to the world. All flesh waxeth old as a garment, and this is the condition of all times: they must die the death. As the green leaves on a tree, some fall and some grow, so is the generation of flesh and blood: one cometh to an end and another is born. For all corruptible things shall fail, and the number of our days are but few and evil, even a span long, and there is an appointed time to man upon earth which we shall not pass. Our life is but a vapor that appeareth for a little while, and afterwards vanisheth away; if we attain unto seventy years it is much, and yet our strength is but labor and sorrow; great travail is created for all men, and a heavy yoke for the children of

Adam, from the day they come from their mother's womb,[77] till they return to the mother of all things. Both he that sitteth on the glorious throne, and he that is beneath in dust and ashes, all must return to the earth from whence they came for man is not lord over the spirit to retain the same, neither can deliver himself in the day of death. But though death can be avoided by none, yet it is causelessly feared by all, partly by our weak nature, shunning the pain that life at parting, or rather sin, not death, layeth upon us, but chiefly by the memory of an evil-passed[78] life, and the horror of the severe Judgment[79] presently to follow; but to those that live godly, death is an advantage, for all things are theirs, and they Christ's, with whom they shall live forever. Amen.

---

[77] *mother's womb*, i.e., the earth.
[78] *evil-passed*: evilly passed.
[79] *the severe Judgment*, i.e., the Last Judgment.

THE DOLEFUL LAY OF CLORINDA

*L*ike many other bereaved women writers in the early modern period—such as Vittoria Colonna, Elizabeth Cook Russell, Marguerite de Navarre, Katherine Philips, and Anne Bradstreet—the countess of Pembroke wrote at least one poem in her initial period of mourning. The cultural pretense that elegy was an unstudied emotional response to loss meant that, unlike more formal genres, it was "accessible to writers of all ages and abilities," as Dennis Kay demonstrates, a form in which they could learn "the components of art and the disciplines of the craft."[1] Her expression of grief was thus unusual not so much in this poetic activity or genre, but in the public attention given to her brother's death, to her own role as mourner, and to this early work. (See page 10.) In *The Ruines of Time* (1591) Spenser claims to have read an elegy that she had written. No one, he says, can write poems mourning Sidney better than his own sister, who "sings with deep heart's sorrowing." His own sorrow is "tempered" with the "dear delight" of enjoying her poetry.[2] As Jacqueline Pearson observes, "the conventional image of an active male writer and a passive female reader has been paraphrased as a more equal relation between male and female poets who are both readers and writers."[3] Spenser's praise of Pembroke's verse is obviously colored by his search for her patronage; he is claiming the high status of being part of this wealthy aristocrat's literary coterie, the select group to whom she would have shown her work in manuscript. He is also celebrating in print the existence of such a coterie and Pembroke's full participation in it as a writer as well as a patron. Her poems obviously circulated beyond Wilton, for three years later she wrote to Sir Edward Wotton, her brother's "dear and special friend," asking him to return his copy of her "passion," or poem of mourning, written in "those sad times" after Sidney's death and given to Wotton "long since."[4] She had lost her only copy, she said. Certainly she may have written more than one poem of mourning, but the only surviving elegy attributed to her is "The Doleful Lay of Clorinda." The simplest explanation would be that she asked Wotton to return his copy

---

[1] Dennis Kay, *Melodious Tears: The English Funeral Elegy from Spenser to Milton* (Oxford: Oxford University Press, 1990), 6.

[2] Spenser, *The Ruines of Time*, lines 318–19.

[3] Jacqueline Pearson, "Women Reading, Reading Women," in *Women and Literature in Britain, 1500–1700*, ed. Wilcox, 87.

[4] Mary Sidney Herbert, countess of Pembroke, to Sir Edward Wotton, endorsed 1594, "Correspondence III," *Collected Works*, 1:286–87.

of her "Lay," which she then reworked, perhaps with Spenser, for inclusion in the *Astrophel* volume of elegies.

The volume of elegies entitled *Astrophel: A Pastoral Elegy Upon the Death of the Most Noble and Valourous Knight, Sir Philip Sidney* does seem to be a collaboration involving Spenser, Lodowick Bryskett (a mutual friend of Spenser and of the Sidney family), and the countess of Pembroke; to their poems were added three more reprinted from *The Phoenix Nest*, an earlier volume that included elegies for Philip Sidney.[5] Spenser introduces the volume with his own elegy, "Astrophel," and provides a one-stanza bridge saying that he will "rehearse," or recite, a poem written by Clorinda, Astrophel's sister. After "The Doleful Lay," Spenser provides a two-stanza bridge, saying that he will first "rehearse" a poem written by Thestylis (Lodowick Bryskett), and then the poems of other mourners. "The Doleful Lay" is set off from the bridge stanzas by elaborate borders; no such decorative borders frame Spenser's "Astrophel" or Bryskett's "The Mourning Muse" (see Plates nos. 4a and 4b). These first three poems in the collection show such remarkable similarities in content and in wording that they must have been deliberately dovetailed. Bryskett's authorship of "The Mourning Muse of Thestylis," entered for publication in 1587, is unquestioned, but in the early twentieth century Ernest de Selincourt challenged Pembroke's authorship of the parallel "Doleful Lay of Clorinda" and attributed it to Spenser.[6] His argument was based on the Spenserian quality of the verse and on his erroneous assumption (at a time when the work of most early modern women writers was unknown) that Pembroke would not have been capable of writing it. This relatively simple poem in six-line stanzas of iambic pentameter rhymed *ababcc*, however,

---

[5] On collaboration between Spenser and Bryskett, see Frederick B. Tromly, "Lodowick Bryskett's Elegies on Sidney in Spenser's *Astrophel* Volume," *RES* ns 37 (1986): 384–88; and Katherine Duncan-Jones, "Astrophel," in *The Spenser Encyclopedia*, ed. A. C. Hamilton, et al. (Toronto: University of Toronto Press, 1990), 74.

[6] For the argument over authorship, see *The Triumph of Death and Other Unpublished and Uncollected Poems by Mary Sidney, Countess of Pembroke (1561–1621)*, ed. Gary F. Waller (Salzburg: University of Salzburg Press, 1977), 53–59, and Waller, *Mary Sidney*, 89–93; "'The Doleful Lay of Clorinda': Literary Context," *Collected Works*, 1:119–32. See also Shannon Miller for additional textual evidence, "Mary Sidney and Gendered Strategies for the Writing of Poetry," in *Write or Be Written. Early Modern Women Poets and Cultural Constraints*, ed. Barbara Smith and Ursula Appelt (Aldershot, England and Burlington, Vt.: Ashgate, 2001), 159. Duncan-Jones, "Astrophel," and Pamela Coren, "Edmund Spenser, Mary Sidney, and the Doleful Lay," *SEL* 42, 1 (2002): 25–41, are among those arguing for Spenser's authorship. Danielle Clarke focuses on the way Spenser "is able to contain and control the figure of the Countess of Pembroke," "'In Sort as She It Sung': Spenser's 'Doleful Lay' and the Construction of Female Authorship," *Criticism* 42 (2000): 451–68.

conforms to her later works in wording and style, if not in complexity.[7] Note, for example, the use of heavy alliteration (as in 49, 95), alliterated noun and adjective (as in 28, 90), intensification of the verb for emphasis (29–30, 32–33), use of questions to structure the work (as in 1–6, 13, 31–32, 43–44, and, most importantly, 55–56 and 65–66), and compound words (43). The old-fashioned "ne" construction (43, 67, 87–88), often thought to be particularly Spenserian, also appears in Pembroke's early version of Psalm 69: "Ne from thy servant hide thy helpful face" (52). Figures of repetition, ubiquitous here (as in 28–29, 35–36, 38–39, 47–48), are usually handled less skillfully than in her later works, including "Angel Spirit." As in "Angel Spirit," Sidney is portrayed with the heavenly choirs (63–64; "Angel Spirit" 59–61). As in *The Triumph of Death*, the moment of death is portrayed by the cropping of a single flower (31–34; *Triumph* 1.115). Several other echoes of her Petrarch translation include symbolic roses and violets for the heavenly soul (71–72; *Triumph* 1.27) and the compound adjective "angel-like" (76; *Triumph* 1.150).[8] There are also Spenserian echoes here, notably to the sad garlands in "November" of *The Shepheardes Calender* ("The Doleful Lay," 41–42) and to the Garden of Adonis in book 3 of *The Faerie Queen* ("The Doleful Lay," 67–88).

"Clorinda" begins with the search for an audience to whom she can tell her grief. She rejects the heavens, because they are ultimately the cause of her brother's death, and those on earth, because they are all too busy with their own sorrows to care about hers. She has no one left to mourn with her, she says, for "none alive like sorrowful remains" (20), probably a reference to Pembroke's mother and father, who had both died in the same year as her brother Philip, and perhaps also to her brother Thomas, who died in 1595. She assumes the role of senior representative of her family and seems to discount her brother Robert as a fellow mourner, perhaps because he was in the Netherlands. In this pastoral literary world she becomes the chief mourner, as she does in "Angel Spirit." At first she can only mourn to herself and to Nature, while the woods, hills, and rivers echo back her song. Later in the poem she instructs the mourning "shepherds' lasses," using the traditional pastoral imagery of the elegy. This "earthly nature" is then contrasted with a "celestial pastoral," as Elaine Beilin notes.[9]

The poem includes the usual elements of lament, praise of the deceased, and consolation. This consolation, traditional in Christian meditations on

---

[7] Hannay, "The Countess of Pembroke as a Spenserian Poet," 41–62; *Collected Works*, 1:119–32.

[8] "Angel-like" 1611, 1617 editions of "Doleful Lay"; "Angelick," 1595.

[9] Beilin, *Redeeming Eve*, 138.

death, is that his soul is not dead, but enjoys eternal bliss in heaven (66–68). In this poem there is no consolation for the speaker herself, who ends as she began, in misery—a traditional contrast between the beloved's joy in paradise and the mourner's sorrow on earth. She does, however, succeed in finding an audience, for she ends in a community of mourners, other "wretches" who "weep and wail, and wear our eyes, / Mourning . . . our own miseries" (95–96). (The search for an audience is eventually completed by the poem's circulation in manuscript and then in print.) "The Doleful Lay" thus enacts a progression from solitary grief to a communal poetic project of commemorating Sidney. That journey from grief to poetry is equally present in the two versions of "Angel Spirit."

COPY-TEXT: "Doleful Lay" (1595). Verbal emendations: 17 wretched (wetched), 35 Great . . . him did see (Creat . . . him see).

[The Doleful Lay of Clorinda]

Ay me, to whom shall I my case complain,
That may compassion[10] my impatient grief?
Or where shall I unfold my inward pain,
That my enriven[11] heart may find relief?
    Shall I unto the heavenly pow'rs it show,
    Or unto earthly men that dwell below?

To heavens? Ah, they, alas, the authors were,
And workers of my unremedied woe:
For they foresee what to us happens here,
And they foresaw, yet suffered[12] this be so.   10
    From them comes good, from them comes also ill,
    That which they made, who can them warn to spill.[13]

To men? Ah, they, alas, like wretched be,
And subject to the heavens' ordinance:
Bound to abide whatever they[14] decree.
Their best redress is their best sufferance.[15]
    How then can they, like wretched, comfort me,
    The which no less need comforted to be?

Then to myself will I my sorrow mourn,
Sith[16] none alive like sorrowful remains: 20
And to myself my plaints[17] shall back return,
To pay their usury[18] with doubled pains.
    The woods, the hills, the rivers shall resound
    The mournful accent of my sorrow's ground.[19]

---

[10] *compassion:* have compassion on, pity.

[11] *enriven:* riven, torn. The form with the prefix is not cited in the *OED*.

[12] *suffered:* permitted.

[13] *warn to spill:* prevent from killing. This is an archaic use of *warn*, not recorded in the *OED* past the sixteenth century.

[14] *they,* i.e., the heavens.

[15] The best remedy people have for their wretchedness is to endure, or suffer, it the best they can.

[16] *Sith:* since.

[17] *plaints:* complaints.

[18] *usury:* in this context, interest paid on a loan, used metaphorically.

[19] *ground:* a line of music above which a descant is sung or played.

Woods, hills, and rivers now are desolate,
Sith he is gone the which them all did grace:
And all the fields do wail their widow state,
Sith death their fairest flow'r did late deface.
    The fairest flow'r in field that ever grew,
    Was Astrophel; that was, we all may rue.[20]   30

What cruel hand of cursed foe unknown,
Hath cropped the stalk which bore so fair a flow'r?
Untimely cropped, before it well were grown,
And clean defaced in untimely hour.
    Great loss to all that ever him did see,
    Great loss to all, but greatest loss to me.

Break now your garlands, O ye shepherds' lasses,
Sith the fair flow'r, which them adorned, is gone:
The flow'r, which them adorned, is gone to ashes,
Never again let lass put garland on.   40
    Instead of garland, wear sad cypress[21] now,
    And bitter elder,[22] broken from the bough.

Ne[23] ever sing the love-lays[24] which he made:
Who ever made such lays of love as he?
Ne ever read the riddles, which he said
Unto yourselves, to make you merry glee.[25]
    Your merry glee is now laid all abed,
    Your merry maker[26] now, alas, is dead.

---

[20] *rue:* think of with sorrow.

[21] *cypress:* a dark conifer associated with mourning.

[22] *elder:* a low tree or shrub.

[23] *Ne:* nor, an archaic form appropriate to the Spenserian quality of this elegy, as in Variant Psalm 69.

[24] *lays:* poems, songs, as in Philip Sidney's *Astrophil and Stella* and *Arcadia.*

[25] *to make you merry glee:* to make merry glee for you.

[26] *maker:* poet, in this context, as in Sidney's *Defence of Poetry,* in *Miscellaneous Prose of Sir Philip Sidney,* ed. Katherine Duncan-Jones and Jan van Dorsten (Oxford: Clarendon Press, 1973), 77.

Death, the devourer of all world's delight,
Hath robbed you and reft[27] from me my joy: 50
Both you and me and all the world he quite
Hath robbed of joyance, and left sad annoy.
    Joy of the world, and shepherds' pride was he,
    Shepherds' hope never like again to see.

O Death, that hast us of such riches reft,
Tell us at least, what hast thou with it done?
What is become of him whose flow'r[28] here left
Is but the shadow of his likeness gone:
    Scarce like the shadow of that which he was,
    Naught like, but that he like a shade did pass.   60

But that immortal spirit, which was decked
With all the dowries of celestial grace:
By sovereign choice from th'heavenly choirs select,[29]
And lineally derived from angels' race,
    Oh, what is now of it become, aread.[30]
    Ay me, can so divine a thing be dead?

Ah no: it is not dead, ne can it die,
But lives for aye,[31] in blissful Paradise:
Where like a new-born babe it soft doth lie,
In bed of lilies wrapped in tender wise,   70
    And compassed all about with roses sweet,
    And dainty violets from head to feet.

There thousand birds all of celestial brood,
To him do sweetly carol day and night:
And with strange notes, of him well understood,
Lull him asleep in angel-like delight;

---

[27] *reft*: robbed, taken.

[28] *flow'r*, i.e., Sidney's literary work or posthumous reputation.

[29] *By sovereign choice . . . select,* i.e., chosen by God.

[30] *aread*: say, interpret. The question about death is answered within a Christian context in 67–96, which express the belief that Sidney's soul is in heaven, the *blissful Paradise* described in 70–78, in contrast with the lamenting natural world in 1–60.

[31] *aye*: ever.

Whilst in sweet dream to him presented be
Immortal beauties, which no eye may see.

But he them sees and takes exceeding pleasure
Of their divine aspects, appearing plain,   80
And kindling love in him above all measure,
Sweet love still joyous, never feeling pain.
    For what so goodly form he there doth see,
    He may enjoy from jealous rancor free.[32]

There liveth he in everlasting bliss,
Sweet spirit never fearing more to die:
Ne dreading harm from any foes of his,
Ne fearing savage beasts' more cruelty.
    Whilst we here, wretches, wail his private lack,
    And with vain vows do often call him back.   90

But live thou there still happy, happy spirit,
And give us leave thee here thus to lament:
Not thee that dost thy heaven's joy inherit,
But our own selves that here in dole are drent.[33]
    Thus do we weep and wail, and wear our eyes,
    Mourning in other's, our own miseries.

---

[32] *from jealous rancor free.* Cf. the reference to heaven as Sidney's haven from Envy
in "Angel Spirit," 60–63.

[33] *dole . . . drent:* grief . . . drowned.

A DIALOGUE BETWEEN TWO SHEPHERDS, THENOT AND PIERS, IN PRAISE OF ASTREA

This pastoral dialogue was evidently written for enactment during Elizabeth's intended visit to Wilton in 1599, although the last two digits of the year are lacking in the original.[1] Such literary performances to welcome a visiting monarch were customary on the queen's progresses to the country homes of the nobility. The queen's progresses were a highly successful public relations campaign, giving thousands of her subjects the opportunity to see her as she journeyed through the countryside with a splendid entourage of hundreds of courtiers and servants. Hosting such a visit was a gamble. Providing suitable food and entertainment was enormously expensive, but it might also bring the hosts into Elizabeth's favor, thereby winning status and perhaps material reward.[2] Young Mary Sidney had been present at the most celebrated of these visits, when her uncle Robert Dudley, earl of Leicester, hosted Elizabeth at Kenilworth in 1575. Philip Sidney had written "A Lady of May" for Elizabeth's visit to Wanstead in the late 1570s and perhaps also "A Dialogue . . . at Wilton."[3] Like these works, Pembroke's "A Dialogue" is in the form of a pastoral debate, or singing match between shepherds, a form that could be performed by two speakers welcoming the monarch.

The form also encourages dialectic between two worldviews; in this case the debate is about the adequacy of language and metaphor to represent the divine, here represented on earth by Elizabeth as divinely appointed monarch (cf. "Even Now," 13). Thenot argues that metaphoric language can express truth; Piers replies that language is inadequate to express the divine.[4] Nine times in this piece Piers gives Thenot the lie, or terms him a liar, an insult that would normally lead to a duel in aristocratic circles; the duel here is with words rather than swords, and at the conclusion Thenot appeals to his "friendship" with Piers.

Pembroke is raising sophisticated philosophical questions here, including the issue of whether the poet was a liar, as Stephen Gosson had charged in his *School of Abuse*, inappropriately dedicated to Philip Sidney, or whether the poet's fictions encourage the reader's moral development, making the poet the

---

[1] Erler, "Davies's *Astraea*," 41–61.

[2] Mary Hill Cole, *The Portable Queen: Elizabeth I and the Politics of Ceremony* (Amherst: University of Massachusetts Press, 1999).

[3] "A Dialogue between Two Shepherds, Uttered in a Pastoral Show, at Wilton," *The Poems of Sir Philip Sidney*, ed. Ringler, 343–44, 517.

[4] On Neo-Platonism vs. Calvinism in the debate, see Waller, *Triumph*, 61–63.

"least liar" as Sidney responded in his *Defence of Poetry*.[5] Helen Hackett suggests that "Piers represents a dogmatic Protestant point of view, from which panegyric is problematic in its potential for idolatrousness."[6] That is, poems praising Elizabeth in traditionally extravagant terms are in danger of sliding into idolatry. Piers does appear to take the extreme position that poetry can never express truth, thereby agreeing with Gosson; that is unlikely to represent Pembroke's own view. The argument may be more subtle, challenging not poetry per se but the standard metaphors used to praise Elizabeth. Of course Pembroke herself is using a mythological comparison by calling the queen "Astrea," the divine virgin goddess associated with justice, whose return would bring back the Golden Age.[7] And she is cleverly using, and surpassing, each of the traditional terms used to praise Elizabeth—she embodies all earthly beauty, personifies wisdom and virtue, brings to her realm peace and prosperity, possesses eternal youth and spring, outshines the sun, exemplifies the best of both female and male qualities, and is renowned for both her military and literary achievement. The reality surpasses language, a traditional motif for panegyric that echoes the argument from writing to silence in *Astrophil and Stella* 70: "Wise silence is best music unto bliss."[8] In its originally intended context, the conclusion also implies that actions speak louder than words, as the queen would be welcomed to Wilton and honored by extravagant hospitality.

The two main topoi, or topics, used in panegyric, the genre of praise, are inexpressibility (the subject is too great for words) and outdoing (the subject is beyond all others who might be compared with her). "A Dialogue" uses both, but begins and ends by using the inexpressibility topos to discuss the philosophic and religious problems inherent in expressing the divine. Thenot begins with the traditional prayers to the Muses for inspiration to raise his work to a higher plane of truth; Piers immediately challenges his "higher" verse as merely more complex, saying that a plain style better represents truth (1–6).[42] Thenot proposes comparing Elizabeth to all glories on earth; Piers

---

[5] Sir Philip Sidney, *A Defence of Poetry*, in *Miscellaneous Prose of Sir Philip Sidney*, ed. Katherine Duncan-Jones and Jan van Dorsten (Oxford: Clarendon Press, 1973), 102.

[6] Helen Hackett, "Courtly Writing by Women," in *Women and Literature in Britain, 1500–1700*, ed. Wilcox, 177.

[7] See Frances A. Yates, *Astraea: The Imperial Theme in the Sixteenth Century* (London: Routledge & Kegan Paul, 1975; repr. Peregrine Books, 1977).

[8] *The Poems of Sir Philip Sidney*, 201.

[9] Cf. George Herbert, "Jordan" (II), "Is there in truth no beauty?" On the Protestant plain style, see Lewalski, *Protestant Poetics and the Seventeenth-Century Religious Lyric*.

responds with the traditional motif of outdoing. Elizabeth is so great that comparisons insult her (7–18). Thenot tries switching from natural to moral comparisons, praising her wisdom and virtue; Piers responds that neither wisdom nor virtue can stand on its own without her mind and her "hand," or power; neither quality has value until it is implemented (19–24). Thenot proposes that Astrea's presence alone will bring good and banish evil; Piers replies that her influence does not require her physical presence (25–30). Thenot then turns to the political realm, explaining that Astrea is England's chief joy and guard against "annoy." (And so she seemed to many in 1599 when Elizabeth was an old woman and the succession was not yet clearly established; many of her subjects did fear an outbreak of civil war after her death, although others longed for a vigorous young king to take her place. But standard flattery of the aging queen said that her death would be devastating for the nation.) Piers attacks the term "chiefest," returning to the topos of outdoing; no one is worth comparing to her (31–36).

Thenot then turns to the praise of Elizabeth as eternal youth and spring, praise that grew louder as her body deteriorated (37–42). Piers's reply hints at mortality (spring is not eternal) and immortality ("Astrea's clime").[10] The movement to heaven is continued in the following stanza, in which Thenot compares Elizabeth to the sun. The sun can be obscured, however, and is therefore inadequate to express the divine (43–48). Thenot then tries praising Elizabeth's dual nature in the doctrine of the queen's two bodies, her physical body (female) and her embodiment of the state (male) (49–54). The similar division between palm and bay trees (50) points to both her military victory (palm) and her poetic achievement (bay). Piers attacks the trees' value as symbol. Increasingly frustrated, Thenot asks why his words are inadequate if his meaning is "true" (55–57), thereby making the same separation between thought and language that Philip Sidney makes in his *Defence of Poetry*. Piers is given the final word. Elizabeth's greatness is beyond thought and therefore beyond language. The last line says that nothing but silence can praise her, but it can also be read as a command to Thenot, "Silence!" Nothing is adequate to praise Elizabeth. The dialogue thus both participates in and questions the conventional praise of Elizabeth.

"A Dialogue" can be read with "Even Now," which was evidently intended for a presentation copy of the *Psalms* for the same visit in 1599, and with her letter thanking Queen Elizabeth for giving her son a position at court. Pembroke addressed her queen in three different literary genres; in each of these genres she praises her in terms that equate her with the divine. Such flattery,

---

[10] Cf. Shakespeare, Sonnet 18: "Shall I compare thee to a summer's day?"

which may seem excessive to twenty-first century readers, is in part court etiquette, in part a rhetorical strategy to gain the queen's favor, and in part the contemporary belief that the monarch did, in some sense, represent God on earth.

"A Dialogue" is written in caudate, or tail rhyme, in ten stanzas of six lines; in each stanza Thenot and Piers are each given two lines of iambic tetrameter followed by one of iambic trimeter with a feminine ending, rhymed *aabccb*. The same form is used in *Antonius*, Act 3, Chorus.

COPY-TEXT: "Dialogue" (1602). Verbal emendations: 34 *there (three)*, 44 *shine (thine)*.

A Dialogue between Two Shepherds, *Thenot* and *Piers*, in Praise of *Astrea*, Made by the Excellent Lady, the Lady Mary, Countess of Pembroke, at the Queen's Majesty's Being at Her House at [Wilton,] Anno 15[99]

Thenot.	I sing divine Astrea's praise.
	O Muses, help my wits to raise
	And heave my verses higher.
Piers.	Thou need'st the truth but plainly tell,
	Which much I doubt[11] thou canst not well,
	Thou art so oft a liar.

Thenot.	If in my song no more I show,	
	Than heav'n, and earth, and sea do know,	
	Then truly I have spoken.	
Piers.	Sufficeth not no more to name,	10
	But being no less, the like, the same,[12]	
	Else laws of truth be broken.	

Thenot.	Then say, she is so good, so fair,
	With all the earth she may compare,
	Not Momus' self denying.[13]
Piers.	Compare may think where likeness holds:
	Naught like to her the earth enfolds.[14]
	I looked to find you lying.

Thenot.	Astrea sees with wisdom's sight,	
	Astrea works by virtue's might,	20
	And jointly both do stay in[15] her.	

---

[11] *doubt*: suspect, fear. Thenot is advising Piers against hyperbole.

[12] 10–11. It is sufficient to name no more comparisons, which are all the same and all inadequate to praise Astrea. The double negative was conventionally used for emphasis.

[13] Which not even Momus, the god of ridicule and censure, can deny.

[14] 16–17. Comparison can be made only between similar things, but there is nothing equal to Astrea on earth. Piers applies the convention of outdoing.

[15] *stay in*. The meter requires that the words be elided as "stain" (mar or disgrace), wordplay anticipating *stain her* in 24. See Erler, "Davies's *Astraea*," 47.

Piers.	Nay, take from them, her[16] hand, her mind,
	The one is lame, the other blind.
	Shall still your lying stain her?

Thenot.	Soon as Astrea shows her face,
	Straight every ill avoids the place,
	And every good aboundeth.
Piers.	Nay, long before her face doth show,
	The last doth come, the first[17] doth go.
	How loud this lie resoundeth!	30

Thenot.	Astrea is our chiefest joy,
	Our chiefest guard against annoy,
	Our chiefest wealth, our treasure.
Piers.	Where chiefest are, there others be;
	To us none else but only she.
	When wilt thou speak in measure?

Thenot.	Astrea may be justly said,
	A field in flow'ry robe arrayed,
	In season freshly springing.
Piers.	That spring endures but shortest time,	40
	This never leaves Astrea's clime.
	Thou liest, instead of singing.

Thenot.	As heavenly light that guides the day,
	Right so doth shine each lovely ray
	That from Astrea flyeth.
Piers.	Nay, darkness oft that light enclouds;
	Astrea's beams no darkness shrouds.
	How loudly Thenot lieth!

Thenot.	Astrea rightly term I may,
	A manly palm, a maiden bay,	50
	Her verdure[18] never dying.

---

[16] *her,* i.e., Astrea's. Without Astrea's hand and mind, wisdom is blind, and virtue lame.

[17] *last . . . first,* i.e., *good* and *ill* (26–27).

[18] *verdure:* fresh greenness, vitality.

Piers.   Palm oft is crooked, bay is low;
          She still upright, still high doth grow.
              Good Thenot, leave[19] thy lying.

Thenot.   Then Piers, of friendship tell me why,
          My meaning true, my words should lie,
              And strive in vain to raise her.

Piers.   Words from conceit[20] do only rise;
          Above conceit her honor flies:
              But silence, naught can praise her.[21]   60

MARY, COUNTESS OF PEMBROKE

---

[19] *leave:* leave off, cease.

[20] *conceit:* thought, understanding, which in the next line Piers says cannot comprehend Astrea's honor.

[21] Piers means primarily that except for silence, nothing can praise Astrea, but he is also giving Thenot advice: "But silence! . . ."

Supplemental Material:

Countess of Pembroke's Letter to Queen Elizabeth

Most sacred Sovereign,

Pardon, I humbly beseech you, this first boldness of your humblest creature, and let it please that divine goodness, which can thus enlive and comfort my life, to vouchsafe to know that not presumption—oh, no—but the vehement working desire of a thankful heart so to acknowledge itself for so high and precious a favor received hath guided my trembling hand to offer these worthless words to your excellent eyes: wherein I would, if any words could, present a thankfulness inexpressible; not only for myself but for my son, who of your Majesty's ever princely grace you are pleased to take into your care, to fashion fit to live in your sight, to add and supply whatsoever want or defect may be in him, for which both my lord and I do humble ourselves at your highness's feet.

And for mine own part remembering (what is of dearest memory) how in my youngest times myself was graced by the same heavenly grace, the same sun which evermore hath power to perfect the greatest imperfection by the rarest example of all perfection, give me leave, humbly I beseech your Majesty, to unfold my comfort, hitherto withheld in the prison of my heart, and now even with tears of joy thus to pour forth my joyfulness finding that unspeakable goodness so begun in me thus continued in mine. What should I say or what can words say for me but that I, who, by a more particular bond, was born and bred, more, your Majesty, than any other creature and do, I protest, desire to live but to serve and observe you, do know that he, participating of the same sprite,[1] must likewise make that his life, his end, his sole care and desire, to which endeavor I do as gladly leave him and give him as ever I was made mother of him and accordingly am to take comfort in him as he shall be blessed in your gracious sight and frame himself wholly to please and serve your most Excellent Majesty to whom all blessedness belongeth. And blessed indeed are they that may behold you. My pen hath now hit upon my part of torment, I that do not, and yet still do behold you with the humblest eyes of my mind's love and admiration.

---

[1] *sprite*: spirit.

I again, and again in all reverent humbleness beg pardon for this fearful boldness, do end with my never-ending prayers. Long, long may that purest light live and shine to his ever-living praise and glory who hath made your Majesty this world's wonder and England's bliss.

Your Highness's

most bound,

the humblest of your creatures,

M. Pembroke[2]

---

[2] Mary Sidney Herbert, countess of Pembroke, to Queen Elizabeth, endorsed "1601." Cecil Papers 90/147. *Collected Works*, 1:290–92.

II.

WORKS CIRCULATED
IN MANUSCRIPT

EVEN NOW THAT CARE

This poem dedicating the Sidney *Psalms* to Queen Elizabeth exists in only one copy that may be the presentation manuscript of the *Psalms* (see "Circulation and Reception of the Texts"), and no contemporary references to the poem have as yet been found. It may well have been written for the queen's eyes only. Pembroke situates herself as the queen's handmaid (90), a reminder that Elizabeth had invited her to serve at court as one of the maids of honor in her youth. She begins by noting the queen's heavy burden as ruler, with the repeated mention of her "cares" as so time-consuming that she would not have time even for the ceremonial presentation of works dedicated to her, and certainly not for reading them, except that she is so accomplished a ruler and a reader (1–18). God has given her such gifts that what would be "toil" for others is a pleasant "exercise" or diversion for her. Pembroke here compliments the queen by saying that she occupies her leisure in literary pursuits and scriptural meditation, activities that are attested to by Elizabeth's own writing.[1] Pembroke may have heard her mother, who was very close to Elizabeth in the early 1560s, talk about her writing, and she may well have seen the queen writing when she herself was one of the queen's young attendants. The poem ends on the same note, praying that Elizabeth will continue to "do what men may sing" in her political actions, as well as "Sing what God doth" in her religious writings.

Pembroke employs an appropriate level of compliment for dedications, but she uses political and religious language, rather than comparisons to mythological figures and the usual hyperbole about Elizabeth's eternal youth and beauty. She praises the queen for her achievements as ruler, for her religious devotion, and for her literary activities. Her praise thus has a strong political component, particularly when joined with "To the Angel Spirit of the Most Excellent Sir Philip Sidney." When she says that the queen is the primary one who must "dispose / What Europe acts in these most active times" (7–8), she is saying that Elizabeth is responsible not only for her own people, but also for the future of Europe (8). This was code for intervention on behalf of European Protestants, which Elizabeth had undertaken primarily by sending English troops under the earl of Leicester to free the Netherlands from Spanish occupation.[2] Pembroke's brother Philip had died in that campaign, which

---

[1] *Elizabeth I: Collected Works*, ed. Leah S. Marcus, Janel Mueller, and Mary Beth Rose. Each of the four chronological sections contains both poems and prayers.

[2] Margaret Hannay, "'Do What Men May Sing': Mary Sidney and the Tradition of Admonitory Dedication," in *Silent but for the Word*, ed. Hannay, 149–65.

the Sidneys believed was doomed by the queen's inadequate support, a lack of support tactfully displaced onto the "envy" of her courtiers as alluded to in "Angel Spirit" (63) and in the *Astrophel* elegies; her brother Robert was still in the Netherlands, taking over Philip's former duties as governor of the garrison town of Flushing. She is thus using admonitory flattery, instructing the monarch while appearing to praise her. Elizabeth was well aware of the convention that praised her for doing what the writer thought that she should do.

The central section of the poem (19–40) concerns the composition of the Sidney *Psalms*. Philip Sidney had begun these metrical paraphrases of the 150 biblical Psalms, but had completed only 1–43 before his death. Pembroke paraphrased Psalms 44–150, including the 22 poems of Psalm 119, so most of the work was hers. She also revised some of her brother's psalms, perhaps in accordance with their previous discussions.[3] She may even have begun working on the *Psalms* with him, since she tells the queen that the *Psalms* had two authors until Sidney's death: "Which once in two, now in one subject go, / The poorer [herself] left, the richer [Philip Sidney] reft away" (21–22); that is, once their work had two authors but unfortunately now only one of those subjects of Elizabeth remains to send her the *Psalms*. The evidence here is ambiguous, however, since her weaving metaphor— he sets the warp, or structural threads, and she wove the pattern (27)—would seem to imply sequential rather than joint composition.

She uses two primary metaphors for their act of translation: citizenship (the *Psalms* are now made English citizens, though they had been born Hebrew) and the more traditional metaphor of clothing.[4] They weave the cloth (27), better than some clothing the Psalms have worn (i.e., previous English psalters), which is presented to the queen to be made into a livery robe, that she can give to those who serve her (34–35).[5] (This may imply that Pembroke expected the queen to circulate the Sidney *Psalms*, though there is no evidence that Elizabeth did so.) The Sidney *Psalms* are thus compared to the needlework or clothing that was traditionally given to the queen as New Years' gifts.[6] These

---

[3] "Major Revisions of Psalms 1–43," *Collected Works*, 2:358–61.

[4] William Hunnis, for example, apologizes that his Psalms wear a "threadbare coat" in his prefatory material to *Seven Sobs of a Sorrowful Soul for Sin* (1583), a metrical version of the penitential psalms. Perhaps someone else, he says, "will shape thee rich array, / And set thee forth as thou deserv'st / with costly jewels gay" (A3v–A4).

[5] Cf. "Angel Spirit" Variant, lines 10–14, specifically addressing the international competition in writing vernacular metrical psalms.

[6] Lisa M. Klein, "Your Humble Handmaid: Elizabethan Gifts of Needlework," *RQ* 50 (1997): 459–93; and Jane Donawerth, "Women's Poetry and the Tudor-Stuart System of Gift Exchange," in *Women, Writing, and the Reproduction of Culture in Tudor and Stuart Britain*, ed. Jane Donawerth, et al. (Syracuse, N.Y.: Syracuse University Press, 2000), 3–18.

"holy garments" of the Psalms are appropriate to all Christian readers, who were traditionally instructed to apply them to the state of their own soul (see pages 180–81) but they are most appropriate to Elizabeth (63–64).

A hint of the Sidneys' frustration at their lack of advancement at court, expressed in the language of land grants, seems to creep into the next lines (35–40), before Pembroke compliments the queen as the appropriate patron for all English poetry, thereby calling on her to encourage and reward the nationalistic project of English language verse (41–48).[7] The Psalms are the most appropriate poems to present to Elizabeth, for her life parallels King David's (51–72). Such comparison of David to the monarch had been frequently employed for previous rulers, especially when presenting scripture, but Elizabeth's life was seen as directly parallel to David in what Protestants interpreted as her persecution by her predecessor, God's intervention in putting her on the throne, and her glorious reign that restored true religion. For example, Thomas Rogers, in *A Golden Chain* (1579), compares David's "foiling of Goliath with your Majesty's overthrowing the Pope; his rooting out of the Philistines with your Majesty's suppressing the Papists; his affliction with your imprisonment; his persecution with your troubles; his singing of godly songs with your godly books; his love of his God, with your promoting his glory and defending of pure religion."[8] They frequently equated the defeat of the Spanish Armada with David's victory over the giant Goliath and over his enemies the Philistines, most notably in Edmund Bunny's *The Coronation of David* (1588).[9] Pembroke uses this Protestant code, but claims that Elizabeth's realm is greater, embracing both the Old World and the New (73–76). God defended her from her enemies when he sent a storm to defeat the Spanish Armada (77–80), though such matters are too high for the poet herself and fit only for royalty ("eagles").

One of Pembroke's rare statements on contemporary gender restrictions appears in her list of paradoxes of Elizabeth's reign—kings must defer to a queen, the Continent to the island of England, men to a woman (81–83). Elizabeth is the unmoved mover (84), a reference to the *primum mobile*, or sphere

---

Esther Inglis, a calligrapher, presented a psalter to Elizabeth for a New Year's gift, also in 1599 and also to support the Protestant cause. See Georgianna Ziegler, "'More Than Feminine Boldness': The Gift Books of Esther Inglis," in *Women, Writing, and the Reproduction of Culture*, 19–37.

[7] Shannon Miller, "Mary Sidney and Gendered Strategies for the Writing of Poetry," in *Write or Be Written*, ed. Smith and Appelt, 169.

[8] Thomas Rogers, "To the Queen's Most Sacred Majesty," *A Golden Chain, Taken out of the Rich Treasure House the Psalms of King David* (1579), A5r–v.

[9] Edmund Bunny of York, *The Coronation of David* (1588), A3v, C4v–D1, L2–3, N2.

that moved the stars. Her reign means that truth is restored, vanity is banished, and England enjoys prosperity at home despite war abroad. These glories of her reign are worthy to be the "subject" of an epic and, in typical word play, "the object of her subjects' joy" (87–88).

The poem concludes with a prayer that Elizabeth may live far past her peers (93) (she had already survived most European rulers of her generation) and that her rule may continue to surpass David's, both in scope and in length, as Elizabeth is both the author of verse praising God and the subject of verse praising her (94–96). By offering her instruction to the queen, Pembroke transforms her role of "handmaid" into that of advisor to the monarch.

The poem is constructed of twelve stanzas of eight lines of iambic pentameter, rhymed *ababbcbc*, like Psalm 45. In the opening section, antithesis is the most prominent literary device, as in "not reading, but receiving" (6), "not weighing" / "but knowing" (11–12), or "the poorer" / "the richer" (22). She also employs both chiasmus (reversal) and polyptoton (the use of the same word in different forms) in her praise of Elizabeth as God's "loved choice" / "chosen love" (54). The wording of both dedicatory poems, "Even Now" and "To the Angel Spirit," can be difficult, largely because it is elliptical, with words deliberately omitted.[10]

COPY-TEXT: "Even Now That Care" (MS. *J*, Tixall MS., Dr. Bent E. Juel Jensen), title of this untitled poem supplied from first line. (The title in the 1962 printing is apparently taken from l. 3.) Verbal emendations: 22 *reft (rest)*, 25 *sighs (signes)*, 40 *Unwealthy (unwalthy)*, 85 *vanity's (vanity)*.

---

[10] Schleiner has shown that such elliptical construction is typical also of Mary Wroth's prose style, *Tudor and Stuart Women Writers*, 260–61.

Plate 1

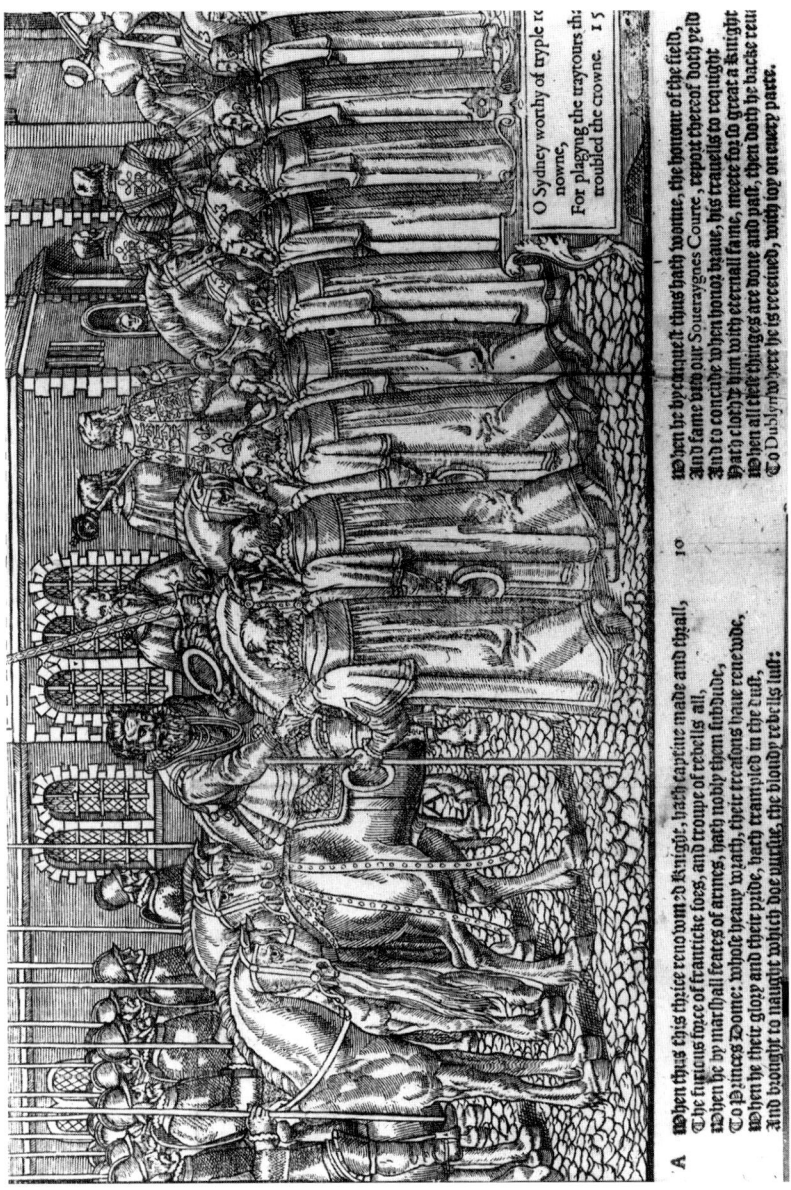

Sir Henry Sidney in Ireland from John Derrick, *The Image of Ireland* (1581), Plate 10.
Courtesy of Edinburgh University Library.

Plate 2

Mary Sidney Herbert, Countess of Pembroke. Miniature by Nicholas Hilliard. Courtesy of the National Portrait Gallery, London.

Plate 3

Mary Sidney Herbert, Countess of Pembroke. Engraving by Simon
van de Passe. Courtesy of the National Portrait Gallery, London.

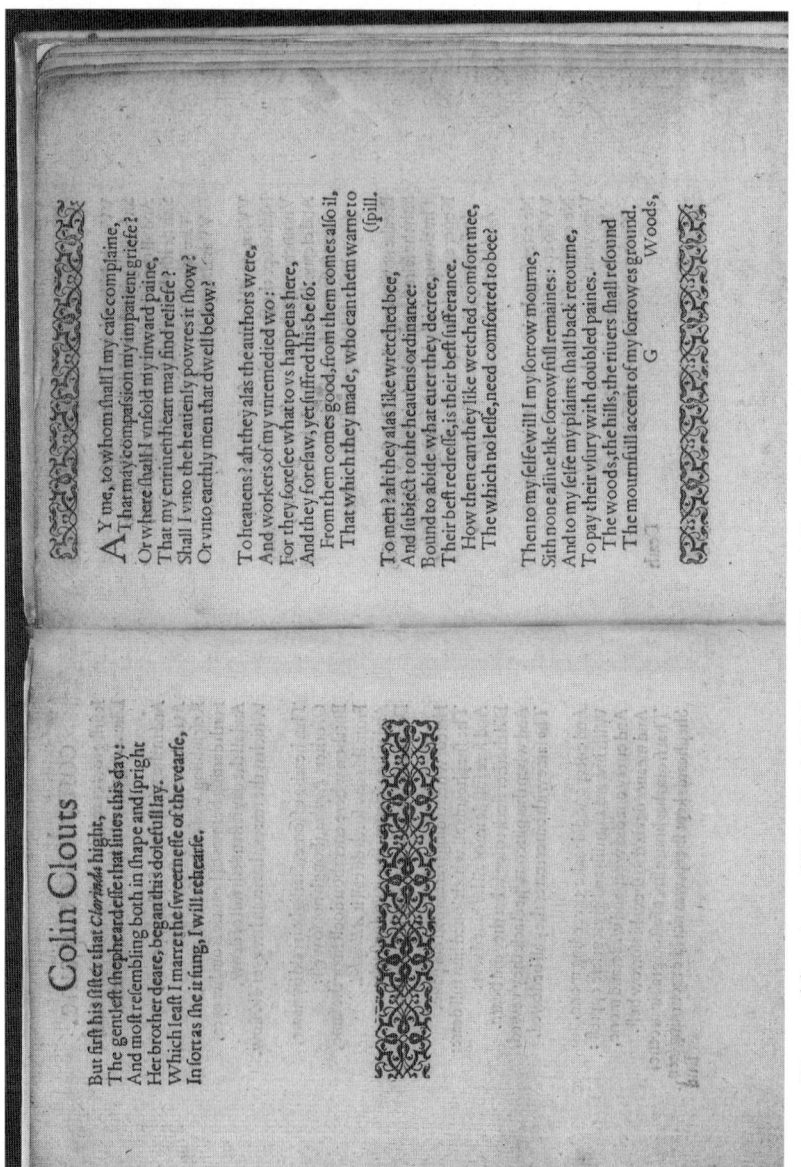

Colin Clouts

But first his sister that *Clorinda* hight,
The gentlest shepheardesse that liues this day:
And most resembling both in shape and spright
Her brother deare, began this dolefull lay.
Which least I marre the sweetnesse of the vearse,
In sort as she it sung, I will rehearse,

AY me, to whom shall I my case complaine,
That may compassion my impatient griefe?
Or where shall I vnfold my inward paine,
That my enriuen heart may find reliefe?
Shall I vnto the heauenly powres it show?
Or vnto earthly men that dwell below?

To heauens? ah they alas the authors were,
And workers of my vnremedied wo:
For they foresee what to vs happens here,
And they foresaw, yet suffred this be so:
From them comes good, from them comes also il,
That which they made, who can them warne to (spill.

To men? ah they alas like wretched bee,
And subiect to the heauens ordinance:
Bound to abide what euer they decree,
Their best redresse, is their best sufferance.
How then can they like wretched comfort mee,
The which no lesse, need comforted to bee?

Then to my selfe will I my sorrow mourne,
Sith none aliue like sorrowfull remaines:
And to my selfe my plaints shall back retourne,
To pay their vsury with doubled paines.
The woods, the hills, the riuers shall resound
The mournfull accent of my sorrowes ground.
    G   Woods,

First publication of "The Doleful Lay of Clorinda" in Edmund Spenser, *Astrophel* (1595). Courtesy of the Brotherton Library, University of Leeds.

Which when she ended had, another swaine
Of gentle wit and daintie sweet deuice:
Whom *Astrophel* full deare did entertaine,
Whilest here he liv'd, and held in passing price,
Hight *Thestylis*, began his mournfull tourne,
And made the *Muses* in his song to mourne.

And after him full many other moe,
As euerie one in order lov'd him best,
Gan dight themselues t'expresse their inward woe,
With dolefull layes vnto the time addrest.
The which I here in order will rehearse,
As fittest flowres to deck his mournfull hearse.

The mourning Muse of Thestylis.

COme forth ye Nymphes come forth, forsake your watry
Forsake your moisy caues, and help me to lament: (bowres,
Helpe me to tune my dolefull notes to gurging sound
Of *Liffies* tumbling streames: Come let salt teares of ours,
Mix with his wat'rs fresh. O come let one consent
Ioyne vs to mourne with wailfull plaints the deadly wound
Which fatall clap hath made; decreed by higher powres.
The dreery day in which they haue from vs yrent
The noblest plant that might from East to West befound.
Mourne, mourn great *Philips* fall, mourn we his wofull end,
Whom spitefull death hath pluckt vntimely from the tree,
Whiles yet his yeares in flowre, did promise worthie fruce.
Ah dreadful *Mars* why didst thou nor thy knight defend?
What wrathfull mood, what fault of ours hath moued thee
Of such a shining light to leaue vs destitute?
Thou with benigne aspect sometime didst vs behold,

G 3   Thou

There thousand birds all of celestiall brood,
To him do sweetly caroll day and night:
And with straunge notes, of him well vnderstood,
Lull him a sleep in Angelick delight;
Whilest in sweet dreame to him presented bee
Immortall beauties, which no eye may see.

But he them sees and takes exceeding pleasure
Of their diuine aspects, appearing plaine,
And kindling loue in him aboue all measure,
Sweet loue still ioyous, neuer feeling paine.
For what so goodly forme he there doth see,
He may enioy from iealous rancor free.

There liueth he in euerlasting blis,
Sweet spirit neuer fearing more to die:
Ne dreading harme from any foes of his,
Ne fearing saluage beasts more enemie:
Whilest we here wretches waile his priuate lack,
And with vaine vowes do often call him back.

But liue thou there still happie, happie spirit,
And giue vs leaue thee here thus to lament:
Nor thee that doest thy heauens ioy inherit,
But our owne selues that here in dole are drent.
Thus do we weep and waile, and wear our eies,
Mourning in others, our owne miseries.

                                        Which

Plate 5

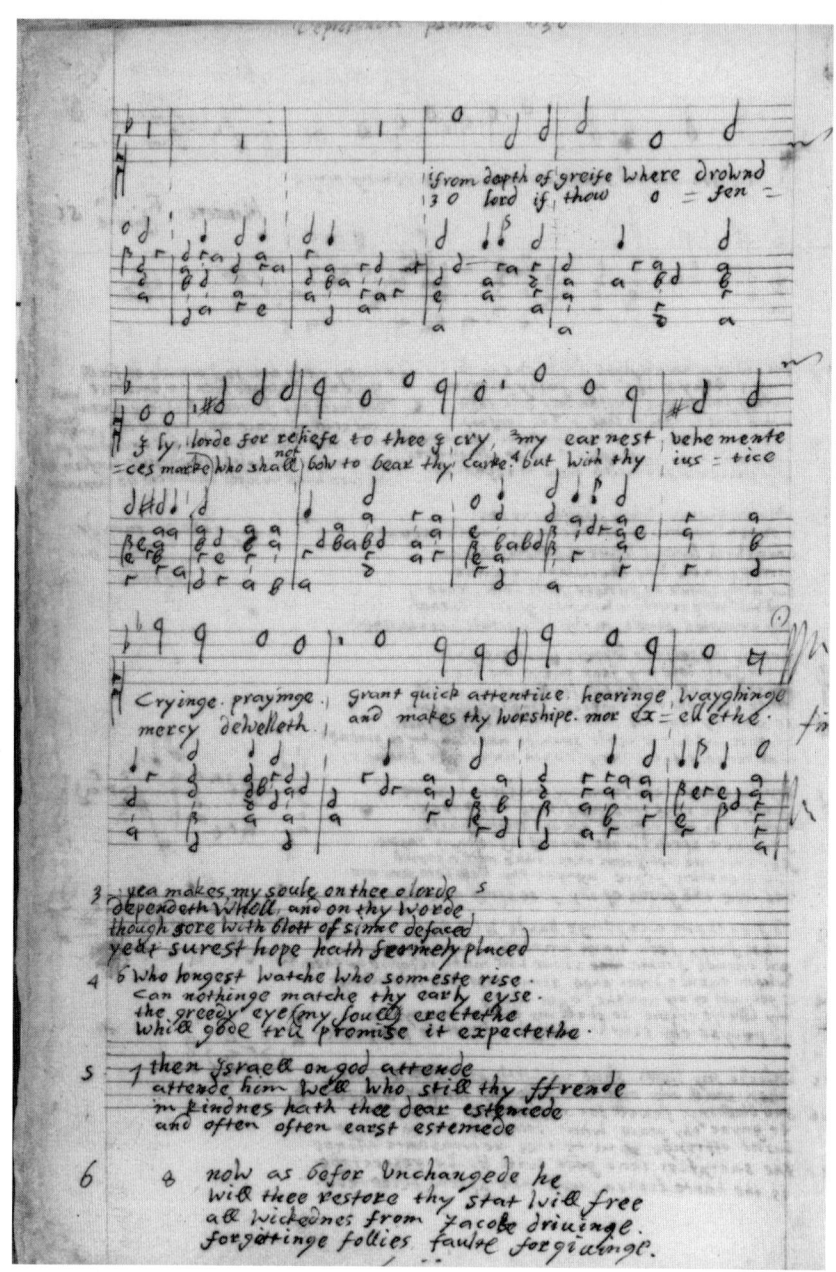

Musical setting of Psalm 130 from British Library ADD 15.117.
By permission of The British Library.

Plate 6

Modernized musical setting of Mary Sidney Herbert's Psalm 130 from British Library 1517. Courtesy of Allan Alexander.

Plate 7

TRIVMPHVS   MORTIS

The Triumph of Death. Courtesy of the Brotherton Library,
University of Leeds.

Even Now That Care

(Dedicatory Poem in the Tixall Manuscript of the Sidney *Psalms*)

Even now that care which on thy crown attends
And with thy happy greatness daily grows
Tells me, thrice sacred Queen, my muse offends,
And of respect to thee the line outgoes.
One instant will, or willing can, she lose,
I say not reading, but receiving rhymes,
On whom in chief dependeth to dispose
What Europe acts in these most active times?[11]

Yet dare I so, as humbleness may dare,
Cherish some hope they shall acceptance find,   10
Not weighing less thy state, lighter thy care,
But knowing more thy grace, abler thy mind.
What heav'nly pow'rs thee highest throne assigned,
Assigned thee goodness suiting that degree:[12]
And by thy strength thy burden so defined,
To others toil, is exercise to thee.

Cares though still great, cannot be greatest still,[13]
Business must ebb, though leisure never flow:
Then these,[14] the posts of Duty and Goodwill,
Shall press to offer what their senders owe,   20
Which once in two, now in one subject go,
The poorer left, the richer reft[15] away,
Who better might (oh, "might": ah, word of woe!)
Have giv'n for me what I for him defray.[16]

---

[11] In this first stanza, the speaker acknowledges that the Muse offends by offering verse (*the line*) that overreaches (*outgoes*): Will the queen be able to spare any time even receiving such a poem (*rhymes*) when she has duties to attend to as head of state in troubled times?

[12] The queen's position and ability as ruler were divinely appointed.

[13] *still*: always, continually. Even a sovereign as busy as the queen may have some moments of leisure.

[14] *these . . . posts,* i.e., rhymes, the Sidney *Psalms*, messengers of personified Duty and Goodwill.

[15] *reft*: robbed, taken.

[16] *defray*: pay out (as partial settlement of the debt to the queen). Cf. 20, 35–36.

How can I name whom[17] sighing sighs extend,
And not unstop[18] my tears' eternal spring?
But he did warp, I weaved this web to end;
The stuff not ours, our work no curious thing,
Wherein yet well we thought the Psalmist King,
Now English denizened, though Hebrew born,   30
Would to thy music undispleased sing,
Oft having worse, without repining worn;[19]

And I the cloth in both our names present,
A livery robe to be bestowed by thee:[20]
Small parcel of that undischarged rent,
From which nor pains nor payments can us free.
And yet enough to cause our neighbors see
We will our best, though scanted in our will:[21]
And those nigh fields where sown thy favors be
Unwealthy do, not else unworthy, till.   40

For in our work what bring we but thine own?
What English is, by many names is thine.
There humble laurels in thy shadows grown
To garland others, would themselves repine.[22]
Thy breast the cabinet,[23] thy seat the shrine,
Where muses hang their vowed memories:
Where wit, where art, where all that is divine
Conceived best and best defended lies,

---

[17] *whom*, i.e., him whom, Philip Sidney.

[18] *unstop*: open.

[19] This line alludes to earlier and inferior metrical psalms in English. Cf. "Angel Spirit" Variant, 10–11.

[20] 27–34. Clothing metaphor. Philip Sidney began the metrical psalms (*did warp*); Pembroke completed the weaving. The substance (*stuff*, or fabric) is not theirs, and neither is their work abstruse or overly subtle (*curious*), but only an attempt to naturalize as English (*denizen*) the work of the Hebrew David (*Psalmist King*), a *livery robe* (court uniform) that the queen can bestow as she sees fit.

[21] *scanted in our will*: restricted in our delight or joy.

[22] 43–44. The *humble laurels* (poems or honors or both) grown in the queen's shadow would lament (*repine*) if used to garland someone other than the queen.

[23] *cabinet*: private study. The line refers both to the queen as private reader of poems and to her position as national patron.

Which if men did not (as they do) confess
And wronging worlds[24] would otherwise consent,   50
Yet here who minds[25] so meet a patroness
For author's state or writing's argument?
A king[26] should only to a queen be sent:
God's loved choice unto his chosen love,
Devotion to devotion's president,
What all applaud, to her whom none reprove.

And who sees aught, but sees how justly square
His haughty ditties to thy glorious days,[27]
How well beseeming[28] thee his triumphs are,
His hope, his zeal, his prayer, plaint, and praise,[29]   60
Needless thy person to their height to raise,
Less need to bend them down to thy degree:
These holy garments each good soul assays,[30]
Some sorting all, all sort to none but thee.[31]

For ev'n thy rule is painted in his reign:
Both clear in right, both nigh by wrong oppressed;

---

[24] *wronging worlds.* Perhaps a reference to non-Protestant countries. But *worlds* may be a scribal error for *words:* thus, even if men did not confess and wronging words did not consent, she would still be best patroness.

[25] 51–52. Yet who here minds (remembers or can call to mind) so appropriate a patroness as the queen, both because of her royal position (*state*) that rivals David's, and because of the content (*writing's argument*) of these metrical versions of psalms traditionally ascribed to David?

[26] *king,* i.e., David, with whom Elizabeth is worthy to be associated (with a further reference to divine appointment in the next line). The comparison is further developed in 57–74 (see also 94). In 55, Elizabeth is further acknowledged the head of the English church (*devotion's president*).

[27] 57–58. And one who sees anything sees how justly David's *haughty ditties* (exalted poems, the *Psalms*) *square* with (match) the queen's *glorious days.*

[28] *beseeming:* suiting, befitting.

[29] *prayer, plaint, and praise.* A reference to the three main types of psalms: prayer, complaint or lament, and praise.

[30] *assays:* tries on.

[31] 63–64. The clothing metaphor of 27–34 is adapted here to the practice of applying the Psalms to one's own life and condition, i.e., trying them on as garments, although as a whole they fit only the queen.

And each at length (man crossing God in vain)
Possessed of place, and each in peace possessed.
Proud Philistines[32] did interrupt his rest,
The foes of heav'n[33] no less have been thy foes: 70
He with great conquest, thou with greater blest;
Thou sure to win, and he secure to lose.[34]

Thus hand in hand with him thy glories walk:
But who can trace them where alone they go?
Of thee two hemispheres[35] on honor talk,
And lands and seas thy trophies jointly show.
The very winds did on thy party blow,
And rocks in arms[36] thy foe men eft[37] defy:
But soft, my muse, thy pitch is earthly low;
Forbear this heav'n, where only eagles fly.[38]   80

Kings on a queen enforced their states to lay;
Mainlands for empire waiting on an isle;
Men drawn by worth a woman to obey;
One moving all, herself unmoved the while:
Truth's restitution, vanity's exile,
Wealth sprung of want, war held without annoy,
Let subject be of some inspired style,
Till then the object of her subjects' joy.[39]

Thy utmost can but offer to her sight
Her handmaid's task, which most her will endears;   90

---

[32] *Philistines*, i.e., David's enemies, the *foes of heav'n* (70). A further reference to the defeat of the Spanish Armada, a victory greater than King David's over his enemies.

[33] *foes of heav'n*. Catholic Spain, whose armada the queen's forces defeated in 1588. Cf. 77–78.

[34] *secure to lose*: invulnerable to loss.

[35] *two hemispheres*, i.e., England and English lands in the New World (namely, Virginia).

[36] 77–78. A storm helped the English by forcing Spanish ships onto the rocks on the coast of the Irish Sea.

[37] *eft*: afterwards.

[38] Refrain from attempting to enter areas appropriate only for monarchs (*eagles*).

[39] 85–88. May Elizabeth's achievements as queen speak for themselves until some *inspired style* be found appropriate and adequate for expressing them. An instance of the modesty topos.

And pray unto thy pains, life from that light
Which lively lightsome court and kingdom cheers,[40]
What wish she may (far past her living peers
And rival still to Judah's faithful King,
In more than he and more triumphant years)
Sing what God doth and do what men may sing.

1599

---

[40] 89–92. The *utmost* or best that the speaker's Muse can do is *but* to offer *her hand-maid's task* to Elizabeth's sight, which *task* her will most prefers; and pray for the Muse's pains, *life from that light* that *cheers* the queen's *lively lightsome* (light-giving, radiant) *court and kingdom.*

TO THE ANGEL SPIRIT
OF THE MOST EXCELLENT SIR PHILIP SIDNEY

*I*n this poem, Pembroke dedicates the *Psalms* to the memory of her brother, who had begun the metrical paraphrase of the Psalms into elegant English verse. Although most of the work was her own, she defers to her brother, praising him as the inspiration for her work and calling her poems the "little streams" in comparison to the "great sea" of his work (32–33). In this stance of humility before his achievement, she stood with others who praised him, and she also alluded to his own disclaimers of "art and skill" in *Astrophil and Stella*. Astrophil's Muse instructs him to stop worrying about art: "look in thy heart and write" (*Astrophil* 1).[1] That is exactly what Pembroke claims to be doing, drawing on the conventional pretense that poems of mourning were spontaneous outpourings of grief.[2] As Helen Wilcox notes, she here casts herself in a "role of the subservient partner whose actions are the result of devoted love," like many other early modern women writers who "represent themselves in a language of relative passivity and emotional dependency rather than of skill or artistic initiative."[3] Such statements are inherently paradoxical, as Pembroke here writes that grief has "stricken [her] dumb" (46).

Such a rhetorical stance need not be taken as a true reflection of her self-assessment. "Sad characters indeed of simple love" (82) she calls her work, yet there is nothing simple about the poem. In handling her pose of grieving female relative, she is modeling her work on classical precedents; her metaphors of "broken bodies, monetary expenditure, emotional reckoning, eternizing conceits, and hyperbolic praise" are, as Wendy Wall notes, adapted from Petrarchan tradition; and she includes the traditional tripartite structure of the elegy—lamentation, praise of the deceased, and consolation.[4] The poem is elegantly constructed in thirteen stanzas of seven lines, rhymed *abba-bba*. She frequently uses enjambment, rather than simpler end-stopped lines, notably across stanzas, as in lines 35–36 and 56–57. Other rhetorical devices typical of her style are internal rhyme (as in 16 and 33), parenthetic repetition used for emphasis (22), compound words (18–20), alliteration (23), word

---

[1] The poem includes numerous other allusions to Philip Sidney's verse. See May, *Elizabethan Courtier Poets*, 180 n. 19.

[2] Kay, *Melodious Tears*, 6.

[3] Helen Wilcox, "'First Fruits of a Woman's Wit:' Authorial Self-Construction of English Renaissance Women Poets," in *Write or Be Written*, ed. Smith and Appelt, 202–3.

[4] Wall, *The Imprint of Gender*, 315. See also Lisa Jardine, *Reading Shakespeare Historically* (London: Routledge, 1996), 143–46; Beilin, *Redeeming Eve*, 148.

play ("adorned" / "adore" 39), polyptoton ("truthful praise"/ "praise to truth confined" 40–41, or "love and zeal" / "zealous love" 26–27). Compare "will" (intent) / "will" (obsolete sense of delight) in "Even Now," 38. She uses various other forms of repetition: to build on an idea, as "thoughts, my burdened thoughts" (34); to indicate the essence of the quality, as "all their all" (32) or "life of life" (74); and for emphasis, as in the repeated command "receive" (84–85). This poem also uses the parallel restatement that is so characteristic of the Psalms. Four synonyms are used in two lines to describe "this account" / "sum"/ "reckoning"/"audit" (43–44), for example, and a subtle variation of the same idea is frequently stated twice in the two halves of the line, as in "My day put out, my life in darkness cast" (58) or "Beyond compare, above all praise" (70), or in successive lines, "no further scope to go, / Nor other purpose" (29–30).

In the decade after Philip Sidney's death, she had been instrumental in publishing the works that had established his literary reputation, and she had served as a patron for other poets who praised Sidney in extravagant terms, including Edmund Spenser. Spenser praised Sidney in *The Ruines of Time* (1591), dedicated to her, and in the collection of elegies by Spenser, Lodowick Bryskett, and others published as *Astrophel* (1595), which includes "The Doleful Lay of Clorinda." (See page 136.) Many of the motifs in "Angel Spirit" also appear in these elegies in the *Astrophel* volume, including the mourning for Sidney as an expression of Protestant "zeal" (26–27), Sidney's surpassing worth (48–49), his apotheosis into heaven (56–61), and the wish that the speaker could die quickly in order to join him in heaven (91). She also adds more personal touches, saying that she dares to combine her muse with his (5), i.e., her writing with his, which is exactly what she did in these Sidney *Psalms*. She emphasizes her position as his sister, one "who knew thee best" (48), though she invokes a personified Truth to demonstrate that she is not partial to her own blood, or family, in praising him; all wise persons know his worth (54–56), and certainly he is celebrated in heaven, where there is "truthful praise" (40) instead of envious slander (61–63). Like their younger brother Robert, she uses imagery of maiming and of bleeding and festering wounds (19–20), alluding to the gangrene of the wound that killed Philip.[5] In this poem, however, the blood—family blood—then becomes her own, as her heart's blood, "fresh bleeding" in the first draft ("Angel Spirit" Variant, 20), is here "dissolved to ink" (79) in a striking metaphor for her own empowerment as a writer. She also insists that "there lives no wit that may thy praise become" (49), thereby putting herself in the company of other writers, all of

---

[5] Robert Sidney, Sonnet 26, in *The Poems of Robert Sidney Edited from the Poet's Autograph Notebook*, ed. P. J. Croft (Oxford: Clarendon Press, 1984), 226.

whom are inadequate to praise Sidney. With such allusions and rhetorical choices, she places her work within the central English and European literary tradition. Her apparent humility thereby masks her self-assertion as a writer, as it does in "Even Now."[6]

"Angel Spirit" is extant in two versions, providing an opportunity for studying Pembroke's methods of composition; the revision retains the same poetic form as the early draft (seven-line stanzas in iambic pentameter rhymed *abbabba*), but there are many changes in content. (See "Process of Revision.") The most significant alterations are the deletion of two stanzas on her grief ("Angel Spirit" Variant, 22–35) and the addition of four stanzas, three on Philip Sidney and his works ("Angel Spirit," 50–70) and one on her own role as writer (78–84). The final two lines, missing from the early draft, may have been on a separate sheet in Daniel's papers and so lost, or she may have deliberately written an abbreviated stanza as Philip Sidney did in several psalms, partial stanzas that she later completed.[7] In the final stanza she eliminates the statement that the *Psalms* are "made only thine" ("Angel Spirit" Variant, 73), thereby allowing more scope to her own role in composition. These alterations, which seem to have been written during the long process of accepting loss, emphasize Philip as a writer whose own works, even in their unfinished state, become his monument, and they shift the self-presentation of the speaker from primarily a grieving relative who spontaneously writes to express loss, to the speaker as a writer who memorializes her brother and carries on his work.

COPY-TEXT: "To the Angel Spirit" (MS. *J*, Tixall MS., Dr. Bent E. Juel Jensen). Verbal emendations of "Angel Spirit": 14 *the (thy)*, 34 *in me (im mee)*, 89 *the highest (thy highest)*.

COPY-TEXT: "To the Angel Spirit," printed variant (1623). Verbal emendations of variant: 6 *stuff (staffe)*, 27 *life-blood (life, blood)*, 51 *sole (soule)*, 63 *praise (prayer)*.

---

[6] Beth Wynne Fisken, "'To the Angell Spirit,'" 266. See also Alexander, "Five Responses to Sir Philip Sidney, 1586–1628," 33; and Schleiner, *Tudor and Stuart Women Writers*, 75–81.

[7] "Major Revisions of Psalms 1–43," *Collected Works*, 2:358–61.

To the Angel Spirit
of the Most Excellent Sir Philip Sidney

(Dedicatory Poem in the Tixall Manuscript of the Sidney *Psalms*)

To thee, pure sprite,[8] to thee alone's addressed
    This coupled work, by double interest thine:[9]
    First raised by thy blest hand, and what is mine
Inspired by thee, thy secret power impressed.[10]
    So dared my Muse with thine itself combine,
    As mortal stuff with that which is divine;
Thy light'ning[11] beams give luster to the rest,

That heaven's king may deign his own, transformed
    In substance no, but superficial 'tire[12]
    By thee put on, to praise—not to aspire   10
To—those high tones so in themselves adorned,
    Which angels sing in their celestial choir,[13]
    And all of tongues[14] with soul and voice admire
These sacred hymns the[15] kingly prophet formed.

Oh, had that soul which honor brought to rest
    Too soon not left and reft[16] the world of all

---

[8] *sprite:* spirit.

[9] The Sidney *Psalms* are literally coupled or joined, since Pembroke's paraphrase of Psalms 44–150 is added to Sidney's Psalms 1–43. The work is yet (paradoxically) doubly Sidney's because he both began it and inspired Pembroke's completion of it.

[10] *thy secret power impressed,* i.e., by thy *power impressed* (urged, pressed into service).

[11] *light'ning:* "giving light," but also "enlightening," with wordplay on "lightning."

[12] *'tire:* attire. Cf. the clothing imagery in "Even Now," 27–34, 63–64. Cf. also *pieced* (as in patched together) in 24 below and *stuff* (fabric) in "Even Now," 28.

[13] See the similar image in "Doleful Lay," 61–64. The reference to angels was added here and in 59–61 when the draft was revised.

[14] *all of tongues,* i.e., all those with knowledge of Greek, Latin, and Hebrew who understand the worth of the biblical Psalms, which the Sidneys have not substantially altered but only dressed in new clothing.

[15] The manuscript reading *thy kingly prophet* is a scribal error: the speaker is addressing the spirit of Philip Sidney, not God. Cf. the similar error in line 89.

[16] *reft:* robbed, deprived.

What man could show, which we perfection call,
This half-maimed[17] piece had sorted[18] with the best.
Deep wounds enlarged, long festered in their gall,
Fresh bleeding smart;[19] not eye—but heart—tears fall.[20]   20
Ah, memory, what needs this new arrest[21]?

Yet here behold (oh, wert thou to behold!)[22]
This[23] finished now, thy matchless Muse begun,
The rest but pieced, as left by thee undone.
Pardon (O blest soul) presumption too, too bold,
If love and zeal[24] such error ill become:[25]
'Tis zealous love, love which hath never done,
Nor can enough in world of words unfold.

And sith[26] it hath no further scope to go,
Nor other purpose but to honor thee,   30
Thee in thy works where all the Graces[27] be,
As little streams with all their all do flow
To their great sea, due tribute's grateful fee,
So press my thoughts, my burdened thoughts in me,
To pay the debt of infinites I owe[28]

---

[17] *half-maimed*, i.e., left unfinished by Sidney.

[18] A subjunctive construction: i.e., would have sorted (associated, consorted).

[19] *fresh bleeding smart*. Ambiguous: either "wounds . . . freshly bleeding, cause pain" (*smart* as a verb; *fresh* as an adverb, a usage attested by the *OED*) or "wounds . . . and fresh, bleeding pain" (*smart* as a noun; cf. 81 below). If the latter reading is adopted, a comma would better replace the semicolon, since "smart" would then be in apposition with "wounds" (19).

[20] *fall*: let fall, drop.

[21] *arrest*: pause.

[22] A similar parenthesis appears in "Even Now," 23.

[23] *This*, i.e., the Sidney *Psalms*.

[24] *zeal* had religious overtones for Protestants and appears in other elegies to represent Philip Sidney as a martyr in the struggle against Catholic Spain.

[25] 25–26. Pardon me if my love and zeal make me fall into the error of presumption.

[26] *sith*: since. Cf. "Angel Spirit" Variant, 43.

[27] *Graces*. The sister-goddesses of classical mythology, bestowers of beauty and charm.

[28] Schleiner observes that the enjambment across stanzas here and elsewhere is intended to "act out the countess's emotional process of trying to become, out of love for her brother, the writer and patron who could step into his harness and carry on," *Tudor and Stuart Women Writers*, 77, 79.

To thy great worth, exceeding Nature's store;
    Wonder of men, sole born perfection's kind,
    Phoenix[29] thou wert, so rare thy fairest mind
Heav'nly adorned, Earth justly might adore,
    Where truthful praise in highest glory shined: 40
    For there alone was praise to truth confined;
And where but there,[30] to live for evermore?

Oh, when to this account, this cast-up[31] sum,
    This reckoning made, this audit of my woe,
    I call my thoughts, whence so strange passions[32] flow,
How works my heart, my senses stricken dumb,
    That would thee more than ever heart could show,[33]
    And all too short[34]! Who knew thee best doth know
There lives no wit that may thy praise become.[35]

Truth I invoke (who scorn elsewhere to move   50
    Or here in aught my blood should partialize),[36]
    Truth, sacred truth, thee sole to solemnize
Those precious rites well known best minds approve:
    And who but doth, hath wisdom's open eyes
    (Not owlly blind the fairest light still flies),
Confirm no less?[37] At least 'tis sealed above

---

[29] *Phoenix.* Mythical bird, symbol of uniqueness since only one existed at a time. A reference to Sidney's rebirth through his works, rising like the phoenix from the ashes of its fiery death.

[30] *there . . . there,* i.e., in heaven.

[31] *cast-up:* calculated.

[32] *passions.* Strong emotions such as the speaker's grief, but also deeply felt poems, particularly elegies, as in the title of Matthew Roydon's "An Elegy, or Friend's Passion, for His Astrophil," printed in Spenser's *Astrophel,* dedicated to the memory of Philip Sidney.

[33] *show:* display, present.

[34] *short:* falling short, inadequate. Cf. "Angel Spirit" Variant, 62.

[35] The inexpressibility topos—that no one can adequately praise, in a becoming or suitable manner, the subject of the elegy—is a common feature of such laments, including other elegies to Philip Sidney. Cf. 70.

[36] *my blood should partialize,* i.e., show partiality to her family.

[37] *And who but doth . . . Confirm no less?* i.e., best minds, those with wisdom's open eyes, instead of the proverbially blind eyes of the owl in daylight, confirm Sidney's worth.

Where thou art fixed among thy fellow lights:[38]
 My day put out, my life in darkness cast,
 Thy angel's soul with highest angels placed
There blessed sings, enjoying heav'n-delights,   60
 Thy Maker's praise: as far from earthy taste
 As here thy works so worthily embraced
By all of worth, where never Envy bites.

As goodly buildings to some glorious end
 Cut off by Fate, before the Graces had
 Each wondrous part in all their beauties clad,
Yet so much done, as art could not amend;
 So thy rare works—to which no wit can add,
 In all men's eyes which are not blindly mad,
Beyond compare, above all praise extend—   70

Immortal monuments of thy fair fame,
 Though not complete, nor in the reach of thought,
 How on that passing[39] piece time would have wrought
Had heav'n so spared[40] the life of life to frame
 The rest. But ah, such loss! Hath this world aught
 Can equal it, or which like grievance brought?
Yet there will live thy ever praised name,[41]

To which these dearest off'rings of my heart,
 Dissolved to ink while pen's impressions move
 The bleeding veins of never dying love,   80
I render here: these wounding lines of smart,
 Sad[42] characters indeed of simple love,

---

[38] *At least 'tis sealed above . . . thy fellow lights,* i.e., Sidney's worth is validated in heaven, where he is now with other spirits; their heavenly light is contrasted with Pembroke's earthly darkness of mourning.

[39] *passing:* surpassing.

[40] *Had heav'n so spared,* i.e., if heaven had so spared.

[41] Sidney will live in his works as well as in heaven. Cf. 78–81: Pembroke's own writings, her heart's blood dissolved in ink, are intended to help his name live forever in his works.

[42] *Sad:* serious, grave.

Not art nor skill which abler wits do prove,
Of my full soul receive the meanest part,[43]
Receive these hymns, these obsequies[44] receive;
    If any mark of thy sweet sprite appear,
    Well are they borne, no title else shall bear.
I can no more: Dear Soul, I take my leave;
    Sorrow still strives, would mount the[45] highest sphere
    Presuming so just cause might meet thee there: 90
Oh happy change, could I so take my leave![46]

BY THE SISTER OF THAT
INCOMPARABLE SIDNEY

---

[43] 81–84. With humility conventional to poems of mourning, Pembroke claims that her lines are artless, spontaneous expressions of grief and that her skill is inferior to Sidney's. Cf. 32–33. *Meanest* has here the sense of "lowest, least."

[44] *hymns:* the Sidney *Psalms*. The *obsequies* are funeral rites, in this case, the dedicatory poems themselves.

[45] The manuscript reading "thy" is a scribal error. The reference is to God's highest sphere (heaven), not Philip Sidney's. Cf. "Angel Spirit" Variant, 75.

[46] Another convention of Christian elegiac verse in which the speaker wishes to be with the person mourned in heaven.

To the Angel Spirit
of the Most Excellent Sir Philip Sidney

(Variant printed in Samuel Daniel's 1623 *Works*)

To thee, pure spirit, to thee alone addressed
Is this joint work, by double interest thine,
Thine by his own, and what is done of mine
Inspired by thee, thy secret power impressed.
My Muse with thine, itself dared to combine
As mortal stuff[1] with that which is divine:
Let thy fair beams give luster to the rest

That Israel's King may deign his own, transformed
In substance no, but superficial 'tire;
And English guised in some sort may aspire   10
To better grace thee what the vulgar formed:
His sacred tones, age after age admire;
Nations grow great in pride and pure desire
So to excel in holy rites performed.[2]

Oh, had that soul which honor brought to rest
Too soon not left and reft the world of all
What man could show, which we perfection call,
This precious piece had sorted with the best.
But ah, wide festered wounds that never shall
Nor must be closed, unto fresh bleeding fall: 20
Ah, memory, what needs this new arrest?

Yet blessed grief, that sweetness can impart
Since thou art blest! Wrongly do I complain:
Whatever weights my heavy thoughts sustain
Dear feels my soul for thee. I know my part
Nor be my weakness to thy rites a stain,

---

[1] "Staff" in "Angel Spirit" Variant is a printer's error. See line 6 in the revised version.

[2] 10–14. See headnote for "Angel Spirit." *Vulgar* in line 11 means "vernacular."

Rites to aright, life-blood would not refrain:[3]
Assist me, then, that life what thine did part.[4]

Time may bring forth what time hath yet suppressed
In whom thy loss hath laid to utter waste;   30
The wrack of time, untimely all defaced,
Remaining as the tomb of life deceased,
Where, in my heart the highest room thou hast;
There, truly there, thy earthly being is placed,
Triumph of death:[5] in life how more than blest.

Behold, oh, that thou were now to behold
This finished long perfection's part begun,
The rest but pieced, as left by thee undone.
Pardon blest soul, presumption overbold,
If love and zeal hath to this error run: 40
'Tis zealous love, love that hath never done,
Nor can enough, though justly here controlled.

But since it hath no other scope to go,
Nor other purpose but to honor thee,
That thine may shine, where all the Graces be;
And that my thoughts (like smallest streams that flow,
Pay to their sea, their tributary fee)
Do strive, yet have no means to quit nor free
That mighty debt of infinites I owe

To thy great worth which time to times enroll,[6]   50
Wonder of men, sole born, sole of thy kind
Complete in all, but heavenly was thy mind,
For wisdom, goodness, sweetness, fairest soul:
Too good to wish, too fair for earth, refined

---

[3] To perform appropriate rites of commemoration, Pembroke would even give her life-blood. Cf. blood as ink in the revised version, 78–80.

[4] The appeal for inspiration is addressed to God, the author of life who parted Philip Sidney from his earthly life.

[5] An allusion to Petrarch's *Trionfo della Morte,* which Pembroke translated.

[6] *Thy great worth* is enrolled by this present time in the annals of time.

For heaven, where all true glory rests confined;
And where but there no life without control?[7]

Oh, when from this account, this cast-up sum,
This reck'ning made the audit of my woe,
Sometime of rase[8] my swelling passions know
How work my thoughts, my sense is stricken dumb   60
That would thee more than words could ever show,
Which all fall short. Who knew thee best do know
There lives no wit that may thy praise become.

And rest fair monuments of thy fair fame,
Though not complete. Nor can we reach, in thought,
What on that goodly piece time would have wrought
Had divers so spared that life (but life) to frame
The rest. Alas, such loss! The world hath naught
Can equal it, nor, oh, more grievance brought,
Yet what remains must ever crown thy name.   70

Receive these hymns, these obsequies receive,
(If any mark of thy secret spirit thou bear)
Made only thine, and no name else must wear.
I can no more: Dear Soul, I take my leave;
My sorrow strives to mount the highest sphere.

---

[7] *control:* censure, fault-finding. Cf. the addition of personified Envy in the revision, 63.

[8] *of rase:* of (e)rasure. The image in 59–62 is an instance of the inexpressibility topos as in the revision, 43–49.

THE PSALMS OF DAVID

The biblical Psalms permeated nearly every aspect of early modern European life. Devout Jews chanted them in Hebrew, even when they had to worship in secret. Catholic nuns and priests sang them in Latin as part of their daily services, and everyone heard psalms read as part of church worship. In the early years of the Protestant Reformation Martin Luther encouraged the musical setting of psalms in the vernacular or common language, "so that the Word of God even by means of song may live among the people."[1] The German psalms were set to popular tunes, printed on broadsides (inexpensive single sheets), and used in congregational singing. In contrast, both French and English metrical psalms began as court verse. The French court, for a time, sang the fashionable psalms of Clément Marot, and the court of Edward VI sang the psalms of Thomas Sternhold. Metrical psalm translation and singing rapidly spread through Europe, as the religious wars forced Protestants from various countries into exile—and therefore into closer contact with each other. Geneva became a center for biblical translation and the composition of metrical psalms. Calvin encouraged his colleague Theodore Beza to complete Marot's work; Sternhold's Psalms were completed by John Hopkins and others. Both works were published in *Les Psaumes mis en rime Français*, and *The Whole Book of Psalms, Collected into English Meter by T. Sternhold, J. Hopkins and Others: Conferred with the Hebrew, with Apt Notes to Sing Them Withal*. The long subtitle of the Sternhold and Hopkins version continues with the proper use of these psalms, both in public worship as *appointed in the Queen's ... Injunctions*, and by *all sorts of people privately for their solace and comfort*. The goal expressed even in this title is to have this sacred song replace *all ungodly songs and ballads, which tend only to the nourishing of vice, and corrupting of youth*. The spiritual goals of both these French and English psalters were thus the same, but their literary methods were quite different. The French *Psaumes* employ more than 100 different poetic forms in a sophisticated verse style, while the English psalter primarily uses the popular ballad meter. The ballad meter was suitable for congregational singing, but it rarely produced poems as elegant as many of the French *Psaumes*. An informal international competition soon sprang up to produce a psalter in one's own language that

---

[1] Martin Luther to Georg Spalatin, 1523, translated in *Luther's Works: American Edition*, ed. U. S. Leupold and H. T. Lehmann (St. Louis, 1955–86), 53:221. On the psalms in Wittenberg, Nuremberg, and Strassburg, see Robin A. Leaver, *"Ghostly Psalmes and Spirituall Songes": English and Dutch Metrical Psalms from Coverdale to Utenhove, 1535–1566* (Oxford: Clarendon Press, 1991), 2–33.

would equal or surpass the literary quality of the *Psaumes*. The production of psalm translations in German, Italian, and Dutch were intertwined with the French and English psalters.

Shortly after Elizabeth came to the throne in November 1558, the Protestant exiles returned and brought with them the Geneva custom of the congregational singing of psalms by large groups of men and women. Bishop John Jewell said that after the service at Paul's Cross, the open-air pulpit in the churchyard of St. Paul's Cathedral, "you may now sometimes see . . . six thousand persons, old and young, of both sexes, all singing together and praising God."[2] Psalm singing rapidly spread through all social classes.[3] Soon educated English fathers and mothers led the household in daily worship that included singing the Sternhold and Hopkins Psalms. Miles Coverdale, who translated the prose psalms still used in the Book of Common Prayer, wanted even uneducated workers—carters and ploughmen—to whistle "Psalms, hymns, and such godly songs as David is occupied withal" and women to sing them as they spin, instead of "*hey nony nony, hey troly loly,* and such like fantasies."[4] Psalm singing did become so popular in England by 1579 that Anthony Gilby complained, in the preface of his translation of Beza's commentaries on the Psalms, that they were being sung more "for fashion sake, than for good devotion and with understanding"; he sought to restore an intellectual rigor to the use of psalms.[5] The hundreds of editions included cheap copies in tiny duodecimo for the poorer classes (equivalent to paperbacks), as well as large elegant folio editions for the wealthy.[6] Yet that did not exhaust the market for psalters, for nearly ninety other psalm versions were published in English between 1535 and 1601, including versions intended for musical performance and versions that emphasized rigorous Hebrew scholarship.[7]

Throughout the religious wars of the sixteenth century, both Catholics and Protestants continued to use the Psalms, but the language was con-

---

[2] Leaver, *Ghoostly Psalmes*, 240–41.

[3] Hamlin, "Very Mete to be Used of all Sortes of People," 37–51.

[4] *Remains of Bishop Coverdale*, ed. George Pearson (Cambridge: Cambridge University Press, 1846), 537.

[5] Anthony Gilby, "The Epistle to the Reader," Theodore Beza, *The Psalms of David, Truly Opened and Explained by Paraphrasis, According to the Right Sense of Every Psalm* (1581), a5.

[6] Hamlin, "Very Mete to be Used of all Sortes of People," 47.

[7] See lists in Rivkah Zim, *English Metrical Psalms: Poetry as Praise and Prayer, 1535–1601* (Cambridge: Cambridge University Press, 1987), 211–59; and Philipp von Rohr-Sauer, *English Metrical Psalms from 1600 to 1660* (Freiburg: Poppen and Ortmann, 1938), 119–24.

tested. The Catholic Church had established as authoritative the Latin Bible of Jerome, usually known as the Vulgate, because when it was translated in the fourth century Latin was the "vulgar," or ordinary, language of the people. Several biblical translations were written in the Anglo-Saxon period, and John Wycliffe translated scripture in the fourteenth century. After Wycliffe's teachings were officially condemned, the "Constitution of Clarendon" (1408) ordered that "no one shall in the future translate on his own authority any text of the holy scripture into the English tongue," which successfully prevented further English biblical translations until the sixteenth century.[8]

A key element of the Protestant Reformation was the study of biblical texts in the original Hebrew and Greek in order to offer fresh translations in contemporary languages. The English law on biblical translation in the mid sixteenth century is complex, reflecting the religious stance of the sovereign. In 1537 the so-called "Matthew's Bible," including the work of Coverdale and of William Tyndale (edited after his death by his friend John Rogers), was licensed by Henry VIII. This version was the basis for the officially sanctioned Great Bible (1539), which included a portrait of Henry VIII on the title page. Thomas Cromwell, the king's vice-regent, ordered all clergy to put it "in some convenient place within the church" where it would be available to all parishioners. Yet because of their Protestant beliefs Coverdale spent much of his life in exile, and both Tyndale (in 1536) and Rogers (in 1555) were executed. Nevertheless, their work became the basis of the Bishops' Bible, sponsored under Elizabeth in 1568, as well the Authorized or King James version in 1611, which was used through the twentieth century. In general, biblical translation was encouraged during the reign of the intensely Protestant young King Edward VI (1547–1553), dangerous during the reign of the intensely Catholic Queen Mary (1553–1558), and encouraged again in the long reign of Queen Elizabeth (1558–1603). Language became such a marker that even the traditional recitation of Psalm 51 before executions became partisan. For example, John Foxe records in the *Book of Martyrs* that when Dr. Rowland Taylor began to recite the psalm in English, the sheriff supervising his execution hit him and ordered, "speak Latin, I will make thee."[9]

---

[8] C. C. Butterworth, *The English Primers (1529–1545): Their Publication and Connection with the English Bible and the Reformation in England* (Philadelphia, 1953), 5.

[9] John Foxe, *The Acts and Monuments of John Foxe*, ed. George Townsend (New York: AMS Press, 1965), 6:700. The work was familiarly known as the *Book of Martyrs*, as it was named in the Sidney account book, De L'Isle MS. U1475 A4/5.

Catholics in France increasingly "disapproved the translation of these Psalms into the vulgar tongues, and scoffed at the singing of them in the reformed Churches," calling them "Geneva jigs and Beza ballets."[10] The sung psalms were used as "battle hymns of the Lord" when French Protestants marched into battle in the religious wars, as Stanford Reid has demonstrated.[11] The ironies of those religious wars are underscored by the use of psalm meditation for comfort by those facing martyrdom on both sides of the conflict, including the Catholic cardinal John Fisher and the Protestant Lady Jane Grey. Usually those facing execution meditated on such penitential psalms, confessing their sins in preparation for death. But Pembroke's uncles John Dudley, earl of Warwick, and Robert Dudley, later earl of Leicester, composed metrical paraphrases of Psalms 55 and 94, prayers of vengeance against their enemies, when they were imprisoned by Queen Mary for their support of Lady Jane Grey.[12] Such a choice underscored their belief, shared by those on both sides of the conflict, that their enemies were God's enemies.

Aside from such politically partisan applications, psalms were used for singing, for personal expression, for religious instruction, and for devotional poetry.[13] Men and women, Catholics and Protestants, were participants in this tradition, although the vernacular, sung psalms became increasingly identified with the Reformation. The typical devout Catholic man would recite psalms as part of the daily offices, but, during the periods when Catholicism was officially banned in England, women carried on most of the devotional practices in Catholic households. One of the paradoxes of gender restrictions was that women faced lesser punishment as recusants, those who refused to participate in the worship of the official Church of England. Most often it was aristocratic women who hid the few priests who ventured into England to lead worship, worship that included the psalms in Latin.[14]

---

[10] George Wither, *A Preparation to the Psalter* (1619), B4v–B5. See Anne Lake Prescott, *French Poets and the English Renaissance: Studies in Fame and Transformation* (New Haven: Yale University Press, 1978), 29–34.

[11] W. Stanford Reid, "The Battle Hymns of the Lord: Calvinist Psalmody of the Sixteenth Century," *Sixteenth Century Essays and Studies* 2 (1971): 36–54; Hannay, *Philip's Phoenix*, 84–105; see also Anne Lake Prescott, "Evil Tongues at the Court of Saul: The Renaissance David as a Slandered Courtier," *JMRS* 21 (1991): 163–86.

[12] *The Arundel Harington Manuscript of Tudor Poetry*, ed. Ruth Hughey (Columbus, Ohio: Ohio State University Press, 1960), 1:338–41, nos. 289 and 290.

[13] Zim, *English Metrical Psalms*, 41.

[14] Frances E. Dolan, *Whores of Babylon: Catholicism, Gender, and Seventeenth-Century Print Culture* (Ithaca, N.Y.: Cornell University Press, 1999), 62–70.

The typical godly Protestant man would recite the Psalms with his family and household in daily worship and include them in his personal devotions. He might whistle the familiar tunes from the Sternhold and Hopkins Psalter while he was at work in his carpentry shop or riding to town for his business. The typical godly Protestant woman might carry a small copy of Sternhold and Hopkins in her pocket as she went about her chores. Her mother or a friend might have embroidered a cover for her psalter with a picture of David and his harp, or with a woman symbolizing "Faith," or with a tulip, representing the soul reaching towards God.[15] She prayed in the words of the Psalms when she was lonely or frightened or felt betrayed. She recited Psalm 22 in the pains of childbirth, identifying with Christ's suffering, and then used the words of the Psalms to celebrate a successful birth or to mourn the baby's death.[16] She used the Psalms to teach her young children to read, and, when her husband was absent, she was the one who led her children and servants in daily worship, including recitation and singing of the Psalms. She sang the Sternhold and Hopkins Psalms while she was spinning, or weeding her garden. If she were a wealthy woman with musical training, she might sing more complex psalm settings as she accompanied herself on her lute.

Singing penitential psalms was considered particularly appropriate for the confession of sins in private worship, a custom that was followed by both Catholics and Protestants. In the seventeenth century the Catholic writer and publisher Richard Rowlands (Verstegan) dedicated his *Odes in Imitation of the Seven Penitential Psalms* (1601) to Catholic Englishwomen with the expressed hope that they would have them set to music; Elizabeth Grymeston did sing these psalms, which she included in her *Miscellanea*.[17] As part of her daily worship the Protestant Grace Sherrington Mildmay daily "spent some time in playing on my lute, and setting songs of five parts thereunto, and practiced my voice in singing of Psalms, in making my prayers to God, and confessing

---

[15] See, for example, Folger STC 2689, copy 1 and copy 2, *The Whole Book of Psalmes* (1639); STC 2661, *The Whole Book of David's Psalmes* (1635). Several of these bindings are reproduced in Frederick A. Bearman, Nati H. Krivatsy, J. Franklin Mowery, *Fine and Historic Bookbindings from the Folger Shakespeare Library* (Washington, D.C.: Folger Shakespeare Library, 1992).

[16] Charlotte F. Otten, "Women's Prayers in Childbirth in Sixteenth-Century England," *Women and Language* 16 (1993): 18–21; see also Helen Wilcox, "'My Soule in Silence'?: Devotional Presentations of Renaissance Englishwomen," in *Representing Women in Renaissance England*, ed. Claude J. Summers and Ted-Larry Pebworth (Columbia: University of Missouri Press, 1997), 15.

[17] Elizabeth Bernye Grymeston, *Miscellanea. Meditations. Memoratives* (London, 1604), F1–H1.

any sins." She evidently sang the *Psalms, Sonnets, and Songs of Sadness and Piety made into Music of Five Parts* (1588) by the famous Catholic composer William Byrd.[18] As we have seen, two of the penitential psalms by Pembroke (51 and 130) were also set for a woman's voice and lute, presumably for such devotional use.

When men and women reflected on their lives in their journals, they often articulated their own experience in the words of the psalms that they had known since infancy. For example, Richard Josselin included in his practical diary that "April 1.2.3. I sow oats.... Lord command a blessing for my hope is in thee" (Ps. 39:7), and the aged Lady Anne Clifford recorded her struggle with her approaching death by writing simply "Ps. 23: 4, 5." To her those numbers immediately signaled comfort: "Yea though I walk through the valley of the shadow of death, I will fear no evil."[19] Such use of the Psalms for personal reflection had been encouraged for many centuries. A statement by Athanasius, one of the early church fathers, was frequently reprinted in English psalters, advising readers, "It is easy . . . for every man to find out in the Psalmes, the motion and state of his own soul."[20] Such "practices of piety are central" to constructions of "Renaissance selfhood," Deborah Shuger argues.[21] Various printings of the Sternhold and Hopkins Psalter included a listing of which psalms were appropriate for which situations—sorrow, joy, betrayal by one's friends, and so on, a list that is now echoed in the prefatory material of the Gideon Bibles placed in hotels. As Matthew Parker phrased the commonplace in his prefatory poem, "Of the Virtue of Psalms":

> In other books where man doth look,
> but others' words seeth he:
> As proper hath this only book,
> most words his own to be.[22]

---

[18] Grace Sherrington Mildmay, *Autobiography*, in *Women Writers in Renaissance England*, ed. Randall Martin (London: Longman, 1997), 220.

[19] *Longman Anthology of British Literature*, ed. David Damrosch, et al. (New York: Longman, 1999), 1:1966; *The Diaries of Lady Anne Clifford*, ed. D. J. H. Clifford (Phoenix Mill, Gloucestershire: Sutton, 1990), 263–67.

[20] *The Whole Book of Psalms, Collected into English Meter by T. Sternhold, J. Hopkins and Others* (Geneva: J. Crespin, 1569), *7v.

[21] Deborah Kuller Shuger, *The Renaissance Bible: Scholarship, Sacrifice, and Subjectivity* (Berkeley: University of California Press, 1994), 190.

[22] Matthew Parker, *The Whole Psalter Translated into English Meter* (London: John Day, 1567), A4^V.

All psalm versions encouraged the reader to identify with the "I" of the Psalms, so that the individual consciousness merged with that of the psalmist.[23] The personal voice of the Psalms thus functioned poetically like that of the sonnet. As Roland Greene observes, the "I" of the Petrarchan sonnet works "to superimpose the subjectivity of the scripted speaker on the reader."[24] The "I" of the Psalms also performs that function, but it becomes even more deeply personal; it also allows the reader to superimpose his or her own subjectivity on the words of the psalm, as they truly become the reader's own. Psalms cross social classes, reflecting the experience of rulers (as in Psalm 101) and of the poor (as in Psalm 86). They express a wide range of emotions including despair, anger, wonder, joy, or gratitude, as they question or challenge or beseech or praise God. As Anne Lake Prescott reminds us, Christians read the Psalms as a dual allegory, of Christ and of the Christian life: "David's infolded voices express Christ and ourselves as well as his own circumstance."[25]

This was even truer for early modern Protestants, because of the emphasis on scriptural translation. If the text is the original Hebrew or the officially approved Latin, it is fixed. If the text can be translated, then it is flexible. Translation inevitably becomes reinterpretation, thereby opening a space for personal reflection. Transforming psalms into vernacular poetry opened even more space for an individual voice, since rhyme and meter required more adaptation. Such paraphrase of the biblical text was considered a form of devotional exercise, as was the reading, recitation, or singing of psalm texts. Some of the Sidneian *Psalms* were, as we have seen, marked for reading in Morning and Evening Prayer, like the official Book of Common Prayer.[26] The translator became invisible, and such poetic versions could be used as the Word of God. This was a tremendous responsibility for the poet.[27]

Composing metrical psalms was also an opportunity to use poetry for the glory of God—and one's native tongue. John Donne alludes to the embarrassment some English poets felt that their church should sing "More hoarse,

---

[23] Although Pembroke is in general careful to use non-gendered language so that the "I" of the Psalms fits any reader, in third person grammatical constructions we occasionally use the traditional masculine form since the Psalms were attributed to King David.

[24] Roland Greene, *Post-Petrarchism: Origins and Innovations of the Western Lyric Sequence* (Princeton, N.J.: Princeton University Press, 1991), 5–6.

[25] Anne Lake Prescott, "King David as a 'Right Poet': Sidney and the Psalmist," *ELR* 19 (1989): 134; see also Lewalski, *Protestant Poetics*, 301–2; Zim, *English Metrical Psalms*, 6, 43–74.

[26] BL MS. Add. 12047; "Manuscripts of the Psalms," *Collected Works*, 1:317–19.

[27] Debra Rienstra and Noel Kinnamon, "Revisioning the Sacred Text," *Sidney Journal* 17 (1999): 53–77.

more harsh than any other." (Pembroke agreed; she let her opinion of the Sternhold and Hopkins Psalms slip in her first version of "Angel Spirit," lines 10–11.) Using the familiar comparison of translation to clothing the original, prominent also in Pembroke's dedication to Elizabeth, Donne laments that the Psalms have been "So well attired abroad, so ill at home."[28] The Sidney *Psalms*, he says, have restored English honor and pointed the way for English devotional verse:

> And who that Psalm [97:1], Now let the Isles rejoice,
> Have both translated, and applied it too,
> Both told us what, and taught us how to do.
> They show us Islanders our joy, our King,
> They tell us why, and teach us how to sing. (lines 18–22)

Philip and Mary Sidney, like the biblical Moses and his sister Miriam, have led the way out of the poetic wilderness and "in forms of joy and art do re-reveal" the Psalms, Donne says, a statement that, as Debra Rienstra observes, "lends the [Sidney] *Psalms* a quasi-inspired status."[29]

Our more secular age finds it difficult to reconstruct a time when metrical psalm translation was as highly valued a literary form as the Petrarchan sonnet. Metrical versions of the penitential psalms were composed by such renowned poets as Thomas Wyatt and Edmund Spenser (Spenser's are now lost). The Book of Psalms was, like Petrarch's sonnets, "a master text" that inspired poets, Greene observes.[30]

Most of the hundreds of psalm translations into European vernacular languages were written by men, but some women did participate in the tradition. (See pages 16–17.) Psalms thus became a foundational discourse for early modern women, one that invited them into a variety of literary genres: because psalms traditionally were used for personal devotion, women could use those words to articulate their own sense of self in forms of life-writing; because psalms traditionally were used for spiritual instruction, women could use those words to undertake a teaching role not unlike that of published ser-

---

[28] Donne, "Upon the Translation of the Psalms," in *John Donne: The Divine Poems*, ed. Gardner, 34; Richard Todd, "'So Well Atyr'd Abroad': A Background to the Sidney-Pembroke Psalter and Its Implications for the Seventeenth-Century Religious Lyric," *Texas Studies in Literature and Language* 29 (1987): 74–93.

[29] Debra Rienstra, "Mary Sidney, Countess of Pembroke, *Psalmes*," in *A Companion to Early Modern Women Writers*, ed. Anita Pacheco (London: Blackwell, 2002), 110–24.

[30] Greene, *Post-Petrarchism*, 19; see also Lewalski, *Protestant Poetics*, 31–53.

mons; because metrical psalms traditionally were used for private and public song, women could use those words to compose poetry.[31]

The countess of Pembroke approached her metrical psalm paraphrase, or more technically metaphrase, as a work of devotion, scholarship, and poetry. As Elaine Beilin observes, to write such divine poems "required not only theological knowledge to make readers think about doctrinal matters, but appropriate forms to make them feel the joys and griefs the poet-prophet experiences."[32] Using the sophisticated French *Psaumes* of Marot and Beza as a literary model, Pembroke typically began her paraphrase by consulting the prose psalms as printed in the Geneva Bible of 1560 and/or Coverdale's Psalms included in the Book of Common Prayer. (Psalm 55 is more indebted directly to the French.) Her first drafts were typically close to these sources. She then usually consulted the Psalm commentaries of Calvin and of Beza (in both Latin and English translation), choosing Beza's interpretations more often than Calvin's, but not slavishly following either. Approaching her work as a scholar, she also seems to have consulted, at one time or another, nearly every psalm version and commentary available to her in English, French, and Latin.[33] Where the commentaries disagreed, she tended to choose the interpretation closest to the Hebrew, suggesting that she consulted with Hebrew scholars (like her former chaplain Gervase Babington) and/or that she had at least rudimentary knowledge of Hebrew herself.[34] It may be significant that at a time when many Christian psalm versions specifically allegorized "Israel" as the "Church," hers does not.[35] Her *Psalms* are, nonetheless, deeply Christian, including her rendering of God's anointed as "Christ" (Psalms 89.126 and 132.69) and numerous reflections on God's "grace" (see particularly Psalm 51).

In the *Psalms* she also signals her debt to English secular poetry, including her echo in Psalm 57.34 of Thomas Wyatt in her phrase, "my lute awake," and of Edmund Spenser in the pastoral similes of Psalm 78, in the recycling of old substance into new form in Psalm 104, and in God's delivery of his people

---

[31] Margaret Hannay, "'So may I with the *Psalmist* truly say': Early Modern English-women's Psalm Discourse," in *Write or Be Written*, ed. Smith and Appelt, 105–34.

[32] Beilin, *Redeeming Eve*, 146.

[33] "*Psalmes*: Literary Context," *Collected Works*, 2:13–32.

[34] Theodore Steinberg, "The Sidneys and the Psalms," *SP* 92 (1995): 1–17; *Collected Works*, 2:16–20; Chanita Goodblatt, "Dialogue and David's Voice."

[35] Cf. Philip Sidney, Psalm 29.24. See R. Gerald Hobbs, "*Hebraica Veritas* and *Traditio Apostolica*: Saint Paul and the Interpretation of the Psalms in the Sixteenth Century," in *The Bible in the Sixteenth Century*, ed. David C. Steinmetz (Durham, N.C.: Duke University Press, 1990), 222–25.

from "error trained" in Psalm 107.[36] Her largest literary debt, as she acknowl-
edges in her dedicatory poems, is to her brother Philip. She may have begun
by working through her brother's versions and making some changes that
they had discussed, particularly the elimination of partial stanzas.[37] A partic-
ularly interesting study is provided by her rendition of Psalm 53, which in the
original is nearly identical to Psalm 14. Her first version is closer to that of her
brother; in her revision the poem became her own. Such increasing indepen-
dence from her models is evident in other revised psalms as well, as she con-
sults additional commentaries and reshapes the poem. She also tends to add
or enhance her usual stylistic elements: alliteration (as in 55.45), frequently
of noun and adjective (as "early east" and multiple other uses throughout
73, or "widest way" and "straitest stay" in 119F.17–18); compound words (as
"never-dying" in 75.26); rhetorical questions (as in 52); parenthetic statement
for emphasis (as in 44.39); polyptoton (as "filthy fault" / "faulty filthiness" in
51.9), and chiasmus (as "sea of light" / "light of sea" in 148.9–10), and other
sophisticated rhetorical figures of repetition. Her 126 different poetic forms
include, among those represented in this edition, rhyme royal (51), three
rhymes repeated throughout (55), Scottish or Spenserian sonnet (100), an orig-
inal form of delayed terza rima (101), alphabetical acrostic couplets (111), acros-
tic (117), a single rhyme for each stanza (119F), quantitative meter (124), and a
Sidneian sonnet form (150).[38] She also includes occasional internal rhyme (as
"lightful" / "flightful" in 139.30). Wordplay abounds in her poems, such as
the complex play on "still" and "will" in Psalm 73. In fact, what may at first
glance seem like simple repetition is typically the use of a word in two dif-
ferent senses, such as God's "right right hand" (63.21), which emphasizes that
God's right hand is also righteous.

She frequently expands the metaphors present in her originals (as the
adder in 58), or smooths abrupt transitions, rethinking the Psalms as Eng-
lish poems as she "*meditated* on the text before her."[39] Her versions can viv-
idly capture an experience, such as the storm where the waves feel so high

---

[36] May, *Elizabethan Courtier Poets*, 209; Hannay, "The Countess of Pembroke as a
Spenserian Poet," 41–62; on Pembroke's allusions to Sidney's verse, see *Collected Works*,
1:67–71 and 323.

[37] Waller, *Triumph*, 18–44; Fisken, "Mary Sidney's *Psalmes*: Education and Wisdom,"
166–83; "Major Revisions of Psalm 1–43," *Collected Works*, 2:358–61.

[38] On her verse forms see Woods, *Natural Emphasis*, 290–302; Alexander, "Five
Responses to Sir Philip Sidney, 1586–1628," 195–96; "Table of Verse Forms," *Collected
Works*, 2:470–83.

[39] Rathmell, *The Psalms of Sir Philip Sidney and the Countess of Pembroke*, xx.

"the stars do drop bedashed with rain" and the ship touches the sky, only to fall abruptly to the center of the earth. Those on board stagger like drunkards (107.65–80). Such expansions frequently reflect her own experience: as a bride in an arranged marriage in Psalm 45; as a participant at Elizabeth's court in the opening of 104; as a woman who has experienced pregnancy, child-birth, miscarriage, and child-rearing (as in 48.17–18; 51.15–18; 58.21–24; 131; and 139.43–63); and as a writer (as in 68, 75, and 119). Her *Psalms* portray a wide range of emotion, like her originals, but one of the dominant notes in hers is celebration. The godly "in Jehovah's presence / Play, sing, and dance" (68.5–6) and worship with a "merry shout" (100.2).

These metrical paraphrases fully engaged Pembroke as a Christian, as a scholar, and as a poet. The work was a joy for her, as we see in her original expansion of Psalm 75:9 ("But I will declare for ever, and sing praises unto the God of Jacob"):

> And I secure shall spend my happy times
> in my, though lowly, never-dying rhymes,
> singing with praise the God that Jacob loveth. (25–27)

Her description of herself as poet combines humility ("lowly" rhymes) with supreme confidence in the worth of her "never-dying rhymes," rhymes that are sanctified because they praise God. She adds the same note at the end of Psalm 45: "Myself thy name in lasting verse will sing." She believes that her divine topic authorizes her voice, a voice that ignores gender restrictions of women's speech, as she prays with the psalmist in Psalm 104.1–2, "Make, O my soul, the subject of thy song / Th'eternal Lord." Such song requires both her most rigorous biblical study as God's "scholar" (Variant 119H.32) and her "utmost skill" (111.2) as a poet.

COPY-TEXTS: *Psalms* (MS. *A*, Penshurst MS., Viscount De L'Isle; variants and Philip Sidney's Psalm XIV: MS. *B*, Bodleian, MS. Rawl. poet. 25; MS. *G*, Trinity College, Cambridge, MS. R. 3. 16; MS. *N*, Bibliothèque de la Sorbonne, MS. 1110). Mainly verbal emendations (MS. *A*, unless otherwise noted): 14.2 (Sidney, MS. *B*) *guilty (omitted)*; XLIV.48 (MS. *B*) *despised (despis'd)*; 51.5 *Oh, cleanse (clense)*; 57.35 *harp (hart)*; 58.5 *Oh (omitted)*; 71.28 *Do (No)*, 71.50 *march assured? (march? assured,)*, 71.69 *sing (ring)*; LXXI.48 (MS. *B*) *Lo! ((Lo!))*; 84.42 *Thou art (that art)*; 88.43 *will (wilt)*; 104.68 *know (knowes)*; 107.13 *who (how)*; 117.7 *H is (H his)*; 119F.29 *with (will)*; 131.6 *Oh (omitted)*.

Psalm 44

The speaker knows the history of God's deliverance in the past, when Israel was empowered to overcome its enemies. Now God has abandoned them and left them to be enslaved and mocked, even though they have continued to obey the covenant. An appeal for God's mercy.

> Lord, our fathers' true relation
>   Often made, hath made us know
> How thy pow'r in each occasion
>   Thou of old for them didst show;
>   How thy hand the pagan foe
>   Rooting hence, thy folk implanting,
>   Leafless made that branch to grow,
>   This to spring, no verdure wanting.[40]
>
> Never could their sword procure them
>   Conquest of the promised land;   10
> Never could their force[41] assure them
>   When they did in danger stand.
>   No, it was thy arm, thy hand,
>   No, it was thy favor's treasure
>   Spent upon thy loved band:
>   Loved, why? For thy wise pleasure.
>
> Unto thee stand I subjected,[42]
>   I that did of Jacob spring:
> Bid then that I be protected,
>   Thou that art my God, my king.[43]   20
>   By that succor thou didst bring,
>   We their pride that us assailed,

---

[40] 5–8. God makes *that branch* (*the pagan foe*) to be *leafless*, while this branch (*thy folk*, or Israel) brings forth *verdure*, i.e., green leaves.

[41] *force*: strength.

[42] I stand under your authority.

[43] *my God, my king.* Cf. George Herbert, "Jordan" (1), 15.

Down did tread, and back did fling,
    In thy name confused and quailed.

For my trust was not reposed
    In my own, though strongest, bow,
Nor my scabbard held enclosed
    That, whence should my safety flow.[44]
    Thou, O God, from every foe
        Didst us shield, our haters shaming: 30
    Thence thy daily praise we show,
        Still thy name with honor naming.

But aloof thou now dost hover,
    Grieving us with all disgrace,
Hast resigned and given over
    In our camp thy captain's place.
    Back we turn, that[45] turned face,
        Flying them, that erst[46] we foiled:
    Lo, our goods (oh, changed case!)
        Spoiled by them that late we spoiled.   40

Right as sheep to be devoured,
    Helpless here we lie alone;
Scatt'ringly by thee out-poured,
    Slaves to dwell with lords unknown.
    Sold we are, but silver none
        Told[47] for us: by thee so prized,
    As for naught to be forgone,[48]
        Graceless, worthless, vile, despised.

By them all that dwell about us,
    Tossed we fly as balls of scorn;   50
All our neighbors laugh, and flout us,
    Men by thee in shame forlorn.
    Proverb-like our name is worn,

---

[44] The sword by which I should make myself safe.
[45] *that*, i.e., we who.
[46] *erst*: once, earlier.
[47] *Told*: counted out, paid.
[48] *forgone*: neglected.

Oh, how fast[49] in foreign places!
    What head-shakings are forborne,
        Wordless taunts and dumb disgraces!

So rebuke before me goeth,
    As myself do daily go;
So confusion on me groweth,
    That my face I blush to show.   60
    By reviling sland'ring foe
        Inly wounded, thus I languish:
Wreakful[50] spite with outward blow
        Anguish adds to inward anguish.

All, this all on us hath lighted,
    Yet to thee our love doth last;
As we were, we are delighted
    Still to hold thy cov'nant fast.
    Unto none our hearts have passed;
        Unto none our feet have slidden;[51]   70
Though us down to dragons cast,
        Thou in deadly shade hast hidden.

If our God we had forsaken,
    Or forgot what he assigned,
If ourselves we had betaken
    Gods to serve of other kind,
    Should not he our doubling find,[52]
        Though concealed and closely lurking,
    Since his eye of deepest mind
        Deeper sinks than deepest working?   80

Surely, Lord, this daily murder
    For thy sake we thus sustain;
For thy sake esteemed no further

---

  [49] *fast:* quickly or firmly.

  [50] *Wreakful:* vengeful.

  [51] *slidden:* slid. Pembroke's use of the disyllabic form predates by more than two centuries the earliest instance cited in the *OED* (1827).

  [52] Would not God have been able to detect any duplicity or apostasy on our part? Cf. 73–76.

Than as sheep, that must be slain.
Up, O Lord, up once again,
    Sleep not ever, slack not ever.
Why dost thou forget our pain?
    Why to hide thy face persevere?[53]

Heavy grief our soul abaseth;
    Prostrate it on dust doth lie.   90
Earth our body fast[54] embraceth;
    Nothing can the clasp untie.
Rise, and us with help supply;
    Lord, in mercy so esteem us,
That we may thy mercy try,[55]
    Mercy may from thrall redeem us.

Psalm XLIV
(Variant: MS. B)

This early version in Woodford's transcription of the working copy of the *Psalms* (see page 21) relies more extensively on the text of the Prayer Book Psalter and the Geneva Bible than does the revision in MS. *A*. The numbers with periods by some of the lines mark the biblical verses, a distinctive feature of MS. *B*. (See also Variant Psalm 71.)

1.   Our fathers, Lord, by hearing
        Have made us understand
    Thy works before their eyes appearing,
        In time gone long ago,
2.   How, rooting nations, them thy hand
        Did plant and, planted, nourish:
    The stock profane did leafless grow;
    The faithful branch did flourish.

3.   Their sword did not procure them
        Possession of the land;   10

---

[53] *persevere.* The meter indicates that the stress is on the second syllable. See similar instances below.

[54] *fast:* closely, tightly.

[55] *try:* prove, test.

Nor more did their own arms assure them
    In doubtful time and place:
    Thy arm it was, it was thy hand,
        Thy favor passing[56] measure
    Sent on them from thy lightsome[57] face.
    Why? Only for thy pleasure.

4.   To thee I stand subjected,
      O God, my only king.
   Let Jacob then by thee protected
        As erst so now remain.   20
5.   By thee our foes we back did fling,
        Thy name us so defended;
   Our feet trod down the rising train[58]
        That ill to us intended.

6.   My trust was not reposed
      In force of bended bow;
   My scabbard did not hold enclosed
        With sword my saving might.
7.   But thou hast kept us from the foe,
        Our haters all confounding.   30
8.   Thee will we praise still day and night,
        Thy name, O God, resounding.

9.   Now thou aloof dost hover
      And dost us quite disgrace
   And utterly hast given over[59]
        Our armies forth to lead.
10. Thou mak'st us show our back for face
      To men with malice boiling,
   Whose troops upon our goods do tread,
        At their own pleasure spoiling.   40

11. As sheep to be devoured
      Thou hast us left alone;

---

[56] *passing:* surpassing.
[57] *lightsome:* light-giving, radiant.
[58] *train:* group of people.
[59] *given over:* ceased.

Thou scatt'ringly hast us out-poured
    Among our heath'nish foes.
12.   Thou sellest us but coin hast none;
    Thy folk thou so hast prized
As things from whence no profit grows
    Base, worthless, vile, despised.

13. To them that are about us
    Thou makest us a scorn   50
That borderers[60] do laugh and flout us
    Who near unto us dwell.
14.   And we a proverb tossed[61] and worn
    By tongues of foreign places,
At whom to nod it suiteth well
    And use all vile disgraces.

15. My shame before me goeth
    As I do daily go;
Confusion so upon me groweth
    That I my face do hide,   60
16.   Fearing to feel the bitter blow
    Rebuking slander giveth,
Wherewith me lord-like, on each side,
    Revengeful malice grieveth.[62]

17. All this on us hath lighted;
    Yet thee to have in mind
We for all this are still delighted
    And hold thy cov'nant fast.
18.   Our hearts have not from thee declined,
    Nor feet away have slidden,   70
19.   Though thou us down to dragons cast,
    In deadly shade hast hidden.

20. If we our God had shifted
    Out of forgetful thought,

---

[60] *borderers:* neighbors, neighboring people.
[61] *tossed:* bandied about.
[62] *grieveth:* troubles (transitive).

If we adoring hands had lifted
    To any god but he,
21.   Should not God seek it out, and sought,
        Find out though closely lurking,
    Since of the deepest hearts his eye
        Descries the deepest working?   80

22. For thy sake sure sustain we
        Thus daily killed to be[63]
    Nor better estimate obtain we
        Than sheep to slaughter prest.[64]
23.   Up, Lord, O Lord, shake sleep from thee,
        Be not far off forever.
24.   Why dost[65] (forgetting us oppressed)
        To hide thy face persevere?

25. Our grieved soul down beaten,
        On lowest dust doth lie;   90
    Our grov'ling belly almost eaten,
        By earth to earth doth cleave.
26.   Oh, rise! With succors[66] us supply;
        Let mercy so esteem us
    That we thy mercy may receive
        From thralldom to redeem us.

Psalm 45

This psalm, traditionally read as an epithalamium or wedding poem for Solomon's marriage to a young Egyptian princess, was often allegorized by Christians as a metaphor for Christ and the Church as his bride. The poet says that he will praise the king (1–8), but first he praises God's justice and might (9–24), emphasizing the need to use force to control rebellious people and reward the righteous; these lines may also suggest the appropriate way for the king

---

[63] 81–82. Surely we endure being killed thus each day for thy sake.

[64] *prest:* ready. Perhaps also "pressed" in the sense of "forced" or "driven."

[65] *dost,* i.e., dost thou.

[66] *succors:* succor, aid. The spelling of this singular form with final "s" reflects the French original, *secours.* Cf. Psalm 71.39.

to rule, with a use of force disturbing to modern readers. The king, like God, also loves justice and hates wrong (25–26). He is anointed with ceremonial perfumed oil (27–32) and surrounded by princesses who wait upon his new bride, who stands beside him in a dress of gold (33–36). The rest of the song is addressed to the bride herself, emphasizing the experience of a young woman facing an arranged marriage, and promising that if she obeys her husband, then she will command many others. Pembroke draws on her own experience both of an arranged marriage that brought her increased wealth and status and also of her days at Elizabeth's court in her description of the duties of the "maids of honor," with some hint of competition among the ladies for "more favor." Pembroke has the poet conclude by promising to immortalize the queen in poetry, although this final verse of the psalm is usually interpreted as a promise to praise the king or God.

> My heart indites an argument of worth,
> The praise of him that doth the scepter sway:
> My tongue the pen to paint his praises forth,
> Shall write as swift as swiftest writer may.
> Then to the king these are the words I say:
>   "Fairer art thou than sons of mortal race:
> Because high God hath blessed thee for aye,[67]
>   Thy lips, as springs, do flow with speaking grace.
>
> Thy honor's sword gird to thy mighty side,
> O thou that dost all things in might excel: 10
> With glory prosper, on with triumph ride,
> Since justice, truth, and meekness with thee dwell.
> So that right hand[68] of thine shall teaching tell
>   Such things to thee as well may terror bring,
> And terror such as never erst[69] befell
>   To mortal minds at sight of mortal king.
>
> Sharp are thy shafts to cleave their hearts in twain
> Whose heads do cast[70] thy conquests to withstand:
> Good cause to make the meaner people fain

---

[67] *for aye*: forever.
[68] *right hand,* metaphorically, righteous hand. Cf. 22–24.
[69] *erst*: before.
[70] *cast*: plan, intend.

With willing hearts to undergo thy hand.[71]   20
Thy throne, O God, doth never-falling stand;
    Thy scepter, ensign of thy kingly might,
To righteousness is linked with such a band,
    That righteous hand still holds thy scepter right.

Justice in love, in hate thou holdest wrong,
    This makes that God, who so doth hate and love,
Glad-making oil, that oil on thee hath flung,[72]
    Which thee exalts thine equals far above.
    The fragrant riches of Sabean[73] grove
        Myrrh, aloes, cassia, all thy robes do smell:[74]   30
    When thou from ivory palace dost remove,
        Thy breathing odors all thy train excel.

Daughters of kings among thy courtly band,
    By honoring thee, of thee do honor hold;[75]
On thy right side thy dearest queen doth stand
    Richly arrayed in cloth of Ophir[76] gold.
    O daughter, hear what now to thee is told;
        Mark what thou hear'st, and what thou mark'st obey:
    Forget to keep in memory enrolled
        The house and folk where first thou saw'st the day.   40

So in the king, thy king, a dear delight
    Thy beauty shall both breed, and bred maintain:[77]
For only he on thee hath lordly right,
    Him only thou with awe must entertain.
    Then unto thee both Tyrus shall be fain

---

[71] God's power, as demonstrated in the way he deals with those who even contemplate rebellion (17–18), also makes those without noble rank (*the meaner people*) glad (*fain*) to submit to his rule (*thy hand*) with *willing hearts.*

[72] *oil on thee hath flung,* i.e., anointed.

[73] *Sabean:* Arabian.

[74] *smell:* have or emit a smell of (*fragrant riches,* etc.), cited as first recorded use in this sense in the *OED.*

[75] The members of the court gain honor by honoring the king.

[76] *Ophir,* a biblical place name, unidentified except as a source of gold.

[77] The queen's beauty will produce and maintain the king's delight.

Presents present, and richest nations mo,[78]
    With humble suit thy royal grace to gain,
        To thee shall do such homage as they owe.

This queen that can a king her father call,
    Doth only she in upper garment shine?   50
Nay, underclothes, and what she weareth all,
    Gold is the stuff, the fashion art divine;
    Brought to the king in robe embroidered fine,
        Her maids of honor[79] shall on her attend
With such, to whom more favor shall assign
        In nearer place their happy days to spend,[80]

Brought shall they be with mirth and marriage joy,
    And enter so the palace of the king:
Then let no grief thy mind, O queen, annoy,
    Nor parents left[81] thy sad remembrance sting.   60
Instead of parents, children thou shalt bring,
    Of partaged[82] earth the kings and lords to be:
Myself thy name in lasting verse will sing,
    The world shall make no end of thanks to thee."

Psalm 51

This psalm is traditionally read as the prayer of King David after he had been rebuked by the prophet Nathan for his adultery with Bathsheba and his murder of her husband (see 2 Sam. 11–12). It has been the most beloved of the seven penitential psalms (the others are 6, 32, 38, 102, 130, and 143), and has been frequently turned into poetry and sometimes set to music. Cf. the versions of Petrarch, Thomas Wyatt, Anne Lock, Queen Mary Stuart, Matthew Parker,

---

[78] 45–46. Tyre and still more (*mo*) of the *richest nations* will be glad to offer gifts. The old form *mo* is retained here for the rhyme.

[79] *maids of honor*: unmarried ladies, usually of noble birth, who attend upon a queen or princess (recorded as first use in the OED).

[80] Pembroke elaborates on the biblical text by seeming to claim that the maids of honor gain favor by their association with the queen herself, with whom they will spend *their happy days*. Some of the women are nearer to the queen than others, which opens up the potential for envy. Cf. the reference to honor derived from the king in 33–34.

[81] *left*, i.e., left behind (when the queen marries the king). Cf. 40.

[82] *partaged*: divided into parts (*OED*, citing this line).

and Richard Rowlands (Verstegan), for example. Pembroke emphasizes the psalm's importance by using rhyme royal, seven lines of iambic pentameter rhymed *ababbcc*. Her version was set for soprano voice and lute in the seventeenth century, probably for a woman's private devotional use.

> O Lord, whose grace no limits comprehend;[83]
> Sweet Lord, whose mercies stand from measure free;
> To me that grace, to me that mercy send,
> And wipe, O Lord, my sins from sinful me.
> Oh, cleanse, oh, wash, my foul iniquity;
> Cleanse still my spots, still wash away my stainings,
> Till stains and spots in me leave no remainings.

> For I, alas, acknowledging do know
> My filthy fault, my faulty filthiness
> To my soul's eye incessantly doth show,[84]   10
> Which done to thee, to thee I do confess,
> Just judge,[85] true witness, that for righteousness
> Thy doom may pass against my guilt awarded,
> Thy evidence for truth may be regarded.[86]

> My mother, lo, when I began to be,
> Conceiving me, with me did sin conceive:
> And as with living heat she cherished me,[87]
> Corruption did like cherishing receive.
> But, lo, thy love to purest good doth cleave,
> And inward truth: which, hardly else discerned,   20
> My truant soul in thy hid school hath learned.[88]

---

[83] *comprehend*: contain, restrict.

[84] *show*: appear.

[85] *Just judge*. The manuscript reading *Just, judge* is plausible, but the parallel construction including *true witness* suggests that the comma after *Just* is a scribal error.

[86] God is presented as the offended party, judge, and witness. The general sense of the passage is that God's judgment (*doom*) as judge and evidence as witness with regard to the speaker's guilt (*awarded* with a just verdict) will be acknowledged as both righteous and true.

[87] In Pembroke's paraphrase the mother cherishes her child even though she inadvertently transmits original sin.

[88] 20–21. *My truant soul*, having *discerned* hardly anything else, has *learned* in God's secret *school* (the speaker's "heart," according to the Geneva Bible) that God loves *purest good* and *inward truth* (19–20).

Then as thyself to lepers hast assigned,
    With hyssop, Lord, thy hyssop, purge me so:[89]
And that shall cleanse the lepry[90] of my mind.
    Make over me thy mercy's streams to flow,
    So shall my whiteness scorn the whitest snow.
        To ear and heart send sounds and thoughts of gladness,
        That bruised bones may dance away their sadness.

Thy ill-pleased eye from my misdeeds avert:
    Cancel the registers my sins contain:[91]   30
Create in me a pure, clean, spotless heart;
    Inspire a sprite[92] where love of right may reign.
    Ah, cast me not from thee; take not again
        Thy breathing grace;[93] again thy comfort send me,
        And let the guard of thy free sprite attend me.

So I to them a guiding hand will be,
    Whose faulty feet have wandered from thy way,
And turned from sin will make return to thee,
    Whom turned from thee sin erst had led astray.
    O God, God of my health,[94] oh, do away   40
        My bloody crime:[95] so shall my tongue be raised
        To praise thy truth, enough cannot be praised.[96]

Unlock my lips, shut up with sinful shame:
    Then shall my mouth, O Lord, thy honor sing.
    For bleeding fuel[97] for thy altar's flame,

---

[89] Hyssop was used for cleansing lepers in Lev. 14.

[90] *lepry*, i.e., leprosy in a figurative sense (*OED*, citing this line).

[91] *registers my sins contain*: records containing my sins.

[92] *sprite*: spirit.

[93] *breathing grace*, i.e., Holy Spirit (according to Christian biblical sources).

[94] *God of my health*. An echo of Anne Lock's version of this psalm (211). The phrase is usually translated as "God of my salvation." *Health*, however, not only recalls the Latin for "health" (*salus*) and "healthy" (*salvus*), as in one of Pembroke's sources, but also reinforces the earlier imagery of leprosy and bruised bones.

[95] *bloody crime*. A reference to David's responsibility for the death of Bathsheba's husband.

[96] *enough cannot be praised*, i.e., cannot be praised sufficiently.

[97] *bleeding fuel*, i.e., animal sacrifices, *burnt-off'rings* (47). Cf. 54–56.

To gain thy grace what boots [98] it me to bring?
Burnt-off'rings are to thee no pleasant thing.
The sacrifice that God will hold respected,
Is the heart-broken soul, the sprite dejected.

Lastly, O Lord, how so I stand or fall,   50
Leave[99] not thy loved Zion to embrace:
But with thy favor build up Salem's[100] wall,
And still in peace, maintain that peaceful place.
Then shalt thou turn a well-accepting face
To sacred fires with offered gifts perfumed:
Till ev'n whole calves on altars be consumed.[101]

Psalm 53

In the biblical text, this psalm is nearly an exact duplicate of Psalm 14. It concerns the folly of the wicked, who are both oblivious to God's oversight as they devour the godly, and ignorant of their own eventual judgment. God is imagined speaking in 9–16; the psalmist addresses God directly in 17–19. Cf. Philip Sidney's version of Psalm 14, below.

"There is no god," the fool doth say,
If not in word, in thought and will:
This fancy rotten deeds bewray,
And studies fixed on loathsome ill.[102]
Not one doth good: from heav'nly hill
Jehovah's eye one wiser mind
Could not discern, that held the way
To understand and God to find.

---

[98] *boots:* avails.

[99] *Leave:* leave off, neglect.

[100] *Salem's:* Jerusalem's. Salem also means "peace" and thus plays on the "peace" and "peaceful place" of the next line.

[101] Sixteenth-century Protestants usually interpreted this final verse metaphorically, so that the offering is "the calves of men's lips," as Calvin says, i.e., praise of God.

[102] *Rotten deeds* and *studies fixed on loathsome ill* are the subjects of *bewray* (reveal); *This fancy,* its object.

"They all have strayed, are cankered[103] all:
    Not one, I say, not one doth good.   10
But[104] senselessness, what should I call
    Such carriage[105] of this cursed brood?
    My people are their bread, their food,
        Upon my name they scorn to cry,
Whom vain affright doth yet appall,
    Where no just ground of fear doth lie."

But on their bones shall wreaked[106] be
    All thy invaders' force and guile,
In vile confusion cast by thee,
    For God himself shall make them vile.   20
    Ah, why delays that happy while
        When Zion shall our saver[107] bring?
The Lord his folk will one day free:
    Then Jacob's house shall dance and sing.

Psalm XIV
(Sir Philip Sidney: MS. B)

1.   The foolish man, by flesh and fancy led,
    His guilty heart with this fond thought hath fed:
        "There is no God that reigneth."
And so thereafter he and all his mates
    Do works which earth corrupt and heaven hates,
        Not one that good remaineth.

2.   Even God himself sent down his piercing eye
    If of this clayey[108] race he could espy
        One that his wisdom learneth.

---

[103] *cankered*: corrupt.

[104] *But*: except.

[105] *carriage*: behavior.

[106] *wreaked*: avenged.

[107] *saver*: "savior."

[108] *clayey*: of "mortal clay." The *OED* cites the first use of this word in reference to the body (as the habitation of the soul) from Sidney's *Defence*.

3.   And, lo, he finds that all astraying went,   10
        All plunged in stinking filth, not one well bent,
           Not one, that God discerneth.

4.   Oh, madness of these folks thus loosely led,
        These cannibals, who as if they were bread
           God's people do devour,
5.   Nor ever call on God! But they shall quake
        More than they now do brag when he shall take
           The just into his power.

6.   Indeed the poor, oppressed by you, you mock;
        Their counsels are your common jesting-stock: 20
           But God is their recomfort.[109]
7.   Ah, when from Zion shall the saver come
        That Jacob, freed by thee, may glad become
           And Israel full of comfort?

Psalm 55

A plea for deliverance from and vengeance against the treachery of a false friend.

My God, most glad to look, most prone to hear,
    An open ear, oh, let my prayer find,
        And from my plaint turn not thy face away.
        Behold my gestures, hearken what I say,
    While uttering moans with most tormented mind,
My body I no less torment and tear.
For, lo, their fearful threat'nings wound mine ear,
    Who griefs on griefs on me still heaping lay,
        A mark[110] to wrath and hate and wrong assigned;
        Therefore, my heart hath all his force[111] resigned   10

---

[109] *recomfort:* comfort, support.

[110] *mark:* target.

[111] *his force,* i.e., its strength. "His" is the regular form of the neuter possessive singular pronoun in the sixteenth century.

To trembling pants; death[112] terrors on me pray;
I fear, nay, shake, nay, quiv'ring quake with fear.

Then say I, oh, might I but cut the wind,
    Borne on the wing the fearful dove doth bear:
        Stay would I not, till I in rest might stay.
        Far hence, oh, far, then would I take my way
    Unto the desert, and repose me there,
These storms of woe, these tempests left behind.
But swallow them, O Lord, in darkness blind,
    Confound their counsels, lead their tongues astray,   20
        That what they mean by words may not appear.
        For mother Wrong within their town each where,[113]
    And daughter Strife their ensigns so display,
As if they only thither were confined.

These walk their city walls both night and day;
    Oppressions, tumults, guiles of every kind
        Are burgesses[114] and dwell the middle near;
        About their streets his masking robes doth wear
    Mischief clothed in deceit, with treason lined,
Where only he, he only bears the sway.   30
But not my foe with me this prank did play,
    For then I would have borne with patient cheer
        An unkind part from whom I know unkind,
        Nor he whose forehead Envy's mark had signed,
    His trophies on my ruins sought to rear,
From whom to fly I might have made assay.[115]

But this to thee, to thee impute I may,
    My fellow, my companion, held most dear,
        My soul, my other self, my inward friend:
        Whom unto me, me unto whom did bind   40
    Exchanged secrets, who together were

---

[112] *death:* death's. The uninflected possessive is a form not unprecedented in early modern English.

[113] *each where:* each place.

[114] *burgesses:* citizens.

[115] *made assay:* tried.

God's temple wont[116] to visit, there to pray.
Oh, let a sudden death work their decay,
    Who speaking fair such cankered malice mind,
      Let them be buried breathing in their bier;
        But purple morn, black ev'n, and midday clear
    Shall see my praying voice to God inclined,
Rousing him up, and naught shall me dismay.

He ransomed me; he for my safety fined[117]
    In fight where many sought my soul to slay;   50
      He, still himself to no succeeding heir
        Leaving his empire shall no more forbear
      But at my motion,[118] all these atheists[119] pay,
By whom, still one,[120] such mischiefs are designed.
Who but such caitiffs[121] would have undermined,
    Nay, overthrown, from whom but kindness mere[122]
      They never found? Who would such trust betray?
      What buttered words! Yet war their hearts bewray.
    Their speech more sharp than sharpest sword or spear
Yet softer flows than balm from wounded rind.[123]   60

But my o'erloaden soul, thyself upcheer,[124]
    Cast on God's shoulders what thee down doth weigh
      Long borne by thee with bearing pained and pined:[125]
        To care for thee he shall be ever kind;
    By him the just in safety held alway
Changeless shall enter, live, and leave the year:
But, Lord, how long shall these men tarry here?
    Fling them in pit of death where never shined
      The light of life, and while I make my stay

---

[116] *wont:* accustomed.
[117] *fined:* paid a penalty or ransom.
[118] *motion:* urging or bidding.
[119] *atheists.* Cf. Geneva (v. 19): "they fear not God."
[120] *still one:* always the same.
[121] *caitiffs:* base persons.
[122] *but kindness mere,* i.e., anything but kindness.
[123] Yet flows more softly than soothing oil from the cut bark of a tree.
[124] *upcheer:* cheer up, encourage (recorded as the first use in the *OED*).
[125] *pined:* tormented or troubled.

On thee, let who[126] their thirst with blood allay   70
Have their life-holding thread so weakly twined
That it, half-spun, death may in sunder shear.[127]

Psalm 57

A psalm of complaint lamenting the treacherous assaults of enemies, but continuing with a plea for deliverance and ending with a song of assurance that God will act. In the biblical text, the verses paraphrased in 31–54 (Psalm 57:7–11) are virtually identical to the verses paraphrased in Psalm 108.1–16 (Psalm 108:1–5).

Thy mercy, Lord, Lord, now thy mercy show:
On thee I lie;
To thee I fly.
Hide me, hive[128] me, as thine own,
Till these blasts be overblown,
Which now do fiercely blow.

To highest God I will erect my cry,
Who quickly shall
Dispatch this all.
He shall down from heaven send   10
From disgrace me to defend
His love and verity.[129]

My soul encaged lies with lions' brood,
Villains whose hands
Are fiery brands,
Teeth more sharp than shaft or spear,
Tongues far better edge do bear
Than swords to shed my blood.

As high as highest heav'n can give thee place,
O Lord, ascend,   20

---

[126] *who,* i.e., those who.

[127] 71–72. An allusion to the Fates of classical mythology, charged with spinning, measuring, and cutting the thread of life.

[128] *hive:* shelter as in a hive (recorded as the first use in the *OED*).

[129] The whole line is the direct object of *send* (10).

And thence extend
With most bright, most glorious show
Over all the earth below,
The sunbeams of thy face.[130]

Me to entangle every way I go
Their trap and net
Is ready set.
Holes they dig but their own holes
Pitfalls make for their own souls:
So, Lord, oh, serve them so.   30

My heart prepared, prepared is my heart
To spread thy praise
With tuned lays:
Wake my tongue, my lute awake,
Thou my harp the consort make,
Myself will bear a part.

Myself when first the morning shall appear,
With voice and string
So will thee sing:
That this earthly globe, and all   40
Treading on this earthly ball,
My praising notes shall hear.

For God, my only God, thy gracious love
Is mounted far
Above each star,
Thy unchanged verity
Heav'nly wings do lift as high
As clouds have room to move.

As high as highest heav'n can give thee place,
O Lord, ascend   50
And thence extend
With most bright, most glorious show
Over all the earth below,
The sunbeams of thy face.

---

[130] Geneva (v. 5): "thy glory." Cf. 54.

Psalm 58

A psalm of complaint against the wicked, including a series of curses against enemies (17–28). The speaker was traditionally assumed to be David, responding to false accusations. Cf. Pembroke's Psalm 82, which has a similar theme about injustice and makes a similar use of question and answer. See also Philip Sidney's Psalm 21.

> And call ye this to utter what is just,
>> You that of justice hold the sov'reign throne?
> And call ye this to yield, O sons of dust,[131]
>> To wronged brethren every man his own?
>>> Oh no: it is your long-malicious will
>> Now to the world to make by practice known
>>> With whose oppression you the balance fill,
> Just to yourselves, indiff'rent else to none.[132]

> But what could they,[133] who ev'n in birth declined
>> From truth and right to lies and injuries?   10
> To show the venom of their cankered[134] mind
>> The adder's image scarcely can suffice.
>>> Nay, scarce the aspic[135] may with them contend,
>> On whom the charmer all in vain applies
>>> His skillfull'st spells: aye missing of his end,[136]
> While she self-deaf[137] and unaffected lies.

> Lord, crack their teeth; Lord, crush these lions' jaws;
>> So let them sink as water in the sand:
> When deadly bow their aiming fury draws,
>> Shiver the shaft ere[138] past the shooter's hand.   20

---

[131] *sons of dust.* Pembroke adds this allusion to Gen. 2:7, the account of the creation of Adam from the dust of the earth.

[132] Added by Pembroke to underscore the partiality of the oppressors.

[133] *But what could they,* i.e., but what else could they do?

[134] *cankered:* corrupt.

[135] *aspic:* asp, serpent.

[136] *aye missing of his end,* i.e., always failing in his purpose.

[137] A reference to the claim in bestiaries that asps supposedly stop their ears with their tails.

[138] *ere past the shooter's hand:* before it moves *past the shooter's hand.* Cf. 23, 27.

So make them melt as the dishoused[139] snail
   Or as the embryo, whose vital band
      Breaks ere it holds, and formless eyes do fail
   To see the sun, though brought to lightful land.

Oh, let their brood, a brood of springing thorns,
   Be by untimely rooting overthrown
Ere bushes waxed,[140] they push with pricking horns,
   As fruits yet green are off by tempest blown:
      The good with gladness this revenge shall see,
   And bathe his feet in blood of wicked one,   30
      While all shall say, "The just rewarded be:
There is a God that carves to each his own."[141]

Psalm 68

A psalm of praise recalling God's past favors to his people, particularly in leading them from Egypt and providing them a new homeland in Canaan. The specific occasion of the psalm has traditionally been thought to be David's taking the Ark of the Covenant to Jerusalem. Pembroke emphasizes the role of women in the celebration of God's power and protection of his people (25–32, 66–67).

Let God but rise, his very face shall cast
   On all his haters flight and disarray:
As smoke in wind, as wax at fire doth waste,
   At God's aspect th'unjust shall flit away.
      The just meanwhile shall in Jehovah's presence
Play, sing, and dance. Then unto him, I say,
      Unto our God, named of eternal essence,[142]
Present yourselves with song, and dance, and play.

Prepare his path, who throned on delights,
   Doth sit a father to the orphan son   10

---

[139] *dishoused:* expelled from its shell, i.e., house (recorded as the first use in the *OED*).

[140] *waxed:* grown.

[141] 31–32. Cf. 1–4. God gives each person what that person deserves.

[142] *named of eternal essence.* Pembroke is following a source like the Geneva gloss (marginal note) on "Jah" or "Jehovah" as referring to God's essential and eternal being.

And in her cause the wronged widow rights:
    God in his holy house late[143] here begun.
      With families he empty houses filleth,
    The prisoner's chains are by his hands undone:
      But barren sand their fruitless labor tilleth,
    Who crossing him rebelliously do run.

O God, when thou in desert didst appear,
    What time[144] thy folk that uncouth journey took,
Heav'n at the sight did sweat with melting fear;
    Earth bowed her trembling knee; mount Sinai shook.   20
      The land bedewed, all wants by thee restored,
    That well thy people might the country brook,[145]
      As to a fold with sheep in plenty stored,
    So to their state thy shepherd's care did look.

There taught by thee in this triumphant song
    A virgin army did their voices try:
"Fled are these kings, fled are these armies strong:
    We share the spoils that weak in house did lie."[146]
      Though late the chimney made your beauties loathed,
    Now shine you shall, and shine more gracefully,   30
      Than lovely dove in clear gold-silver clothed,
    That glides with feathered oar through wavy[147] sky.

For when God had (that this may not seem strange[148])
    Expelled the kings with utter overthrow,
The very ground her mourning clouds did change

---

[143] *late:* lately, recently.

[144] *What time:* at which time.

[145] *brook:* possess.

[146] We who remained weak at home share the spoils. Pembroke substitutes the first person plural for the second person in her sources and thus seems to identify here and in subsequent lines with the women. See pages 24–25 for the earlier version.

[147] *wavy:* full of waves (of the air, clouds, etc.), recorded as the first use in this sense in the *OED*.

[148] *that this may not seem strange.* The character of the conquered land (35–36 describe the land, not the atmosphere) changes to accord with God's expulsion of the kings and their armies (33–34), and Canaan thus becomes more habitable and less threatening to its new possessors, the Israelites.

To weather clear, as clear as Salmon[149] snow.
    Bashan,[150] huge Bashan, that so proudly standest,
Scorning the highest hills as basely low,
    And with thy top so many tops commandest,
Both thou, and they, what makes ye brave it so?   40

This mountainet,[151] not you, doth God desire:
    Here he intends his lodging's plot to lay;
Hither Jehovah will himself retire
    To endless rest and unremoved stay.
    Here twice ten thousands, doubled twice he holdeth,
Of hooked chariots, clad in war's array:
    And hence more might, more majesty unfoldeth,
Than erst he did from Sinai mount display.

Ascended high, immortal God thou art,
    And captives' store thou hast led up with thee   50
Whose gathered spoils to men thou wilt impart:
    Nay, late thy rebels, now thy tenants be.
    Blest be the Lord, by whom our bliss increaseth,
The God of might by whom we safety see:
    God, our strong God, who us each way releaseth,
And ev'n through gates of death conducts us free.

God of his enemies the head shall wound
    And those proud looks that stiff in mischief go.
"From Bashan safe, and from the deep undrowned,
    I brought thee once, and oft I will do so."   60
    This said by him, thy foot in blood was stained,
Thy dogs' tongues dyed in blood of slaughtered foe:
    And God, my king, men saw thee entertained
In sacred house with this triumphant show.

---

[149] *Salmon.* Mount Salmon (Calvin) or Canaan (Geneva).

[150] *Bashan.* A mountain in the area east of Galilee. Cf. Beza, "O mount Bashan! God had not chosen thee, but the mount Zion unto himself."

[151] *This mountainet,* i.e., the little mountain of Zion, not noted for its height. The *OED* cites this line in the entry on "mountainet."

In vanguard marched who did with voices sing;
The rearward[152] loud on instruments did play
The battle maids and did with timbrels ring:[153]
　　And all in sweet consort did jointly say,
　　　　"Praise God, the Lord, of Jacob you descended,
　　Praise him upon each solemn meeting day:　　　　　　　70
　　　　Benjamin, little,[154] but with rule attended,
　　Judah's brave lords, and troops in fair array,

Stout Naphtali with noble Zebulun:[155]
And sith our might thy bidding word did make,
Confirm, O God, what thou in us hast done,
　　From out thy house, and that for Salem's sake.
　　　　So kings bring gifts, so in thy check their ending
　　These furious, wanton bulls and calves shall take,[156]
　　　　These arrow-armed bands, which us offending,
　　Are now so ready war to undertake.　　　　　　　　　80

They shall bring silver stooping humbly low,
　　Egypt's great peers with homage shall attend:
And Ethiop with them shall not foreslow[157]
　　To God with speed like service to commend.
　　　　Then kingdoms all to God present your praises,
　　And on the Lord your singing gladness spend:
　　　　Above the heav'n of heav'ns his throne he raises,
　　And thence his voice, a voice of strength doth send.

Then of all strength acknowledge God the well,[158]
　　With brave magnificence and glory bright,　　　　　　90
Shining no less on loved Israel
　　Than showing in the clouds his thund'ring might.
　　　　Thou from the shrine where Jacob thee adoreth,

---

[152] *The rearward,* i.e., in the rear-guard (recorded as the first use in this transferred sense in the *OED*).

[153] 66 67. Pembroke, unlike most of her sources, has the instrumental music played solely by the women.

[154] *little,* i.e., the youngest—of the sons of Jacob.

[155] *Naphtali, Zebulun*: Tribes of Galilee.

[156] 77–78. The subject of *shall take* is *their ending.*

[157] *foreslow:* be slow.

[158] Then acknowledge God the source (*well*) of all strength.

All folk, O God, with terror dost affright:
    He (praised be he) with strength his people storeth,
    His force[159] it is, in which their forces fight."

Psalm 71

The speaker recalls having trusted in God even from earliest infancy (16–21)
and, now in old age, prays for renewal of God's help and favor, ending with a
promise to sing in praise of God's deliverance of one who relies on him. Cf.
George Herbert, "The Flower."

Lord, on thee my trust is grounded:
Leave me not with shame confounded;
      But in justice bring me aid.
Let thine ear to me be bended:
Let my life from death defended
      Be by thee in safety stayed.

Be my rock, my refuge tower,
Show thy unresisted power,
      Working now thy wonted[160] will:
Thou, I say, that never feignest[161]   10
In thy biddings but remainest
      Still my rock, my refuge still.

O my God, my sole help-giver,
From this wicked[162] me deliver,
      From this wrongful, spiteful man:
In thee trusting, on thee standing,
With my childish understanding,
      Nay, with life my hopes began.

Since imprisoned in my mother
Thou me freed'st, whom have I other   20
      Held my stay[163] or made my song?

---

[159] *force:* strength.
[160] *wonted:* accustomed.
[161] *feignest:* make fictitious statements or dissemble.
[162] *this wicked:* this wicked person. Cf. 15.
[163] *stay:* support.

Yea, when all me so misdeemed,[164]
I to most a monster seemed,
    Yet in thee my hope was strong.

Yet of thee the thankful story
Filled my mouth; thy gracious glory
    Was my ditty long the day.[165]
Do not then, now age assaileth,
Courage, verdure, virtue faileth,
    Do not leave me cast away.   30

They by whom my life is hated,
With my spies[166] have now debated
    Of their talk, and, lo, the sum:
"God," say they, "hath him forsaken.
Now pursue, he must be taken;
    None will to his rescue come."

O my God, be not absented:
O my God, now, now presented
    Let in haste thy succors[167] be:
Make them full[168] disgraced, shamed,   40
All dismighted, all defamed,[169]
    Who this ill intend to me.

As for me, resolved to tarry
In my trust, and not to vary:
    I will heap thy praise with praise
Still with mouth thy truths recounting,
Still thy aids, though much surmounting
    Greatest sum that number lays.

---

[164] *misdeemed:* misjudged.

[165] *long the day:* all the day long.

[166] *my spies:* those who spy on the speaker. The addition of the spies to the biblical text was perhaps influenced by Pembroke's awareness of intrigues in the Elizabethan court.

[167] *succors:* aid.

[168] *full:* fully, totally.

[169] *dismighted:* deprived of might, rendered powerless (*OED*, citing this line); *defamed:* dishonored.

Nay, my God, by thee secured
Where will I not march assured?   50
    But[170] thy truth, what will I hold,
Who by thee from infant cradle
Taught still more, as still more able,[171]
    Have till now thy wonders told?

Now that age hath me attainted,[172]
Age's snow my head hath painted,
    Leave me not, my God, forlorn.
Let me make thy might's relation,[173]
To this coming generation,
    To this age as yet unborn.   60

God, thy justice highest raised,
Thy great works as highly praised,
    Who thy peer, O God, doth reign?
Thou into these woes dost drive me;
Thou again shalt hence revive me.
    Lift me from this deep again.

Thou shalt make my greatness greater,
Make my good with comfort better;
    Thee my lute, my harp shall sing:[174]
Thee, my God, that never slidest   70
From thy word but constant bidest,
    Jacob's holy heav'nly king.

So my lips all joy declaring,
So my soul no honor sparing,
    Shall thee sing by thee secure,

---

[170] *But*: except for.

[171] *as still more able,* i.e., having continually grown in my ability. Pembroke adds the image of the cradle (52) and thus reinforces the speaker's lifelong reliance on God.

[172] *attainted*: accused or disgraced; tainted or stained, hence a pun connecting with *painted* (56).

[173] Let me present an account of thy might.

[174] *sing.* A number of manuscripts and the biblical text have this verb, which is more in keeping with references to verbal praise elsewhere in the poem. MS. *A* has "ring," probably Davies's error.

So my tongue all times, all places,
Tell thy wreaks[175] and their disgraces,
Who this ill to me procure.

Psalm LXXI
(Variant: MS. B)

The draft status of this early version is indicated partly by the anomalous rhyme scheme in stanza 5. The numbers with periods by some of the lines mark the biblical verses, a distinctive feature of MS. *B*.

1.   On thee my trust is grounded.
            Lord, let me never be
               With shame confounded,
2.   But set me free
And in thy justice rescue me;
Thy gracious ear to me-ward[176] bend
              And me defend.

3.   Be thou my rock, my tower,
            My ever safe resort,
               Whose saving power   10
                 Hath not been short[177]
To work my safety, for my fort
On thee alone is built; in thee
              My strongholds be.

4.   Me, O my God, deliver
            From wicked, wayward hand:
5.   God, my help-giver
               On whom I stand
And stood since I could understand,
Nay, since by life I first became   20
             What now I am.

---

[175] *wreaks:* acts of vengeance (against the speaker's enemies).
[176] *to me-ward:* toward me.
[177] *short:* insufficient, inadequate.

6.   Since prisoned in my mother
By thee I prison brake,[178]
I trust no other,
No other make
My stay, no other refuge take.
Void of thy praise no time doth find
My mouth and mind.

7.   Men for a monster took me,
Yet hope of help from thee   30
Never forsook me:
8.   Make then by me
All men with praise extolled may see
Thy glory, thy magnificence,
Thy excellence.[179]

9.   When feeble years do leave me
No stay of other sort,
Do not bereave me
Of thy support
And fail not then to be my fort   40
When weakness in me killing might
Usurps his[180] right.

10.   For now against me banded,
My foes have talked of me;
Now unwithstanded[181]
Who their spies be
Of me have made a firm decree:
11. "Lo! God to him hath bid adieu.
Now then pursue.

---

[178] *brake:* broke.

[179] 32–35. Cause then all people to see thy glory, magnificence, and excellence extolled with my praise.

[180] *his: might*'s (41). *Might* is vulnerable to dangerous, overpowering *weakness*.

[181] *unwithstanded:* unopposed (but not recorded in the *OED*, which does cite "unwithstood" with a similar meaning). In Pembroke's paraphrase of 45–47, the *spies* seem to be making a report (*decree*) to the enemies, concerning the speaker's current vulnerability. Cf. the revision, MS. *A*, 31–36.

Pursue," say they, "and take him.   50
    No succor can he win,
      No refuge make him."[182]
12.   O God, begin
To bring with speed thy forces in.
Help me, my God, my God, I say
    Go not away,

13.   But let them be confounded
    And perish by whose hate
     My soul is wounded,
      And in one rate   60
Let them all share in shameful state
Whose counsels as their farthest end[183]
    My wrong intend.

14.   For I will still persevere
    My hopes on thee to raise.
     Augmenting ever
      Thy praise with praise,
15. My mouth shall utter forth always
Thy truths, thy helps, whose sum surmounts
    My best accounts.   70

16.   Thy force keeps me from fearing,
    Nor ever dread I aught,
     Thy justice bearing
      In mindful thought
17. And glorious acts which thou hast taught
Me from my youth, and I have shown
    What I have known.

18.   Now age doth overtake me
    And paint my head with snow,
     Do not forsake me   80
      Until I show
The ages which succeeding grow

---

[182] *make him,* i.e., make for himself.
[183] *farthest end:* ultimate goal or purpose.

And every after-living wight[184]
    Thy pow'r and might.

19.   How is thy justice raised
    Above the height of thought!
    How highly praised
     What thou hast wrought!
Sought let be all that can be sought,
None shall be found, nay none shall be,   90
    O God, like thee.

20.   What if thou down didst drive me
    Into the gulf of woes?
    Thou wilt revive me
     Again from those,
And from the deep which deepest goes
Exalting me again, wilt make
    Me comfort take.

21.   My greatness shall be greater
    By thee, by comfort thine   100
    My good state better.
22.   O lute of mine,
To praise his truth thy tunes incline.
My harp, extol the holy one
    In Judah known.

23.   My voice, to my harp join thee.
    My soul saved from decay,
    My voice, conjoin thee.
24.   My tongue each day
In all men's view his justice lay   110
Who hath disgraced and shamed so
    Who[185] work my woe.

---

[184] *wight*: person.
[185] *Who*, i.e., those who.

Psalm 73

The subject of this wisdom psalm is the same problem that is presented in the Book of Job: the suffering of the godly in the face of the unchecked pride of the wicked. The speaker begins with a complaint concerning God's apparent desertion of the righteous while the unrighteous prosper (1–42), then pleads for a hearing (43–48), and finally, from within God's "house," makes a statement of assurance—that God will continue both to show favor to the godly and to punish the wicked—and a pledge to remain faithful and sing God's praise (49–84). Cf. Philip Sidney, Psalm 37, and George Herbert, "The Collar." As in the latter particularly, the speaker's meditation leads to self-examination and self-knowledge (37–45, 61–69, 76–78).

> It is most true that God to Israel,[186]
> > I mean to men of undefiled hearts,
> > Is only[187] good, and naught but good imparts.
> Most true, I see, albe[188] almost I fell
> > From right conceit into a crooked mind
> > And from this truth with straying steps declined:
> For, lo, my boiling breast did chafe and swell
> > When first I saw the wicked proudly stand,
> > Prevailing still in all they took in hand.
> And sure no sickness dwelleth where they dwell: 10
> > Nay, so they guarded are with health and might,
> > It seems of them death dares not claim his right.
>
> They seem as privileged from others' pain:
> > The scourging plagues which on their neighbors fall
> > Torment not them, nay, touch them not at all.
> Therefore with pride, as with a gorgeous chain,
> > Their swelling necks encompassed they bear;
> > All clothed in wrong, as if a robe it were;
> So fat become, that fatness doth constrain
> > Their eyes to swell: and if they think on aught,   20
> > Their thought they have, yea, have beyond their thought.[189]

---

[186] Cf. *Astrophil* 5 and the opening of Beza's translation. See Hannay, "Incorporating Women Writers into the Survey Course: Mary Sidney's Psalm 73 and *Astrophil and Stella* 5," 133–38.

[187] *only:* uniquely. Only God is good.

[188] *albe:* albeit, although.

[189] They attain their desires and even more than they hope for.

They wanton grow, and in malicious vein
  Talking of wrong, pronounce as from the skies!
  So high a pitch[190] their proud presumption flies.

Nay heav'n itself, high heav'n, escapes not free
  From their base mouths; and in their common talk
  Their tongues no less than all the earth do walk.
Wherefore ev'n godly men, when so they see
  Their horn of plenty[191] freshly flowing still,
  Leaning to them, bend from their better will.   30
And thus, they reasons frame: "How can it be
  That God doth understand, that he doth know,
  Who sits in heav'n, how earthly matters go?"
See here the godless crew, while godly we
  Unhappy pine,[192] all happiness possess:
  Their riches more, our wealth still growing less.

Nay, ev'n within myself, myself did say,
  "In vain my heart I purge, my hands in vain[193]
  In cleanness washed I keep from filthy stain,[194]
Since thus afflictions scourge me every day: 40
  Since never a day from early east is sent,
  But brings my pain, my check, my chastisement."
And shall I then these thoughts in words bewray?[195]
  Oh, let me, Lord, give never such offense
  To children thine that rest in thy defense.
So then I turned my thoughts another way,
  Sounding if I this secret's depth might find;
  But cumbrous[196] clouds my inward sight did blind.

---

[190] *pitch,* the height to which a falcon or other bird of prey soars before swooping down on its prey (*OED,* citing this line as an example of the figurative sense).

[191] *Their horn of plenty,* i.e., a cornucopia representing the prosperity of the wicked (recorded as the first use of the phrase in the *OED*).

[192] *pine:* languish. The godly languish while the *godless crew* (34) *all happiness possess.*

[193] The speaker's earlier feeling that his pursuit of righteousness has been in vain is countered later by his understanding of the ultimate vanity of the dreams of the unrighteous (58–60).

[194] Cf. Psalm 51.4–11.

[195] *bewray:* reveal, expose.

[196] *cumbrous:* obstructing, troublesome.

Until at length nigh weary of the chase,
    Unto thy house I did my steps direct:[197]   50
    There, lo, I learned what end did these expect,
And what but that in high, but slippery place,
    Thou didst them set, whence, when they least of all
    To fall did fear, they fell with headlong fall?
For how are they in less than moment's space
    With ruin overthrown, with frightful fear
    Consumed so clean, as if they never were?
Right as a dream, which waking doth deface,
    So, Lord, most vain thou dost their fancies make,
    When thou dost them from careless[198] sleep awake.   60

Then for what purpose was it, to what end,
    For me to fume with malcontented heart,
    Tormenting so in me each inward part?
I was a fool (I can it not defend)
    So quite deprived of understanding might,
    That as a beast I bore me[199] in thy sight.
But as I was, yet did I still attend,
    Still follow thee, by whose upholding hand,
    When most I slide, yet still upright I stand.[200]
Then guide me still, then still upon me spend   70
    The treasures of thy sure advice, until
    Thou take me hence into thy glory's hill.

Oh, what is he will teach[201] me climb the skies,
    With thee, thee good, thee goodness to remain?
    No good on earth doth my desires detain.
Often my mind and oft my body tries
    Their weak defects. But thou, my God, thou art
    My endless lot and fortress of my heart.
The faithless fugitives who thee despise,
    Shall perish all, they all shall be undone,   80

---

[197] Cf. the imagery of "path" and "way" in Psalm 119.

[198] *careless:* without care—or the kind of afflictions that plague the speaker.

[199] *bore me:* bore myself, behaved.

[200] 67–69. Cf. Herbert, "The Collar," 33–36, where there is a similar acknowledgment that the speaker's sense of alienation from God has been illusory.

[201] *what is he will teach,* i.e., who is there who will teach?

Who leaving thee to whorish idols run.
But as for me, naught better in my eyes
Than cleave to God, my hopes in him to place,
To sing his works while breath shall give me space.

Psalm 82

A call to judgment of those who have been given temporal authority by God, the true judge of the world, to rule as his deputies on earth, but who have neglected their obligation to deal justly with God's people. Cf. Psalm 73 and the four poems titled "Affliction" in George Herbert's *The Temple.*

Where poor men plead at princes' bar,[202]
Who gods (as God's vicegerents[203]) are:
The God of gods hath his tribunal pight,[204]
Adjudging right
Both to the judge and judged wight.[205]

"How long will ye just doom[206] neglect?
How long," saith he, "bad men respect?
You should his own unto the helpless give,
The poor relieve,
Ease him with right, whom wrong doth grieve.   10

You should the fatherless defend;
You should unto the weak extend
Your hand, to loose and quiet his estate[207]

---

[202] *bar:* the bar of justice.

[203] *God's vicegerents,* i.e., those appointed by God to govern in his stead. Cf. 21–22. The final lines (26–30) make clear that the power of princes derives solely from God, who retains ultimate authority and makes earthly rulers accountable to him for their conduct.

[204] *hath his tribunal pight,* i.e., has pitched (placed or established) his law court.

[205] *wight:* person.

[206] *ye,* i.e., the princes, God's vicegerents, whom God addresses in 6–25; *doom:* judgment.

[207] *to loose and quiet his estate.* By *estate* Pembroke seems to intend both "condition" and "property." *Loose* and *quiet* would then also mean "rescue" and "soothe," as well as "release" and "settle," as in settle a dispute or *debate* (15).

Through lewd[208] men's hate
Entangled now in deep debate.

This should you do: but what do ye?
You nothing know, you nothing see:
No light, no law;[209] fie, fie, the very ground
Becomes unsound,
So right, wrong, all, your faults confound.[210]   20

Indeed to you the style I gave
Of gods, and sons of God, to have:
But err not, princes: you as men must die;
You that sit high,
Must fall, and low, as others lie."[211]

Since men are such, O God, arise:
Thyself most strong, most just, most wise,
Of all the earth king, judge, disposer be,
Since to decree
Of all the earth belongs to thee.   30

Psalm 84

Traditionally thought to have been composed by King David in exile, this psalm expresses the joy of serving in God's glorious temple.

How lovely is thy dwelling,
Great God, to whom all greatness is belonging!
To view thy courts far, far from any telling[212]
My soul doth long and pine with longing.
Unto the God that liveth,

---

[208] *lewd:* wicked.

[209] 16–18. Cf. Psalm 119 O.1–3, where the psalmist swears to uphold God's law and follow God's word as a lamp that guides his feet.

[210] 18–20. In Pembroke's paraphrase, the *ground* seems to be metaphorical: that on which a system is founded. The unjust rule of the princes blurs fundamental moral distinctions and puts all in jeopardy.

[211] 23–25. The princes are reminded of their mortality and of the certainty of God's judgment by which the unjust rulers will *fall* (25) from their high eminence and lie as low as others stretched out in death.

[212] *far from any telling,* i.e., beyond the ability of anyone to describe.

The God that all life giveth,[213]
My heart and body both aspire,
Above delight, beyond desire.

Alas, the sparrow knoweth
The house where free and fearless she resideth;   10
Directly to the nest the swallow goeth,
Where with her sons she safe abideth.
Oh, altars thine, most mighty
In war, yea, most almighty:
Thy altars, Lord, ah, why should I
From altars thine excluded lie?

Oh, happy who remaineth
Thy household-man and still thy praise unfoldeth!
Oh, happy who himself on thee sustaineth,
Who to thy house his journey holdeth!   20
Me seems I see them going
Where mulberries are growing:
How wells they dig in thirsty plain,[214]
And cisterns make for falling rain.

Me seems I see augmented
Still troop with troop, till all at length discover
Zion, where to their sight is represented
The Lord of hosts, the Zion lover.
O Lord, O God, most mighty
In war, yea, most almighty: 30
Hear what I beg; hearken, I say,
O Jacob's God, to what I pray.

Thou art the shield us shieldeth:
Then, Lord, behold the face of thine anointed.
One day spent in thy courts more comfort yieldeth
Than thousands otherwise appointed.
I count it clearer pleasure
To spend my age's treasure

---

[213] 5–6. God is eternal and also gives and sustains life. Cf. Psalm 68.7.
[214] 21–23. The Geneva Bible notes that "Bacá" ("of mulberry trees") was a "barren place," so wells would be required for supplying water there.

Waiting a porter at thy gates
Than dwell a lord with wicked mates. 40

Thou art the sun that shineth;
Thou art the buckler, Lord, that us defendeth:
Glory and grace Jehovah's hand assigneth
And good without refusal sendeth
To him who truly treadeth
The path[215] to pureness leadeth.
O Lord of might, thrice blessed he
Whose confidence is built on thee.

Psalm 88

The psalmist complains of the suffering he endures because of God's punishment and apparent alienation and because of the desertion and disaffection of former friends.

My God, my Lord, my help, my health,[216]
To thee my cry
Doth restless fly,
Both when of sun the day
The treasures doth display,[217]
And night locks up his golden wealth.

Admit to presence what I crave;
Oh, bow thine ear
My cry to hear,
Whose soul with ills and woes 10
So flows, so overflows,
That now my life draws nigh the grave.

---

[215] *The path*: the path that. Cf. the imagery of paths, ways of righteousness throughout the Psalms, especially in Psalm 68 and the various sections of Psalm 119.

[216] *my health*. An alternative reading (in Latin: *Deus salutis meae*) in one of Pembroke's sources to "my salvation" in most of the other sources. It is also a reading that occurs in some of the Hebrew manuscripts. Cf. Psalm 51.40.

[217] 4–5. An inversion for the sake of the meter: Both when the day doth display the treasures of the sun. *His* in line 6 also refers to the sun.

With them that fall into the pit[218]
    I stand esteemed,
    Quite forceless deemed,[219]
        As one who free from strife,
        And stir[220] of mortal life,
Among the dead at rest doth sit.

Right like unto the murdered sort,
    Who in the grave
    Their biding[221] have,
        Whom now thou dost no more
        Remember as before,
Quite, quite cut off from thy support.

Thrown down into the grave of graves[222]
    In darkness deep
    Thou dost me keep:
        Where lightning of thy wrath
        Upon me lighted hath,
All overwhelmed with all thy waves.

Who did know me, whom I did know,
    Removed by thee
    Are gone from me:
        Are gone? That is the best:
        They all me so detest,
That now abroad I blush to go.

My wasted eye doth melt away
    Fleeting amain[223]
    In streams of pain
        While I my prayers send,

20

30

40

---

[218] *pit:* grave.
[219] *forceless deemed:* judged weak.
[220] *stir:* bustle or activity (*OED,* citing this line).
[221] *biding:* residence or dwelling.
[222] *grave of graves,* i.e., the deepest, darkest of graves.
[223] *amain:* at full speed or at once.

While I my hands extend,
To thee, my God, and fail no day.[224]

Alas, my Lord, will then be time,[225]
    When men are dead,
    Thy truth to spread?
        Shall they, whom death hath slain,
        To praise thee live again,
And from their lowly lodgings climb?

Shall buried mouths thy mercies tell,
    Dust and decay   50
    Thy truth display?
        And shall thy works of mark[226]
        Shine in the dreadful dark,
Thy justice where oblivions dwell?[227]

Good reason then I cry to thee,
    And ere[228] the light
    Salute thy sight,[229]
        My plaint to thee direct.
        Lord, why dost thou reject
My soul and hide thy face from me?   60

Ay me, alas, I faint, I die,
    So still, so still,
    Thou dost me fill,
        And hast from youngest years,
        With terrifying fears,
That[230] I in trance amazed do lie.

---

[224] *and fail no day,* i.e., the speaker does not fail to make his supplication to God each day.

[225] *will then be time,* i.e., *will* there *then be time* to spread God's truth when men are dead (44–45)? "Wilt" in MS. *A* is probably Davies's error.

[226] *of mark:* of note, i.e., remarkable, worth noticing.

[227] Shall *thy justice* also *shine* (53) where things forgotten (*oblivions*) dwell?

[228] *ere:* before.

[229] Cf. Beza: "I do prevent [anticipate] the morning light in pouring forth my prayers."

[230] *That:* so that.

All over me thy furies passed;
  Thy fears my mind
  Do fretting[231] bind,
    Flowing about me so,   70
    As flocking[232] waters flow:
No day can overrun[233] their haste.

Who erst[234] to me were near and dear
  Far now, oh, far
  Disjoined are,
    And when I would them see,
    Who my acquaintance be,
As darkness they to me appear.

Psalm 100

A psalm of praise, originally intended as celebration of God as king—who cares for his people as a shepherd cares for his flock—and presented as part of a temple entrance liturgy. One of two sonnets, this one Scottish or Spenserian, among Pembroke's paraphrases. See also Psalm 150.

O all you lands, the treasures of your joy
  In merry shout upon the Lord bestow:
Your service cheerfully on him employ,
  With triumph song into his presence go.
  Know first that he is God, and after know
This God did us, not we ourselves create:
  We are his flock, for us his feedings[235] grow;
We are his folk, and he upholds our state.
With thankfulness, oh, enter then his gate;
  Make through each porch of his your praises ring. 10
All good, all grace, of his high name relate,
  He of all grace and goodness is the spring.
Time in no terms his mercy comprehends;[236]
From age to age his truth itself extends.

---

[231] *fretting:* rubbing, chafing.
[232] *flocking:* gathering in great numbers, flooding.
[233] *overrun:* exceed, outlast, outrun.
[234] *erst:* formerly.
[235] *feedings:* pastures.
[236] *terms:* fixed periods; *comprehends:* contains.

Psalm 101

The *appointed* king, traditionally thought to be David, vows that when he receives the crown he will rule righteously and will not tolerate unrighteousness and that he will prepare for the part with study of virtue. Cf. the description in Psalm 82 of the unjust rulers who fail in their duties as God's *vicegerents*. The sixteenth-century courtly context of Pembroke's paraphrase is unmistakable, particularly in her use of words like *counselors* (16) and *officers* (17). This psalm thus becomes part of the tradition of the "mirror for princes," or instructions for the monarch. Pembroke emphasizes the cluster of images on hearts and tongues (6, 11ff.).

When, now appointed king, I king shall be,
    What mercy then, what justice use I will,
I here, O Lord, in song protest to thee.

Till that day come thou me the crown shalt give,
    Deep study I on virtue will bestow:
And pure in heart at home retired live.

My lowly eye shall level at[237] no ill:
    Who fall from thee with me not one shall stand;
Their ways I shall pursue with hatred still.

Mischievous heads far off from me shall go;   10
    Malicious hearts I never will admit,[238]
And whisp'ring biters[239] all will overthrow.

Ill shall I brook[240] the proud ambitious band,
    Whose eyes look high, whose puffed hearts do swell,[241]
But for truth-tellers seek and search the land.

Such men with me my counselors shall sit;
    Such evermore my officers shall be:
Men speaking right and doing what is fit.

---

[237] *lowly:* humble; *level at:* aim at.

[238] *never will admit,* i.e., will never allow into my presence.

[239] *whisp'ring biters,* i.e., secretly slandering backbiters or deceivers.

[240] *brook:* tolerate.

[241] *swell,* i.e., with pride. The two halves of the line correspond metaphorically to the double description of the *band* in line 13 as *ambitious* and *proud,* respectively.

No fraudulent[242] within my house shall dwell:
    The cunning coining[243] tongue shall in my sight   20
Be not endured, much less accepted well.[244]

As soon as I in all the land shall see
    A wicked wretch, I shall him hate outright;
And of vile men Jehovah's city free.

Psalm 102

The second of the four penitential psalms paraphrased by Pembroke, Psalm 102 is a complaint concerning the speaker's *woes* (13) that are so severe as to cause *sharpest pain* (10) and emaciation (13–14, 19–20). Isolated and despairing, he prays for deliverance, both of Israel (of which he is assured in 55–60) and of himself personally (73–78).

    O Lord, my praying hear;
        Lord, let my cry come to thine ear.
  Hide not thy face away,
        But haste, and answer me,
  In this my most, most miserable day,
        Wherein I pray and cry to thee.

    My days as smoke are past;
        My bones as flaming fuel waste,
  Mown down in me, alas,
        With scythe of sharpest pain.   10
My heart is withered like the wounded grass;
    My stomach doth all food disdain.

    So lean my woes me leave,
        That to my flesh my bones do cleave:
  And so I bray and howl,
        As use to howl and bray

---

[242] *No fraudulent:* no fraudulent person.

[243] *coining:* lying.

[244] 16–21. The speaker acknowledges his obligation both to govern virtuously and to surround himself with others who will fulfill their responsibilities honestly and justly.

The lonely pelican and desert owl,
  Like whom I languish long the day.[245]

  I languish so the day,
    The night in watch I waste away;   20
Right as the sparrow sits,
    Bereft of spouse, or son,
Which irked alone with dolor's deadly fits[246]
    To company will not be won.

  As day to day succeeds,
    So shame on shame to me proceeds
From them that do me hate,
    Who of my wrack[247] so boast,
That wishing ill, they wish but my estate,
    Yet think they wish of ills the most.[248]   30

  Therefore my bread is clay;
    Therefore my tears my wine allay.[249]
For how else should it be,
    Sith thou[250] still angry art,
And seem'st for naught to have advanced me,
    But me advanced to subvert?

  The sun of my life-days[251]
    Inclines to west with falling rays,
And I as hay am dried,
    While yet in steadfast seat   40
Eternal thou eternally dost bide,
    Thy memory no years can fret.[252]

---

[245] *long the day:* all the day long.

[246] *dolor's deadly fits:* deadly fits of dolor (sorrow).

[247] *wrack:* downfall, misfortune.

[248] 29–30. The speaker's enemies use his condition (*my estate*) as a curse on others and think it the greatest of ills to be wished on anyone.

[249] *allay:* dilute.

[250] *thou,* i.e., God.

[251] *my life-days:* the days of my life.

[252] *fret:* devour (figuratively), diminish.

Oh, then at length arise;
　　On Zion cast thy mercy's eyes.
Now is the time that thou
　　To mercy shouldst incline
Concerning her: O Lord, the time is now
　　Thyself for mercy didst assign.

　　Thy servants wait the day
　　When she,[253] who like a carcass lay　　　　　　50
Stretched forth in ruin's bier,[254]
　　Shall so arise and live,
That nations all Jehovah's name shall fear,
　　All kings to thee shall glory give.

　　Because thou hast anew
　　Made Zion stand, restored to view
Thy glorious presence there,
　　Because thou hast, I say,
Beheld our woes and not refused to hear
　　What wretched we did plaining[255] pray,　　　　60

　　This of record shall bide[256]
　　To this and every age beside.[257]
And they commend thee shall
　　Whom thou anew shalt make,
That from the prospect of thy heav'nly hall
　　Thy eye of earth survey did take,

　　Heark'ning to prisoners' groans,
　　And setting free condemned ones,
That they,[258] when nations come,

---

[253] *she*, i.e., Zion (44, 56), linked with Salem (Jerusalem) in 71. Interpreted by sixteenth-century commentators as the Church.

[254] *bier*. Perhaps in the sense of "tomb," as *in* suggests.

[255] *plaining*: complaining, lamenting.

[256] God's deliverance shall endure in the *record* of his acts.

[257] *beside*: besides.

[258] *they*, i.e., the *prisoners* and *condemned ones*, who, when released, can serve to *record* God's honor (71–72).

And realms to serve the Lord,   70
In Zion and in Salem might become
Fit means his honor to record.

But what is this if I
In the mid way should fall and die?[259]
My God, to thee I pray,
Who canst my prayer give.
Turn not to night the noontide of my day,
Since endless thou dost ageless live.

The earth, the heaven stands[260]
Once founded, formed by thy hands: 80
They perish, thou shalt bide;
They old, as clothes shall wear,[261]
Till changing still, full change shall them betide,
Unclothed of all the clothes they bear.

But thou art one, still one:[262]
Time interest in thee hath none.
Then hope, who godly be,
Or come of godly race:
Endless your bliss, as never ending he,
His presence your unchanged place.   90

Psalm 104

An exuberant psalm of praise of God's creative and sustaining power.

Make, O my soul, the subject of thy song
Th'eternal Lord: O Lord, O God of might,

---

[259] What will God's delivering Israel mean to the speaker if he himself perishes in the middle of his life? Cf. *the noontide of my day* (77).

[260] The use of a third-person singular verb with a compound subject is not uncommon in sixteenth-century writings, including Shakespeare's plays.

[261] Cf. Beza: "All these things, I say, how stable so ever they seem, are worn by little and little, as the garment is by long use, whilst that at the length they be changed by thee from the form that we now see, as a garment cast off."

[262] *one*: unique, preeminent. God is the one true God ("I am that I am," Exodus 3:14) and will remain so eternally (*still*), an idea developed in the concluding lines.

To thee, to thee, all royal pomps[263] belong;
    Clothed art thou in state[264] and glory bright.
    For what is else this eye-delighting light,
But unto thee a garment wide and long,
    The vaulted heaven but a curtain right,
A canopy, thou over thee hast hung?

The rafters that his parlor's roof sustain,
    In chevron[265] he on crystal waters binds;   10
He on the winds, he on the clouds doth reign,
    Riding on clouds, and walking on the winds,
    Whose winged blasts, his word as ready finds
To post from him, as angels of his train,[266]
    As to effect the purposes he minds
He makes no less the flamy fire fain.

By him the earth a steadfast base doth bear,
    And steadfast so, as time nor force can shake,
Which once round waters garment-like did wear,
    And hills in seas did lowly lodging take.   20
    But seas from hills a swift descent did make,
When swelling high by thee they chidden[267] were:
    Thy thunder's roar[268] did cause their conduits quake,
Hast'ning their haste with spur of hasty fear.

So waters fled, so mountains high did rise,
    So humble valleys deeply did descend,
All to the place thou didst for them devise,
    Where bounding[269] seas with unremoved end,

---

[263] *pomps:* splendid displays or celebrations.

[264] *in state:* with great pomp and solemnity. God is portrayed in royal garb sitting under the canopy of state, like Queen Elizabeth.

[265] *In chevron:* in a chevron shape, with a bar bent like two rafters touching one another.

[266] 13–14. God's word finds the *winged blasts* of the winds as ready as his company of angels *to post* (go on a mission) *from him.* The imagery is further developed in 15–16, where the *fire* is said to be just as glad (*fain*) to do God's bidding.

[267] *chidden:* rebuked.

[268] *Thy thunder's roar,* i.e., the roar of thy thunder (although the plural possessive is also possible). Cf. similar constructions in 31–32.

[269] *bounding:* God's act of setting limits of the *seas.*

Thou badst[270] they should themselves no more extend,
To hide the earth which now unhidden lies: 30
    Yet from the mountains' rocky sides didst send
Springs' whisp'ring murmurs, rivers' roaring cries.[271]

Of these the beasts which on the plains do feed
    All drink their fill; with these their thirst allay[272]
The asses wild and all that wildly breed;
    By these[273] in their self-chosen mansions stay
    The free-born fowls, which through the empty way
Of yielding air wafted with winged speed,
    To art-like notes of nature-tuned lay
Make earless bushes give attentive heed.   40

Thou, thou of heav'n the windows dost unclose,[274]
    Dewing the mountains with thy bounty's rain:
Earth great with young her longing doth not lose;[275]
    The hopeful ploughman, hopeth not in vain.
    The vulgar[276] grass, whereof the beast is fain,
The rarer, herbman for himself hath chose:
    All things in brief, that life in life maintain,
From Earth's old bowels fresh and youngly grows:

Thence wine, the counter-poison[277] unto care;
    Thence oil, whose juice unplaits[278] the folded brow;   50
Thence bread, our best, I say not daintiest fare,
    Prop yet of hearts, which else would weakly bow;
    Thence, Lord, thy leaved people bud and blow,[279]

---

[270] *badst:* commanded (second person singular).

[271] 17–32. A recounting of God's act of creating the earth (*once* [19]). Cf. Genesis 1:9–10.

[272] *allay:* satisfy.

[273] *By these,* i.e., beside the springs and rivers.

[274] *unclose:* open.

[275] Pembroke develops the image of pregnancy from Psalm 104:13 that speaks mainly only of "bringing forth."

[276] *vulgar:* common, ordinary. Cf. the contrast with the *rarer* vegetation preferred by the *herbman* (46).

[277] *counter-poison:* antidote.

[278] *unplaits:* unwrinkles. The brow is wrinkled (*folded*) with *care* (49).

[279] *leaved people:* trees; *blow,* bloom.

Whose princes thou, thy cedars, dost not spare[280]
    A fuller draught of thy cup to allow,
That highly raised above the rest they are.

Yet highly raised they do not proudly scorn
    To give small birds an humble entertain,[281]
Whose brickle[282] nests are on their branches borne,
    While in the firs the storks a lodging gain.   60
    So highest hills rock-loving goats sustain
And have their heads with climbing traces worn;
    That safe in rocks the coneys[283] may remain,
To yield them caves, their rocky ribs are torn.

Thou mak'st the moon, the empress of the night,
    Hold constant course with most inconstant face;
Thou mak'st the sun the chariot-man of light,[284]
    Well know the start and stop of daily race.
    When he[285] doth set and night his beams deface,
To roam abroad wood-burgesses delight,   70
    Lions, I mean, who roaring all that space,
Seem then of thee to crave their food by right.

When he returns they all from field retire,
    And lay them down in cave, their home, to rest:
They rest, man stirs to win a workman's hire,
    And works till sun have wrought his way to west.
    Eternal Lord, who greatest art and best,
How I amazed thy mighty works admire!

---

[280] The *cedars* are God's *princes*, i.e., noblest of trees. Pembroke adds the class distinction and also the sense of obligation that the noble cedars show to the humbler birds in providing them places to nest (57–59).

[281] *entertain:* entertainment, reception.

[282] *brickle:* brittle.

[283] *coneys:* rabbits.

[284] 65–67. Pembroke adds elements from secular poetry and classical mythology in describing the inconstant moon and the chariot of the sun.

[285] *he:* the sun (67). At night creatures of a different sort become active (69–75). Cf. 73.

Wisdom in them hath every part possessed,
Whereto in me, no wisdom can aspire.[286]   80

Behold the earth: how there thy bounties flow!
    Look on the sea extended hugely wide:
What wat'ry troops, swim, creep, and crawl, and go,[287]
    Of great and small, on that, this, every side!
    There the sail-winged ships on waves do glide;
Sea-monsters there their plays and pastimes show:
    And all at once in seasonable tide[288]
Their hungry eyes on thee their feeder throw.

Thou giv'st, they take; thy hand itself displays,
    They filled feel the plenties of thy hand: 90
All darkened lie deprived of thy rays,
    Thou tak'st their breath, not one can longer stand.[289]
    They die, they turn to former dust and sand,
Till thy life-giving sprite[290] do must'ring raise
    New companies, to reinforce each band,
Which still supplied, never whole decays.[291]

So may it, oh, so may it ever go,
    Jehovah's works his glorious gladness be,
Who touching mountains, mountains smoking grow,
    Who eyeing earth, earth quakes with quivering knee.[292]   100
    As for myself, my silly[293] self, in me
While life shall last, his worth in song to show

---

[286] 78–80. By adding the first person, Pembroke intensifies the contrast between God's wise governance of his creation and the human inability to comprehend it, except to the extent of acknowledging and admiring it. Cf. Psalm 139.20–21.

[287] *go:* walk.

[288] *tide:* time.

[289] 89–92. The stark contrast between the images of sustenance and mortality emphasizes the absolute nature of God's power over all creatures.

[290] *sprite:* spirit. The manuscript reading is "sp'rit," but we have retained "sprite" elsewhere and have adopted it here for the sake of consistency.

[291] 93–96. Cf. the process of change depicted in Edmund Spenser's "Garden of Adonis" in *The Faerie Queene,* 3.6.35–38.

[292] 99–100. Volcanoes and earthquakes also attest to God's might.

[293] *silly:* deserving of pity, helpless.

I framed[294] have a resolute decree,
And thankful be, till being I forgo.[295]

Oh, that my song might good acceptance find:
    How should my heart in great Jehovah joy!
Oh, that some plague this irreligious kind,
    Ingrate to God, would from the earth destroy!
    Meanwhile, my soul, incessantly employ
To high Jehovah's praise my mouth and mind: 100
    Nay, all (since all his benefits enjoy)
Praise him whom bands of time nor age can bind.[296]

Psalm 107

One of the liturgical psalms, in which the congregation is invited to praise
God's sustaining power. The varied refrain in 33–38, 49–54, and 81–86 corre-
sponds to the biblical text (verses 8–9, 15–16, 21–22, and 31–32).

Oh, celebrate Jehovah's praise,[297]
    For gracious he and good is found;
And no precinct,[298] no space of days
    Can his great grace and goodness bound.
    Say you with me, with me resound
        Jehovah's praise with thankfulness,
    Whose bands of peril he unbound,
        When tyrant's hate did you oppress.

How many, and how many times,[299]
    From early east, from evening west,   10
From thirsty coasts, from frosty climes,

---

[294] *framed:* composed.

[295] *till being I forgo,* i.e., until I die.

[296] *Time* and *age* may not be redundant since such apparent synonyms rarely are in
Pembroke's work, but may be distinguished as time in general (in contrast to eternity) and
a particular length of human time, respectively.

[297] *praise:* praiseworthiness.

[298] *precinct:* boundary or limit.

[299] Part of the exclamatory construction in 9–12: How many of his people and how
often God has delivered...!

Hath he dispersed[300] brought to rest!
How many saved, who deep distressed
    And straying far from path and town,
With want and drought so sore were pressed[301]
    That drought well near[302] their lives did drown!

They cried to him in woeful plight;
    His succor sent did end their woe.
From error trained[303] he led them right
    And made to peopled places go.   20
    Such then in song his mercies show,
        His wonders done to men display,
    Who in the hungry hunger so,
        So doth in thirsty thirst allay.[304]

How many fast imprisoned lie
    In shade of death and horror blind,
Whose feet as iron fetters tie,
    So heavy anguish clogs their mind,
    Whom though the Lord did rebels find,
        Despising all he did advise,   30
    Yet when their heart with grief declined,
        How helpless quite and hopeless lies!

They[305] cry to him in woeful plight;
    His succor sent doth end their woe.
From death to life, from dark to light
    With broken bolts[306] he makes them go.
    Such then in song his mercy show,
        His wonders done to men display;

---

[300] *dispersed:* those who have been dispersed.

[301] *pressed:* oppressed.

[302] *well near:* very nearly. Pembroke adds the paradoxical imagery: *drought* nearly drowned (destroyed) them.

[303] *error trained.* Cf. Spenser, *The Faerie Queene,* 1.1.18.9: "Error's endless train." Cf. *Folly's train* below (42).

[304] 23–24. Who doth *allay* (satisfy) *hunger* in the *hungry* and *thirst* in the *thirsty.*

[305] *They,* i.e., the *rebels* (29), who cry to God for help only in times of need.

[306] *bolts.* Pembroke substitutes *bolts* for "bonds" in the biblical sources and thus anticipates the imagery of the gates in 39–40.

The gates of brass who breaketh so,
　　So makes the iron yield them way.　　　　　　　40

How many wantonly misled,
　　While fools, they follow Folly's train,
For sin confined to their bed,
　　This guerdon[307] of their folly gain!
　　Their loathing soul doth food refrain,[308]
　　　　And hardly, hardly failing breath
　　Can now his ending gasp restrain
　　　　From ent'ring at the gate of death.

They cry to him in woeful plight;
　　His succor sent doth end their woe.　　　　　　　50
His word puts all their pain to flight
　　And free from sickness makes them go.
　　Such then in song his merçy show,
　　　　His wonders done to men display;
　　Tell gladly of his works they know
　　　　And sacrifice of praises pay.

How many mounting winged tree[309]
　　For traffic leave retiring land
And on huge waters busied be,
　　Which bankless[310] flow on endless sand!　　　　60
　　These, these indeed, well understand,
　　　　Informed by their fear-open eye,
　　The wonders of Jehovah's hand
　　　　While on the waves they rocking lie.

He bids and straight on moisty main
　　The blust'ring tempest falling flies.

---

[307] *guerdon*: reward. An ironic reference to the illness suffered by the foolish sinners.

[308] *refrain*: avoid, give up.

[309] *mounting winged tree*: boarding a ship with sails. The *OED* cites this line as the first recorded use of *winged* in the sense of having sails.

[310] *bankless*: without banks, as if infinite (predating the earliest entry in the *OED* [1612]).

The stars do drop bedashed[311] with rain,
 So huge the waves in combat[312] rise.
Now ship with men do touch the skies,
 Now down, more down than center[313] falls;   70
Their might doth melt, their courage dies,
 Such hideous fright each sense appalls.

For now the whirlwind makes them wheel;
 Now stopped in midst of broken round,
As drunkards use, they stagg'ring reel,
 Whose head-lame feet[314] can feel no ground.
What helps to have a pilot sound,
 Where wisdom wont to guide the stern,
Now in despairful danger drowned,
 With wisdom's eye can naught discern?[315]   80

They cry to him in woeful plight;
 His succor sent doth end their woe.
Of seas and winds he parts the fight;
 To wished port with joy they row.
Such then in song his mercies show,
 His wonders done to men display:
Make people's press[316] his honor know,
 At princes' thrones his praise bewray.

How many wheres[317] doth he convert
 Well-watered grounds to thirsty sand,   90
And salts the soil[318] for wicked heart

---

[311] *bedashed:* dashed about (*OED*), or splashed *with rain.* In 67–68, Pembroke intensifies the biblical imagery by describing the storm as so violent that the waves rise as high as the stars.

[312] *combat,* i.e., the fight between wind and sea. Cf. 83.

[313] *center:* the center of the earth.

[314] *head-lame feet,* i.e., feet made unsteady by minds disturbed by fear.

[315] 77–80. What help is it to have an expert *pilot* when *wisdom,* which is needed to steer the ship but which is now *drowned* in danger-induced despair caused by fear of the storm, can see nothing?

[316] *people's press:* throng of people.

[317] *wheres:* places.

[318] *salts the soil,* i.e., makes the soil infertile, barren.

The dwellers bear that till the land!
How oft again his gracious hand
    To wat'ry pools doth deserts change
And on the fields that fruitless stand
    Makes trickling springs unhoped range!

Suppose of men that live in want
    A colony he there do make:
They dwell, and build, and sow, and plant,
    And of their pains great profit take.   100
    His blessing doth not them forsake,
        But multiplies their children's store:
    Nay, ev'n their cattle, for their sake,
        Augments in number more and more.

They stand while he their state sustains:
    Then comes again that harmful day
Which brings the interchange of pains
    And their increase turns to decay.
    Nor strange:[319] for he exiled stray
        Makes greatest kings, scorned where they go: 110
    The same from want the poor doth way,[320]
        And makes like herds their houses grow.

See this, and joy this thus to see,
    All you whose judgments judge aright;[321]
You whose conceits distorted be,
    Stand mute, amazed at the sight.
    How wise were he, whose wisdom might
        Observe each course the Lord doth hold,
    To light in men his bounty's light,
        Whose providence doth all enfold!   120

---

[319] *Nor strange,* i.e., nor is the change of fortune just described strange, surprising.

[320] *way:* cause to go, proceed. As if in a revolution of the medieval image of the Wheel of Fortune, God causes both the powerful *kings* (110) and the powerless *poor* (111) to change their state.

[321] *aright:* rightly, justly.

Psalm 111

A psalm of praise that focuses on God's deliverance of his people from Egypt.
The form is an alphabetical acrostic; there is no "J" in early modern usage.

At home, abroad, most willingly I will
Bestow on God my praise's utmost skill:
Chanting[322] his works, works of unmatched might,
Deemed so by them, who in their search delight.[323]
Endless the honor to his pow'r pertains,[324]
From end as far his justice eke[325] remains.
Gracious and good and working wonders so,[326]
His wonders never can forgotten go.
In hungry waste[327] he fed his faithful crew,
Keeping his league[328] and still in promise true.   10
Lastly his strength he caused them understand,[329]
Making them lords of all the heathens' land.
Now what could more each promise, doom, decree,
Of him confirm sure, just, unmoved to be![330]
Preserved his folk, his league eternal framed,[331]
Quake then with fear when holy he is named.
Reverence of him is perfect wisdom's well:[332]
Stand in his law, so[333] understand you well.
The praise of him (though wicked hearts repine[334])
Unbounded bides, no time can it define.   20

---

[322] *Chanting:* singing.

[323] Judged *of unmatched might* by those who *delight* in the study (*search*) of God's works.

[324] The honor that pertains to God's power is endless.

[325] *From end as far,* i.e., endless; *eke:* also.

[326] *so:* so that.

[327] *waste:* wilderness (through which Israel wandered in the Exodus from Egypt).

[328] *league:* covenant. Cf. 15.

[329] Finally he made them (caused them to) understand his strength.

[330] 13–14. Now what could more confirm the certainty, justice, and permanence of God's promises, judgments, and decrees than his own acts.

[331] A pair of absolute constructions: *his folk* (having been) *preserved*, his covenant (having been) made eternal.

[332] *well:* source, origin.

[333] *so:* thus. Cf. Beza: "Therefore this is the chief point, and the very sum of true wisdom, *To fear the Lord.* They certainly are truly wise, whosoever do obey his commandments: and his praise, though it be despised of the wicked, yet shall it remain for ever."

[334] *repine:* complain, feel or manifest discontent.

Psalm 117

Another acrostic psalm, in which the first letter of each line spells out *PRAIS THE LORD*.

> P raise him that aye[335]
> R emains the same:
> A ll tongues display
> I ehovah's[336] fame.
> S ing all that share
> T his earthly ball:
> H is mercies are
> E xposed to all,
> L ike as the word
> O nce he doth give,   10
> R olled in record,[337]
> D oth time outlive.

Psalm 119

This long psalm is composed in the biblical text of twenty-two sets of eight verses (octaves), each beginning with a different letter of the Hebrew alphabet. Each octave is a separate but related meditation on God's law (*promise, word, doctrine,* etc.) as a guide to the righteous. Pembroke paraphrases each octave as a separate poem and according to convention, assigns each an English letter (in alphabetical order), which begins the first line in each case. Psalm 119 F begins with a plea for grace to see the defeat of the speaker's enemies (1–12) and continues with an assertion of trust in God's *doctrine* (13–24) and a promise to persist in studying and following the way of righteousness (25–32).

F

> Frankly[338] pour, O Lord, on me
> Saving grace, to set me free:

---

[335] *aye:* always, ever.

[336] *I ehovah's:* Jehovah's. We have retained the "I" (the usual spelling of "J" in the sixteenth century) to preserve the acrostic.

[337] Enrolled in the *record* of God's Word.

[338] *Frankly:* freely.

That supported I may see
Promise truly kept by thee.

That to them who me defame,
Roundly I may answer frame:
Who because thy word and name
Are my trust, thus seek my shame.

Thy true word, oh, do not make
Utterly my mouth forsake: 10
Since I thus still waiting wake,
When thou wilt just vengeance take.

Then, lo, I thy doctrine pure,
Sure I hold, will hold more sure:
Naught from it shall me allure,
All the time my time shall dure.[339]

Then as brought to widest way
From restraint of straitest stay,
All their thinking night and day:
On thy law my thoughts shall lay.   20

Yea, then unto any king
Witness will I anything
That[340] from thee can witness bring:
In my face no blush shall spring.

Then will I set forth to sight
With what pleasure, what delight,
I embrace thy precepts right,
Whereunto all love I plight.[341]

Then will I, with either hand,
Clasp the rules of thy command: 30
There my study still shall stand,
Striving them to understand.

---

[339] *dure:* endure.
[340] *That,* i.e., I who.
[341] *plight:* pledge.

K

The speaker, certain of God's justice from past experience, asks both for full understanding of God's commands and for vengeance against enemies so that others may acknowledge and joy in the favor shown to him.

Knit and conformed by thy hand
    Hath been every part of me:[342]
Then make me well to understand,
Conceiving all thou dost command.
    That when me thy fearers see,
        They for me may justly joy:
    Seeing what I looked[343] from thee
    On thy word I now enjoy.

O Lord, thy judgments just I know;
    When thy scourges scourged me,   10
Thou, in that doing, naught didst show
That might thy promise overthrow.[344]
    Let me then thy comfort see
        Kindly sent as thou hast said;
    Bring thy mercy's life[345] from thee:
    On thy laws my joys are laid.

Let blame and shame the proud betide
    Falsely who subverted me,
Whose[346] meditations shall not slide,
But fast[347] in thy commandments bide.   20
    So shall I thy fearers see
        On my part[348] who know thy will:
    While I purely worship thee,
        Blot nor blush my face shall fill.

---

[342] 1–2. Cf. Psalm 139.43–56, where God's fashioning of the embryo is more elaborately developed.

[343] *looked:* looked for, expected.

[344] 9–12. Even when the speaker was being punished by God, he saw nothing that might counter the fundamental justice of God's dealings with him.

[345] *thy mercy's life:* the life of thy mercy.

[346] *Whose,* i.e., the speaker's (the antecedent is *me* in the previous line).

[347] *fast:* firm.

[348] *On my part:* on my side.

O

The speaker swears, as before, to follow the light of God's law, even when subject to treacherous enemies, and promises offerings of praise for past blessings.

> Oh, what a lantern, what a lamp of light
>   Is thy pure word to me
> To clear my paths and guide my goings right!
>   I swore and swear again,
>   I of the statutes will observer be,
>   Thou justly dost ordain.
>
> The heavy weights of grief oppress me sore:[349]
>   Lord, raise me by thy word,
> As thou to me didst promise heretofore.
>   And this unforced praise   10
>   I for an off'ring bring, accept, O Lord,
>   And show to me thy ways.
>
> What if my life lie naked[350] in my hand,
>   To every chance exposed!
> Should I forget what thou dost me command?
>   No, no, I will not stray
>   From thy edicts though round about enclosed
>   With snares the wicked lay.
>
> Thy testimonies as mine heritage,
>   I have retained still: 20
> And unto them my heart's delight engage,
>   My heart which still doth bend,
>   And only bend to do what thou dost will,
>   And do it to the end.

---

[349] *sore:* intensely, severely.

[350] *naked:* exposed to danger. Cf. Beza: "my life is exposed to all casualties as though I did carry it in my hand."

Psalm 124

This is one of a set of liturgical psalms, called Songs of Ascents (120 to 134), that were apparently used in temple celebrations. Pembroke paraphrased the first eight of this subgroup, Psalms 120 to 127, in quantitative meter, without rhyme. Psalm 124 is in iambics; hanging indentation and rhyming of lines 1 and 11 indicate structural divisions. Alternative, rhymed versions of Psalms 120 to 127 (probably not by Pembroke) are preserved in MSS. *G* and *M*.

> Say, Israel, do not conceal a verity,
>> Had not the Lord assisted us,
> Had not the Lord assisted us what time[351] arose
>> Against us our fierce enemies,
> Us all at once long since they had[352] devoured up:
>> They were so fell,[353] so furious.
> If not,[354] the angry gulfs, the streams most horrible
>> Had drowned us: so drowned us,
> That in the deep been tombed, at the least on the deep
>> Had tumbled our dead carcasses.[355]   10
> But, Lord, what honor shall thy people yield to thee,
>> From greedy teeth delivered,
> Escaped as the fowl, that oft breaking the grin,[356]
>> Beguiles the fowler's wiliness?
> For sure this is thy work, thy name protecteth us,
>> Who heav'n and earth hast fashioned.

---

[351] *what time:* at the time that, when.

[352] *had:* would have. Cf. 8, 10.

[353] *fell:* fierce.

[354] *If not.* A continuation of the parallel construction begun in line 2: If the Lord had not assisted us. . . .

[355] 9–10. If God had not assisted, our corpses (*dead carcasses*) would have been buried (*tombed*) in the *deep* water, or at least would have *tumbled* (been thrown down in confusion) on the water.

[356] *grin:* trap, snare. Israel is the *fowl*; the pursuing Egyptians are the *enemies* (4), the wily *fowler* (14).

Psalm 124
(Variant: MS. G)

This rhymed alternative (probably not by Pembroke) to the version in MS. *A* appears in MSS. *G* and *M* and is printed here from MS. *G*. The revision seems to have been made for congregational singing; it can in fact be sung to the Genevan tune (Old Hundredth) familiar in the doxology "Praise God from whom all blessings flow."

> If thou, O Lord, hadst not our right
> Maintained by thy great power and might,
> If thou with us hadst not uprose
> Against our mortal deadly foes,
>
> We swallowed up alive had[357] been
> So bitter was their rage and spleen;[358]
> The waters on us had prevailed,
> Our soul had sunk, our life had failed;
>
> The waters deep of proud men high[359]
> O'erwhelmed our souls had suddenly: 10
> But praised be God, not as a prey
> Unto their teeth cast us away.[360]
>
> Our soul hath now escaped free
> Even as poor birds from fowlers be:
> The snare is broke, and we are fled
> And from their hands delivered.

---

[357] *had:* would have. Cf. 7, 8, 10.

[358] *spleen:* violent ill-nature.

[359] In this version, the deep waters seem to be metaphorical, referring to the *mortal deadly foes* (4), as in the Prayer Book Psalter: "The deep waters of the proud." While the apparently synonymous terms in a phrase like *mortal deadly* are usually complementary in Pembroke's paraphrases, they seem here to be merely redundant since neither the context nor the sources encourage the interpretation that the enemies are themselves mortal and that they are deadly to others.

[360] 11–12. Praised be God, who did not cast us away as a prey unto their teeth.

Our help and hope, therefore, shall rest
   In thee, O Lord, forever blest:
     Who heav'n and earth and all of[361] naught
     By thy great power hast made and wrought.   20

Psalm 124
(Book of Common Prayer)

1. If the Lord himself had not been on our side (now may Israel say), if the Lord himself had not been on our side when men rose up against us,

2. They had swallowed us up quick, when they were so wrathfully displeased at us.

3. Yea, the waters had drowned us, and the stream had gone over our soul.

4. The deep waters of the proud had gone even over our soul.

5. But praised be the Lord, which hath not given us over for a prey unto their teeth.

6. Our soul is escaped even as a bird out of the snare of the fowler; the snare is broken, and we are delivered.

7. Our help standeth in the name of the Lord, which hath made heaven and earth.

Psalm 130

Another of the penitential psalms, this psalm acknowledges the speaker's faults, but trusting in God's justice tempered with mercy, prays for forgiveness. This paraphrase was also set to music in the same manuscript containing the setting of Psalm 51. (See Plates nos. 5 and 6.)

    From depth of grief
       Where drowned I lie,
    Lord, for relief
       To thee I cry:
    My earnest, vehement, crying, praying,
    Grant quick, attentive hearing, weighing.[362]

---

[361] *of:* out of, from. A reference to creation *ex nihilo,* or out of nothing.
[362] *weighing:* considering.

O Lord, if thou
    Offenses mark,[363]
Who shall not bow
    To bear the cark?[364]   10
But with thy justice mercy dwelleth,
And makes thy worship more, excelleth,[365]

Yea, makes my soul
    On thee, O Lord,
Dependeth whole,[366]
    And on thy word,
Though sore[367] with blot of sin defaced,
Yet surest hope hath firmly placed.

Who longest watch,
    Who soonest rise,   20
Can nothing match
    The early eyes,
The greedy eyes my soul erecteth,[368]
While God's true promise it expecteth.

Then, Israel,
    On God attend:
Attend him well,
    Who still thy friend,
In kindness hath thee dear esteemed,[369]
And often, often erst[370] redeemed.   30

---

[363] *mark:* notice, take account of.

[364] *cark:* burden.

[365] And mercy makes thy worship more excellent. Cf. Geneva (v. 3): "If thou, O Lord, straitly markest iniquities, O Lord, who shall stand?"

[366] *whole.* wholly.

[367] *sore:* intensely, severely. The line modifies *soul* (13), not *word* (16).

[368] *erecteth:* lifts up, raises.

[369] *dear esteemed:* dearly (at a high rate or price) valued.

[370] *erst:* formerly. *Erst* indicates that *often, often* is not an empty doublet: God has often redeemed Israel (the people addressed here), as he often redeemed past generations.

Now, as before,
Unchanged he
Will thee restore,
Thy state will free,
All wickedness from Jacob driving
Forgetting follies, faults forgiving.

Psalm 131

The psalmist uses the image of a weaned child to express his humility and trust in God.

A lofty heart, a lifted eye,
Lord, thou dost know I never bare:[371]
Less have I borne in things too high
A meddling mind or climbing care.
Look how the weaned babe doth fare:
Oh, did I not? Yes, so did I:
None more for quiet might compare
Ev'n with the babe that weaned doth lie.
Hear then and learn, O Jacob's race,
Such endless trust on God to place.   10

Psalm 131
(Variant: MS. N)

Thou, Lord, for thou dost know,
Canst well my witness be:
My heart was never apt to climb,
Nor I at any time
Did arrogantly go,
Meddling in things too great, too high for me.

Nay, thou canst witness well
So far was thought of pride,
As proud the weaned infant is
Who first the breast doth miss: 10

---

[371] *bare:* bore. The old form is retained here for the rhyme.

Such pride,[372] I say, did dwell
    In me, as doth in weaned babe abide.

Unmoved I quiet lay
    With care but how to rest:
        And now I wish, that as did I,
           All Jacob would rely
And make their trustful stay
    On him, now still, who greatest is and best.

Psalm 137

A lament of the Israelites in exile in Babylon and a plea for vengeance against their captors, who have taunted them about their songs in praise of distant Zion, God's holy hill.

Nigh seated where the river flows
    That wat'reth Babel's[373] thankful plain,
Which then our tears in pearled rows
    Did help to water with their rain,
The thought of Zion bred such woes,
    That though our harps we did retain,
        Yet useless and untouched there
        On willows only hanged they were.

Now while our harps were hanged so,
    The men whose captives then we lay   10
Did on our griefs insulting go,
    And more to grieve us, thus did say:
"You that of music make such show,
    Come sing us now a Zion lay."
        Oh no, we have nor voice, nor[374] hand
        For such a song, in such a land.

Though far I lie, sweet Zion hill,
    In foreign soil exiled from thee,

---

[372] *Such pride.* Only so much pride as there is in a weaned child, i.e., no pride at all.
[373] *Babel's*: Babylon's.
[374] *nor . . . nor*: neither . . . nor.

Yet let my hand forget his[375] skill,
    If ever thou forgotten be;
And let my tongue fast[376] glued still
    Unto my roof[377] lie mute in me,
        If thy neglect[378] within me spring,
        Or aught I do, but Salem sing.[379]

20

But thou, O Lord, shalt not forget
    To quit the pains of Edom's race,[380]
Who causelessly yet hotly set[381]
    Thy holy city to deface,
Did thus the bloody victors whet[382]
    What time[383] they entered first the place:
        "Down, down with it[384] at any hand
        Make all plat pays,[385] let nothing stand."

30

And, Babylon, that didst us waste,[386]
    Thyself shalt one day wasted be;
And happy he who what thou hast
    Unto us done, shall do to thee,
Like bitterness shall make thee taste,
    Like woeful objects cause thee see:
        Yea, happy who thy little ones
        Shall take and dash against the stones.

40

---

[375] *his,* i.e., its, my hand's.

[376] *fast:* firmly, tightly.

[377] *my roof:* the roof of my mouth.

[378] *thy neglect,* i.e., neglect of thee.

[379] Or if I do anything (*aught*) except sing of Jerusalem (*Salem*).

[380] To repay (*quit*) the efforts of the Edomites, who were thought to have been in league with the Babylonians.

[381] *set:* began.

[382] *whet:* encourage. The Edomites voice their support of the Babylonian assault on Jerusalem in 31–32.

[383] *What time:* when.

[384] *it,* i.e., God's holy city, Jerusalem. Lines 31–32 are the war cry of those who laid the city waste.

[385] *plat pays.* A French phrase meaning "flat land" or as in some manuscripts of the *Psalms* "flat plain."

[386] *waste:* lay waste, destroy.

Psalm 139

The psalmist meditates on God's all-knowing, all-seeing power, and protesting his trust in God's personal care for him even from the womb, prays for deliverance from his enemies.

> O Lord, in me there lieth naught,
>> But to thy search revealed lies:[387]
>>> For when I sit
>>> Thou markest it;[388]
>> No less thou notest when I rise;
> Yea, closest closet of my thought
>> Hath open windows to thine eyes.

> Thou walkest with me when I walk,
>> When to my bed for rest I go,
>>> I find thee there   10
>>> And everywhere:
>> Not youngest thought in me doth grow,
> No, not one word I cast to talk,
>> But yet unuttered thou dost know.[389]

> If forth I march, thou go'st before;
>> If back I turn, thou com'st behind:
>>> So forth nor back[390]
>>> Thy guard I lack,
>> Nay, on me too, thy hand I find.[391]
> Well I thy wisdom may adore,   20
>> But never reach with earthy mind.[392]

> To shun thy notice, leave thine eye,
>> Oh, whither might I take my way?

---

[387] 1–2. *naught . . . lies*: Nothing except what *lies revealed* to thy *search*.

[388] You take note of it.

[389] 13–14. *No*, there is *not one word* I intend (*cast*) to speak, except you *know* it, still *unuttered*. A statement of God's omniscience.

[390] *So forth nor back*: thus, neither forth nor back.

[391] 15–19. Not only does God go before and follow behind, but he also guides the speaker with the touch of his hand.

[392] The speaker can admire, but never fully comprehend God's wisdom. Cf. Psalm 104.78–80.

To starry sphere?[393]
Thy throne is there.
To dead men's undelightsome[394] stay?
There is thy walk, and there to lie
Unknown, in vain I should assay.[395]

O sun, whom light nor flight can match,[396]
Suppose thy lightful, flightful[397] wings
Thou lend to me,
And I could flee
As far as thee the evening brings:
Ev'n led to west he would me catch,
Nor should I lurk[398] with western things.

Do thou thy best, O secret night,
In sable veil to cover me:
Thy sable veil
Shall vainly fail;
With day unmasked my night shall be,[399]
For night is day, and darkness light,
O father of all lights,[400] to thee.

Each inmost piece in me is thine:
While yet I in my mother dwelt,
All that me clad
From thee I had.
Thou in my frame[401] hast strangely dealt;

30

40

---

[393] A reference to the theory of the spheres in Ptolemaic astronomy.

[394] *undelightsome:* not delightful, unpleasant. This is the only recorded instance in the *OED.*

[395] 22–28. There is no way to avoid God's presence or all-seeing eye.

[396] Nothing can *match* the *light* or *flight* of the *sun. Flight* here seems to be clarified in 30–35.

[397] *flightful:* well adapted for flight. This is the only instance of the use of the word in this sense cited in the *OED.*

[398] *lurk:* hide.

[399] My *night* shall be *unmasked* with the coming of *day.*

[400] *father of all lights.* Cf. James 1:17.

[401] *my frame:* my framing, the forming of my body.

Needs in my praise thy works must shine[402]
So inly them my thoughts have felt.

Thou how my back was beam-wise laid   50
   And raft'ring of my ribs dost know:
      Know'st every point
      Of bone and joint,
   How to this whole these parts did grow,
In brave embroid'ry fair arrayed,
   Though wrought in shop[403] both dark and low.[404]

Nay, fashionless, ere form I took,
   Thy all and more beholding eye
      My shapeless shape
      Could not escape: 60
   All these, with times appointed by,
Ere one had being, in the book
   Of thy foresight, enrolled did lie.[405]

My God, how I these studies[406] prize,
   That do thy hidden workings show
      Whose sum is such,
      No sum so much:[407]
   Nay, summed as sand they sumless grow!
I lie to sleep, from sleep I rise,
   Yet still in thought with thee I go.   70

---

[402] Thy works needs must shine in my praise. In this construction, *needs* is adverbial.

[403] *shop:* the womb.

[404] Pembroke's elaboration of the psalmist's statement that God formed him in his mother's womb is drawn from details in several of her sources, but the tone and intensity of the passage are her own. See Rathmell, *The Psalms of Sir Philip Sidney and the Countess of Pembroke,* xix–xx.

[405] Cf. Beza: "Even then, I say, thou didst behold me, when I was yet an unfashioned lump without shape: and all this my fashioning, and also the very time appointed thereunto, was set down in thy book, before that any part of that workmanship was made."

[406] *these studies.* Pembroke here develops the speaker's study as scientific exploration of God's *hidden workings* (65). See *Collected Works,* 2.17.

[407] No number can express God's numberless works. Cf. 68.

My God, if thou but one wouldst kill,
    Then straight would leave my further chase
        This cursed brood
        Inured to blood,[408]
    Whose graceless taunts at thy disgrace
Have aimed oft, and hating still
    Would with proud lies, thy truth outface.[409]

Hate not I them, who thee do hate?
    Thine, Lord, I will the censure be.
        Detest I not   80
        The cankered[410] knot,
    Whom I against thee banded see?
O Lord, thou know'st in highest rate
    I hate them all as foes to me.

Search me, my God, and prove my heart,
    Examine me, and try my thought:
        And mark[411] in me
        If aught there be
    That hath with cause their anger wrought.
If not (as not) my life's each part,   90
    Lord, safely guide from danger brought.

Psalm 143

The last of the penitential psalms. Acknowledging his sinfulness, the speaker appeals to God that he will act out of *honor, justice, mercy* (51) and deliver him from his foes and the torment they cause him.

    Hear my entreaty, Lord; the suit,[412] I send,
    With heed attend.

---

[408] 71–74. The sense is that if God would demonstrate his power by killing one of the speaker's pursuers, then the whole group, accustomed (*Inured*) *to blood* (violence, murder), would cease chasing him any further. *My . . . chase* means *chase* (pursuit) of me.

[409] *outface:* contradict (*OED,* citing this line).

[410] *cankered:* corrupt, malignant.

[411] *mark:* notice, observe.

[412] *suit:* supplication or petition. This, along with *entreaty* and *audience* (6), particularly, reinforce the courtly context of the paraphrase.

And as my hope and trust is[413]
Reposed whole in thee,
So in thy truth and justice
Yield audience to me.
And make not least beginning
To judge thy servant's sinning:
For, Lord, what living wight
Lives sinless in thy sight?   10

Oh, rather look with ruth upon my woes,
Whom ruthless foes
With long pursuit have chased,
And chased at length have caught,
And caught, in tomb have placed
With dead men out of thought.[414]
Ay me! What now is left me?
Alas, all knowledge reft[415] me,
All courage faintly fled,
I have nor heart nor head.   20

The best I can[416] is this, nay, this is all:
That I can call
Before my thoughts, surveying
Time's evidences old,
All deeds with comfort weighing
That thy handwriting[417] hold.
So hand and heart conspiring
I lift, no less desiring
Thy grace I may obtain,
Than drought desireth rain.   30

Leave then delay, and let his[418] cry prevail
Whom force doth fail.

---

[413] The use of a singular verb with a compound subject is not unprecedented in early modern English.

[414] *out of thought:* no longer remembered.

[415] *reft:* taken from.

[416] *can:* can do.

[417] *thy handwriting.* The sources have some form of the expression "thy handiwork."

[418] *his,* i.e., the speaker's. *One* in 34 also refers to the speaker.

Nor let thy face be hidden
From one who may compare
With them whose death hath bidden
Adieu to life and care.
My hope, let mercy's morrow
Soon chase my night of sorrow.
My help,[419] appoint my way
I may not wand'ring stray.[420]   40

My cave, my closet where I wont[421] to hide
In troublous tide:[422]
Now from these troubles save me,
And since my God thou art,
Prescribe how thou wouldst have me
Perform my duty's part.
And lest awry I wander
In walking this Meander,[423]
Be thy right sprite my guide[424]
To guard I go not wide. [425]   50

Thy honor, justice, mercy crave of thee,
O Lord, that me
Revived thou shouldst deliver
From pressure of my woes,
And in destruction's river
Engulf and swallow those
Whose hate thus makes in anguish
My soul afflicted languish:
For meet it is so kind
Thy servant should thee find.   60

---

[419] 37, 39. *My hope . . . My help*, i.e., God.

[420] An elliptical construction: So that I may not. . . .

[421] *wont*: am accustomed.

[422] *tide*: time.

[423] *this Meander*. A winding river in Phrygia. The *OED* cites this as the first recorded instance of the figurative use of the word to mean a "winding or labyrinthine course."

[424] Subjunctive: May *thy right sprite* (Holy Spirit) be. . . .

[425] Stand guard, so that I do not stray.

Psalm 148

A celebration of God as creator and a call to all created things, but particularly God's people (51–54), to acknowledge their dependence on him and to sing his praises.

> Inhabitants of heav'nly land,
>> As loving subjects praise your king:
> You that among them highest stand,
>> In highest notes Jehovah sing.
>> Sing, angels all on careful[426] wing,
>>> You that his heralds fly,
>> And you whom he doth soldiers bring
>>> In field his force[427] to try.

> Oh, praise him sun, the sea of light,
>> Oh, praise him moon, the light of sea.[428]　　　　10
> You pretty stars in robe of night
>> As spangles twinkling do as they.
>> Thou sphere within whose bosom play
>>> The rest that earth emball,[429]
>> You waters banked with starry bay,
>>> Oh, praise, oh, praise him all.

> All these, I say, advance that name,
>> That doth eternal being[430] show:
> Who bidding, into form and frame,
>> Not being yet, they all did grow,[431]　　　　20
>> All formed, framed, founded so,
>>> Till age's utmost date,[432]

---

[426] *careful:* full of care, to do God's bidding. Cf. the angels as heralds and soldiers here with the more general reference to their function in Psalm 104.13–14.

[427] *force:* strength, power.

[428] 9–10. The sun is the source (*sea*) of light; the reflected light of the moon lights the sea.

[429] A reference to Ptolemaic astronomy: *thou sphere* is the sphere of fixed stars, which contains all the others that surround (*emball*) the earth in the center.

[430] *eternal being.* Cf. Psalm 68.7.

[431] 19–20. Cf. Variant Psalm 124.19–20.

[432] The heavens will endure till the end of time.

They place retain, they order know,
   They keep their first estate.

When heav'n hath praised, praise earth anew:[433]
   You dragons first, her deepest guests;
Then soundless[434] deeps, and what in you
   Residing low or moves or[435] rests;
   You flames affrighting mortal breasts;
      You stones that clouds do cast;   30
   You feathery snows from winter's nests;
      You vapors, sun's appast;[436]

You boist'rous winds, whose breath fulfills
   What in his word his will sets down;
Ambitious mountains, courteous hills;
   You trees that hills and mountains crown,
   Both you that proud of native gown[437]
      Stand fresh or tall to see,
   And you that have your more renown,
      By what you bear, than be;   40

You beasts in woods untamed that range,
   You that with men familiar go;
You that your place by creeping change,
   Or airy streams with feathers row;
   You stately kings, you subjects low,
      You lords and judges all,
   You others whose distinctions show,
      How sex or age may fall:

All these, I say, advance that name
   More high than skies, more low than ground.   50

---

[433] After heaven has praised God, then the earth should *praise . . . anew*. There follows a roll call of all creation, including dragons who live in deep caves; sea creatures and plants; the four elements of fire, water, air and earth; trees; wild and domesticated animals; reptiles; birds; and people of both sexes, all ages, and all social ranks.

[434] *soundless:* unfathomable (recorded as the first use in the *OED*).

[435] *or . . . or:* either . . . or.

[436] *appast:* food.

[437] *native gown:* foliage. The reference in the biblical text is to cedars, in contrast to fruit trees, which have more *renown* from *what* they *bear* (39–40).

And since advanced by the same
    You Jacob's sons stand chiefly bound;
    You Jacob's sons be chief to sound
      Your God Jehovah's praise.
    So fits them well on whom is found,
      Such bliss on you he lays.

Psalm 150

The concluding psalm is a doxology, a song of praise that emphasizes the use of music in worship. This is the second of Pembroke's sonnets among her psalm paraphrases. Cf. Psalm 100.

Oh, laud the Lord, the God of hosts commend,
    Exalt his pow'r, advance his holiness:
    With all your might lift his almightiness;
Your greatest praise upon his greatness spend.

Make trumpet's noise in shrillest notes ascend;
    Make lute and lyre his loved fame express;
    Him let the pipe, him let the tabret[438] bless,
Him organ's breath, that winds or waters lend.

Let ringing timbrels[439] so his honor sound,
    Let sounding cymbals so his glory ring,   10
    That in their tunes such melody be found
As fits the pomp of most triumphant king.

Conclude: by all that air or life[440] enfold,
    Let high Jehovah highly be extolled.

---

[438] *tabret:* small tabor, or drum.

[439] *timbrels:* tambourines or similar small hand-held drums.

[440] *air or life.* Cf. Calvin's distinction between creatures who merely breathe and human beings, who have life in a sense that makes them superior to other sentient beings.

THE TRIUMPH OF DEATH

Mary Sidney learned Italian as a child, evidently both from her mother, who was fluent enough in Italian to speak to European ambassadors in that language, and from a tutor. Knowledge of Italian was nearly as important for a highly-educated Englishwoman as knowledge of Latin, for while Latin was the international language of scholarship, law, religion, and diplomacy, Italian was internationally recognized as the language of literature. Three giants towered over Italian literature: Dante, Petrarch, and Boccaccio, as Philip Sidney recognized in his *Defence of Poetry* (74). Francis Petrarch (1304–74) was celebrated in England not for his major Latin works: his epic *Africa* on Scipio Africanus; his Roman biographies, *De viris illustribus*; or his dialogues of comfort in adversity, *De remediis utriusque fortunae*. Rather, he was known primarily for his series of Italian sonnets written to his beloved Laura, the *Rime sparse*. The Petrarchan sonnet tradition had been brought to England by Sir Thomas Wyatt and by Henry Howard, earl of Surrey, and the first English sonnet sequence was evidently a meditation on Psalm 51 by Anne Lock, but it was Philip Sidney's sequence *Astrophil and Stella* that established the vogue for sonnets in England. Hundreds of sonnets and more than fifty sonnet sequences followed, most notably those by Edmund Spenser and William Shakespeare; several other members of Mary Sidney Herbert's family also wrote sonnets, including her younger brother Robert, and her niece Mary Wroth, although so far as we know she herself wrote only two sonnets, her metrical paraphrases of Psalms 100 and 150. Her son William is not known for writing in the traditional, fourteen-line sonnet form, although several of his poems (with varying line lengths) were titled as sonnets in John Donne the Younger's 1660 edition of William Herbert's poems.

Instead, she turned to *Il Trionfi*, or the *Triumphs*, of Petrarch. Frequently printed with the *Rime sparse*, the *Triumphs* could be read as a continuation of the sonnets, recounting Petrarch's love for Laura.[1] Petrarch began, perhaps as early as 1338, by portraying himself as love's captive in *The Triumph of Love*. In *The Triumph of Chastity* Laura's chastity defeats Cupid; in *The Triumph of Death*, probably begun in the year of her death (1348), Death apparently defeats the chaste Laura. However, in *The Triumph of Fame*, her reputation

---

[1] For possible structural links between the *Triumphs* and book 3 of Petrarch's *Secretum* (a series of three confessional dialogues between the author and St. Augustine), see Hans Baron, *Petrarch's Secretum: Its Making and Its Meaning* (Cambridge, Mass.: The Medieval Academy of America, 1985), 113–14.

defeats Death. *The Triumph of Time* appears to give the victory to Time, but in the concluding *Triumph of Eternity* (composed six months before his own death in 1374) she lives forever. Like Dante's *Divine Comedy*, the *Triumphs* include a dream vision, in which Laura appeared to Petrarch even as Beatrice appeared to Dante. Like the *Divine Comedy*, the *Triumphs* could be read as moral allegory. The meditations on Death, in particular, combined Christian and Senecan ideas in a way that was obviously of comfort to Renaissance readers. (See similar attitudes in *A Discourse of Life and Death*.) The most famous passage in the *Triumphs* is the *ubi sunt* (or "where are") section from *The Triumph of Death* (Chapter 1.79–84). This meditation on Death's victory is echoed in English from *Beowulf* and "The Wanderer" through Renaissance literature and even to the twentieth-century war protest song, "Where have all the flowers gone?"[2]

Pembroke may have known two fragments and one complete English translation of the *Trionfi* that had appeared in print. The first extant translation is Surrey's short excerpt, "Such wayward ways hath love" (*Triumph of Love*, 3.151–87). She may also have known the few lines from the *ubi sunt* passage of the *Triumph of Death* that were translated anonymously in *The Praise of Nothing* (1585), although her translation does not appear to be indebted to it. She apparently had read the long-winded couplets in the translation (pub. 1554) by Henry Parker, Lord Morley, but would have been most unlikely to have seen the manuscript of the full translation by William Fowler, Secretary to Queen Anne of Scotland (1587–1588). During her years at court she may have seen or at least learned of Elizabeth's youthful translation of the first 90 lines of *The Triumph of Eternity* into quatrains. Certainly Pembroke was the first to undertake the challenging task of translating the *Triumphs* into English in Petrarch's original form, *terza rima* (*aba*, *bcb*, etc.). Despite a few minor errors (see the notes), her translation is remarkably accurate to the Italian and matches the content *terzina* by *terzina*.

Even though most English readers had never read *The Triumphs* themselves, most educated people were probably familiar with its general content through a visual tradition. The usual imagery is that of an allegorical figure (of Love, Chastity, Death, Fame, Time, or Eternity) enthroned on a chariot pulled by allegorical beasts, surrounded by a crowd of victims similar to those that Petrarch lists; the details, however, are not necessarily accurate to the poem. (See Plate no. 7.) Such imagery was seen not only in the illustrations in printed editions of the *Triumphs*, but also in thousands of artworks, including paintings, drawings, tapestries, miniatures, frescos, medals, birth trays,

---

[2] The most familiar Continental version is François Villon's lament for dead ladies, "Où sont les neiges d'antan?"

marriage chests, illustrated psalters, glass cups, majolica dishes, and statues. Pembroke had no doubt seen such artworks, as well as Henry VIII's famous tapestries based on the *Triumphs* at Westminster, Windsor, and Hampton Court. The idea of the triumph also appears in other literature known to her, including Philip Sidney's parody in the triumph of Artesia in the *New Arcadia*, and in Spenser's *Faerie Queene*, particularly the triumphal procession of Lucifera (Pride) and the six other Deadly Sins in the House of Pride (book 1), the Masque of Cupid in the House of Busirane (book 3), and the procession of the Seasons in the Mutability Cantos (book 7). Pembroke herself emphasizes the idea of the triumph in her translation of *Antonius*, wherein both Antony and Cleopatra prefer death to the shame of being exhibited in Caesar's triumph (see Argument and lines 1847–68).

She also knew of the use of the *Triumphs* to praise Elizabeth, who had been celebrated as the heroine of the *Triumph of Chastity* in her 1578 progress in Suffolk, and more importantly, in the 1581 tilt (ceremonial combat) the *Four Foster Children of Desire*, or the "Fortress of Perfect Beauty," in which Philip Sidney appeared. The imagery of such praise became exceedingly complex, as imagery of the chaste Laura was intertwined with that of the virgin queen, the goddess Astrea (see "A Dialogue"), biblical figures (see "Even Now"), and with various traditional symbols of virginity, like the sieve, the pearl, and the ermine.

We do not know whether or not she completed her translation of the *Triumphs*, because her translation of *The Triumph of Death* was preserved by chance. It exists only in one slightly inaccurate scribal transcription of papers sent by her cousin John Harington to Lucy Harington Russell, countess of Bedford, with an accompanying letter, dated 29 December 1600, that praises Mary Sidney Herbert for her *Psalms* but does not mention the *Triumphs*. That manuscript includes just three of Pembroke's Psalms (51, 104, and 137), so it may also include just a portion of her Petrarch translation. It is thus quite possible that she translated all of the *Triumphs*.

Even for *The Triumph of Death* this one extant manuscript may not be a fully reliable record of the final state of Pembroke's text. If we allow for simple scribal error, the large number of places where emendation can be supported, as well as other irregularities of rhyme (e.g., 2.74) and meter (e.g., 1.95, 2.45, 2.187), suggest that the unique Petyt text (which is itself a copy of a copy) may derive from an early draft of a work in progress. Compare the incomplete state of Variant Psalm 71, as well as the anomalous texts of many of the Psalms in one of the British Library copies, MS. Additional 12047, which was owned by Harington, who may perhaps have seen Pembroke's writings at various stages of composition.

The possibility that this transcription of a copy of a draft is not complete also means that we cannot assume that there was a special significance for her in this one *Triumph*, yet it is of particular interest in the history of English Petrarchism, for it gives the dead Laura a voice, one amplified by a female translator. Chapter one recounts her death from Petrarch's perspective, but in chapter two the spirit of Laura appears to him and gives her own perspective on his love and on her death. "Her" words, of course, are still the words of Petrarch and are wish fulfillment, so that her primary motivation is her love for him; nevertheless, *The Triumph of Death* allows the beloved woman to become a speaking subject rather than just the passive object of the poet's affection. (Philip Sidney's *Astrophil and Stella* also gives the woman a voice, at least in the songs.) Pembroke's translation enlarges Laura's voice and agency in subtle ways, thereby preparing for *Pamphilia to Amphilanthus*, her niece's sonnet sequence in a female voice, and for subsequent English women writers.[3] Undoubtedly, Laura's words did express the frustration that many women felt when they were constrained to silence, when the only word permitted them was "no," despite the lover's pleas and accusations of unkindness. Laura says that his love, expressed so loudly, did not give him more pain than her own secret love for him gave her (2.135–47), and that by her alternate demonstration of disdain and affection, she kept his love virtuous. Her "no" is thus portrayed as costly to herself, but she is proud that her reason overcame her desire—and his (2.97–102). Laura thus encounters the same conflict between passion and reason that Cleopatra does in *Antonius*, but she chooses reason and leads her lover to God, rather than choose passion that would cause his destruction and her own. Both Laura and Cleopatra, however, are portrayed as strong, eloquent women who defeat death through their nobility and resulting fame.[4]

In modernizing the text, we have benefited from consulting the editions by Gavin Alexander: "*The Triumph of Death*: A Critical Edition in Modern Spelling . . . ," *Sidney Journal* 17 (1999): 2–18, and "*The Triumph of Death* (c. 1600)," *Sidneiana, Copia, CERES*, 20 Sept. 1999, <http://www.english.cam. ac.uk/ceres/sidneiana/triumph.htm>.

COPY-TEXT: *Triumph of Death* (Library of the Inner Temple, Petyt MS. 538. 43. 14, fols. 286r–289v). Verbal emendations: 1.25 *seemed (send)*, 1.55 *eye . . . attends*

---

[3] On women poets regendering the Petrarchan tradition, see particularly Ilona Bell, *Elizabethan Women and the Poetry of Courtship* (Cambridge: Cambridge University Press, 1998); William J. Kennedy, *Authorizing Petrarch* (Ithaca, N.Y.: Cornell University Press, 1994), 114–94; Mary B. Moore, *Desiring Voices: Women Sonneteers and Petrarchism* (Carbondale, Ill.: Southern Illinois University Press, 2000).

[4] Beilin, *Redeeming Eve*, 128, 131–37; Lamb, *Gender and Authorship*, 129–40.

(eyes . . . attend), 1.76 *Cathay (Gattay),* 1.86 *find (dye),* 1.102 *task (talke),* 1.120 *sing (spring),* 2.4 *sprinkle (sprintle),* 2.5 *Tithonus' (Tithons),* 2.18 *On pleasing (vnpleasing),* 2.81 *leaving (loving),* 2.83 *eyes (eye),* 2.97 *Thou (Tho),* 2.104 *our (or* [perhaps a spelling variant]*),* 2.105 *thee then (thee),* 2.110 *acceptance now, now (acceptance; now),* 2.130 *fame (flame),* 2.158 *fire (fires),* 2.178 *See (Shee).*

We have added the following designations to clarify speakers:

> *D=Death*
> *L=Laura*
> *P=Petrarch*
> *C=Company of Women Mourners*

THE TRIUMPH OF DEATH,
Translated out of Italian by the Countess of Pembroke

The First Chapter

That gallant lady,[5] gloriously bright,
 The stately pillar once of worthiness,
 And now, a little dust, a naked sprite,
Turned from her wars a joyful conqueress:
 Her wars, where she had foiled the mighty foe,
 Whose wily stratagems the world distress,
And foiled him, not with sword, with spear or bow,
 But with chaste heart, fair visage, upright thought,
 Wise speech, which did with honor linked go:
And love's new plight to see strange wonders wrought   10
 With shivered bow, chaste arrows, quenched flame,
 While here some slain, and there lay others caught.
She, and the rest, who in the glorious fame
 Of the exploit, her chosen mates, did share,
 All in one squadronet close ranged came—[6]
A few, for nature makes true glory rare,
 But each alone (so each alone did shine)
 Claimed whole historian's, whole poet's care.
Borne in green field, a snowy ermiline
 Colored with topazes, set in fine gold   20
 Was this fair company's unfoiled sign.[7]
No earthly march, but heavenly, did they hold;
 Their speeches holy were, and happy those
 Who so are borne, to be with them enrolled.

---

[5] *That gallant lady.* In the preceding *Triumph of Chastity*, Laura, the *joyful conqueress* (1.4) has defeated Cupid, *the mighty foe* (1.5). In chapter 1 of the present *Triumph* she is herself overthrown by Death, a woman in black (1.31), who speaks in 1.34–48, 59–60, 62–69.

[6] Laura is accompanied by a little squadron of other virtuous women who have likewise overcome Cupid through chastity.

[7] The *green field* of the women's banner has been traditionally interpreted as youth (cf. 2.68), and the ermine (*ermiline*) and *topazes* as symbols of chastity or purity. An alternative interpretation of the color green associates it with the laurel and steadfast virtue. The banner is *unfoiled*, or undefeated, and perhaps also unfurled.

Clear stars they seemed, which did a sun unclose,[8]
     Who hiding none, yet all did beautify
     With coronets decked with violet and rose:
And as gained honor filled with jollity
     Each gentle heart, so made they merry cheer,[9]
     When, lo, an ensign sad I might descry,   30
Black, and in black, a woman did appear,[10]
     Fury with her, such as I scarcely know
     If like at Phlegra with the giants were.[11]
[D] "Thou, dame," quoth she, "that doth so proudly go,
     Standing upon thy youth and beauty's state,
     And of thy life, the limits dost not know:
Lo, I am she, so fierce, importunate,
     And deaf and blind, entitled oft by you,[12]
     You, whom with night ere evening I amate.[13]
I, to their end, the Greekish nation drew,   40
     The Trojan first, the Roman afterward,
     With edge and point of this my blade I slew.
And no barbarian my blow could ward,[14]
     Who stealing on with unexpected wound,
     Of idle thoughts have many thousand marred.
And now no less to you-ward am I bound,
     While life is dearest, ere[15] to cause you moan,
     Fortune some bitter with your sweets compound."
[L] "To this, thou right or interest hast none,
     Little to me, but only to this spoil,"[16]   50
     Replied then she, who in the world was one.[17]

---

[8] *unclose:* disclose.

[9] As honor filled each *gentle heart* with jollity, so *made they merry cheer.*

[10] Death.

[11] *Phlegra* was the valley of Thessaly where the giants assaulted Mt. Olympus; Jupiter retaliated with thunderbolts.

[12] I am she whom you call *fierce, importunate, deaf and blind.*

[13] *amate:* dishearten.

[14] *ward:* ward off, deflect.

[15] *ere:* before. Death will strike before Fortune brings some bitterness into Laura's sweet life.

[16] *spoil,* i.e., Laura's body. In 1.49–50 Laura counters Death's threats with the assurance that her soul is immortal.

[17] *one:* unique, preeminent.

"This charge of woe on others will recoil,
    I know, whose safety on my life depends:
    For me, I thank who shall me hence assoil."[18]
As one whose eye some novelty attends,
    And what it marked not first, it spied at last,
    New wonders with itself, now comprehends,
So fared the cruel, deeply over-gast[19]
    With doubt a while, then spoke, *[D]* "I know them now.
    I now remember when my teeth they passed."   60
Then with less frowning, and less darkened brow,
    "But thou that lead'st this goodly company,
    Didst never yet unto my scepter bow.
But on my counsel if thou wilt rely,
    Who may enforce[20] thee, better is by far
    From age and age's loathsomeness to fly.
More honored by me, than others are
    Thou shalt thee find: and neither fear nor pain
    The passage shall of thy departure bar."
[L] "As likes that Lord, who in the heav'n doth reign,   70
    And thence, this all doth moderately guide:
    As others do, I shall thee entertain."
So answered she, and I withal[21] descried
    Of dead appear a never-numbered sum,
    Pest'ring[22] the plain, from one to th'other side,
From India, Spain, Cathay,[23] Morocco come,
    So many ages did together fall,
    That worlds were filled, and yet they wanted[24] room.
There saw I, whom their times did happy call,
    Popes, emperors, and kings, but strangely grown   80
    All naked now, all needy beggars all.

---

[18] *assoil:* release, absolve. In 1.52–54 Laura claims that only those who survive her will be pained by her death, which she views as the freeing of her soul from its mortal imprisonment. Cf. *Discourse*, part 2, "Meditation on Death," page 127.

[19] *over-gast:* terrified, afraid. In 1.55–59 Death is momentarily but *deeply* overcome by Laura's strength and eloquence. The *cruel* (the cruel one) recovers, however, when in 1.59–60 she recognizes those whom she has devoured.

[20] *enforce:* force, compel.

[21] *withal:* also.

[22] *Pest'ring:* crowding.

[23] *Cathay:* China.

[24] *wanted:* lacked.

Where is that wealth? Where are those honors gone:
    Scepters, and crowns, and robes, and purple dye,
    And costly miters, set with pearl and stone?
O wretch, who dost in mortal things affy![25]
    (Yet who but doth?) and if in end they find
    Themselves beguiled, they find but right, say I.
What means this toil?[26] O blind, O more than blind:
    You all return, to your great mother,[27] old,
    And hardly leave your very names behind.   90
Bring me, who doth your studies well behold,
    And of your cares not manifestly vain,
    One let him tell me, when he all hath told.
So many lands to win, what boots the pain,
    And on strange lands, tributes to impose,
    With hearts still greedy, their own loss to gain?
After all these, wherein you winning lose
    Treasures and territories dear bought with blood;
    Water and bread hath a far sweeter close.
And gold and gem gives place to glass and wood: 100
    But lest I should too long digression make
    To turn to my first task I think it good.
Now that short, glorious life her leave to take
    Did near unto the utmost instant go,
    And doubtful step,[28] at which the world doth quake.
Another number than themselves did show
    Of ladies, such as bodies yet did lade:[29]
    If Death could piteous be, they fain would know.
And deep they did in contemplation wade
    Of that cold end, presented there to view,   110
    Which must be once, and must but once be made.

---

[25] *affy*: trust. All wretched people trust in *mortal things*, only to find *themselves beguiled* (87), or fooled, by their transience.

[26] *toil*: snare or activity.

[27] *great mother*: the earth, which is old.

[28] *doubtful step*. A reference to the lack of certainty concerning one's salvation or damnation after death.

[29] *ladies, such as bodies yet did lade*, i.e., women who were alive, whose bodies still burdened (*did lade*) their souls. They are among the *careful crew* (1.112) who are present as observers of Laura's good death.

All friends and neighbors were this careful crew,
 But Death with ruthless hand one golden hair
 Chosen from out those amber tresses drew,[30]
So cropped the flower, of all this world most fair,
 To show upon the excellentest thing
 Her[31] supreme force, and for no hate she bare.
How many drops did flow from briny spring,
 In who there saw those sightful fountains dry,[32]
 For whom this heart so long did burn[33] and sing.   120
For her in midst of moan and misery,
 Now reaping once what virtue's life did sow,
 With joy she sat retired silently.
[C] "In peace," cried they, "right mortal goddess, go,"
 And so she was,[34] but that in no degree
 Could Death entreat, her coming to foreslow.
What confidence for others, if that she
 Could fry and freeze in few nights' changing cheer[35]
 O human hopes, how fond and false you be.
And for this gentle soul, if many a tear   130
 By pity shed, did bathe the ground and grass,
 Who saw, doth know; think thou, that dost but hear.
The sixth of April,[36] one o'clock,[37] it was
 That tied me once, and did me now untie,
 Changing her copy;[38] thus doth Fortune pass.

---

[30] The act of plucking a single hair as a representation of the moment of death is familiar from *Aeneid*, 4.698–705.

[31] *Her*, i.e., Death's.

[32] Many tears flowed from the eyes of those who witnessed Laura's dry eyes, a sign of her faith in the immortality of her soul. Cf. 1.121–23.

[33] *burn*: Petrarch's heart burns with love. Cf. 2.94–95.

[34] *And so she was*, i.e., Laura was a *mortal goddess* (cf. 2.19), and yet her divinity (virtuous nature) could not make Death delay in claiming her body.

[35] *changing cheer*, i.e., suffering. If even Laura can suffer the tormenting fevers and chills of death, then who can hope to escape them?

[36] *The sixth of April*. The date has triple significance as referring to the day of the present encounter of Petrarch and Laura's spirit, the day of her death, and the day on which Petrarch fell in love with her. Cf. 1.134.

[37] *one o'clock*. An imprecise translation of what in the Italian means "the first hour" after sunrise.

[38] *Changing her copy*: changing her (Fortune's) style or course of action.

None so his thrall, as I my liberty,
  None so his death, as I my life do rue,
  Staying with me, who fain from it[39] would fly.
Due to the world, and to my years was due,
  That I, as first I came, should first be gone,   140
  Not her leaf quailed, as yet but freshly new.[40]
Now for my woe, guess not by't, what is shown,
  For I dare scarce once cast a thought thereto,
  So far I am off, in words to make it known.[41]
[C] "Virtue is dead, and dead is beauty too,
  And dead is courtesy," in mournful plight,
  The ladies said: "And now, what shall we do?
Never again such grace shall bless our sight;
  Never like wit, shall we from woman hear
  And voice, replete with angel-like delight."   150
The soul now prest[42] to leave that bosom dear,
  Her virtues all uniting now in one,
  There, where it passed did make the heavens clear.
And of the enemies[43] so hardly none,
  That once before her showed his face obscure
  With her assault, till Death had thorough gone.[44]
Passed plaint[45] and fear when first they could endure
  To hold their eyes on that fair visage bent,
  And that despair had made them now secure.[46]
Not as great fires violently spent,   160
  But in themselves consuming, so her flight
  Took that sweet sprite, and passed in peace content,

---

[39] *it,* i.e., life.

[40] Petrarch should have died before Laura, who was younger than he: her leaf was killed (*quailed*), even though it was still green. Cf. 2.68.

[41] Inexpressibility topos; Petrarch's words are not adequate to describe his pain.

[42] *prest:* ready, eager.

[43] *enemies.* In Petrarch, *avversari* (adversaries), glossed by in modern editions as "devils" (*demoni*).

[44] 154–56. An elliptical construction: And so there was present not one of those enemies that once showed their obscure faces before her, till Death had completed (*thorough gone with*) her assault. . . .

[45] *plaint:* complaint, lamentation.

[46] 157–59. Another elliptical construction: Not until *plaint and fear* had passed, nor until *despair* had made them now certain (*secure*) of her death, could the mourners endure to look at *that fair visage bent.*

Right like unto some lamp of clearest light,
    Little and little wanting nutriture,[47]
    Holding to end a never-changing plight.[48]
Pale? No, but whitely, and more whitely pure
    Than snow on windless hill, that flaking falls:
    As one, whom labor did to rest allure.
And when that heav'nly guest those mortal walls[49]
    Had left, it naught but sweetly sleeping was   170
    In her fair eyes: what folly dying calls.
Death fair did seem to be in her fair face.

MARY SIDNEY, COUNTESS OF PEMBROKE

The Second Chapter of The Triumph of Death

That night, which did the dreadful hap[50] ensue
    That quite eclipsed, nay, rather did replace
    The sun[51] in skies, and me bereave of view,
Did sweetly sprinkle through the airy space
    The summer's frost, which with Tithonus' bride,[52]
    Cleareth of dream the dark, confused face,
When, lo, a lady, like unto the tide[53]
    With orient jewels crowned, from thousands mo[54]
    Crowned as she, to me, I coming spied:
And first her hand, sometime desired so,   10
    Reaching to me, at once she sighed and spake,
    Whence endless joys yet in my heart do grow:

---

[47] *nutriture:* nourishment.

[48] 160–65. Death comes, not as a violent fire, but as a gradually fading light.

[49] *heav'nly guest . . . mortal walls,* i.e., the soul . . . the body.

[50] *the dreadful hap:* the death of Laura.

[51] *The sun:* Laura. Cf. 2.87.

[52] *Tithonus' bride,* Aurora, goddess of the dawn and wife of Tithonus. Cf. 2.178–80. Since the original, *Tithons,* would make the line a syllable short, it probably represents a scribal slip.

[53] *a lady,* Laura, approaching Petrarch as a spirit from heaven; *the tide,* the time, the hour of dawn.

[54] *mo:* more. Laura emerges from a throng of other spirits.

[L] "And know'st thou her, who made thee first forsake
    The vulgar path and ordinary trade,
    While her their mark thy youthful thoughts did make?"
Then down she sat, and me sit down she made—
    Thought, wisdom, meekness in one grace did strive—
    On pleasing bank in bay and beech's shade.
[P] "My goddess, who me did, and doth revive,
    Can I but know?" I sobbing answered,   20
    "But art thou dead—ah, speak—or yet alive?"
[L] "Alive am I: and thou as yet art dead,[55]
    And as thou art shalt so continue still
    Till by thy ending hour, thou hence be led.
Short is our time to live, and long our will:
    Then let with heed, thy deeds and speeches go,
    Ere that approaching term his course[56] fulfill."
Quoth I, *[P]* "When this our light to end doth grow,
    Which we call life (for thou by proof hast tried),
    Is it such pain to die? That, make me know."   30
[L] "While thou," quoth she, "the vulgar make thy guide,
    And on their judgments (all obscurely blind)
    Dost yet rely, no bliss can thee betide.
Of loathsome prison to each gentle mind
    Death is the end: and only who employ
    Their cares on mud, therein displeasure find.
Even this my death, which yields thee such annoy,
    Would make in thee far greater gladness rise,
    Couldst thou but taste least portion of my joy."
So spoke she with devoutly fixed eyes   40
    Upon the heavens; then did in silence fold
    Those rosy lips, attending there[57] replies:
[P] "Torments invented by the tyrants old,
    Diseases, which each part torment and toss,
    Causes that death we most bitter hold."
[L] "I not deny," quoth she, "but that the cross[58]

---

[55] Laura's paradox—she, who has died, is alive in heaven, while Petrarch, who yet lives, is dead on the earth—is both Christian and Neoplatonic. The idea is anticipated at the end of chapter 1, "what folly dying calls" (1.171).

[56] *Ere:* before; *term:* time of life; *his course,* i.e., the course of one's lifetime.

[57] *there,* perhaps "their." The sense would be that the lips have become silent, awaiting replies to their earlier speech.

[58] *cross,* i.e., the suffering that comes before death (2.47).

Preceding death, extremely martyreth,
 And more the fear of that eternal loss.[59]
But when the panting soul in God takes breath,
 And weary heart affecteth heavenly rest,   50
 An unrepented sigh, not else, is death.
With body,[60] but with spirit ready prest,
 Now at the furthest of my living ways,
 There sadly uttered sounds[61] my ear possessed:
'Oh, hapless he who counting times and days
 Thinks each a thousand years, and lives in vain
 No more to meet her while on earth he stays,
And on the water now, now on the main
 Only on her doth think, doth speak, doth write,
 And in all times one manner still retain.'   60
Herewith, I thither cast my failing sight,
 And soon espied, presented to my view,
 Who oft did thee restraining, me incite.
Well I her face, and well her voice I knew,
 Which often did my heart reconsolate,
 Now wisely grave, then beautifully true.[62]
And sure, when I was in my fairest state,
 My years most green, myself to thee most dear,
 Whence many much did think and much debate
That life's[63] best joy was all most bitter cheer   70
 Compared to that death, most mildly sweet,
 Which comes to men, but comes not everywhere.
For I that journey passed with gladder feet
 Than he from hard exile that homeward goes
 (But only ruth of thee) without regreet."[64]

---

[59] *the fear of that eternal loss:* the fear of losing salvation.

[60] *With body* probably goes with the next line: "With my body now at the end of its life, but with my spirit ready and eager (*prest*) . . . ," in an evident echo of Matthew 26:41 (Geneva Bible), "the spirit indeed is ready but the flesh is weak."

[61] *sadly uttered sounds:* the sounds of Petrarch's grieving. In 2.55–60 Laura recalls her thoughts concerning the way her death affected Petrarch. The repeated *her* (2.57, 59) is Laura's reference to herself.

[62] 62–66: According to most commentators, Laura refers here to the counsel of an unnamed female friend or confidante, a convention of courtly literature.

[63] *That life,* i.e., youth, Laura's "green years," the greatest joys of which are bitter.

[64] Only pity (*ruth*) of Petrarch's grief at her parting caused Laura any regret. The unusual spelling of "regret" as *regreet* was perhaps intended as an eye rhyme.

[P] "For that faith's sake time once enough did show,
    Yet now to thee more manifestly plain
    In face of him who all doth see and know,
Say, lady, did you ever entertain
    Motion or thought more lovingly to rue   80
    (Not leaving[65] honor's height) my tedious pain?
For those sweet wraths, those sweet disdains in you,
    In those sweet peaces written in your eyes,
    Diversely many years my fancies drew."[66]
Scarce had I spoken, but in lightning-wise,
    Beaming, I saw that gentle smile appear,
    Sometimes[67] the sun of my woe-darkened skies.
Then sighing, thus she answered, *[L]* "Never were
    Our hearts but one, nor never two shall be.
    Only thy flame I tempered with my cheer:[68]   90
This only way could save both thee and me;
    Our tender fame[69] did this support require:
    The mother had a rod, yet kind is she.
How oft this said my thoughts: 'In love, nay, fire
    Is he: now to provide must I begin,
    And ill providers are fear and desire.'
Thou saw'st what was without, not what within.
    And as the brake the wanton steed doth tame,
    So this did thee from thy disorders win.
A thousand times wrath in my face did flame,   100
    My heart meanwhile with love did inly burn,
    But never will, my reason overcame:
For if woe-vanquished once, I saw thee mourn,
    Thy life, our honor, jointly to preserve,
    Mine eyes to thee then sweetly did I turn.

---

  [65] *leaving:* deserting, or, in this context, violating standards of honorable conduct. The original, "loving," is probably a scribal slip.

  [66] After acknowledging Laura's *faith* (2.76), now confirmed before God (2.78), Petrarch asks for clarification of her love for him since he experienced diverse responses from her (2.82–84).

  [67] *Sometimes:* formerly.

  [68] *cheer:* behavior.

  [69] *tender fame:* vulnerable reputation.

But if thy passion did from reason swerve,
    Fear in my words and sorrow in my face
    Did then to thee for salutation serve.
These arts I used with thee; thou ran'st this race;
    With kind acceptance now, now sharp disdain;   110
    Thou know'st, and hast it sung in many a place.
Sometimes thine eyes pregnant with teary rain
    I saw, and at the sight, 'Behold, he dies
    But if I help,' said I, 'the signs[70] are plain.'
Virtue for aid did then with love advise:
    If spurred by love, thou took'st some running toy,[71]
    'So soft a bit,' quoth I, 'will not suffice.'
Thus glad and sad, in pleasure and annoy,
    Hot red, cold pale; thus far I have thee brought
    Weary, but safe, to my no little joy."   120
Then I with tears, and trembling: [P] "What it sought
    My faith hath found, whose more than equal meed[72]
    Were this; if this, for truth could pass my thought."
[L] "Of little faith!" quoth she. "Should this proceed,
    If false it were or if unknown, from me?"
    The flames withal seemed in her face to breed.[73]
[L] "If liking in mine eyes the world did see
    I say not, now, of this; right fain I am,
    Those chains that tied my heart well liked me.[74]
And well me likes (if true it be) my fame,   130
    Which far and near by thee related goes,
    Nor in thy love could aught but measure blame.
That only failed;[75] and while in acted woes
    Thou needs wouldst show, what I could not but see,
    Thou didst thy heart to all the world disclose.

---

[70] *But if*: unless; *the signs*: the signs indicating what would have happened to Petrarch without Laura's intervention.

[71] *some running toy*: some cursory composition, or poem, as the word is used by Pembroke in her letter to Wotton (*Correspondence* III, *Collected Works*, 1:287).

[72] *meed*: reward.

[73] Laura responds with disdainful heat (2.124–26) to Petrarch's apparent doubt concerning the strength of her love for him (2.121–23).

[74] *liked me*: pleased me. Cf. *me likes* in 130.

[75] 132–33. Laura could find nothing to blame in Petrarch's love except for (*but*) his failure to maintain moderation (*measure*).

Hence sprang my zeal, which yet distemp'reth thee,
    Our concord such in everything beside,
    As when united love and virtue be.
In equal flames[76] our loving hearts were tried,
    At least when once thy love had notice got: 140
    But one to show, the other sought to hide.
Thou didst for mercy call with weary throat;
    In fear and shame, I did in silence go.
    So[77] much desire became of little note.
But not the less becomes concealed woe,
    Nor greater grows it uttered, than before:
    Through fiction, truth will neither ebb nor flow.
But cleared I not the darkest mists of yore
    When I thy words alone did entertain
    Singing for thee, 'My love dares speak no more'?   150
With thee my heart,[78] to me I did restrain
    Mine eyes; and thou thy share canst hardly brook,
    Leesing by me the less, the more to gain,[79]
Not thinking if a thousand times I took
    Mine eyes from thee, I many thousands cast
    Mine eyes on thee; and still with pitying look,
Whose shine no cloud had ever overcast,
    Had I not feared in thee those coals to fire
    I thought would burn too dangerously fast.
But to content thee more ere I retire   160
    For end of this, I something will thee tell,
    Perchance agreeable to thy desire:
In all things fully blest, and pleased well,
    Only in this I did myself displease:
    Born in too base a town for me to dwell.
And much I grieved, that for thy greater ease,

---

[76] *equal flames.* Pembroke omits Petrarch's *quasi,* "almost." See William J. Kennedy, *The Site of Petrarchism* (Baltimore: The Johns Hopkins University Press, 2003).

[77] *So:* thus.

[78] *With thee my heart,* i.e., Laura had given her heart to Petrarch, although she did not openly acknowledge the gift (2.151–52).

[79] The general sense seems to be that Petrarch could only with difficulty find value in (*hardly brook*) Laura's silent gift of her heart (his *share*), whereas he had less to lose from her conduct (*by me*) and more to gain from it than he realized, as she explains further in 2.154–59. *Leesing* probably has the sense of "losing" in this context.

At least, it stood not near thy flow'ry nest,
Else far enough, from whence I did thee please.[80]
So might the heart on which I only rest,
Not knowing me, have fit itself elsewhere,   170
And I less name, less notice have possessed."
[P] "Oh, no," quoth I, "for, me, the heavens' third sphere
To so high love advanced by special grace,
Changeless to me, though changed thy dwelling were."[81]
[L] "Be as it will, yet my great honor was,
And is as yet," she said. "But thy delight
Makes thee not mark how fast the hours do pass.
See from her golden bed Aurora bright
To mortal eyes returning sun and day
Breast-high above the ocean, bare to sight.   180
She to my sorrow, calls me hence away,
Therefore thy words in time's short limits bind,
And say in brief, if more thou have to say."
[P] "Lady," quoth I, "your words most sweetly kind
Have easy made whatever erst[82] I bare,
But what is left of you to live behind.[83]
Therefore to know this, my only care,[84]
If slow or swift shall come our meeting-day."
She parting said, [L] "As my conjectures are,
Thou without me long time on earth shalt stay."   190

MARY SIDNEY, COUNTESS OF PEMBROKE

---

[80] Laura acknowledges the discrepancy between her provincial birthplace, which was near Avignon, and Petrarch's noble Florence, "Firenze" or "Fiorenze," punning on the Italian, *fiorito* ("flowery") in her phrase, *thy flow'ry nest*.

[81] Petrarch assures Laura that his love for her was ordained by heaven and thus is not affected by the place where she dwells, perhaps with a reference to her current heavenly dwelling place.

[82] *erst*: formerly.

[83] A difficult line. The Italian translates literally as "but living without you is harsh and difficult for me" (William J. Kennedy, private correspondence).

[84] This line is lacking a syllable, perhaps because the scribe omitted "is" following "this." See Alexander's emended editions.

BIBLIOGRAPHY

MARY SIDNEY HERBERT, COUNTESS OF PEMBROKE

Works

"A Dialogue between Two Shepherds, *Thenot* and *Piers*, in Praise of *Astrea*," in *A Poetical Rhapsody Containing, Diverse Sonnets, Odes, Elegies, Madrigals, and Other Posies, Both in Rhyme, and Measured Verse*, ed. Francis Davison. London: printed by V. Simmes for J. Baily, 1602; repr. 1608, 1611, 1621.

A Discourse of Life and Death, Written in French by Philip Mornay; Antonius: A Tragedy Written Also in French by Robert Garnier. Both Done in English by the Countess of Pembroke. London: printed by J. Windet for William Ponsonby, 1592.

A Discourse of Life and Death: Written in French by Philip Mornay. Done in English by the Countess of Pembroke. London: printed by R. Field for William Ponsonby, 1600; repr. 1606, 1607, 1608.

"The Doleful Lay of Clorinda," in Edmund Spenser, *Astrophel. A Pastoral Elegy upon the Death of the Most Noble and Valorous Knight, Sir Philip Sidney.* London: printed by T. Creede for William Ponsonby, 1595.

"To the Angel Spirit," an early version by Mary Sidney Herbert found with Samuel Daniel's papers and erroneously included in *The Whole Works of Samuel Daniel Esquire in Poetry*. London: printed by N. Okes for Simon Waterson, 1623.

The Tragedy of Antony. Done into English by the Countess of Pembroke. London: printed by P. Short for William Ponsonby, 1595.

Modern Editions

Antonius [1592], ed. Marvin Spevak. *A New Variorum Edition of Shakespeare: Antony and Cleopatra*, 475–524. New York: MLA, 1990.

The Collected Works of Mary Sidney Herbert, Countess of Pembroke, ed. Margaret P. Hannay, Noel J. Kinnamon, and Michael G. Brennan. 2 vols. Oxford: Clarendon Press, 1998.

The Countess of Pembroke's Antonie [1592], ed. Alice Luce. Weimar: Verlag von Emil Felber, 1897.

The Countess of Pembroke's Translation of Philippe de Mornay's Discourse of Life and Death, ed. Diane Bornstein. Detroit: Michigan Consortium for Medieval and Early Modern Studies, 1983.

Isabella Whitney, Mary Sidney and Aemilia Lanyer: Renaissance Women Poets, ed. Danielle Clarke. London: Penguin Books, 2000. ("Even Now That Care," "To the Angel Spirit," "A Dialogue," *The Triumph of Death*, and a selection of psalms.)

Mary Sidney Herbert: Translation of Philippe de Mornay, A Discourse of Life and Death; Antonius, a Tragedie by R. Garnier. Facsimile. Intro. Gary F. Waller. Vol. 6, The Early Modern Englishwoman: Part One. Aldershot, England, and Burlington, Vt.: Ashgate, 1996.

The Psalmes of David Translated into Divers and Sundry Kinds of Verse, More Rare and Excellent for the Method and Varity Than Ever Yet Hath Been Done in English. Begun by . . . Sir Philip Sidney, Knt. and Finished by the Right Honorable the Countess of Pembroke. Chiswick: printed by C. Whittingham for R. Triphook, 1823.

The Psalms of Sir Philip Sidney and the Countess of Pembroke, ed. J. C. A. Rathmell. New York: New York University Press, 1963.

Rock Honeycomb. Broken Pieces of Sir Philip Sidney's Psalter. Bibliotheca Pastorum, Vol. 2, ed. John Ruskin. London: Ellis and White, 1877.

The Sidney Psalms, ed. R. E. Pritchard. Manchester: Carcanet, 1992. (Includes twelve psalms by Philip Sidney and fifty by Mary Sidney Herbert.)

"To the Angel Spirit of the Most Excellent Sir Phillip Sidney." In *The Poems of Sir Philip Sidney*, ed. William Ringler, 267–69. Oxford: Clarendon Press, 1962.

The Tragedy of Antony [1595], ed. Geoffrey Bullough. *Narrative and Dramatic Sources of Shakespeare*, 5: 358–405. New York: Columbia University Press, 1966.

"*The Triumph of Death*: A Critical Edition in Modern Spelling of the Countess of Pembroke's translation of Petrarch's *Trionfo della Morte*," ed. Gavin Alexander. *Sidney Journal* 17 (1999): 2–18.

The Triumph of Death and Other Unpublished and Uncollected Poems by Mary Sidney, Countess of Pembroke (1561–1621), ed. Gary F. Waller. Salzburg: University of Salzburg Press, 1977.

Two Poems by the Countess of Pembroke, ed. Bent Juel-Jensen. Oxford: Privately printed, 1962. ("Even Now That Care" and "To the Angel Spirit.")

The Works of Mary Sidney, Countess of Pembroke, ed. Robert G. Barnwell. London: John Wilson, 1865. (*Antonius, A Discourse of Life and Death*, "The Doleful Lay," and six psalms, as well as the misattributed "Our Saviour's Passion.")

Selections from Mary Sidney Herbert's works appear in nearly all anthologies of early modern literature published since 1984; for appearance in anthologies prior to 1984, see Josephine A. Roberts's bibliography below.

Online Resources

Mary Sidney Herbert, Countess of Pembroke: <http://users.mhc.edu/facultystaff/nkinnamo/pembroke/MSHHomeR.htm>

Renaissance Women Online: <http://www.wwp.brown.edu/texts/rwoentry.html>

Renascence Editions. The Tragedy of Antony, transcribed by R. Bear: <http://uoregon.edu/~rbear/antonie.html>

The Triumph of Death, transcribed and edited by Gavin Alexander. *Sidneiana:* <http://www.english.cam.uk/ceres/sidneianna/triumph.htm.

Biographies

Hannay, Margaret P. *Philip's Phoenix: Mary Sidney, Countess of Pembroke.* New York: Oxford University Press, 1990.

Young, Frances B. *Mary Sidney, Countess of Pembroke.* London: David Nutt, 1912.

Nearly all biographies of Philip and Robert Sidney include Mary Sidney Herbert, particularly in discussions of her role in the publication of Philip Sidney's works. See the annotated bibliography at the website Sir Philip Sidney, On Line <http://www.slu.edu/colleges/AS/ENG/sidney/>.

Bibliographies

Roberts, Josephine A. "Recent Studies in Women Writers of Tudor England, Part II: Mary Sidney, Countess of Pembroke." *ELR* 14 (1984): 426–39. Repr. and updated in *Women in the Renaissance: Selections from "English Literary Renaissance,"* ed. Kirby Farrell, Elizabeth H. Hageman, and Arthur F. Kinney, 245–58 and 265–69. Amherst: University of Massachusetts Press, 1988.

Travitsky, Betty. "ITER/MRTS Bibliography of English Women Writers, 1500–1630." <http://www.itergateway.org> (subscribers only) Forthcoming.

White, Micheline. "Recent Studies in Women Writers of Tudor England, 1485–1603 (mid-1993–mid-1999): Mary Sidney Herbert, Countess of Pembroke (1561–1621)." *ELR* 30 (2000): 480–84.

Ziegler, Georgianna M. "Recent Studies in Women Writers of Tudor England, 1485–1603 (1990–mid-1993): Mary Sidney Herbert, Countess of Pembroke (1561–1621)." *ELR* 24 (1994): 237–38.

Critical Studies

Acheson, Katherine O. "'Outrage Your Face': Anti-theatricality and Gender in Early Modern Closet Drama by Women." *Early Modern Literary Studies* 6.3 (January 2001): 7.1–16.

Alexander, Gavin. "Five Responses to Sir Philip Sidney, 1586–1628." Ph.D. diss., University of Cambridge, 1996. Chapter 1: "The Countess of Pembroke's Conclusions," 12–54; Appendix, "The Countess of Pembroke's Verse Forms," 195–201.

———. "Mary Sidney Herbert: *The Psalmes, The Triumph* and the Scribes." *Sidney Journal* 16 (1998): 16–30.

———. "A New Manuscript of the Sidney Psalms: A Preliminary Report." *Sidney Journal* 18 (2000): 43–56.

Ballard, George. *Memoirs of Several Ladies of Great Britain Who Have Been Celebrated for Their Writings or Skill in the Learned Languages, Arts and Sciences*, ed. Ruth Perry. Oxford: W. Jackson, 1752; repr. Detroit: Wayne State University, 1985.

Ballaster, Ros. "The First Female Dramatists." In *Women and Literature in Britain, 1500–1700*, ed. Helen Wilcox, 267–90. *Antonius* 269–73. Cambridge: Cambridge University Press, 1996.

Beauchamp, Virginia Walcott. "Sidney's Sister as Translator of Garnier." *Renaissance News* 10 (1957): 8–13.

Beilin, Elaine. *Redeeming Eve: Women Writers of the English Renaissance*. Chapter 5: "The Divine Poet: Mary Sidney, Countess of Pembroke," 121–50. Princeton: Princeton University Press, 1987.

Bell, Ilona. *Elizabethan Women and the Poetry of Courtship*. Cambridge: Cambridge University Press, 1998.

Bennet, Lyn. *Women Writing of Divinest Things: Rhetoric and the Poetry of Pembroke, Wroth, and Lanyer*. Pittsburgh, Pa.: Duquesne University Press, 2004.

Bergeron, David M. "Women as Patrons of English Renaissance Drama." In *Patronage in the Renaissance*, ed. Guy Fitch Lytle and Stephen Orgel, 274–90. Princeton: Princeton University Press, 1981.

Bornstein, Diane. "The Style of the Countess of Pembroke's Translation of Philippe de Mornay's *Discours de la vie et de la mort*." In *Silent but for the Word: Tudor*

Women as Patrons, Translators, and Writers of Religious Works, ed. Margaret P. Hannay, 126–48. Kent, Ohio: Kent State University Press, 1985.

Bottalla, Paola. "'Formes of Joy and Art': Le traduzioni dei Salmi di Mary Sidney, Contessa di Pembroke." In *Poesia e memoria poetica: Scritti in onore di Grazia Caliumi*, ed. Giovanna Silvani and Bruno Zucchelli, 139–67. Parma, Italy: University of Parma, 1999.

Brennan, Michael G. "The Date of the Countess of Pembroke's Translation of the Psalms." *RES* 33 (1982): 434–36.

———. "'First Rais'de by Thy Blest Hand, and What Is Mine / Inspired by Thee': The 'Sidney Psalter' and the Countess of Pembroke's Completion of the Sidneian *Psalms*." Conference Proceedings of "Protestant Men, Protesting Women: The Sidneys in Renaissance Society" at the University of Dundee on 10 April 1996. *Sidney Journal* 14 (1996): 37–46.

———. "Licensing the Sidney Psalms for the Press in the 1640s." *N&Q* 31 (1984): 304–5.

———. *Literary Patronage in the English Renaissance: The Pembroke Family*. London: Routledge, 1988.

———. "The Literary Patronage of the Herbert Family, Earls of Pembroke, 1550–1640." D.Phil. diss., Brasenose College, Oxford, 1982.

———. "Nicholas Breton's *The Passions of the Spirit* and the Countess of Pembroke." *RES* 38 (1987): 221–27.

———. "The Queen's Proposed Visit to Wilton House in 1599 and the 'Sidney Psalms.'" *Sidney Journal* 21 (2003): 1–28.

———. *The Sidneys of Penshurst and the Monarchy: 1500–1700*. Aldershot, England, and Burlington, Vt.: Ashgate (forthcoming, 2005).

———. "'We Have the Man Shakespeare with Us': Wilton House and *As You Like It*." *Wiltshire Archaeological Magazine* 80 (1986): 225–27.

Brennan, Michael G., and Noel J. Kinnamon. *A Sidney Chronology, 1554–1654*. London: Palgrave Macmillan, 2003.

Briley, John. "Mary Sidney—A Twentieth-Century Reappraisal." In *Elizabethan and Modern Studies Presented to Professor Willem Schrickx*, ed. J. P. Vander Motten, 47–56. Ghent: Seminarie voor Engelse en Amerikaanse Literatuur, 1985.

Bulloch, Mary M. "Mary Sidney, Countess of Pembroke: An Elizabethan Historiette." Paper read at the Young Women's Association of Belmont Congregational Church, Aberdeen. 11 February 1895.

Burgess, Irene Stephanie. " The Sidneys: Family, Writing, and Subjectivity." Ph.D. diss., State University of New York, Binghamton, 1994.

———. "'The Wreck of Order' in Early Modern Women's Drama." *Early Modern Literary Studies* 6.3 (January 2001): 1–24.

Buxton, John. *Elizabethan Taste*. London: Macmillan, 1963.

———. *Sir Philip Sidney and the English Renaissance*. Chapter 6: "The Countess of Pembroke," 173–204. London: Macmillan, 1954.

Camden, Carroll. *The Elizabethan Woman*. Mamaroneck, N.Y.: Paul P. Appel, 1975.

Catty, Jocelyn. *Writing Rape, Writing Women in Early Modern England: Unbridled Speech*. London: Macmillan, 1999.

Clark, Emma. "Metaphors of Motherhood: Claiming Back the Female Body in the Poems of Mary Sidney and Mary Wroth." *Women's Writing* 8 (2001): 263–73.

Clarke, Danielle. "'In Sort as She It Sung': Spenser's 'Doleful Lay' and the Construction of Female Authorship." *Criticism* 42 (2000): 451–68.

———. "'Lover's Songs Shall Turne to Holy Psalmes': Mary Sidney and the Transformation of Petrarch." *Modern Language Review* 92. 2 (1997): 282–94.

———. *The Politics of Early Modern Women's Writing*. London: Longman, 2001.

———. "The Politics of Translation and Gender in the Countess of Pembroke's *Antonie*." *Translation & Literature* 6 (1997): 149–66.

Coogan, Robert. "Petrarch's *Trionfi* and the English Renaissance." *SP* 67 (1970): 306–27.

Coren, Pamela. "Edmund Spenser, Mary Sidney, and the 'Doleful Lay.'" *SEL* 42 (2002): 25–41.

Davis, Joel. "Multiple Arcadias and the Literary Quarrel between Fulke Greville and the Countess of Pembroke." *SP* 101 (2004): 401–30.

DeNeef, A. Leigh. "'The Ruines of Time': Spenser's Apology for Poetry." *SP* 76 (1979): 262–71.

Distiller, Natasha. "'Philip's Phoenix'? Mary Sidney Herbert and the Identity of Author." In *The Anatomy of Tudor Literature: Proceedings of the First International Conference of the Tudor Symposium*, ed. Mike Pincombe, 112–29. Aldershot, England, and Burlington, Vt.: Ashgate, 1998.

Donawerth, Jane. "Women's Poetry and the Tudor-Stuart System of Gift Exchange." In *Women, Writing, and the Reproduction of Culture in Tudor and Stuart Britain*, ed. Mary Burke, Jane Donawerth, Linda L. Dove, and Karen Nelson, 3–18. Syracuse, N.Y.: Syracuse University Press, 2000.

Duncan-Jones, Katherine. "Pyramus and Thisbe: Shakespeare's Debt to Moffett Cancelled." *RES* 32 (1981): 296–301.

———. "Stoicism in *Measure for Measure*: A New Source," *RES* 28 (1977): 441–46.

Edmond, Mary. "Pembroke's Men." *RES* 25 (1974): 129–36.

Eliot, T. S. "Apology for the Countess of Pembroke." In *The Use of Poetry and the Use of Criticism*, 37–52. London: Faber and Faber, 1933.

——. "Seneca in Elizabethan Translation." In *Selected Essays: New Edition*, 51–88. New York: Harcourt, Brace, 1950.

Eriksen, Roy T. "George Gascoigne's and Mary Sidney's Versions of Psalm 130." *Cahiers Elisabéthains: Late Medieval and Renaissance Studies* 36 (1989): 1–9.

Erler, Mary C. "Davies's *Astraea* and Other Contexts of the Countess of Pembroke's 'A Dialogue,'" *SEL* 30 (1990): 41–61.

Ferguson, Margaret. "Sidney, Cary, Wroth." In *A Companion to Renaissance Drama*, ed. Arthur F. Kinney, 482–506. London: Blackwell, 2002.

Fisken, Beth Wynne. "'The Art of Sacred Parody' in Mary Sidney's *Psalmes*." *Tulsa Studies in Women's Literature* 8 (1989): 223–39.

——. "The Education of Mary Sidney." Ph.D. diss., Rutgers University, 1979.

——. "Mary Sidney's *Psalmes*: Education and Wisdom." In *Silent but for the Word: Tudor Women as Patrons, Translators, and Writers of Religious Works*, ed. Margaret P. Hannay, 166–83. Kent, Ohio: Kent State University Press, 1985.

——. "'To the Angell Spirit. . .': Mary Sidney's Entry into the 'World of Words.'" In *The Renaissance Englishwoman in Print: Counterbalancing the Canon*, ed. Anne M. Haselkorn and Betty S. Travitsky, 263–75. Amherst: University of Massachusetts Press, 1990.

Freer, Coburn. "The Countess of Pembroke in a World of Words." *Style* 5 (1971): 37–56.

——. "Mary Sidney, Countess of Pembroke." In *Women Writers of the Renaissance and Reformation*, ed. Katharina A. Wilson, 481–521. Athens, Ga.: University of Georgia Press, 1987.

——. *Music for a King: George Herbert's Style and the Metrical Psalms*. Baltimore: Johns Hopkins University Press, 1972.

Frontain, Raymond-Jean. "Translating Heavenwards: 'Upon the Translation of the Psalmes' and John Donne's Poetics of Praise." *Explorations in Renaissance Culture* 22 (1996): 103–25.

Gibson, Wendy. "Sidney's Two Riddles." *N&Q* 24 (1977): 520–21.

Goldberg, Jonathan. *Desiring Women Writing: English Renaissance Examples*. Part Two, "The Countess of Pembroke's Literal Translation," 114–31. Stanford, Calif.: Stanford University Press, 1997.

———. *Sodometries: Renaissance Texts/Modern Sexualities*. Stanford, Calif.: Stanford University Press, 1992.

Green, Reina. "Eroticizing Virtue: The Role of Cleopatra in Early Modern Drama." In *Women as Sites of Culture: Women's Roles in Cultural Formation from the Renaissance to the Twentieth Century*, ed. Susan Shifrin, 93–103. Aldershot, England, and Burlington, Vt.: Ashgate, 2002.

H. T. R. "Mary Sidney and Her Writings." *Gentlemen's Magazine* 24 (1845): 129–36, 254–59, 364–70.

Hackett, Helen. "Courtly Writing by Women." In *Women and Literature in Britain, 1500–1700*, ed. Helen Wilcox, 169–89. Cambridge: Cambridge University Press, 1996.

Hamlin, Hannibal. *Psalm Culture and Early Modern English Literature*. Cambridge: Cambridge University Press, 2004.

Hannay, Margaret P. "The Countess of Pembroke as a Spenserian Poet." In *Pilgrimage for Love: Essays in Early Modern Literature in Honor of Josephine A. Roberts*, ed. Sigrid M. King, 41–62. Tempe, Ariz.: MRTS, 1999.

———. "'Do What Men May Sing': Mary Sidney and the Tradition of Admonitory Dedication." In *Silent but for the Word: Tudor Women as Patrons, Translators, and Writers of Religious Works*, ed. Margaret P. Hannay, 149–65. Kent, Ohio: Kent State University Press, 1985.

———. "Elizabeth Ashburnham Richardson's Meditation on the Countess of Pembroke's *Discourse*." *EMS* 9 (2000): 114–28.

———. "'House-confined Maids': The Presentation of Woman's Role in the *Psalmes* of the Countess of Pembroke." *ELR* 24 (1994): 44–71.

———. "'How I These Studies Prize': The Countess of Pembroke and Elizabethan Science." In *Women, Medicine and Science, 1500–1700*, ed. Lynette Hunter and Sarah Hutton, 108–21. Phoenix Mill, Gloucestershire: Sutton Publishing Ltd, 1997.

———. "Incorporating Women Writers into the Survey Course: Mary Sidney's Psalm 73 and *Astrophil and Stella* 5." In *Approaches to Teaching Shorter Elizabethan Poetry*, ed. Patrick Cheney and Anne Lake Prescott, 133–38. New York: MLA, 2000.

———. "Mary Sidney, Countess of Pembroke." In *Teaching Tudor and Stuart Women Writers*, ed. Susanne Woods and Margaret Hannay, 135–44. New York: MLA, 2000.

———. "Mary Sidney Herbert, Countess of Pembroke." In *Dictionary of Literary Biography: Sixteenth-Century British Nondramatic Writers*, ed. David

Richardson, 184–93. Vol. 167. Third Series. Detroit: Bruccoli Clark Layman, 1996.

———. "Mary Sidney and Scribal Publication." In *Women's Writing and The Circulation of Ideas: Manuscript Publication in England, 1550–1800*, ed. George Justice and Nathan Tinker, 17–49. Cambridge: Cambridge University Press, 2002. First published as "'Bearing the livery of your name': the Countess of Pembroke's Agency in Print and Scribal Publication." *Sidney Journal* 18 (2000): 1–34.

———. "'O Daughter Heare': Reconstructing the Lives of Aristocratic Englishwomen." In *Attending to Women in the Renaissance*, ed. Betty Travitsky and Adele Seeff, 35–63. Newark: University of Delaware Press, 1994.

———. "Patronesse of the Muses." (Section repr. from *Philip's Phoenix.*) In *Readings in Renaissance Women's Drama: Criticism, History, and Performance 1594–1998*, ed. S. P. Cerasano and Marion Wynne-Davies, 142–55. London: Routledge, 1998.

———. "'Princes You as Men Must Dy': Genevan Advice to Monarchs in the *Psalmes* of Mary Sidney." *ELR* 19 (1989): 22–41.

———. "'So May I with the *Psalmist* Truly Say': Early Modern Englishwomen's Psalm Discourse." In *Write or Be Written: Early Modern Women Poets and Cultural Constraints*, ed. Barbara Smith and Ursula Appelt, 105–34. Aldershot, England, and Burlington, Vt.: Ashgate, 2001.

———. "'This Moses and This Miriam': The Countess of Pembroke's Role in the Legend of Sir Philip Sidney." In *Sir Philip Sidney's Achievements*, ed. M. J. B. Allen, Dominic Baker-Smith, and Arthur F. Kinney, 217–26. New York: AMS Press, 1990.

———. "'Unlock My Lipps': The *Miserere Mei Deus* of Anne Vaughan Lok and Mary Sidney Herbert, Countess of Pembroke." In *Privileging Gender in Early Modern England*, ed. Jean R. Brink. *Sixteenth-Century Essays and Studies.* Kirksville, Mo.: Sixteenth Century Journal Publishers, 23 (1993): 19–36.

———. "Unpublished Letters by Mary Sidney, Countess of Pembroke." *Spenser Studies* 6 (1985): 165–90.

———. "'When Riches Growes': Class Perspective in the Pembroke's *Psalmes.*" In *Women, Writing, and the Reproduction of Culture in Tudor and Stuart Britain*, ed. Mary Burke, Jane Donawerth, Linda L. Dove, and Karen Nelson, 77–97. Syracuse, N.Y.: Syracuse University Press, 2000.

———. "'Your Vertuous and Learned Aunt': The Countess of Pembroke as a Mentor to Lady Wroth." In *Reading Mary Wroth: Representing Alternatives in Early Modern England*, ed. Naomi Miller and Gary Waller, 15–34. Knoxville: University of Tennessee Press, 1991.

Hiller, Geoffrey G. "'Where Thou Doost Live, There Let All Graces Be': Images of the Renaissance Woman Patron in Her House and Rural Domain." *Cahiers Elisabéthains* 40.2 (1991): 37–52.

Hogrefe, Pearl. *Tudor Women: Commoners and Queens*. Ames: Iowa State University Press, 1975.

——. *Women of Action in Tudor England*. Chapter 5: "Mary Sidney Herbert, Countess of Pembroke," 105–35. Ames: Iowa State University Press, 1977.

Holaday, Allan. "William Browne's Epitaph on the Countess of Pembroke." *Philological Quarterly* 28. 4 (1949): 495–97.

Hopkins, Lisa. "*A Midsummer Night's Dream* and Mary Sidney." *English Language Notes* 41 (2004): 23–28.

Juel-Jensen, Bent. "Contemporary Collectors XLIII." *The Book Collector* 15 (1966): 152–74.

——. "The Tixall Manuscript of Sir Philip Sidney's and the Countess of Pembroke's Paraphrase of the Psalms." *The Book Collector* 18 (1969): 222–23.

Kay, Dennis. *Melodious Tears: The English Funeral Elegy from Spenser to Milton*. Oxford: Oxford University Press, 1990.

Kinnamon, Noel J. "Emendations in G. F. Waller's Edition of the Countess of Pembroke's *Psalms*." *American Notes & Queries* 22 (1984): 66–70.

——. "God's 'Scholer': The Countess of Pembroke's Psalmes and Beza's *Psalmorum Davidis . . . Libri Quinque*." *N&Q* 44 (1997): 85–88.

——. "A Note on Herbert's 'Easter' and the Sidneian Psalms." *George Herbert Journal* 1 (1978): 44–48.

——. "Notes on the Psalms in Herbert's *The Temple*." *George Herbert Journal* 4 (1981): 10–29.

——. "The Peniarth Manuscript of the Sidney Psalms." *National Library of Wales Journal* 28 (1993–1994): 279–84.

——. "The Sidney Psalms: The Penshurst and Tixall Manuscripts." *EMS* 2 (1990): 139–61.

Kinney, Clare. "'Love Which Hath Never Done': The Countess of Pembroke's Elegies and the Apology for Copia." *Sidney Journal* 21 (2003): 31–40.

Kissileff, Beth P. "'The Soul in Paraphrase': Early Modern Lyric and the Psalms." Ph.D. diss., University of Pennsylvania, 1998.

Klein, Lisa M. *The Exemplary Sidney and the Elizabethan Sonneteer*. Chapter 4: "*Delia*, the Countess of Pembroke, and the Literary Career of Samuel Daniel," 136–70. Newark: University of Delaware Press, 1998.

Krontiris, Tina. "Mary Herbert: Englishing a Purified Cleopatra." In *Readings in Renaissance Women's Drama: Criticism, History, and Performance 1594–*

1998, ed. S. P. Cerasano and Marion Wynne-Davies, 156–66. London: Routledge, 1998.

——. *Oppositional Voices: Women as Writers and Translators of Literature in the English Renaissance.* London: Routledge, 1992.

Lamb, Mary Ellen. "The Countess of Pembroke and the Art of Dying." In *Women in the Middle Ages and the Renaissance: Literary and Historical Perspectives,* ed. Mary Beth Rose, 207–26. Syracuse, N.Y.: Syracuse University Press, 1986.

——. "The Countess of Pembroke's Patronage." *ELR* 12 (1982): 162–79.

——. "The Countess of Pembroke's Patronage." Ph.D. diss., Columbia University, 1976.

——. *Gender and Authorship in the Sidney Circle.* Madison: University of Wisconsin Press, 1990.

——. "The Myth of the Countess of Pembroke: The Dramatic Circle." *Yearbook of English Studies* 11 (1981): 194–202.

Lever, Tresham. *The Herberts of Wilton.* London: John Murray, 1967.

Lewalski, Barbara Kiefer. *Protestant Poetics and the Seventeenth-Century Religious Lyric.* Princeton: Princeton University Press, 1979.

Lewis, Janette Seaton. "'The Subject of All Verse': An Introduction to the Life and Work of Mary Sidney Herbert, the Countess of Pembroke." Ph.D. diss., UCLA, 1976.

Lifschutz, Ellen St. Sure. "David's Lyre and the Renaissance Lyric: A Critical Consideration of the Psalms of Wyatt, Surrey, and the Sidneys." Ph.D. diss., University of California, Berkeley, 1980.

Long, Percy W. "Spenseriana: *The Lay of Clorinda.*" *MLN* 31 (1916): 79–82.

MacArthur, Janet. "Ventriloquizing Comfort and Despair: Mary Sidney's Female Personae in *The Triumph of Death* and *The Tragedy of Antony.*" *Sidney Newsletter and Journal* 11 (1990): 3–13.

May, Steven W. *The Elizabethan Courtier Poets: The Poems and Their Contexts.* Columbia: University of Missouri Press, 1991; repr. Asheville, N.C.: Pegasus Press, 1999.

——. "Two Unpublished Letters by Mary Herbert, Countess of Pembroke." *EMS* 9 (2000): 88–97.

Mazzola, Elizabeth A. "Brothers' Keepers and Philip's Siblings: The Poetics of the Sidney Family." *Criticism* 41 (1999): 513–42.

——. *Favorite Sons: The Politics and Poetics of the Sidney Family.* London: Palgrave, 2003.

McBride, Kari Boyd. "Remembering Orpheus in the Poems of Aemilia Lanyer." *SEL* 38 (1998): 87–108.

———. "Sacred Celebration: The Patronage Poems." In *Aemilia Lanyer: Gender, Genre, and the Canon*, ed. Marshall Grossman, 60–82. Lexington, Ky.: University Press of Kentucky, 1998.

McCarthy, Penny. "'Milsop Muses' or Why Not Mary?" *SEL* 40 (2000): 21–39.

Miller, Shannon. "Mary Sidney and Gendered Strategies for the Writing of Poetry." In *Write or Be Written: Early Modern Women Poets and Cultural Constraints*, ed. Barbara Smith and Ursula Appelt, 155–76. Aldershot, England, and Burlington, Vt.: Ashgate, 2001.

Montgomery, Deborah Hope. "The Art of Translation: Mary Sidney's Means to Political, Religious, and Personal Expression." Ph.D. diss., California State University, Fresno, 1998.

Morrison, Mary. "Some Aspects of the Treatment of the Theme of Antony and Cleopatra in Tragedies of the Sixteenth Century." *JES* 4 (1974): 113–25.

Morton, Lynn Moorhead. "'Vertue Cladde in Constant Love's Attire': The Countess of Pembroke as a Model for Renaissance Women Writers." Ph.D. diss., University of South Carolina, 1993.

Newcomb, E. A. "The Countess of Pembroke's Circle." Ph.D. diss., University of Wisconsin, 1938.

Norland, Howard B. "Englishing Garnier: Mary Sidney's *Antonie* and Daniel's *Cleopatra*." *Tudor Theatre: Emotion in the Theatre*. Collection Theta 3, 161–69. Bern: Peter Lang, 1996.

O'Connell, Michael. "'Astrophel': Spenser's Double Elegy." *SEL* 11 (1971): 27–35.

Osgood, Charles W. "The Doleful Lay of Clorinda." *MLN* 35 (1920): 90–96.

Padel, John. "Shakespeare's Sonnets, the Sidney and Herbert Families: A Reply to M. E. Lamb." *Sidney Newsletter & Journal* 3. 2 (1982): 3–12.

Patton, Elizabeth. "Seven Faces of Cleopatra." In *Teaching Tudor and Stuart Women Writers*, ed. Susanne Woods and Margaret Hannay, 289–94. New York: MLA, 2000.

Pritchard, R. E. "Sidney's Dedicatory Poem: 'To the Angel Spirit of the Most Excellent Sir Philip Sidney.'" *Explicator* 54 (1995): 2–4.

Raber, Karen. *Dramatic Difference: Gender, Class, and Genre in the Early Modern Closet Drama*. Newark: University of Delaware Press, 2001.

Rathmell, J. C. A. "Explorations and Recoveries—Hopkins, Ruskin, and the *Sidney Psalter*." *London Magazine* 6 (1959): 51–66.

Rees, D. G. "Petrarch's 'Trionfo della Morte' in English." *Italian Studies* 7 (1952): 82–96.

Richards, Jennifer. "Philip Sidney, Mary Sidney, and Protestant Poetics." Conference Proceedings of "Protestant Men, Protesting Women: The Sidneys in Renaissance Society" at the University of Dundee on 10 April 1996. *Sidney Journal* 14 (1996): 28–36.

Rienstra, Debra. "Aspiring to Praise: The Sidney-Pembroke Psalter and the English Religious Lyric." Ph.D. diss., Rutgers University, 1995.

———. "Dreaming Authorship: Aemilia Lanyer and the Countess of Pembroke." In *Discovering and (Re)Covering the Seventeenth Century Religious Lyric*, ed. Eugene Cunnar and Jerry Johnson, 80–103. Pittsburgh, Pa.: Duquesne University Press, 2001.

———. "Mary Sidney, Countess of Pembroke, *Psalmes.*" In *A Companion to Early Modern Women's Writing*, ed. Anita Pacheco, 110–124. London: Blackwell, 2002.

Rienstra, Debra, and Noel Kinnamon. "Circulating the Sidney-Pembroke Psalter." In *Women's Writing and the Circulation of Ideas: Manuscript Publication in England, 1550–1800*, ed. George Justice and Nathan Tinker, 50–72. Cambridge: Cambridge University Press, 2002. First published as "Revisioning the Sacred Text," *Sidney Journal* 17 (1999): 53–77.

Rix, Herbert David. "Spenser and the 'Doleful Lay.'" *MLN* 53 (1938): 261–65.

Roberts, Josephine A. "The Huntington Manuscript of Lady Mary Wroth's Play, *Loves Victorie.*" *HLQ* 46 (1983): 156–74.

Robertson, Jean. "Drayton and the Countess of Pembroke." *RES* 16 (1965): 49.

Rowe, Kenneth Thorpe. "The Countess of Pembroke's Editorship of the *Arcadia.*" *PMLA* 54 (1939): 122–38.

———. "The Love of Sir Philip Sidney for the Countess of Pembroke." *Papers of the Michigan Academy of Science, Arts and Letters* 25 (1939): 579–95.

Rowton, Frederic. *The Female Poets of Great Britain Chronologically Arranged with Copious Selections and Critical Remarks.* 1853. Facsimile, ed. Marilyn L. Williamson. Detroit: Wayne State University Press, 1981.

Sanders, Eve Rachele. *Gender and Literacy on Stage in Early Modern England.* Chapter 3 [on *Antonius*]: "She Reads and Smiles," 89–137. Cambridge: Cambridge University Press, 1998.

Sandhaug, Christina. "Conceit beyond Expectation: Mary Sidney's Rhyming Rhetoric in Psalm 55 *Exaudi, Deus.*" *Nordlit: Arbeidstidsskrift i litteratur* 6 (1999): 105–18.

Schanzer, Ernest. "*Antony and Cleopatra* and the Countess of Pembroke's *Antonius*." *N&Q* 21 (1956): 152–54.

Schleiner, Louise. *Cultural Semiotics, Spenser, and the Captive Woman*. Bethlehem, Pa.: Lehigh University Press, 1995.

———. "Placing Elizabethan Poetry: Some Classroom Ideas." In *Approaches to Teaching Shorter Elizabethan Poetry*, ed. Patrick Cheney and Anne Lake Prescott, 123–27. New York: MLA, 2000.

———. *Tudor and Stuart Women Writers*, Chapter 3: "Authorial Identity for a Second-Generation Protestant Aristocrat: The Countess of Pembroke," 52–81. Bloomington: Indiana University Press, 1994.

Schnell, Lisa Jane. "'The Fetter'd Muse': Renaissance Women Writers and the Idea of a Literary Career." Ph.D. diss., Princeton University, 1990.

Seaton, Janette Lewis. "'The Subject of All Verse': An Introduction to the Life and Work of Mary Sidney Herbert, Countess of Pembroke." Ph.D. diss., UCLA, 1976.

Seronsy, Cecil C. "Another Huntington Manuscript of the Sidney Psalms." *HLQ* 29 (1966): 109–16.

Shea, Colleen. "Literary Authority as Cultural Criticism in Aemilia Lanyer's *The Authors Dreame*." *ELR* 32 (2002): 386–407.

Sheppeard, Sallye Jeannet. "The Forbidden Muse: Mary Sidney Herbert and Renaissance Poetic Theory and Practice." Ph.D. diss., Texas Women's University, 1980.

———. "Mary Herbert's 'A Dialogue between Two Shepherdes': A Study in Renaissance Poetic Method." *Proceedings of the Conference of College Teachers of English of Texas* 46 (1981): 17–21.

———. "Toward a Reassessment of the Psalms of David within Renaissance Poetry." *Publications of the Mississippi Philological Association* (1988): 143–52.

Skretkowicz, Victor. "Mary Sidney Herbert's *Antonius*, English Philhellenism and the Protestant Cause." *Women's Writing* 6 (1999): 7–26.

———. "Protestant Men, Protesting Women—A Sidney Family Discourse." Conference Proceedings of "Protestant Men, Protesting Women: The Sidneys in Renaissance Society" at the University of Dundee on 10 April 1996. *Sidney Journal* 14 (1996): 3–13.

Smith, Hallett. "English Metrical Psalms in the Sixteenth Century and Their Literary Significance." *HLQ* 9 (1946): 249–71.

Steinberg, Theodore. "The Sidneys and the Psalms." *SP* 92 (1995): 1–17.

Steppat, Michael. "Shakespeare's Response to Dramatic Tradition in *Antony and Cleopatra*." In *Shakespeare: Text, Language, Criticism: Essays in Honour of Marvin Spevack*, ed. Bernhard Fabian and Kurt Tetzeli von Rosador. Hildesheim and New York: Olms-Weidmann, 1987.

Straznicky, Marta. "'Profane Stoical Paradoxes': *The Tragedie of Mariam* and Sidneian Closet Drama." *ELR* 24 (1994): 104–34.

Swaim, Kathleen. "Contextualizing Mary Sidney's Psalms." *Christianity and Literature* 48 (1999): 253–73.

Thomson, Patricia. "The Literature of Patronage, 1580–1630." *Essays in Criticism* 11 (1952): 267–84.

Tilyou, Elizabeth Mary. "Ficinian Elements in Selected Poems of Mary Sidney Herbert, Countess of Pembroke." In *Neglected English Literature: Recusant Writings of the 16th–17th Centuries*, ed. Dorothy L. Latz, 49–58. Salzburg: University of Salzburg Press, 1997.

Todd, Richard. "Humanist Prosodic Theory, Dutch Synods, and the Poetics of the Sidney-Pembroke Psalter." *HLQ* 52 (1989): 273–93.

———. "'So Well Attyr'd Abroad': A Background to the Sidney-Pembroke Psalter and Its Implications for the Seventeenth-Century Religious Lyric." *Texas Studies in Literature and Language* 29 (1987): 74–93.

Trill, Suzanne. "Engendering Penitence: Nicholas Breton and 'the Countesse of Penbrooke.'" In *Voicing Women: Gender and Sexuality in Early Modern Writing*, ed. Kate Chedgzoy, Melanie Hansen and Suzanne Trill, 25–44. Keele, Staffordshire: Keele University Press, 1996.

———. "Religion and the Construction of Femininity." In *Women and Literature in Britain, 1500–1700*, ed. Helen Wilcox, 30–55. Cambridge: Cambridge University Press, 1996.

———. "Sixteenth-century Women's Writing: Mary Sidney's Psalmes and the 'Femininity of Translation.'" In *Writing and the English Renaissance*, ed. Suzanne Trill and William Zunder, 140–58. London: Longman, 1996.

———. "Spectres and Sisters: Mary Sidney and the 'Perennial Puzzle' of Renaissance Women's Writing." In *Renaissance Configurations: Voices, Bodies, Spaces, 1580–1690*, ed. Gordon McMullan, 191–211. London: Macmillan, 1998.

Walker, Kim. *Women Writers of the Renaissance*. Chapter 4: "'Some inspired stile': Mary Sidney, Countess of Pembroke," 72–100. London: Twayne, 1996.

Wall, Wendy. *The Imprint of Gender: Authorship and Publication in the English Renaissance*. Ithaca, N.Y.: Cornell University Press, 1993.

———. "Our Bodies/Our Texts? Renaissance Women and the Trials of Authorship." In *Anxious Power: Reading, Writing, and Ambivalence in Narrative by Women*, ed. Carol J. Singley and Susan Elizabeth Sweeney, 51–71. Albany, N.Y.: State University of New York Press, 1993.

Waller, Gary F. "The Countess of Pembroke and Gendered Reading." In *The Renaissance Englishwoman in Print: Counterbalancing the Canon*, ed. Anne M. Haselkorn and Betty S. Travitsky, 327–45. Amherst: University of Massachusetts Press, 1990.

———. *Mary Sidney, Countess of Pembroke: A Critical Study of Her Writings and Literary Milieu*. Salzburg: University of Salzburg Press, 1979.

———. "Mary Sidney's '...Two Shepherds.'" *American Notes & Queries* 9 (1971): 100–102.

———. "A 'Matching of Contraries': Ideological Ambiguity in the Sidney Psalms." *Wascana Review* 9 (1974): 124–33.

———. *The Sidney Family Romance: Mary Wroth, William Herbert, and the Early Modern Construction of Gender*. Detroit: Wayne State University Press, 1993.

———. "Struggling into Discourse: The Emergence of Renaissance Women's Writing." In *Silent but for the Word: Tudor Women as Patrons, Translators, and Writers of Religious Works*, ed. Margaret P. Hannay, 238–56. Kent, Ohio: Kent State University Press, 1985.

———. "The Text and Manuscript Variants of the Countess of Pembroke's Psalms." *RES* 26 (1975): 1–18.

———. "'This Matching of Contraries': Bruno, Calvin and the Sidney Circle." *Neophilologus* 56 (1972): 331–43.

———. "'This Matching of Contraries': Calvinism and Courtly Philosophy in the Sidney Psalms." *English Studies* 55 (1974): 22–31.

Weiner, Seth. "The Quantitative Poems and the Psalm Translations: The Place of Sidney's Experimental Verse in the Legend." In *Sir Philip Sidney: 1586 and the Creation of a Legend*, ed. Jan van Dorsten, Dominic Baker-Smith, and Arthur F. Kinney, 193–220. Leiden: Brill, 1986.

Wentersdorf, Karl P. "The Origin and Personnel of the Pembroke Company." *Theatre Research International* 5 (1979–80): 45–68.

Wilcox, Helen. "'First Fruits of a Woman's Wit:' Authorial Self-Construction of English Renaissance Women Poets." In *Write or Be Written: Early Modern Women Poets and Cultural Constraints*, ed. Barbara Smith and Ursula Appelt, 199–221. Aldershot, England, and Burlington, Vt.: Ashgate, 2001.

———. "'Whom the Lord with Love Affected': Gender and the Religious Poet, 1590–1633." In *'This Double Voice': Gendered Writing in Early Modern England*, ed. Danielle Clarke and Elizabeth Clarke, 185–207. London: Macmillan Press, 2000.

——, ed. *Women and Literature in Britain, 1500–1700.* Cambridge: Cambridge University Press, 1996.

Williams, Franklin F., Jr. "The Literary Patronesses of Renaissance England." *N&Q* 207 (1962): 364–66.

Wilson, Katharina M., ed. *Women Writers of the Renaissance and Reformation.* Athens, Ga.: University of Georgia Press, 1987.

Witherspoon, Alexander Maclaren. *The Influence of Robert Garnier on Elizabethan Drama.* New Haven: Yale University Press, 1924.

Woods, Susanne. *Natural Emphasis: English Versification from Chaucer to Dryden.* San Marino, Calif.: Huntington Library, 1984.

——. "Vocation and Authority: Born to Write." In *Aemilia Lanyer: Gender, Genre, and the Canon,* ed. Marshall Grossman, 83–98. Lexington, Ky.: University Press of Kentucky, 1998.

Wynne-Davies, Marion. "'For *Worth,* Not Weakness, Makes in Use but One': Literary Dialogues in an English Renaissance Family." In '*This Double Voice*': *Gendered Writing in Early Modern England,* ed. Danielle Clarke and Elizabeth Clarke, 164–84. London: Macmillan Press, 2000.

——. "'So Much *Worth* as Lives in You': Veiled Portraits of the Sidney Women." Conference Proceedings of "Protestant Men, Protesting Women: The Sidneys in Renaissance Society" at the University of Dundee on 10 April 1996. *Sidney Journal* 14 (1996): 45–55.

Wynne-Davies, Marion, and Susan Cerasano, eds. *Readings in Renaissance Women's Drama: Criticism, History, and Performance 1594–1998.* London: Routledge, 1998. (Reprints *Antonius* sections from Hannay, *Philip's Phoenix,* and from Krontiris, *Oppositional Voices,* as well as Churchyard's and Daniel's poems to Mary Sidney Herbert.)

Zim, Rivkah. *English Metrical Psalms: Poetry as Praise and Prayer, 1535–1601.* Chapter 6: "'A Heavenly Poesie . . . Of That Lyricall Kind': Part Two—The Countess of Pembroke," 185–210. Cambridge: Cambridge University Press, 1987.

MRTS

MEDIEVAL AND RENAISSANCE TEXT AND STUDIES

is the major publishing program of the
Arizona Center for Medieval and Renaissance Studies
at Arizona State University, Tempe, Arizona

MRTS emphasizes books that are needed—
editions, translations, and major research tools—
but also welcomes monographs
and collections of essays on focused themes.

MRTS aims to publish the highest quality scholarship
in attractive and durable format at modest cost.